The
Java/C++
Cross-Reference Handbook

Frederick F. Chew

To Join a Prentice Hall PTR Internet mailing list, point to:
http://www.prenhall.com/mail lists/

Hewlett-Packard Company

ISBN 0-13-848318-3

90000

Prentice Hall PTR
Upper Saddle River, NJ 07458

9 780138 483180

Library of Congress Cataloging in Publication Data

Chew, Frederick F.
  The Java/C++ cross-reference handbook/Frederick F. Chew.
    p. cm.
  Includes bibliographical references and index.
   ISBN 0-13-848318-3
   1. Java (computer program language) 2. C++ (Computer program)
language) I. Title
QA76.73.J38C48 1997
005.13'3—DC21   97-29164
                                                 CIP

Acquisitions editor: Karen Gettman
Editorial assistant: Barbara Alfieri
Editorial/Production supervision: Nicholas Radhuber
Cover design: Bruce Kenselaar
Cover design director: Jerry Votta
Marketing manager: Dan Rush
Manufacturing manager: Julia Meehan
Manager, Hewlett-Packard Press: Patricia Pekary

Published by Prentice Hall PTR
Prentice-Hall, Inc.
A Simon & Schuster Company
Upper Saddle River, New Jersey 07458

Prentice Hall books are widely used by corporations and government agencies for training, marketing, and resale.

The publisher offers discounts on this book when ordered in bulk quantities.
For more information, contact: Phone: 800-382-3419; Fax: 201-236-7141; e-mail:
corpsales@prenhall.com; or write to:
Corporate Sales Department
Prentice Hall PTR
One Lake Street
Upper Saddle River, NJ 07458.

Printed in the United States of America
10 9 8 7 6 5 4 3 2 1

ISBN 0-13-848318-3

Prentice-Hall International (UK) Limited, *London*
Prentice-Hall of Australia Pty. Limited, *Sydney*
Prentice-Hall Canada Inc., *Toronto*
Prentice-Hall Hispanoamericana, S.A., *Mexico*
Prentice-Hall of India Private Limited, *New Delhi*
Prentice-Hall of Japan, Inc., *Tokyo*
Simon & Schuster Asia Pte. Ltd., *Singapore*

This book is dedicated to Mom and Dad.

"To look back all the time is boring.
Excitement lies in tomorrow."
—*Natalia Makarova*

Contents

Chapter 3:

The Class: Blueprint for Object Creation, 62

Chapter 4:

Inheritance: Up and Down the Class Hierarchy, 108

Chapter 5:
Run-Time Type Information, 165

Chapter 6:
Dealing with the Unexpected: Exception Handling, 183

Chapter 10:

Networking the Java Environment, 403

Preface

The Story Behind this Book

At the time of this writing, I have been an employee of the Hewlett-Packard Company for over fifteen years. Over the years I have worked in many entities, played different roles and have experienced many changes within the company. My technical literary journey started when I had joined HP's North American Response Center around 1987, where I became a member of a personal computer support team. During that period, I had contributed articles to the now defunct *HP PC Communicator*, a pocket-size journal that was delivered to HP customers. Since then, I have written articles for *HP Professional, Interact* and *hp-ux/usr* magazines. The latter two are publications of INTEREX, an organization representing all HP trade customers.

During that period of my career, I had also joined an internal company program called "HP AHEAD." HP AHEAD is an after-hours training program to benefit HP employees, a sort of community college within the company for those who work around the San Francisco Bay Area. The program is a great way for employees with special expertise to share their knowledge and broaden their horizons. For myself, I have been engaged in after-hours instruction for over ten years and have designed, developed and delivered five courses. The latest and most recent work is a comprehensive course I call *Objects++: C++ Programming Fundamentals,* a course to help the experienced C programmer enter the world of C++ programming.

Now, the reader might be wondering what technical instruction and technical writing has to do with this book. For some years, I have dreamt of becoming an author, but I was not sure if I was up to the task. In many ways, writing a book is like developing a course, except the discipline, effort and the risks are immensely greater. Compared to writing an article, writing a book is an effort of a titanic scale.

In January 1995, I had an article about C++ exception handling published in INTEREX's *hp-ux/usr* magazine. Shortly after the article's release, Pat Pekary of Hewlett-Packard Professional Books had given me a call to congratulate me on the article. Up to then, I did not know, nor had I ever worked with Pat. The amazing thing about the entire conversation was that she had actually encouraged me to write a book!

It is extremely rare in life that someone you do not know actually approaches you and tells you that you have "the right stuff." Too often, individuals with great potential are discouraged or denied the opportunity to excel because they are not chosen by, or part of, a special nobility. I thank Pat for opening the door to make my dream of becoming an author possible. In addition, I hope my example will lend encouragement and hope to other individuals with the same dreams.

Acknowledgments

For myself, writing this book was a great, personal mission requiring an extraordinary amount of planning, patience, and persistence. I believe any author will testify that these virtues are absolutely necessary for success. However, despite all of the hard work of the individual author, it is the team effort of all concerned who make the book a reality. Toward this effort, I would like to acknowledge the hard-working people at Prentice Hall for making the mission a wonderful success. My thanks to Nicholas Radhuber for keeping the production of the book on track, to Mary Franz for making the book the most customer-friendly product it could be, and to Miles Williams for his imaginative and witty idea of the graphic that adorns the front cover of the book. Last, but not least, my thanks goes to all who have reviewed or given feedback to improve the content and clarity of the book.

The Audience for the Book

This book is for the software professional who has anything to do with software development: development, instruction, learning or consulting. I have written this book in the same spirit that I developed and taught my C++ course. In other words, this work is to serve as a bridge to help seasoned professionals of an established technology (C++) embrace and become proficient in a rising technology (Java).

To say that Java is merely a rising technology is probably an understatement. In the very short time since its formal release, there has been tremendous interest in this Internet technology. Businesses that are interested in publicizing their products and services on the World Wide Web are competing to find Java-knowledgeable developers. For software professionals, the possibilities for career growth and financial gain have never been better.

In this day and age, a software professional cannot afford to be complacent, otherwise he will be left behind in the employment marketplace. Unfortunately, many of the new technologies are not easily learned or mastered. It takes initiative and long-term dedication to become proficient at a new skill.

There are those who would give the impression that Java is simply another dialect of C++. However, beyond the many syntactic similarities, writing a meaningful Java application with only C++ experience is not trivial. There are many C++ constructs, semantics and practices that do not apply to the Java environment. Conversely, there are elements in Java that have no equivalents in C++.

However, an experienced C++ developer is in a good position to integrate Java into his technical skill set. It is mostly a matter of unlearning some things, understanding the equivalent things, learning some new things, changing habits and a lot of practice. The purpose of this book is to address these aspects and to demonstrate the differences <u>by example</u>. I believe this is where my book differs from other Java books: I do not merely talk about the differences between Java and C++, I demonstrate them. I believe this approach will shorten the learning curve tremendously and help the developer internalize the subtle, but important, differences between the two languages.

For the experienced C language developer who has yet to enter the world of object-oriented programming with either C++ or Java, this book will guide the developer into both languages. Learning both of these popular languages will give the traditional, procedural language programmer valuable skills in the technical marketplace.

The Organization of the Book

The heart of the book compares the language features of C++ and Java. The first six chapters discuss and demonstrate the syntactic and semantic features of both languages.

- Chapter 1 gives an overview of the environmental differences surrounding a C++ application versus a Java application.

- Chapter 2 discusses the literals, keywords, operators and basic constructs of both languages.

- Chapter 3 focuses on how each language implements the notion of the `class`.

- Chapter 4 introduces how inheritance is supported in both languages. In addition, this chapter discusses supporting constructs like member access restrictions, virtual functions and abstract classes.

- Chapter 5 discusses how to obtain run-time type information about an object in either language.

- Chapter 6 covers the exception handling mechanism in both languages. This chapter demonstrates how to regulate the flow of control when exceptions are thrown.

The last four chapters go beyond the standard features of the languages to compare services typically required by any application. Such services include functions or classes to support file input-output, window control layout and network programming. The comparisons span multiple platforms, where a Java example is compared to a popular, native C or C++ example from UNIX or Microsoft Windows NT™.

- Chapter 7 compares the C++ `iostream` class framework with the Java stream classes of package `java.io`.

- Chapter 8 discusses multiprocessing versus multithreading, with the main focus on how to do the latter in Java.

- Chapter 9 discusses how events could be trapped in message-driven environments such as Microsoft Windows NT™ and Java. In addition, a major portion of the chapter is devoted to window layout management in Java as compared to OSF Motif™.

- Chapter 10 discusses and demonstrates how to do client-server programming with sockets in both Java and C.

The Sample Programs

The great majority of the Java and C++ sample programs were conceived from a Microsoft Windows NT™ environment (version 3.51 or higher). All of these programs come with sources, bytecode files or executables. All of these samples should work fine in the Windows 95™ environment.

At the time of the actual writing, all of the Java samples were built with Symantec Café™ 1.0 and version 1.0.2 of the Java Developers Kit™ (JDK). Since the book had entered production, the JDK has undergone a major revision to 1.1. All of the Java samples have been tested with JDK 1.1.1 and, with the exception of a handful, have been verified to work with the new version. For the corner cases, version 1.1.1-specific examples have been provided on the media.

The great majority of the C++ samples from Windows NT™ were composed with Microsoft Visual C++ 4.0™. Since this version of the Microsoft compiler does not support all of the ISO/ANSI exception handling specifications, there are a few examples that are more suited to the Borland C++ 5.0™ compiler. The Borland-specific example is noted as such in the comment header at the top of the source file.

A small handful of C sample programs were created on a HP-UX 9.0 environment. These programs come with sources and shell scripts to create the executables. The sources and scripts must be network copied to a UNIX environment with a utility like FTP. The OSF Motif™-based examples require certain development libraries to be in place before the executables can be built.

For directory structure and installation instructions, please refer to the section entitled *About the Software* at the end of this book.

Interesting Web Sites

There is certainly no shortage of information about Java from different Internet sources. The following uniform resource locators (URLs) will keep the user current with the latest news, products, fads and tips about Java:

```
http://www.sun.com/
http://java.sun.com/
http://www.hp.com/gsyinternet/hpjdk/
http://www.javaworld.com/
http://www.gamelan.com/
http://www.sigs.com/jro/
```

Many of the above sites have hyperlinks to other sites on Java.

About the Icons

Sprinkled throughout the book are graphical icons that serve to emphasize certain passages in the text. Such icons may draw the reader's attention to warnings, recommended practices or simply the fact that a program listing is available from the distribution media. Below are the icons and their meaning:

This icon is a warning. In other words, be watchful of pitfalls.

This icon is a note or observation. The connotation is neither negative nor positive.

This icon represents enlightenment. The point emphasized is a recommended software engineering practice.

About the Author

Frederick F. Chew is a graduate of the University of Santa Clara and has a B.S. degree in mathematics. He has been an employee of the Hewlett-Packard Company for over fifteen years and is currently an Information Technology Engineer with Hewlett-Packard's Asia-Pacific Geography. He is also a C++ instructor with the HP AHEAD program and is a contributor of articles on object-oriented software development to INTEREX's hp-ux/usr magazine.

CHAPTER 1

Beyond Appearances: Different by Design

Applications or Applets?

One of the very special features of Java is that it was designed to be a programming language for the Internet. With Java you can write either stand-alone applications, i.e., applications that can be executed from the operating environment or *applets*, pieces of code that are embedded in HTML home pages. Applets are activated when a user visits a home page containing the applets with the help of Java-aware browsers like Netscape Navigator 2.0™ or higher. As an internet programming language, Java has this unique ability not found in any traditional programming language such as Pascal, C, C++ or Smalltalk.

Java is considered a purely object-oriented language because the programmer must think in terms of objects, which represent encapsulated entities of attributes and behaviors. The notion of a `class` is the blueprint from which actual objects or instances are created. Java looks a lot like C++ because it has acquired some of the features and much of the syntax of its predecessor.

On the other hand, C++ is a multi-paradigm language, because virtually every feature of ANSI C is part of the C++ specification. That means that one can use C++ like C, i.e., use it like a procedural language or use it with the modern, object-oriented approach (by designing and writing classes). As experience has shown, this flexibility of C++ has made it very difficult for many C traditionalists to do a successful "paradigm shift" into object orientation. Many traditional procedural language methodologies and recommended practices are simply obstacles to developing a sound, object-oriented outlook.

Figure 1-1

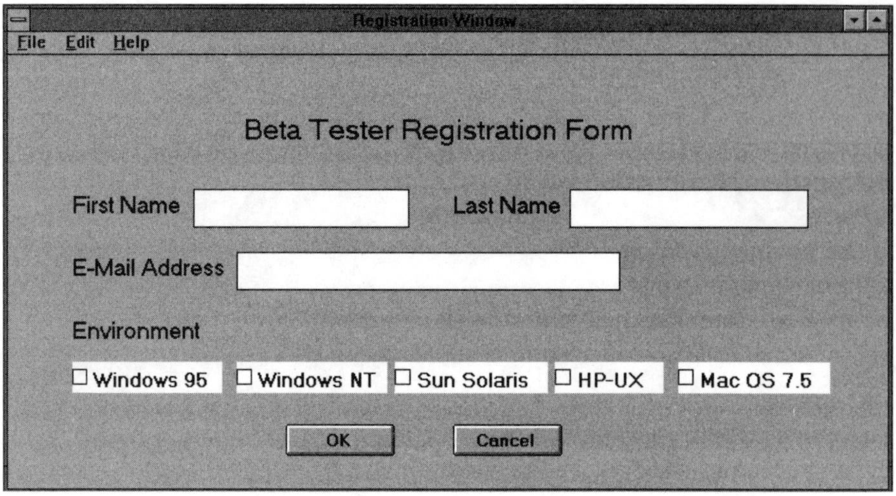

Figure 1-1 and the following code fragments illustrate the basic structure of a stand-alone Java program:

Listing 1-1: RegistrationApplicationDemo.java

```java
import java.awt.*;

public class RegistrationApplicationDemo extends Frame {

    private Menu fileMenu;
    private Menu editMenu;
    private Menu helpMenu;

    private Label registrationTitle;
    private Label firstName;
    private Label lastName;
    private Label email;
    private TextField firstNameField;
    private TextField lastNameField;
    private TextField edit1;
    private Label environment;
    private Checkbox win95;
    private Checkbox winnt;
```

```
    private Checkbox solaris;
    private Checkbox hpux;
    private Button OKButton;
    private Button cancelButton;
    private Checkbox macOS7;

    public RegistrationApplicationDemo() {

        super("Registration Window");
        ...
        setLayout(null);
        addNotify();
        resize(insets().left + insets().right + 717, insets().top +
         insets().bottom + 395);
        registrationTitle=new Label("Beta Tester Registration
         Form");
        registrationTitle.setFont(new Font("Dialog",Font.PLAIN,24));
        add(registrationTitle);
        registrationTitle.reshape(insets().left + 186,insets().top +
         46,342,32);
         ...
        OKButton=new Button("OK");
        OKButton.setFont(new Font("Dialog",Font.BOLD,14));
        add(OKButton);
        OKButton.reshape(insets().left + 234,insets().top +
         306,90,26);
        cancelButton=new Button("Cancel");
        cancelButton.setFont(new Font("Dialog",Font.BOLD,14));
        add(cancelButton);
        cancelButton.reshape(insets().left + 372,insets().top +
         306,90,26);
        show();
        }

public static void main(String args[]) {
        new RegistrationApplicationDemo();
        }

}   // end of class RegistrationApplicationDemo
```

The above illustration is a simple Java window application to gather user data. I
am not going to discuss the details of the associated code fragment since all of
the essentials will be handled in the rest of the book. However, I will draw the
reader's attention to the following:

* Within the source file, there is one primary class and that is
  RegistrationApplicationDemo.

- Class `RegistrationApplicationDemo` has a method called `main()` that has modifiers `public` and `static`. The method returns no value (`void`) and takes a single argument (`String args[]`). Method `main()` is the entry point for a stand-alone Java program (just as `main()` is the entry point in traditional C and C++ programs).

- The method `RegistrationApplicationDemo()` is a no-argument constructor. A constructor is a special method for initializing the variable members (like `registrationTitle`, `firstName`, `lastName`, etc.).

- The `import` statement at the top of the sample source is the mechanism by which existing classes within packages can be linked into the program. In this example, all the classes of package `java.awt` (the *Abstract Window Toolkit*) are being referenced.

- The source file containing the code must be named `RegistrationApplicationDemo.java`. When this file is successfully compiled (`java RegistrationApplicationDemo.java`), a bytecode file named `RegistrationApplicationDemo.class` will be created. The bytecode file can be run by entering:

  ```
  java   RegistrationApplicationDemo
  ```

  from the command line.

Figure 1–2 illustrates how the same functionality in the form of an applet would appear from Netscape Navigator™ 2.0. Code fragments for the applet follow the illustration.

Listing 1–2: RegistrationAppletDemo.java

```java
import java.awt.*;
import java.applet.*;

public class RegistrationAppletDemo extends Applet {

    private Label registrationTitle;
    private Label firstName;
    private Label lastName;
    private Label email;
    private TextField firstNameField;
    private TextField lastNameField;
    private TextField edit1;
    private Label environment;
    private Checkbox win95;
    private Checkbox winnt;
```

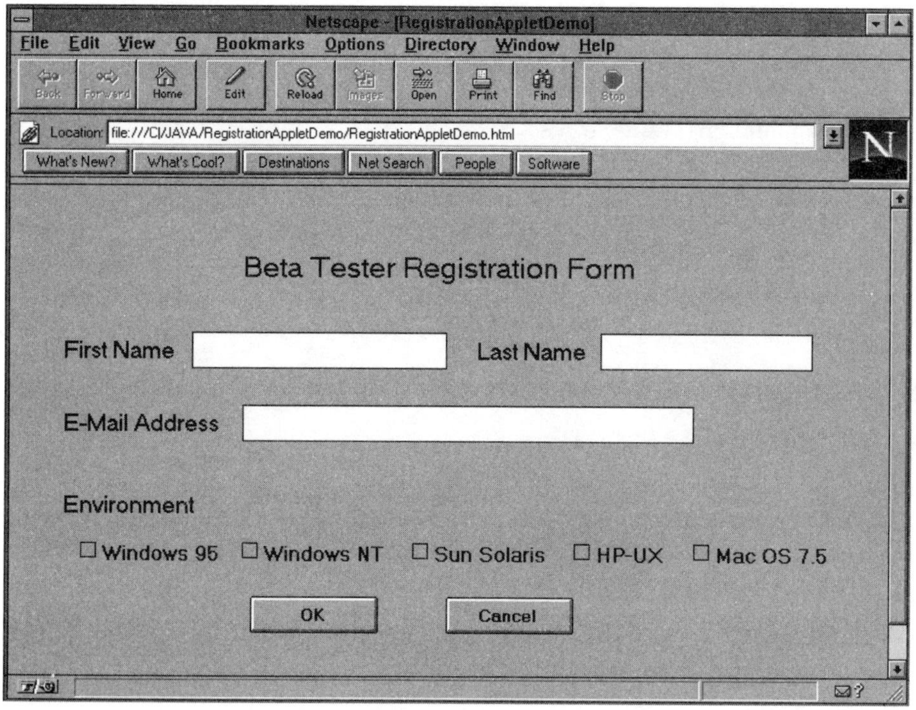

Figure 1–2

```
private Checkbox solaris;
private Checkbox hpux;
private Button okButton;
private Button cancelButton;
private Checkbox macOS7;

public void init() {

    super.init();

    setLayout(null);
    resize(704,382);
    registrationTitle=new Label("Beta Tester Registration
     Form");
    registrationTitle.setFont(new
     Font("Dialog",Font.PLAIN,24));
    add(registrationTitle);
    registrationTitle.reshape(182,37,343,30);
```

```
    ...
    okButton=new Button("OK");
    okButton.setFont(new Font("Dialog",Font.BOLD,14));
    add(okButton);
    okButton.reshape(189,322,105,30);
    cancelButton=new Button("Cancel");
    cancelButton.setFont(new Font("Dialog",Font.BOLD,14));
    add(cancelButton);
    cancelButton.reshape(350,322,105,30);
    }

}   // end of class RegistrationAppletDemo
```

The key features to note about applets are the following:

- The entry point to start the applet is a method called init() in class RegistrationAppletDemo. This method is typically used to instantiate the window controls, assign them attributes and position them on the window.

- The primary class, RegistrationAppletDemo, must be a subclass of class Applet (note the extends keyword). A subclass inherits the non-private variable members and methods of a parent class.

- In addition to all of the classes of the java.awt package, all of the classes of the java.applet package must also be imported.

- Like the stand-alone application, all of the source file naming conventions still apply for applets.

In the case of applets, the bytecode file must be called from HTML code. A sample HTML file might look like:

```
<HTML>
<HEAD>
<TITLE> RegistrationAppletDemo </TITLE>
</HEAD>
<BODY>
<APPLET CODE="RegistrationAppletDemo.class" WIDTH=660
HEIGHT=400>
</APPLET>
</BODY>
</HTML>
```

Java-aware browsers like Netscape Navigator™ 2.0 or higher support a tag called APPLET. The CODE parameter is used to reference the bytecode file (in this case, RegistrationAppletDemo.class). The APPLET tag must be qualified with required parameters WIDTH and HEIGHT (the width and height of the applet display area in pixels).

The Java Virtual Machine

For years software developers have been striving to write programs that will run on any operating environment of any hardware platform. As far as portable computer languages go, the C language has served this objective very well. This is due to the availability of C compilers for many operating systems. As a modern, multi-paradigm descendant of C, the C++ language is very close to a formal industry standard and enjoys the same widespread support as its predecessor.

Twenty years ago, programs written in a language like C with its standard ANSI function libraries were the norm for stand-alone mainframe environments. The source code could be taken from one vendor's environment and it could be expected to compile, link and run with predictable behavior on a different vendor's environment.

However, times have changed. Different operating systems running on different brands of hardware are expected to interoperate in a harmonious fashion. The big picture is no longer a homogenous environment where the executable code is binary compatible for all systems. Furthermore, code that runs from one section of the environment are often dependent on a variety of different function or class libraries (like OSF Motif™ or Microsoft Foundation Classes™). The result is a situation where it is no longer simple to port applications without investing in large development teams and dealing with tacky maintenance and support issues.

To answer the need for interoperability, Sun Microsystems invented the Java language with its collection of standard classes (called *packages*) and Sun released the Java Developer's Kit 1.0™ into the public domain in May 1996. The packages also include support for networking and windowing (graphical user interface development).

Unlike C or C++, Java source code is compiled into *bytecode*, <u>not</u> native machine code. Each environment that supports stand-alone Java applications would have a program called a *virtual machine* that is capable of interpreting and executing the bytecode file. From the point of view of the Java application, every operating environment appears the same. For example, if I have a stand-alone Java application called `CommandLineDemo` in the form of a bytecode file called `CommandLineDemo.class`, I would execute it from the command line by typing:

```
java   CommandLineDemo
```

followed by the enter key. Without altering `CommandLineDemo.class`, I can copy this file to any environment with Java virtual machine support and expect the execution to provide predictable and consistent results. This is portability at its finest!

In addition to portability for stand-alone applications, the Java language is also designed to accommodate Java-aware internet browsers like Netscape Navigator™ 2.0. Such browsers have a built-in Java virtual machine. Java code, which are embedded within Hypertext Markup Language home pages, are called applets and they are dynamically retrieved and executed when users visit Java-based internet sites. This arrangement gives internet service providers a powerful technology to greatly enhance their Web pages so they can reach customers throughout the world.

The idea of the virtual machine is not a new one. For years, it has been a key component of the Smalltalk language environment. However, Smalltalk has enjoyed only limited success. Certainly, the inclusion of Java support in popular browsers like Netscape Navigator™ will give Java a promising future.

Memory Management: Public Service or Do It Yourself?

One of the biggest differences between Java and C++ is that Java has a built-in mechanism called garbage collection. Garbage collection is a scheme to reuse memory when it is no longer referenced by any variables. Unlike C++, the programmer need not worry about explicitly freeing the memory.

One of the most tricky and troublesome areas of C and C++ programming is the failure to deallocate dynamic memory when it is no longer needed. A C or C++ programmer must always be very conscientious about freeing heap memory or else memory exhaustion will cause a program (or an entire operating system) to "hang." For this reason, the designers of Java chose to take this worry away from the programmer so that the resulting applications would be more reliable.

In Java, objects are created or instantiated from a class with the keyword `new`. Simply declaring a variable of a certain type without having the variable reference a real object is insufficient. For example,

```
List list1;
```

simply declares a variable called `list1`, which is a reference to a scrolling `List` object. However, an actual scrolling `List` object has yet to be instantiated. If we continue with the following line:

```
list1 = new List();
```

we will have `list1` reference an instantiated `List` object. The argument following keyword `new` is a legal constructor (`List()`) defined for the class of the object.

The Java garbage collector will come into play at some point after the object goes out of scope. The statements above would be within some enclosing block, say:

```
{
...
```

```
List list1;
list1 = new List();
...
}
```

When execution reaches the right brace (}), the reference variable `list1` would go out of scope and, provided the memory previously referenced by `list1` is not referenced by anything else, the garbage collector will put that memory back into the free pool.

Within your Java programs, it is possible to explicitly call the garbage collector. That is done with the statement:

```
System.gc();
```

As I had mentioned, C++ has no automatic garbage collection. The programmer must do his own clean up. The equivalent to using `new` in Java is to use the keywords `new` and `delete` in C++. If I were to rewrite the above Java code in C++, it would look like:

```
{
...
List * list1;
list1 = new List;
...
delete list1;
}
```

In C++, the `new` operator returns a pointer to the object (in this case, a dynamically created object of class `List`). In this example, I am also using a pre-defined no-argument constructor for class `List`. In C++, when there are no arguments, I simply write `List` (and not `List()`, because of clashes with functions called conventions). Before I reach the right brace (}), I must call the `delete` operator to free the dynamic memory I had allocated for pointer `list1`.

The C++ `new` and `delete` operators are also used in the constructors and destructors of a class. The following is a simple example:

```
class Person {
public:
    Person(char * nm);
    ~Person();
    // more member functions
private:
    char * name;
};

Person::Person(char * nm) {                    // constructor
name = new char[strlen(nm)+1];
strcpy(name,nm);
}
```

```
Person::~Person() {              // destructor
delete []   name;
}
```

In the only constructor for class `Person`, `Person(char *)`, I had dynamically allocated memory for the pointer variable name. The constructor is invoked when an instance of `Person` is instantiated, as in:

```
{
Person p1("Freddie");            // p. 1 is an automatic object
...
}
```

To balance this out, `delete` must be used in the destructor. The destructor for a `Person` instance would be invoked when the instance goes out of scope. In the above example, instance `p1` would go out of scope when execution reaches the right brace (`}`).

Note: The idea of providing garbage collection for a programming language is not new. Garbage collection has been available in languages like Smalltalk at least since the 1970s.

Printing to the Standard Output Device

Java and C++ each has different ways to display information on the standard output device. Almost every sample program in this book uses the standard output device, so it is important to understand a little about how this is done in each language.

Every C language programmer should be familiar with the standard `printf()` function. An example is as follows:

```
int qty = 5;
double price_per_unit = 0.25;
double total_price = qty * price_per_unit;
char * prompt = " and the total cost is ";

printf("There are %d pears, each costing %4.2f%s%4.2f\n",
          qty, price_per_unit, prompt, total_price);
```

The output on the standard output device would be:

```
There are 5 pears, each costing 0.25 and the total cost is 1.25
```

One of the traditional problems with `printf()` is that the format descriptors (which begin with a %) must correspond to the subsequent arguments by type, or else there will be runtime problems. For the example, the matching begins with the second argument from the left. The `%d` matches `qty`, the first `%4.2f` matches `price_per_unit`, `%s` matches `prompt` and the second `%4.2f` matches `total_price`.

Another problem with `printf()` is that the number of arguments need not match the number of format descriptors. The C compiler would not complain about such discrepancies. Again, this could lead to subtle or strange runtime errors.

To correct this historical problem from C, both C++ and Java support type-safe linkage. In other words, the number of arguments, the type of each argument and the order of the arguments must match the argument list of the function (or *method*, as a function is called in Java). If there is a violation of these rules, the compiler would flag the call to the function (or method) as an error.

Now, the name of the function plus the argument list constitute a *signature* of the function. In both Java and C++ it is possible to overload a function, i.e., a function with a given name could have multiple implementations. By specifying a function name and passing arguments of differing types in a given order, the compiler tries to determine which implementation is requested.

With this in mind, we can rewrite the above `printf()` statement in Java as follows:

```
int qty = 5;
double price_per_unit = 0.25;
double total_price = qty * price_per_unit;
String prompt = new String(" and the total cost is ");

System.out.print("There are ");
System.out.print(qty);
System.out.print(" pears, each costing ");
System.out.print(price_per_unit);
System.out.print(prompt);
System.out.println(total_price);
```

Executing the Java code will produce exactly the same output as above with `printf()`. Basically, these are the main features of the Java code:

- `System` is a special class that is a platform-independent way of representing standard input (`System.in`), standard output (`System.out`) and standard error (`System.err`). Since all of the variables and methods of the class are declared `static`, no objects may be instantiated from the class. In other words, there is exactly one object of `System` and that is `System` itself.

- `System.out` represents a `PrintStream` object. `PrintStream` is a standard Java input-output class. The public interface of class `PrintStream` includes the following overloaded methods:

```
void print(char s[]);    // prints an array of ASCII charac
                            ters

void print(int);         // prints an integer as ASCII charac
                            ters

void print(double);      // prints a double-precision floating
                            point number as ASCII characters

void print(String);      // prints a String object as ASCII
                            characters

void println(double);    // prints a double-precision floating
                            point number as

                         // ASCII characters followed by a
                            newline character
```

The `print` method is an example of an overloaded method, i.e., it is defined for different argument lists. Each argument list for `print` has one argument, but each signature is distinguished by a unique type.

Now, there is a way to abbreviate the effort to output the data with a single Java statement and that is:

```
System.out.println("There are "+qty+" pears, each costing "
    +price_per_unit+prompt+total_price);
```

Normally, operator overloading is not possible in Java and there is no mechanism to perform operator overloading. However, there is one small exception to this and that is the use of the + for string concatenation. The + operator for string concatenation has the same precedence and associatively (left to right) as its more familiar role as the binary addition operator.

Note that when the string concatenation operator + is applied to other primitive (built-in) types like `int`, `double` and array of `char`, the conversion to a `String` object is automatic. For user-defined objects, the `toString()` method must be applied to explicitly convert the object to a string.

The equivalent to the Java example in C++ would look like:

```
cout<<"There are "<<qty<<" pears, each costing "
    <<price_per_unit<<prompt<<total_price<<endl;
```

Unlike Java, C++ allows the overloading of operators. Here, the traditional left shift operator << has been overloaded to facilitate the writing of data (called *insertion*). Specifically,

- The `cout` variable is a pre-defined, global `ostream` object that represents the standard output device.

- The `ostream` class represents the output stream, which the user can think of as a flow of data to a destination (which could be a file, a network connection, a data structure in memory, etc.). The `ostream` object has these public interfaces defined:

```
ostream & operator<<(const char *);   // return is a refer-
                                       ence to an ostream

ostream & operator<<(int);            // return is a refer-
                                       ence to an ostream

ostream & operator<<(double);         // return is a refer-
                                       ence to an ostream
```

The special C++ keyword `operator` plus the actual operator symbol (`operator<<`) takes the place the function name (after all, an operation is a function). The `<<` operator is left-to-right associative. As a simplified example, if we take part of the `cout` statement above, say:

```
cout<<"There are "<<qty<<" pears, each costing ";
```

the statement can be rewritten as:

```
(((cout<<"There are ")<<qty)<<" pears, each costing ");
```

which, in turn, can be rewritten with the dot (.) operator as:

```
(((cout.operator<<("There are ")).operator <<(qty)) .opera-
tor <<(" pears, each costing "));
```

which matches the syntactic format of the overloaded operator prototypes.

- Finally, `endl` is what is known as a *manipulator* in C++. Manipulators are used to control the behaviors of streams in C++. The `endl` manipulator will put a newline character (`'\n'`) into the internal buffer of the `cout` object and flush the contents of the buffer to the output device. Depending on various implementations of C++, a newline character alone may not flush the internal buffer. The `endl` manipulator will assure that the buffer is flushed.

CHAPTER

2

- Identifiers
- The Keywords of Java and C++
- The Char Type
- The Boolean Type
- The Built-In Types
- An Overview of the Operators
- The Order of Evaluation of the Operands
- The Role of the Semicolon
- Flow of Control: Branching
- Flow of Control: Iteration
- Flow of Control: The `break` and `continue` Keywords
- Setting Up Arrays
- Array of Arrays
- Declaring an Array of a Type
- Passing Parameters into Functions or Methods
- Passing Arguments from the Command Line
- Macros, the `const` Keyword and the `final` Keyword.
- Comment Delimiters
- Documenting Java Code with JavaDoc

The Basics of the Languages

Identifiers

An identifier is simply a name a programmer chooses to represent a variable, a method (function), a class, an interface or a package in Java or C/C++. The following are legal identifiers in either Java or C/C++:

```
a
index
Student5
miles_per_hour
DATABASE_BUSY
_name
```

An identifier must begin with an alphabetic or underscore (_) and an identifier is case sensitive. In both Java and C/C++, the following are <u>illegal</u>:

```
time@junction
4you
```

Special characters like the tilde (~), at sign (@) and vertical slash (|) cannot be used to compose an identifier. In addition, an identifier must not begin with a digit.

In addition to the above, there are Java features that may not be available in some C++ implementations. It is legal to name identifiers with the dollar sign ($) in Java and allow identifiers to exceed 32 characters:

```
$money
more$money
the_total_number_of_sheep_on_the_ranch
```

The Keywords of Java and C++

Keywords are considered part of a language and cannot be used as identifiers. While Java and C++ have many keywords in common, Java has some that are not in C++. In addition, not all of the reserved keywords of Java are currently used.

The following keywords are common to both languages:

break	case	catch	char	class
const	continue	default	do	double
else	float	for	goto	if
int	long	new	private	protected
public	return	short	static	switch
throw	try	void	volatile	while

The keywords *const* and *goto* are currently undefined in Java and are not used.

The following keywords are specific to Java:

abstract	boolean	byvalue	cast	extends
final	finally	future	generic	implements
import	inner	instanceof	interface	native
null	operator	outer	package	rest
super	synchronized	this	throws	transient
var				

The keywords *byvalue, cast, future, generic, inner, operator, outer, rest* and *var* are currently undefined in Java and are not used.

In addition, the following are not really keywords in Java, but they represent special values:

false	null	true

Finally, the following keywords are specific to C or C++ and are not in Java:

auto	enum	extern	friend	inline
register	signed	sizeof	struct	typedef
union	unsigned			

The Char Type

In C and C++, the character is represented by a single byte (eight bits) in the form of the built-in char type. With eight bits, a maximum of 256 characters could be represented and, over the years, the ASCII collating sequence has been the accepted ordering of these characters.

On the other hand, Java has adopted Unicode, a two-byte standard for character representation. Each Unicode character is a sixteen-bit unsigned value. With Unicode, as many as 65,536 characters could be represented! This means that many modern non-Roman languages, like Chinese and Korean, can be accommodated very comfortably.

The ASCII collating sequence is actually a subset of Unicode and this sequence appears as the first 128 characters in the Unicode sequence. In Latin 1 character set (ISO 8859-1), which is also part of Unicode, it appears as the first 256 characters of the sequence.

In both Java and C++, the '\', or backslash character, is used as an escape character to help represent special characters, such as the backspace, newline, single quote and double quote. The following special characters are shared by both Java and C++:

```
\n      newline
\r      carriage return
\b      backspace
\t      tab
\f      formfeed
\'      single quote
\"      double quote
\\      backslash
```

A statement such as:

```
char backspace = '\b';
```

would declare a char variable called `backspace` and have it initialized to \b (the character is bounded within single quotes).

C and C++ have a few additional special characters that are not available in Java. They are:

```
\a      bell
\?      question mark
\v      vertical tab
```

In Java, there is a special way to represent a character by its value in hexadecimal. For instance, the declaration:

```
char alpha = '\u0391';
```

means that the char variable `alpha` is initialized to the character corresponding to hexadecimal value 391 (931 in decimal), which is a capital Greek alpha. The \u in Java denotes a hexadecimal number. The entire Unicode sequence would range from '\u0000' to '\uFFFF'.

The Boolean Type

Java has a built-in type called *boolean*, which is used to test conditions. A boolean has only two values: *true* or *false*, both of which are keyword values in Java. The boolean type uses only one bit for storage and is <u>not</u> an integral type (as in C). Java boolean types cannot be promoted or casted to an integral type. Consider the following:

```
boolean status = true;
```

In the above, I declare a boolean variable called `status` and it is initialized to `true`.

In C and C++, programmers and library vendors have always simulated a boolean type by doing the following:

```
#define   FALSE   0
#define   TRUE    1
```

or

```
enum boolean { FALSE, TRUE }
```

These schemes have lead to many inconsistencies in practice. In an attempt to resolve these inconsistencies, the ISO/ANSI committee recently added a new built-in type to C++ called *bool* (<u>not</u> *boolean*). The following examples show how this new type is used in C++:

```
bool  status = true;
bool * flag = &status;
```

Unlike the Java boolean type, the *bool* type is an integral type. Value *true* can be promoted to 1 and value *false* can be promoted to 0. In an expression, a zero assignment is converted to *false* and a non-zero assignment is converted to *true*.

The Built-In Types

The Java language has eight built-in primitive data types. The language specification is very precise about the sizes and properties of each type. They are:

Type	Size	Description
boolean	1 bit	A boolean can either be true or false. It cannot be cast to another type, such as int.

Type	Size	Description
char	16-bit unsigned integer	Each char is a Unicode code.
byte	8-bit signed two's complement	Range is -128 to 127.
short	16-bit signed two's complement	Range is -32768 to 32767.
int	32-bit signed two's complement	Range is -2147483648 to 2147483647.
long	64-bit signed two's complement	Range is -2^{63} to $2^{63} - 1$.
float	32-bit IEEE 754 single-precision	Range is about -3.4E38 to +3.4E38. Accuracy is about six to seven significant decimal places.
double	64-bit IEEE 754 double-precision	Range is about -1.7E308 to +1.7E308 Accuracy is about 14 to 15 significant decimal places.

Being of fixed size, all of the Java types are platform-independent. Unlike C and C++, Java does not have a `sizeof` operator. The predictability of the sizes for the primitive types makes Java programs highly portable.

In contrast, not all of the built-in types of C and C++ are of fixed size. The fundamental or built-in types of C++ land in two categories: integer types and floating types. The basic integer types include `char`, `short`, `int` and `long`. The floating types include `float`, `double` and `long double`. Each of the integer types may be explicitly declared *signed* or *unsigned*, i.e., the high-order bit may be treated as a sign bit. A char by itself may be understood to be signed or unsigned, depending on the vendor's implementation on the target platform.

The following table describes each of the C++ built-in types with typical sizes (a byte is eight bits):

Type	Size	Description
char	1 byte	Without the unsigned or signed qualification, a char may have a range of −128 to 127 on some systems and a range of 0 to 255 on others.
short	2 bytes	
int	2 or 4 bytes	Actual size varies with the machine.
long	4 or 8 bytes	Actual size varies with the machine.
float	4 bytes	Single precision.
double	8 bytes	Double precision.
long double	12 or 16 bytes	Actual size varies with the machine.

There is also a type called void, which represents an empty set of values. No object or variable of type void can be declared. It is used as the return type for functions that do not return a value.

The actual size in bytes of a type for any platform can be found by using the sizeof operator, as in:

```
cout<<sizeof(int)<<endl;
cout<<sizeof(long)<<endl;
cout<<sizeof(Employee)<<endl;
```

where Employee is some user-defined type.

The sizeof operator can also be applied to a pointer to a type, such as:

```
cout<<sizeof(long *)<<endl;
cout<<sizeof(float *)<<endl;
cout<<sizeof(Employee *)<<endl;
```

The sizeof a pointer to a type will return the amount of memory (in bytes) required to contain an address of that type.

Another variation of the use of sizeof is to apply this operator to the reference of an object, like:

```
cout<<sizeof(long double &)<<endl;
cout<<sizeof(Employee &)<<endl;
```

In this case, the sizeof operator will return the amount of memory required to contain the referenced object (or instance), not the reference to the type.

An Overview of the Operators

Nearly all of the operators of Java originate from ANSI C. In addition, Java has a few that are unique to Java itself. Likewise, C++ uses all of the operators of ANSI C and includes a number of its own. In this section, we will browse the operators of both languages, starting with those of C++ (from the highest level of precedence to the lowest):

Table 2-1 - C++ Operators

Associativity	Oper- ator	Description	Example
Level 17			
R-to-L	::	Global Scope Resolution	::name
L-to-R	::	Class Scope Resolution	cname::member
Level 16			
L-to-R	.	Member Selection	cobject.member
L-to-R	->	Member Selection	pobject->member
L-to-R	[]	Subscripting	expr[expr]
L-to-R	()	Function Call	expr(expr_list)
L-to-R	()	Type Construction	type(expr_list)
L-to-R	sizeof	Size of Object	sizeof (expr)
L-to-R	sizeof	Size of Type	sizeof (type)
Level 15			
R-to-L	++	Pre-Increment	++lvalue
R-to-L	—	Pre-Decrement	—lvalue
R-to-L	++	Post-Increment	lvalue++
R-to-L	—	Post-Decrement	lvalue—
R-to-L	~	Bitwise NOT	~expr
R-to-L	!	Logical NOT	!expr
R-to-L	-	Unary Minus	-expr
R-to-L	+	Unary Plus	+expr
R-to-L	&	Address of	&lvalue
R-to-L	*	De-reference	*expr
R-to-L	()	Type Conversion (cast)	(type)expr
R-to-L	new	Allocate Heap Memory	new type
R-to-L	delete	Free Heap Memory	delete pointer
R-to-L	delete []	Free Heap Memory Array	delete [] pointer
Level 14			
L-to-R	.*	Member Pointer Selection	cobject.*member_ptr

Table 2-1 - C++ Operators *Continued*

Associativity	Oper- ator	Description	Example
L-to-R	->*	Member Pointer Selection	pobject->*member _ptr
Level 13			
L-to-R	*	Multiply	expr * expr
L-to-R	/	Divide	expr / expr
L-to-R	%	Modulo	expr % expr
Level 12			
L-to-R	+	Add (Binary Plus)	expr + expr
L-to-R	-	Subtract (Binary Minus)	expr - expr
Level 11			
L-to-R	<<	Shift Left	value << expr
L-to-R	>>	Shift Right	value >> expr
Level 10			
L-to-R	<	Less Than	expr < expr
L-to-R	<=	Less Than or Equal	expr <= expr
L-to-R	>	Greater Than	expr > expr
L-to-R	>=	Greater Than or Equal	expr >= expr
Level 9			
L-to-R	==	Equal	expr == expr
L-to-R	!=	Not Equal	expr != expr
Level 8			
L-to-R	&	Bitwise AND	expr & expr
Level 7			
L-to-R	^	Bitwise Exclusive OR	expr ^ expr
Level 6			
L-to-R	|	Bitwise Inclusive OR	expr | expr
Level 5			
L-to-R	&&	Logical AND	expr && expr
Level 4			
L-to-R	||	Logical Inclusive OR	expr || expr

Table 2-1 - C++ Operators *Continued*

Associativity	Operator	Description	Example
Level 3			
L-to-R	?:	Arithmetic IF	expr ? expr : expr
Level 2			
R-to-L	=	Assignment	lvalue = expr
R-to-L	*=	Multiply and Assign	lvalue *= expr
R-to-L	/=	Divide and Assign	lvalue /= expr
R-to-L	%=	Modulo and Assign	lvalue %= expr
R-to-L	+=	Add and Assign	lvalue += expr
R-to-L	-=	Subtract and Assign	lvalue -= expr
R-to-L	<<=	Shift Left and Assign	lvalue <<= expr
R-to-L	>>=	Shift Right and Assign	lvalue >>= expr
R-to-L	&=	Bitwise AND and Assign	lvalue &= expr
R-to-L	|=	Bitwise OR and Assign	lvalue |= expr
R-to-L	^=	Bitwise XOR and Assign	lvalue ^= expr
Level 1			
L-to-R	,	Comma (sequencing)	expr, expr

Java has a very similar hierarchy of operator precedence and associativity. The following is a table of the Java operators:

Table 2-2 - Java Operators

Associativity	Operator	Description	Example
Level 15			
R-to-L	new	Object Allocation	new type(expr_list)
Level 14			
L-to-R	.	Member Selection	cobject.member
L-to-R	[]	Subscripting	expr[expr]
L-to-R	()	Method Call	expr(expr_list)
Level 13			
R-to-L	++	Pre-Increment	++lvalue
R-to-L	—	Pre-Decrement	—lvalue
R-to-L	++	Post-Increment	lvalue++

Table 2-2 - Java Operators *Continued*

Associativity	Operator	Description	Example
R-to-L	—	Post-Decrement	lvalue—
R-to-L	-	Unary Minus	-expr
R-to-L	+	Unary Plus	+expr
R-to-L	~	Bitwise NOT	~expr
R-to-L	!	Logical NOT	!expr
R-to-L	()	Type Conversion (cast)	(type)expr
Level 12			
L-to-R	*	Multiply	expr * expr
L-to-R	/	Divide	expr / expr
L-to-R	%	Modulo	expr % expr
Level 11			
L-to-R	+	Add (Binary Plus)	expr + expr
L-to-R	+	String Concatenation	expr + expr
L-to-R	-	Subtract (Binary Minus)	expr - expr
Level 10			
L-to-R	<<	Shift Left	value << expr
L-to-R	>>	Shift Right with Sign Extension	value >> expr
L-to-R	>>>	Shift Right with Zero Extension	value >>> expr
Level 9			
L-to-R	instanceof	Type Comparison	expr instanceof type
L-to-R	<	Less Than	expr < expr
L-to-R	<=	Less Than or Equal	expr <= expr
L-to-R	>	Greater Than	expr > expr
L-to-R	>=	Greater Than or Equal	expr >= expr
Level 8			
L-to-R	==	Equal	expr == expr
L-to-R	!=	Not Equal	expr != expr
Level 7			
L-to-R	&	Bitwise AND	expr & expr
L-to-R	&	Boolean AND	expr & expr
Level 6			
L-to-R	^	Bitwise Exclusive OR	expr ^ expr
L-to-R	^	Boolean Exclusive OR	expr ^ expr

Table 2-2 - Java Operators *Continued*

Associativity	Operator	Description	Example
Level 5			
L-to-R	|	Bitwise Inclusive OR	expr | expr
L-to-R	|	Boolean Inclusive OR	expr | expr
Level 4			
L-to-R	&&	Boolean AND	expr && expr
Level 3			
L-to-R	||	Boolean OR	expr || expr
Level 2			
L-to-R	?:	Boolean IF	expr ? expr : expr
Level 1			
R-to-L	=	Assignment	lvalue = expr
R-to-L	*=	Multiply and Assign	lvalue *= expr
R-to-L	/=	Divide and Assign	lvalue /= expr
R-to-L	%=	Modulo and Assign	lvalue %= expr
R-to-L	+=	Add and Assign	lvalue += expr
R-to-L	+	String Concatenation and Assign	lvalue += expr
R-to-L	-=	Subtract and Assign	lvalue -= expr
R-to-L	<<=	Shift Left and Assign	lvalue <<= expr
R-to-L	>>=	Shift Right with Sign Extension and Assign	lvalue >>= expr
R-to-L	>>>=	Shift Right with Zero Extension and Assign	lvalue >>= expr
R-to-L	&=	Bitwise AND and Assign	lvalue &= expr
R-to-L	|=	Bitwise OR and Assign	lvalue |= expr
R-to-L	^=	Bitwise XOR and Assign	lvalue ^= expr

Operator precedence specifies the order in which operations are performed. Associatively determines the direction that the operations are performed when the expression contains operators of equal precedence. For instance, the given expression:

```
total = 2 * item1 + 20 / item2;
```

has four binary operators: *, /, + and =. Since * and / have the highest precedence, these operations would be performed first. Since * and / are of equal precedence, the * would be done first and then the / (given that * and / are left-to-right associative). Since + has higher precedence than =, the + would then be performed on the resulting product and quotient. Finally, the sum on the right side of the = would then be assigned to variable `total`.

Observe that Java has far fewer operators than C++. This is mainly because the Java language designers have chosen to eliminate many of the troublesome and controversial features of C++ so that Java would be straightforward and consistent as an object-oriented language.

Because Java has no pointers, operators like ->, &, *, .*, ->* would be totally meaningless in Java. The first three operators (the member selection operator for pointer variables, the address operator and the dereference operator) are frequently found in C or C++ code:

```
class  A {
public:
     A();
    ~A();
     int max(int, int);
     int strcmp(const char *, const char *);
     ...
     int value;
};

void foo()
{
int num1 = 50;
int num2 = 55;
int * pnum1 = &num1;
A     obj_a;
A *   pobj_a = &obj_a;
...
pobj_a ->max(num1, num2);
...
cout<<*pnum1<<endl;
...
}
```

The pointer-to-member operators (.* and ->*) are somewhat obscure and redundant features in C++. Basically, these operators allow one to reference a member of a class with a special identifier. For instance, if we enhance the above by adding more statements to the body of `foo()`:

```
int A::*pvalue;       // pvalue is a pointer to int in class A
pvalue = &A::value;   // pvalue now points to data member value in
                         class A
int (A::*getMax)      // getMax is a pointer to a function of class A;
(int, int);            it takes two  int's and returns an int
getMax = &A::max;     // getMax now points to member function A::max
```

we can then write statements like:

```
obj_a.*pvalue = 15;   // means the same as obj_a.value = 15;
(obj_a.*getMax)       // means the same as obj_a.max(num1, num2);
(num1, num2);

(pobj_a->*getMax)     // means the same as pobj_a->max(num1, num2);
(num1, num2)
```

The C++ scope operator *(::)* is also non-existent in Java. The scope operator is used to refer to a specific global or class data member or member function in C++. For instance, if we expand on the above example by defining a subclass B from class A:

```
class B : public A {
public:
    B();
   ~B();
    int strcmp(const char *, const char *);
    char * strcpy(char *, const char *);
    . . .
private:
    . . .
};

void main()
{
B obj_b;
const char * s1 = "Good Dining!";
const char * s2 = "Good Dining.";
char s3[80];

obj_b.strcmp(s1, s2);
. . .
obj_b.A::strcmp(s1,s2);
. . .
::strcpy(s3, s1);
. . .
}
```

Class B has a member function called `strcmp(const char *, const char *)` which returns an `int`. Variable `obj_b` is an instance of B and the statement:

```
obj_b.strcmp(s1, s2);
```

means that `obj_b` is calling the `strcmp` implementation of class B (with the use of the dot (.) operator). Class B overrides an inherited implementation of the same function name and signature of class A. The instance `obj_b` can call the class A implementation by using the class name and scope operator:

```
obj_b.A::strcmp(s1,s2);
```

The scope operator can also be used by itself to refer to a function. For instance,

```
::strcpy(s3, s1);
```

is another way to write "`strcpy(s3,s1),`" which refers to the standard, non-member function implementation found in the ANSI C library (which is part of C++). Note that whenever the scope operator is used by itself, it refers to some non-member function (a typical C-style function that is not associated with any class).

The `sizeof` operator found in C and C++ are also not available in Java. Basically, `sizeof` is used to return the size (in bytes) of a type, pointer or instance of an object. This operator is not necessary in Java because each primitive type in Java has a clearly defined size.

Java also does not have a `delete` operator to free heap memory previously allocated for objects like in C++. That is because dynamic memory deallocation is performed automatically by a garbage collector in Java. In C++, dynamic memory management is the responsibility of the developer and `delete` would be used to complement the `new` operator. For example,

```
class Person {
public:
    Person();
    Person(char * nm);
    ~Person();
            // more member functions
private:
    char * name;
};

Person::Person() {
name = new char[strlen("Nameless")+1];
strcpy(name, "Nameless");
}

Person::Person(char * nm) {
name = new char[strlen(nm)+1];
strcpy(name,nm);
}

Person::~Person() {
delete [] name;
}

void main()
{
Person freddie("Freddie");
Person * robert = new Person("Robert");
Person * students = new Person[10];
```

```
. . .
delete robert;
delete []students;
}
```

In the above example, `robert` points to a dynamically allocated instance of `Person` and `students` points to an array of ten `Person` objects. After these variables have served their purposes, `delete` is called to return the memory to the heap. Note that "`delete []`" is used for <u>arrays</u> of dynamically allocated objects. For automatic object `freddie`, its destructor (`Person::~Person`) is called when the variable goes out of scope.

In Java, the right shift operator (>>) is used to do a *signed* right shift, meaning that the value of the sign bit will fill the high bits as shifting occurs. On the other hand, the >>> operator means to perform an *unsigned* right shift, meaning that the high bits are zero filled (including the sign bit). The >>> operator is totally unique to Java and does not exist in C++.

In C++, the meaning of the right shift operator (>>) is very ambiguous. It could be either a signed shift or an unsigned shift, depending on the particular vendor's implementation. This ambiguity is a historical obstacle to portability.

The left shift operator (<<) will perform a left shift with zeros filling the lower bits. The lower order bits will also shift into the sign bit. A <<< operator does not exist.

The following example shows the effects of shifting a few variables of type `int` (a signed 32-bit quantity in Java):

Listing 2-1: BitShiftDemo1.java

```java
public class BitShiftDemo1 {

    public static void main(String argv[]) {
    int num1 = 16;
    System.out.println("num1 = "+num1);
    num1 = num1>>2;
    System.out.println("num1 = "+num1);

    int num2 = 3;
    System.out.println("num2 = "+num2);
    num2 = num2<<2;
    System.out.println("num2 = "+num2);

    int num3 = -16;
    System.out.println("num3 = "+num3);
    num3 = num3>>2;
    System.out.println("num3 = "+num3);

    int num4 = -3;
```

```
        System.out.println("num4 = "+num4);
        num4 = num4>>2;
        System.out.println("num4 = "+num4);

        int num5 = 0x40000000;    // 1073741824 in decimal
        System.out.println("num5 = "+num5);
        num5 = num5<<1;
        System.out.println("num5 = "+num5);

        int num6 = 0xFFFFFFFF;    // Two's complement: -1
        System.out.println("num6 = "+num6);
        num6 = num6>>>1;
        System.out.println("num6 = "+num6);
        }
}
```

```
Output:

num1 = 16
num1 = 4
num2 = 3
num2 = 12
num3 = -16
num3 = -4
num4 = -3
num4 = -1
num5 = 1073741824
num5 = -2147483648
num6 = -1
num6 = 2147483647
```

In the above example, num1 initially contained 16 or the binary bit pattern 00010000. Shifting right two places resulted in 00000100, which is 4.

In the case of num5 above, num5 initially had value 1073741824 or $2^{30} - 1$. When a single shift to the left took place, the sign bit became enabled. The resulting value became -2147483648 or -2^{31} (which is found by inverting the lower 31 bits and adding 1, which is the two's complement).

In the case of num6, its initial value was -1 (the sign bit was enabled). When the first >>> operation was applied, the 1 of the sign bit moved one position to the right and the sign bit received a zero, which resulted in the positive integer, 2147483647 or $2^{31} - 1$.

 Warning: The >>> operator does not work as one would expect for negative values contained within variables of primitive types byte and short, each of which has a size less than the size of an int (32 bits). For instance, suppose we have the following:

```
short aShort = -1;
System.out.println("aShort = "+aShort);
aShort >>>= 1;
System.out.println("aShort = "+aShort);
```

The following would be the output:

```
aShort = -1
aShort = -1
```

Wait! After a single unsigned shift to the right, isn't variable aShort supposed to contain 32767? Well, as things turn out, the short was implicitly promoted to the canonical size of an int <u>before</u> the shift. After the shift had taken place, the int was truncated back to a short:

```
0xFFFF          (What aShort initially contained)
0xFFFFFFFF      (Implicit promotion to an int)
0x7FFFFFFF      (After shifting once to the right)
0xFFFF          (Truncation back to a short)
```

Unfortunately, in such situations, the >>> operator is useless. To obtain the effect of an unsigned right shift, one writes a statement such as:

```
aShort = (short)((aShort & 0xFFFF)>>1);
```

The effect of the bitwise & is to zero out the bits of the upper two bytes before the shift takes place. After that, we would get the expected value of 32767. The Java sample program, BitShiftDemo2, illustrates this point and can be found on the included media.

Java also has another operator called instanceof, which is not found in C++. This operator is used to determine whether an object is of a particular user-defined type. For example, if we have:

```
if (str1 instanceof  String)
    System.out.println("str1 is a String");
```

the expression "str1 instanceof String" would return true and print out the line "str1 is a String" if str1 is of class String. The instanceof operator can only be applied to an object that is known to be within a hierarchy of classes. In practical terms, instanceof is used to determine if it is safe to cast the object to a specialized (subclass) type. We will explore this operator further when I discuss *Run Time Type Information*.

Unlike C, Java does not have the comma (,) operator for grouping expressions. In C, we could have something like:

```
foo(num1, num2, (num3 = 5, num4 = 3 * num3));
```

where the third argument to function foo is (num3 = 5, num4 = 3 * num3), which evaluates to 15.

However, the comma operator can be simulated in Java for loops. This is the only place where this C-like feature is permissible:

```
int b = 20;
for (int a = 0; a < 10; a++, b-) {
        System.out.println("a = "+a);
        System.out.println("b = "+b);
        }
```

The + operator in Java takes on the special meaning of string concatenation and is frequently used with the `String` class, which is part of the default `java.lang` package. Unlike C++, Java does not support operator overloading for user-defined classes. The use of the + operator for string concatenation is the only exception to this rule in Java.

The Order of Evaluation of the Operands

While C and C++ have well-defined rules for operator precedence and associativity, the same cannot be said for the order of evaluation of operands within an expression. For instance, if we are given the following C++ code:

```
int add_and_increment(int val1, int val2)
{
return (val1 + val2 + 1);
}

void main()
{
int x = 5;
int y;
int m = 10;
int n;

y = x + x++;                            // Statement #1
// At this point, does y contain 10 or 11?

n = add_and_increment(m, m++);          // Statement #2
// At this point, does n contain 21 or 22?
}
```

Within the first statement, which part of the right-hand side gets evaluated first, x or x++? If x gets evaluated first, then the temporary value on the right-hand side would be 5 + 5, or 10. However, if x++ gets evaluated first, the temporary value would be 6 + 5, or 11.

A similar dilemma holds true for the second statement. Within the argument list, is the m evaluated first or the m++? If m is evaluated first, then the second statement could be logically rewritten as:

```
int temp;
temp = m++;
n = add_and_increment(temp, temp);
```

which is equivalent to a left-to-right evaluation and the variable n would contain
21. However, if the m++ portion is evaluated first, then the second statement
could be logically rewritten as:

```
int temp;
temp = m++;
n = add_and_increment(m, temp);
```

which is equivalent to a right-to-left evaluation and the variable n would contain
22.

Given these two choices, which is the correct one? As it turns out, that depends
on the compiler you have and the vendor's implementation. The order of evaluation of the operands was left undefined in the C and C++ standards so that
vendors are free to optimize their compilers in the way they see fit.

This sort of situation, where one sub-expression could influence the outcome
of another sub-expression, is called a side effect. Knowledgeable and experienced C and C++ programmers make a point to avoid coding statements
with side effects because such code is not portable (even between different
memory models of the same compiler of the same platform!). Unfortunately,
such troublesome code can still be found in many industries that use C or
C++.

The designers of Java chose to eliminate this portability issue by declaring that
the order of evaluation of the operands will be from left to right. So, if we have
the following equivalent Java code:

Listing 2-2: OrderEvaluationDemo.java

```
public class OrderEvaluationDemo {

    static int add_and_increment(int val1, int val2) {
    return (val1 + val2 + 1);
    }

    public static void main(String argv[]) {
    int x = 5;
    int y;
    int m = 10;
    int n;

    System.out.println("At start, x = "+x);
    y = x + x++;
    System.out.println("At end, x = "+x+", y = "+y+"\n");

    System.out.println("At start, m = "+m);
    n = add_and_increment(m, m++);
```

```
    System.out.println("At end, m = "+m+", n = "+n+"\n");
    }
}
```

The results that would be displayed would be:

```
At start, x = 5
At end, x = 6, y = 10

At start, m = 10
At end, m = 11, n = 21
```

Note: Even though the designers of Java chose to provide a language that is safer to use for the programmer, it is still a good idea to avoid writing statements with interdependent sub-expressions. Highly abbreviated code is difficult to read and understand, especially if it is going to be supported by people who are unfamiliar with your work (or you may be that support person and you forget what you had done after one year).

The Role of the Semicolon

In C, C++ and Java, the executable statement is terminated with the semicolon (;). The following are some sample C statements:

```
x = abs(v) + abs(w);
printf("The result is %d\n", x);
```

The semicolon is also used for do-while loops, such as:

```
long index = 200;
do {
        draw(index, index/2);
        index-;
        } while (index > 0);
```

However, there is a difference in the way the semicolon is used between C++ and Java. In C++, the body of a class definition must be terminated with the semicolon. For example,

```
class Pair {
public:
    Pair(x, y);
    void setX(int);
    void setY(int);
    int getX();
    int getY();
    ...
private:
```

```
    int x;
    int y;
};   // semicolon required here
```

In Java, the class definition is written in a similar way, except the semicolon can
be omitted! The following is the Java equivalent to class `Pair`:

Listing 2-3: Pair.java

```
public class Pair {
    public Pair(int x_value, int y_value) {
        setX(x_value);
        setY(y_value);
    }
    public int getX() {
        return x;
    }
    public int getY() {
        return y;
    }
    public void setX(int x_value) {
        x = x_value;
    }
    public void setY(int y_value) {
        y = y_value;
    }
    private int x;
    private int y;

    public static void main(String args[]) {
        Pair pt = new Pair(-50, 450);
        System.out.println("pt = ("+pt.getX()+",
        "+pt.getY()+")");
    }
}   // semicolon not required
```

C++ programmers who are new to Java are often puzzled by the lack of the
semicolon as I've shown above.

Flow of Control: Branching

The if/else and switch statements are syntactically identical between Java and
C/C++. Below is a typical if/else construct for Java:

```
if (a <= 5)        // conditional expression
    System.out.println("a = "+a);
else
    System.out.println("a is greater than 5");
```

In C or C++, the test for the conditional expression results in either zero (false) or non-zero (true), which are integral values. However, in Java, the conditional must evaluate to a boolean type, which has either a value of *true* or *false*. A boolean type cannot be cast to an integral type. Hence, something such as:

```
int value;
value = 1;
if  (value)//                             Error  in  Java
    System.out.println("Is true...\n");
```

will <u>not</u> compile.

The *switch* statement is used to test a conditional expression for multiple alternatives. The conditional expression must evaluate to a `char`, `byte`, `short` or `int`. For example:

```
int category = 4;

switch (category) {
    case 1:
        System.out.println("Fish");
        break;
    case 2:
        System.out.println("Birds");
        break;
    case 3:
        System.out.println("Reptiles");
        break;
    case 4:
        System.out.println("Mammals");
        break;
    default:
        System.out.println("Unknown");
        break;
};
```

In the above example, the string `Mammals` would be written to the standard output. The `break` keyword is used to exit the switch statement and prevent processing from continuing into the next case.

Flow of Control: Iteration

The constructs to support iteration and looping in Java are identical to those of C and C++. The `for` and `while` keywords of C/C++ are also available in Java. The `for` loop is typically used to iterate through a sequence, in order to pass the elements of an array to other methods. The following is a Java example:

```
for (int index = 0; index < 20; index++) {
    System.out.println("The string object at index"+index+" is ");
    System.out.println(msg[index]+"\n");
    }
```

The above is a typical example where an int called index is declared and initial-ized to zero to start the iteration process. The iteration proceeds as long as the con-dition (index < 20) is true. Each pass would increment index by 1. The result is the outputting of all the String objects from a String array called msg.

For the above example, the variable index is defined for the for loop and its lifetime is only valid within the body of the loop. Once the loop com-pletes, the index variable goes out of scope. This is one of the important dif-ferences between Java and C/C++. In C/C++, the index variable would not be out of scope until processing reaches the end of the function body that contains the for loop. The equivalent to the above in C++ would be some-thing like:

```
{

for (int index = 0; index < 20; index++) {
    cout<<"The string object at index"<<index<<" is ");
    cout<<msg[index]<<"\n");
 }


cout<<"Loop completed, index = "<<index<<endl; // legal -
                                                index still//
                                                in scope in C++

// index will exit scope at the '}'
}
```

In both Java and C++, the initial condition of a for loop must be true before processing enters the loop. The for loop would be bypassed if the initial condi-tion is false. This is also the case with the following form of the while construct (Java example):

```
index = 0;
while  ( index < 20) {
    System.out.println("The string object at index"+index+" is ");
    System.out.println(msg[index]+"\n");
    index++;
 }
```

Like the for loop examples, the condition (index < 20) is checked first before the loop is entered. There is also a second form of the while loop (Java exam-ple):

```
int index = 20;
 do {
      System.out.println("Index = "+index+"\n");
      index++;
    } while (index < 20);
```

The loop begins with the do keyword and the conditional clause is placed after the body of the loop. In this case, the body of the loop is performed at least once since the condition is checked <u>after</u> processing the body. In the above example, the body of the loop is executed exactly once, even though the condition (index < 20) is false on initial entry.

Both forms of the while loop apply to Java and C/C++. A sample program called Iteration (both Java and C++ versions) can be found on the supplied media.

Flow of Control: The **break** and **continue** Keywords

Programmers often use iteration to find the first occurrence of an element of interest. In this case, the break keyword is very useful. Basically, it is a restricted form of goto to exit the immediate enclosing loop. The following is an example in Java:

Listing 2-4: BreakDemo.java

```java
public class BreakDemo {

    public static void main(String args[]) {

        String subject[] = new String[10];
        subject[0] = new String("geography");
        subject[1] = new String("history");
        subject[2] = new String("mathematics");
        subject[3] = new String("biology");
        subject[4] = new String("fitness");
        subject[5] = new String("dining");
        subject[6] = new String("sports");
        subject[7] = new String("travels");

        for (int index = 0; index<8; index++) {
            if (subject[index].equals("sports")) {
                System.out.println("Subject "+subject[index]+"
                is at index "+
                    index);
                break;
            }
        }
    }
}
```

As the example shows, we are given a pre-initialized array of String objects called subject and we want to know if one of the elements contains "sports." As we loop through each element we examine the content of each

String object with the `equals` method to see if it matches the string
`"sports."` If so, a message indicating the desired subject and index is printed
on the standard output device and we break from the loop. The following is the
result:

```
Subject sports is at index 6
```

There is also a `continue` keyword for the purposes of going to the end of a `for`
block so that the next iteration can begin immediately. The following is an example where the contents of all the members of array `subject` is outputted except
the one with `"sports"`:

Listing 2-5: ContinueDemo.java

```java
public class ContinueDemo {

    public static void main(String args[]) {
        String subject[] = new String[8];
        subject[0] = new String("geography");
        subject[1] = new String("history");
        subject[2] = new String("mathematics");
        subject[3] = new String("biology");
        subject[4] = new String("fitness");
        subject[5] = new String("dining");
        subject[6] = new String("sports");
        subject[7] = new String("travels");
        subject[8] = new String("chemistry");
        subject[9] = new String("computers");

        for (int index = 0; index<8; index++) {
            if (subject[index].equals("sports"))
                continue;
            else
                System.out.println("Subject "+subject[index]+"
                is at index "+
                    index);
        }
    }
}
```

The following is the output:

```
Subject geography is at index 0
Subject history is at index 1
Subject mathematics is at index 2
Subject biology is at index 3
Subject fitness is at index 4
Subject dining is at index 5
```

```
Subject travels is at index 7
```

Both Java and C++ support the use of the break and continue keywords in the manner demonstrated.

Setting Up Arrays

The array is a collection of contiguous data items of the same type. Practically every modern programming language supports arrays in some fashion. The syntax for arrays in C and C++ is highly varied because of the conceptual relationship to pointers. In Java, there are no pointers and the whole scheme for declaring arrays is simplified. Consider the following Java example:

Listing 2-6: ArrayDemo..java

```java
public class ArrayDemo {

    public static void main(String args[]) {
        int num[];                                            /* (1) */
        num = new int[10];
        for (int index = 0; index < 10; index++) {   /* (2) */
            num[index] = 3 * index;
        }
        for (int index = 0; index < 10; index++) {   /* (3) */
            System.out.println("Element #"+index+" =
            "+num[index]+"\n");
        }
                                                     /* (4) */
        System.out.println("Number of elements of array =
        "+num.length+"\n");
    }
}
```

One of the first things that is different about the declaration of arrays in Java is that no size is specified with the identifier! The line:

```java
int num[];
```

means that num is an array of type int. The next line:

```java
num = new int[10];
```

means that num refers to ten contiguous memory locations, where each location is of type int. This memory allocation is done with the use of the new operator. To simplify matters, the declaration and initialization could be combined into one statement:

```java
int num[] = new int[10];
```

At this point, each element of num still has no value. These memory locations must be initialized and that is done with the for loop at comment /* (2) */.

After printing out the contents of the num array, the size is displayed at the end. All arrays record their own sizes with the `length` attribute (which is `public` and `final`, meaning that all methods of all classes may read this attribute, but cannot change it). The size is found by the expression "`num.length`" as displayed at comment /* (4) */.

The equivalent to the above in C++ would look like:

Listing 2-7: ArrayDemo.cpp

```cpp
#include <iostream.h>

void main() {

int num[10];

for (int index = 0; index < 10; index++) {
    num[index] = 3 * index;
    }
for (index = 0; index < 10; index++) {
    cout<<"Element #"<<index<<" = "<<num[index]<<endl;
    }

cout<<"Number of elements of array =
"<<sizeof(num)/sizeof(int)<<endl;
}
```

The `sizeof` operator of C or C++ is used to determine the number of elements array num could contain.

Note: One of the biggest differences between Java and C/C++ is that Java provides protection against array overruns while C/C++ does not. In the above C++ example, if I were to make a slight change to the first `for` loop as follows:

```cpp
for (int index = 0; index < 11; index++) {
    num[index] = 3 * index;
    }
```

The compiler would compile the code, run and generate some runtime error indicating attempted access to unallocated memory (num[10]). Such classical problems in C or C++ are typically very difficult to find.

On the other hand, if the equivalent occurred in Java, the program would terminate with the message:

```
java.lang.ArrayIndexOutOfBoundsException: 10
        at ArrayDemo.main(ArrayDemo.java:10)
```

Array overruns in Java are handled by the throwing and catching of exceptions. Exception handling is also available in C++, but Java strongly enforces its use for the sake of reliability. A later chapter is devoted to how exceptions work.

Array of Arrays

In Java, it is also possible to declare an array of an array, or what some might call a multidimensional array. The following is an example:

Listing 2-8: TwoDArrayDemo1.java

```java
public class TwoDArrayDemo1 {

    public static void main(String args[]) {

        int cell[][]  = new int[3][];                    /* (1) */
        for (int row = 0; row < 3; row++)                /* (2) */
            cell[row]  = new int[5];

        for (int row = 0; row < 3; row++)                /* (3) */
            for (int column = 0; column < 5; column++)
                cell[row][column]  = column + row;

        for (int row = 0; row < 3; row++) {
            for (int column = 0; column < 5; column++)
                System.out.print("["+row+","+column+"]="+cell
                [row][column]+"\t");
            System.out.println();
        }
    }
}
```

The output appears as:

```
[0,0] = 0    [0,1] = 1    [0,2] = 2    [0,3] = 3    [0,4] = 4
[1,0] = 1    [1,1] = 2    [1,2] = 3    [1,3] = 4    [1,4] = 5
[2,0] = 2    [2,1] = 3    [2,2] = 4    [2,3] = 5    [2,4] = 6
```

At comment /* (1) */, we are declaring variable cell to be an array of an array of int and it is initialized to three rows, each with an indefinite number of columns. The first for loop (comment /* (2) */) allocates for each row five columns. With the help of an outer for loop and an inner for loop (comment /* (3) */), each member of cell is assigned an int value.

In the above example, statements /* (1) */ and /* (2) */ could also have been combined as one:

```java
int cell[][]  = new int[3][5];
```

Note: In Java, as each dimension of a multidimensional array is instantiated, the most significant dimensions must be instantiated first. For the above example, the following would <u>not</u> be legal:

```
int cell[][] = new int[][5];
```

The next example is a variation of the previous one. It is possible to initialize each member of the two-dimensional array by using lists of constants as follows:

```
public class TwoDArrayDemo2 {

    public static void main(String args[]) {

        int cell[][] = { {-3, -6, -9, -12, -15},     /* (1) */
                         {4, 12, 16, 20, 24},
                         {-5, 15, -20, 25, -30} };

        for (int row = 0; row < 3; row++) {
            for (int column = 0; column < 5; column++)
             System.out.print("["+row+","+column+"]=
             "+cell[row][column]+"\t");
            System.out.println();
            }
        }
    }
```

Each row is bounded by a set of braces ({}) and the entire array of arrays is also bounded by the braces (comment /* (1) */).

Declaring an Array of a Type

The angled brackets representing arrays can also be used in a different context. Consider the following:

Listing 2-9: ArrayTypeDemo.java

```
public class ArrayTypeDemo {

    static int [] [] create2DArray() {
        int [] grid[] = new int[3][];

        for (int row = 0; row < 3; row++) {
            grid[row] = new int[5];
            for (int column = 0; column < 5; column++)
                grid[row][column] = column + row;
            }

        return grid;
        }
```

```java
public static void main(String args[]) {

    int [] [] cell;
    cell = create2DArray();

    for (int row = 0; row < 3; row++) {
        for (int column = 0; column < 5; column++)
        System.out.print("["+row+","+column+"]="+cell
        [row][column]+"\t");
        System.out.println();
        }

    }

}
```

The above is a variation of an example" of the previous topic, "Array of Arrays." In this example, the activity of declaring and initializing a two-dimensional array was separated into a method called `create2DArray()`. There are some interesting points about this particular method:

- Within the body of the method, the statement:

  ```java
  int [] grid[] = new int[3][];
  ```

  declares variable `grid` to be an array of type `array of int`. Note that when the angled brackets are placed to the left of the identifier, the notion of array applies to the type.

- The return type of `create2DArray` is a `type of array of array of int`:

  ```java
  static int [] [] create2DArray()
  ```

  The body of `create2DArray` returns `grid`, which is a reference to an array of array of int. Note that in Java, this approach of returning local data is safe since the information is created on the heap and not on the stack. Furthermore, automatic garbage collection will insure that the memory will be deallocated when it is no longer useful.

- Finally, within method `main` of class `ArrayTypeDemo`, we see the following statements:

  ```java
  int [] [] cell;
  ```

  ```java
  cell = create2DArray();
  ```

  Variable `cell` is declared to be of type `array of array of int` and it is assigned to refer to the memory returned by `create2DArray()`. Note that since method main is `static`, it can only call other static methods, which is why `create2DArray` was qualified as static.

The following is roughly an equivalent to the above in C++:

Listing 2-10: ArrayTypeDemo.cpp

```cpp
#include <iostream.h>
#include <stdio.h>
#include <stdlib.h>

const int ROW_SIZE = 3;
const int COL_SIZE = 5;

typedef int * IntPtr;

void create2DArray(int ** grid, int row_size, int col_size) {

for (int row = 0; row < row_size; row++) {
   for (int column = 0; column < col_size; column++)
      grid[row][column] = column + row;
      }
}

void main() {

int ** cell;

cell = new IntPtr[ROW_SIZE];

for(int index = 0; index < ROW_SIZE; index++)        /* (1) */
   cell[index] = new int[COL_SIZE];

create2DArray(cell, ROW_SIZE, COL_SIZE);

for (int row = 0; row < ROW_SIZE; row++) {            /* (2) */
   for (int column = 0; column < COL_SIZE; column++)
     cout<<"["<<row<<","<<column<<"]="<<cell[row][column]
       <<"\t";
   cout<<endl;
   }

delete [] cell;
}
```

In the above, I had chosen to use memory from the heap instead of the stack to approximate the equivalent example in Java. This C++ example differs from its Java equivalent in the following ways:

- The implementation of arrays in C++ has a close correlation with pointers. The declaration:

  ```cpp
  int ** cell;
  ```

is essentially equivalent to int `cell[][]` in Java. The next statement:

```
cell = new IntPtr[ROW_SIZE];
```

establishes three locations (of size int `*`) representing three rows. The new operator in this case allocates memory from the heap and returns an int `**` (pointer to a pointer of int).

In the first `for` loop (comment /* (1) */), each of the three rows (of type int `*`) is assigned to point to an `array of int` of size COL_SIZE.

The allocation of storage in this example is done outside of function `create2DArray()` since it is recommended practice to perform both the allocation and deallocation within the same body of the calling function (`main` in this case). This discipline would help deal with memory leaks.

- The `create2DArray` function in this example does not return any value. Rather it takes three arguments, of which the first is of type int `**`. The body of the `main` function passes variable `cell` into `create2DArray`, where the two-dimensional array actually gets values assigned to each location.

- Each location of the two-dimensional array cell is then displayed (comment /* (2) */). Since C++ has no automatic garbage collection, the programmer has to make a point of deallocating the heap memory previously allocated for `cell`. This is done with the statement:

```
delete [] cell;
```

The angled bracket notation in the statement indicates the deallocation of an array and not a single object. The statement will also perform a cascaded deallocation of all subobjects within the larger subobjects.

 Warning: In C++, a statement such as:

```
delete cell;
```

does <u>not</u> necessarily mean:

```
delete [] cell;
```

Since `cell` was declared to be an array of something, the first statement may <u>not</u> perform a cascaded deallocation of memory (it depends on the vendor's implementation). This usage is undefined in C++. If you had allocated an array of any type, the second statement is the proper one to use.

Passing Parameters into Functions or Methods

The basic syntax and structure of a function in C, C++ and Java are fundamentally identical:

```
return_value    function_name(arg1, arg2,...)
{

// body of executable statements

}
```

In Java, all functions must be associated with some class and they are called *methods*. In C++, functions associated with a class are called *member functions*. Traditional C functions and functions not associated with any C++ class are simply called *non-member functions*.

The function name and its argument list constitute the *signature* of the function. The argument list is the function's interface to the outside world since it is the entry point for incoming parameters.

Parameter passing varies somewhat between Java and C++. From the perspective of Java,

- There are no pointers as in C or C++.

- Built-in types (called *primitive data types*) are always passed by value.

- Object types (like the classes that are part of the standard Java packages) are always passed by reference.

Java variables that represent object types are called *reference* variables and those that represent built-in types are called *non-reference* variables. The following sample program demonstrates these two types of Java variables.

Listing 2-11: ParameterPassingDemo.java

```
import java.awt.Point;     // Class Point is part of the standard
                           Java AWT package

public class ParameterPassingDemo {

    public static void swap_by_value(int x, int y) {
    int temp;
    temp = x;
    x = y;
    y = temp;
    }

    public static void exchange_coordinates_by_reference(Point
    pt) {
```

```java
        int temp = pt.x;
        pt.x = pt.y;
        pt.y = temp;

        System.out.println("\n Inside exchange_coordinates_by_refer
         ence...");
        System.out.println("\n pt.x = " + pt.x);
        System.out.println("\n pt.y = " + pt.y);
        }

        public static void main(String argv[]) {

                int num1 = -30;
                int num2 =  45;

                System.out.println("\n Before calling
                 swap_by_value...");
                System.out.println("\n num1 = "+num1);
                System.out.println("\n num2 = "+num2);

                swap_by_value(num1,num2);

                System.out.println("\n After calling swap_by_value...");
                System.out.println("\n num1 = "+num1);
                System.out.println("\n num2 = "+num2);

                Point aPoint = new Point(-50,300);

                System.out.println("\n Before calling exchange_coordi
                 nates_by_reference...");
                System.out.println("\n aPoint.x = " + aPoint.x);
                System.out.println("\n aPoint.y = " + aPoint.y);

                exchange_coordinates_by_reference(aPoint);

                System.out.println("\n After calling exchange_coordi
                 nates_by_reference...");
                System.out.println("\n aPoint.x = " + aPoint.x);
                System.out.println("\n aPoint.y = " + aPoint.y);
                }
        }

Output:

Before calling swap_by_value...
num1 = -30
num2 = 45

After calling swap_by_value...
```

```
num1 = -30
num2 = 45

  Before calling exchange_coordinates_by_reference...
  aPoint.x = -50
  aPoint.y = 300

  Inside exchange_coordinates_by_reference...
  pt.x = 300
  pt.y = -50

  After calling exchange_coordinates_by_reference...
  aPoint.x = 300
  aPoint.y = -50
```

In the above Java program, num1 and num2 are non-reference variables of built-in type int. In an attempt to swap the contents of the two variables, num1 and num2 are passed into method swap_by_value. However, the swapping never took place within function main() because **copies** of num1 and num2 are passed into swap_by_value.

The same program also had instantiated and initialized a Point object aPoint (defined in package java.awt.Point) to point (-50,300). The Point class is an object type and, consequently, aPoint is a reference variable. When aPoint was passed into a method called exchange_coordinates_by_reference, the method swapped the contents of the x and y coordinates of the argument. In this case, a change was reflected inside aPoint of main() when the method had completed.

It is important to note that a reference variable is really an address to the object and not the object itself. When aPoint was passed into exchange_coordi-nates_by_reference, the address of the object and **not** a copy of the object was passed. This notion in Java is semantically equivalent to how reference variables and pointer variables work in C++. In terms of syntax and usage, Java reference variables are very close to C++ references.

With the above in mind, let us look at an equivalent example written in C++:

Listing 2-12: ParameterPassingDemo.cpp

```cpp
#include <iostream.h>

class Point {
public:
    Point();
    Point(int,int);
    void setCoordinates(int,int);
    int getX() const;
    int getY() const;
```

```
private:
    int x;
    int y;
};

Point::Point() : x(0), y(0) {
}

Point::Point(int x_value, int y_value) : x(x_value), y(y_value) {
}

void Point::setCoordinates(int x_value, int y_value) {
x = x_value;
y = y_value;
}

int Point::getX() const {
return x;
}

int Point::getY() const {
return y;
}

void swap_by_value(int x, int y) {
int temp;
temp = x;
x = y;
y = temp;
}

void swap_by_pointer(int * x, int * y) {
int temp;
temp = *x;
*x = *y;
*y = temp;
}

void swap_by_reference(int & x, int & y) {
int temp;
temp = x;
x = y;
y = temp;
}

void exchange_coordinates_by_reference(Point & pt) {
int x_val = pt.getX();
int y_val = pt.getY();
pt.setCoordinates(y_val,x_val);
```

```
cout<<"\nInside exchange_coordinates_by_reference...\n";
cout<<"pt.x = "<<pt.getX()<<endl;
cout<<"pt.y = "<<pt.getY()<<endl;
}

void main(int argc, char ** argv)
{
int num1 = -30;
int num2 =  45;
int num3 = -15;
int num4 =  55;
int * num5;
int * num6;
int & num7 = num1;
int & num8 = num2;

cout<<"\nBefore calling swap_by_value...\n";
cout<<"num1 = "<<num1<<endl;
cout<<"num2 = "<<num2<<endl;

swap_by_value(num1,num2);

cout<<"\nAfter calling swap_by_value...\n";
cout<<"num1 = "<<num1<<endl;
cout<<"num2 = "<<num2<<endl;

num5 = &num3;
num6 = &num4;

cout<<"\nBefore calling swap_by_pointer...\n";
cout<<"*num5 = "<<*num5<<endl;
cout<<"*num6 = "<<*num6<<endl;

swap_by_pointer(num5,num6);

cout<<"\nAfter calling swap_by_pointer...\n";
cout<<"*num5 = "<<*num5<<endl;
cout<<"*num6 = "<<*num6<<endl;

cout<<"\nBefore calling swap_by_reference...\n";
cout<<"num7 = "<<num7<<endl;
cout<<"num8 = "<<num8<<endl;

swap_by_reference(num7,num8);

cout<<"\nAfter calling swap_by_reference...\n";
cout<<"num7 = "<<num7<<endl;
cout<<"num8 = "<<num8<<endl;
```

```
Point aPoint(-50,300);

cout<<"\nBefore calling exchange_coordinates_by_reference...\n";
cout<<"aPoint.x = "<<aPoint.getX()<<endl;
cout<<"aPoint.y = "<<aPoint.getY()<<endl;

exchange_coordinates_by_reference(aPoint);

cout<<"\nAfter calling exchange_coordinates_by_reference...\n";
cout<<"aPoint.x = "<<aPoint.getX()<<endl;
cout<<"aPoint.y = "<<aPoint.getY()<<endl;

}
```

Output:

```
Before calling swap_by_value...
num1 = -30
num2 = 45

After calling swap_by_value...
num1 = -30
num2 = 45

Before calling swap_by_pointer...
*num5 = -15
*num6 = 55

After calling swap_by_pointer...
*num5 = 55
*num6 = -15

Before calling swap_by_reference...
num7 = -30
num8 = 45

After calling swap_by_reference...
num7 = 45
num8 = -30

Before calling exchange_coordinates_by_reference...
aPoint.x = -50
aPoint.y = 300

Inside exchange_coordinates_by_reference...
pt.x = 300
pt.y = -50

After calling exchange_coordinates_by_reference...
aPoint.x = 300
aPoint.y = -50
```

In C++, built-in or user-defined (object) types can be passed by value, by pointer or by reference. The example above employs a user-defined type for class `Point`.

Like the Java equivalent, the `swap_by_value` function above does not exchange the contents of `num1` and `num2` since copies of both variables are passed into the function. Consequently, `num1` and `num2` are not changed after `swap_by_value` completes.

The contents of `num5` and `num6` are actually swapped when they are passed into the `swap_by_pointer` function. In the function's signature, the `int * ` notion means `"pointer to an int."` Within the body of the function, the `*` is used as the dereference operator (e.g., `*x` means the `"contents of pointer variable x"`).

Similarly, the contents of variables `num7` and `num8` are swapped when they are passed into the `swap_by_reference` function. Within the function's signature, `int &` means a `"reference to an int."` The ampersand (`&`) does not mean `"address of"` (as in the statement `location = &bldg;`). Reference variables must be initialized upon declaration and are part of C++ but not C. Reference variables spare the programmer from having to remember to dereference variables to extract content.

Finally, the `exchange_coordinates_by_reference` function above takes a reference to user-defined type `Point`. Like the equivalent Java example, the contents of the x and y coordinates are exchanged within object `aPoint` in `main()`.

Passing Arguments from the Command Line

C and C++ programmers will be surprised to find that stand-alone Java applications recognize and count the command line arguments differently. The following is a simple Java application to display and count command line arguments:

Listing 2-13: CommandLineDemo.java

```java
public class CommandLineDemo {

    public static void main(String argv[]) {

    if (argv.length > 0)   {
        for (int index = 0; index < argv.length; index++)
            System.out.println("\nArgument #"+index+" is
            "+argv[index]);
            System.out.println("\nTotal number of arguments:
            "+argv.length);
            }
    else
```

```
        System.out.println("\nNo arguments were entered!");
    }
}
```

Since class `CommandLineDemo` is declared public, the `public` modifier key-word in `public static void main(String argv[])` means that the method `main()` is accessible to all classes from the same or different packages (a package is a logical grouping of related classes). The `static` keyword means that the method `main()` belongs to the class `CommandLineDemo` and not merely to instances of class `CommandLineDemo`. However, the most interesting feature of `main()` is that it takes an array of `String` objects within its signa-ture. This is in contrast to the C or C++ function `void main(int argc, char ** argv)`, where `argc` is the number of arguments on the command line. In Java, there is no need for `argc` since arrays have an implicit `public`, `final` variable called `length` that will give the total number of elements.

The method `main()` is defined within a class called `CommandLineDemo` and the bytecode file that will be produced is called `CommandLineDemo.class` (from source file `CommandLineDemo.java`). If we execute the file from the command line by typing:

```
java CommandLineDemo The clear blue sky
```

we will obtain the following output:

```
Argument #0 is The
```

```
Argument #1 is clear
```

```
Argument #2 is blue
```

```
Argument #3 is sky
```

```
Total number of arguments: 4
```

The first argument (number zero) is `"The"`

Warning: The virtual machine program *java* and the bytecode file `CommandLineDemo` (with implicit extension .`class`) do **not** count as argu-ments!

Compare this simple Java application with its equivalent in C++:

Listing 2-14: CommandLineDemo.cpp

```cpp
#include <iostream.h>
void main(int argc, char ** argv) {
```

```
    if (argc > 0)  {
        for (int index = 0; index < argc; index++)
            cout<<"\nArgument #"<<index<<" is "<<argv[index];
            cout<<"\nTotal number of arguments: "<<argc;
    }
    else
        cout<<"\nNo arguments were entered!";

}
```

Executing the program from the command line:

```
CommandLineDemo The clear blue sky
```

we would obtain the following results:

```
Argument #0 is CommandLineDemo
Argument #1 is The
Argument #2 is clear
Argument #3 is blue
Argument #4 is sky
Total number of arguments: 5
```

In C and C++, the first argument (number zero) is always the name of the executable program.

Macros, the `const` Keyword and the `final` Keyword.

Since the birth of pre-ANSI C to this day, C programmers have taken advantage of the C preprocessor mechanism to write macros that simulate named constants. Such macros might look like:

```
#define DB_GOOD_IO          0
#define DB_TABLE_BUSY       -10
#define DB_TABLE_FULL       -20
...
#define PENNY               .01
#define NICKEL              .05
#define DIME                .10
#define QUARTER             .25
...
#define TITLE               "Beta Registration Form"
```

The actions of the preprocessor precede the compilation process and are not part of the compiler. The `#define` keyword is a directive to find all strings and substrings of the first argument (like QUARTER) and substitute them with the second argument (in this case, .25). Programmers use macros because they are more descriptive than the actual representation of the constant value. Furthermore, such macros are normally placed into a header (.h) file so that any changes to the actual value can be made easily.

With ANSI C (and with C++), the const keyword was introduced. The const keyword is a qualifier for variables like the following:

```
const float quarter = .25;
```

The variable quarter is of type const float and it is initialized to .25 upon declaration (const variables must always be initialized). The const keyword in this context means that we cannot assign a new value to quarter later in the program.

```
quarter = .50;      //  This is an illegal assignment!
```

The const keyword can also be applied to pointers. For instance, we might have something like:

```
char * const subject = "Dining";
```

We would read variable subject as "a const pointer to char," meaning that the pointer (address) is read-only, but the content pointed to is changeable (<u>not</u> const). Hence,

```
subject[0] = 'M';
```

is a legal assignment, while:

```
char * category = "Recreation";
subject = category;      // Illegal!
```

is an illegal assignment, since subject is a const pointer (cannot change the address).

A variation to this discussion is the possibility that we can have const pointers to content that is also const. For example,

```
const char * const trademark = "Gamma Publications";
```

is read as "a const pointer to const char," which means that both the address and the content it references is const (cannot be changed through assignment).

Java does not have macros since it does not have any preprocessor. Its equivalent of the ANSI C and C++ const keyword is a keyword called final. The following is an example of its usage:

Listing 2-15: RegistrationAppletDemo.java

```
public class RegistrationAppletDemo extends Applet {
    ...
    final String TITLE = new String("Beta Tester Registration
    Form");

    public void init() {

        super.init();
        setLayout(null);
```

```
        resize(704,382);
        registrationTitle=new Label(TITLE);
        ...
        }
...
}  // end of class RegistrationAppletDemo
```

The variable TITLE is a reference to a String object and it has been qualified as final, meaning that the content of TITLE cannot be changed. Like const variables of C++, final variables of Java must also be initialized to a value or instance (in this case, an instance of String).

One constraint about the use of final is that local variables cannot be declared final. For instance, if we modify the init() method above to look like:

```
public void init() {

        final int MAX_CONTROLS = 20;    // Illegal!  Compilation
        Error!

        super.init();
        ...
        }
```

the declaration for MAX_CONTROLS would fail since MAX_CONTROLS is local to method init().

Note: In Java 1.1, the rules regarding final variables have changed. The following points are amendments to the rules regarding final variables:

- It is now possible to declare blank variables, i.e., it is no longer mandatory to initialize the final variable upon declaration:

```
final String TITLE;                 // This is now OK
```

Within some method of the class, the blank final variable can be assigned a value or an object *once:*

```
TITLE = new String ("Beta Tester Registration");
```

Any attempt to have TITLE refer to a different String object later will result in a compilation error.

Final variables can be local to a method, so final int MAX_CONTROLS = 20; of the init() method above would be legal under Java 1.1. In addition, formal parameters of a method can be declared final and given a single assignment within the body of the method.

Comment Delimiters

Conscientious documentation of one's work is just as important as following good coding practices. Chances are you work in a large organization and there are others who will need to read and support your code. Furthermore, your comments will help remind you of work you did months earlier.

Comments or non-executable text are not processed by the compiler. Comments can be bounded by delimiters /* and */. Furthermore, text which follows a // is also treated as comments. Both of these styles are applicable to Java and C++. For example,

```
/*
This program will enable support center engineers to browse the
history of calls made by contract customers.
*/
```

```
version = 7.2;      // 7.2 is assigned to variable version
```

There is another style of commenting that is only applicable to Java. Called JavaDoc comments, this form begins with /** and ends with */. The following is an example:

```
/**
 *      Program: Vacation Browser (vacation.java)
 *
 *      Author: Frederick F. Chew
 *
 *      Description: This applet will allow a user to scan popular
 *                   vacation sites available from Cyber Travels,
 *                   Inc.
 *
 *                   (more comments)
 *
 */
```

The comments above could be part of a Java application or applet source file. The Java Developers Kit™ has a program called JavaDoc that could process the comments into a Hypertext Markup Language (HTML) reference page. This page can then be viewed through any Java-enabled browser, such as Netscape Navigator™ 2.0 or higher.

Documenting Java Code with JavaDoc

JavaDoc is very handy utility to convert your JavaDoc-aware comments into online HTML documentation. To see how this utility works, let us first look at a partial listing of a Java source file called CommandLineDemo.java:

```
/**
 *
 * Program: CommandLineDemo
 *
 * Author: Frederick F. Chew
 *
 * Description: This program is for displaying the arguments
```

```
 *  entered on the command line. In addition, the total number of
 *  arguments is also displayed.
 *
 */

public class CommandLineDemo {

    /**
     *
     * main: The entry point for a standalone Java program.
     *
     */

    public static void main(String argv[]) {

    // more code

    }
}
```

From the command line, we would run JavaDoc as follows:

```
javadoc CommandLineDemo.java
```

The result will be a number of HTML files of which the main one will be CommandLineDemo.html. Figure 2-1 shows what the user would see when CommandLineDemo.html is loaded into Netscape Navigator™.

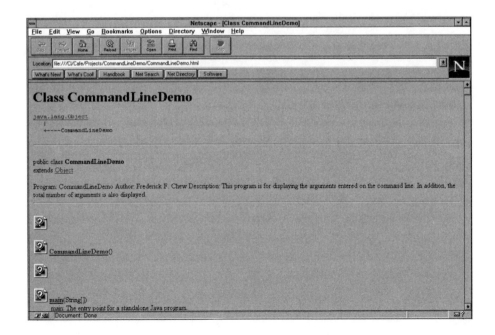

Figure 2-1

CHAPTER

3

The Class: Blueprint for Object Creation

A Basic Overview of the Class

Regardless of whether you are programming in Java or C++, the *class* is the basic blueprint for object creation. The class models a real world entity, an idea or an event. Provided it is well-conceived, it is supposed to be an encapsulated unit of attributes and behaviors. By encapsulated we mean that the attributes, which represent the internal state of the object, are concealed from the outside world. Any access to those attributes would be through the behaviors, if that is what the class designers intend.

It is important to note that the terms *attributes* and *behaviors* each have many synonyms, depending on the context. In C++, attributes are commonly called *data members* and behaviors are *member functions*. In Java, the respective terms are *variables* (*instance* or *class*) and *methods*. In subsequent discussions, I will be using terminology appropriate to each language.

In this discussion, we will get an overview of the basic syntax for a class in both Java and C++. In this overview we will not embroil ourselves in too many details too soon. Concepts like inheritance and polymorphism will be explained and demonstrated in a later chapter.

The syntax for a class has similarities in both languages, but there are also some important differences. Let us start by looking at a simple example for Java:

Listing 3–1: OrderPair.java

```java
import java.lang.*;

public class OrderPair {

    public OrderPair(int x_value, int y_value) {
```

```
        setX(x_value);
        setY(y_value);
        }
    public int getX() {
        return x;
        }
    public int getY() {
        return y;
        }
    public void setX(int x_value) {
        x = x_value;
        }
    public void setY(int y_value) {
        y = y_value;
        }
    public void printXY() {
        System.out.println("("+getX()+","+getY()+")");
        }

    private int x;
    private int y;

    public static void main(String args[]) {
      OrderPair pair[] = {
                    new OrderPair(-4,4), new OrderPair(7,17),
                    new OrderPair(19,25), new OrderPair(-9,21),
                    new OrderPair(37, -93), new OrderPair(-15, 72)
                    };
        for (int index = 0; index < pair.length; index++)
            pair[index].printXY();
        }   // end of main

}   // end of class OrderPair
```

- The following characteristics can be observed about the Java class syntax:

  ```
  public class OrderPair
  ```

  The name of the class follows the `class` keyword and in this example it is called `OrderPair`. The keyword `public` is one of several possible *access modifiers*. In this case, `public` means that class `OrderPair` can be accessed by any class outside the package containing `OrderPair`. A *package*, which I will discuss later, is a logical collection of related classes.

- The class `OrderPair` has a body that is bounded by a set of braces (`{` and `}`):

  ```
  public class OrderPair {

      public OrderPair(int x_value, int y_value) {
  ```

```
        . . .
      }
  public int getX() {
      . . .
      }
  public int getY() {
      . . .
      }
  public void setX(int x_value) {
      . . .
      }
  public void setY(int y_value) {
      . . .
      }
  public void printXY() {
      . . .
      }

  private int x;
  private int y;

  public static void main(String args[]) {
      OrderPair pair[] =                        {/* (1) */
              new OrderPair(-4,4), new OrderPair(7,17),
              new OrderPair(19,25), new OrderPair(-9,21),
              new OrderPair(37, -93), new OrderPair(-15, 72)
              };
      for (int index = 0; index < pair.length; index++)
          pair[index].printXY();
  }  // end of main

}  // end of class OrderPair
```

The body encompasses the *variables* and *methods* of the class. Each method name takes an argument list, may return a type and may be qualified with an access modifier (in this case, all `public`, which means that the methods may be accessed outside the class). The variables, x and y, are of type `int` and are also qualified with access modifiers (in this case, `private`, which means they can only be accessed by methods of class `OrderPair` and no other classes).

In this example all of the variables are *instance variables* and all of the methods are *instance methods*. By *instance*, we mean that the variables and methods pertain to individual objects created from the class. We know that these are instance variables and instance methods because the `static` keyword is <u>not</u> used (we will examine `static` later). To use instance methods, one must first create objects of the class such as the array of `OrderPair` (refer to `/* (1) */`) in method `main`.

- This example illustrates only one class, but it is certainly possible to define more than one class within the same source file. However, in Java there can be only one main class and the name of that class would match the file name for the source. Since OrderPair is the only class in this example, the source file name would be called OrderPair.java. Java also has other naming rules and rules of how source files should be located within a hierarchical file system.

- The entry point to begin the execution of a stand-alone Java program is a method called main(), which is implemented by the main class of the source file. The method main() must always have the following signature, return type and modifiers:

```
public static void main(String args[])
```

While the main() method for the class in question may not be used by other programs, class developers often implement this method as a "driver" to test the other methods of the class.

Java class OrderPair is implicitly derived from class *Object* (standard C++ classes do not have a common, great ancestor base class). However, the subject of inheritance will be explained in a later chapter.

- In Java, an array records the number of elements it contains with a read-only variable called length. The expression pair.length means to get the number of elements of array pair.

- Finally, at the top of the source file are import statements. The import keyword is part of Java and is analogous to the C/C++ preprocessor #include directive (which is not part of the C or C++ languages). The import statement is used to integrate Java classes already in existence. The statement:

```
import java.lang.*;
```

means to link in all the classes of package java.lang (the standard language class library). Actually, this statement is not really necessary in this example since java.lang is implicitly imported. I have shown this statement explicitly to illustrate that existing classes can be integrated into new code.

Now, let us look at essentially the same class written in C++:

Listing 3-2: OrderPair1.cpp

```cpp
#include <iostream.h>

class OrderPair {
public:
    OrderPair(int x_value, int y_value) {
        setX(x_value);
        setY(y_value);
```

```
        }
    int getX() {
        return x;
        }
    int getY() {
        return y;
        }
    void setX(int x_value) {
        x = x_value;
        }
    void setY(int y_value) {
        y = y_value;
        }
    void printXY() {
        cout<<"("<<getX()<<","<<getY()<<")"<<endl;
        }
private:
    int x;
    int y;
};

void main(int argc, char ** argv) {

OrderPair pair[] = {
                    OrderPair(-4,4), OrderPair(7,17),
                    OrderPair(19,25), OrderPair(-9,21),
                    OrderPair(37, -93), OrderPair(-15, 72)
                    };
for (int index = 0; index < sizeof(pair)/sizeof(OrderPair);
  index++)
      pair[index].printXY();
}
```

- On first glance, the two programs are quite similar. The C++ program differs from the Java equivalent in the following way:

  The name of the class still follows the class keyword, but there are <u>no</u> modifiers as you have seen with Java:

```
class OrderPair {
public:
    OrderPair(int x_value, int y_value) {
        ...
        }
    int getX() {
        ...
        }
    int getY() {
        ...
        }
    void setX(int x_value) {
        ...
```

```
        }
    void setY(int y_value) {
        ...
        }
    void printXY() {
        ...
        }
private:
    int x;
    int y;
}; // terminated with a semicolon
```

The body of the class is still bounded by braces ({ and }), but it is terminated with a semicolon (;), whereas this is not necessary in Java. Another important difference is that the public and private access modifiers for the variables (called *data members* in C++) and methods (called *member functions* in C++) are written with the semicolon (e.g., private:) and encompass the members within its region (the region ends with the beginning of the next modifier). In the example above, all of the member functions are public, meaning that all subclasses and unrelated classes can access those members with the dot (.) operator. On the other hand, the data members are private, meaning that only the member functions of OrderPair can access those members.

- The entry point for the start of execution of a C++ program is the function main(), which is <u>not</u> a member function of any class:

```
void main(int argc, char ** argv) {

OrderPair pair[] = {
                    OrderPair(-4,4), OrderPair(7,17),
                    OrderPair(19,25), OrderPair(-9,21),
                    OrderPair(37, -93), OrderPair(-15, 72)
                    };

for (int index = 0; index < sizeof(pair)/sizeof(OrderPair);
 index++)
        pair[index].printXY();
}
```

Unlike the main() method of class OrderPair from the Java example, the C++ main non-member function accepts two arguments within its signature. The variable argc is the number of arguments passed to the program and variable argv represents the actual array of string (char *) arguments. In Java, the only argument is an array of type String. Since each Java array keeps track of the number of elements through a special read-only variable called length, there is no need for an equivalent to argc.

Within the body of function main(), the variable pair represents an array of OrderPair and it is initialized with a list of OrderPair objects. The only constructor of OrderPair is used to create each member.

In the `for` loop of `main`, the number of elements of the array is calculated by taking the total byte size of the array divided by the byte size of one `OrderPair` object. This takes the place of the array `length` variable of Java.

* Unlike Java programs, C and C++ programs still rely on a preprocessor to inform the compiler of global variables, functions and classes originating from external binary code files. In C++ programs, a standard library to include would be all of the `iostream` classes and their methods. That is represented by the preprocessor statement:

```
#include <iostream.h>
```

The `iostream.h` file is a header file that contains all of the required declarations. This library provides the definition of `cout`, which is a global `iostream` object for standard output and support for $<<$ as an insertion operator.

A Strictly C++ Style for Writing a Class

The C++ example for class `OrderPair` of the previous topic was not exactly written in a form that caters to recommended industry practices. It was written to help the reader visualize the obvious differences between the two languages. A better version of the previous C++ example would look like:

Listing 3-3: OrderPair2.cpp

```cpp
#include <iostream.h>

class OrderPair {
public:
    OrderPair(int x_value, int y_value);          // member function
                                                  //    prototypes

    int getX() const;
    int getY() const;
    void setX(int x_value);
    void setY(int y_value);
    void printXY() const;
private:
    int x;
    int y;
};

// member function implementations

OrderPair::OrderPair(int x_value = 0, int y_value = 0) :
 x(x_value), y(y_value) {
}

inline int OrderPair::getX() const {
```

```
return x;
}

inline int OrderPair::getY() const {
return y;
}

inline void OrderPair::setX(int x_value) {
x = x_value;
}

inline void OrderPair::setY(int y_value) {
y = y_value;
}

inline void OrderPair::printXY() const {
cout<<"("<<getX()<<","<<getY()<<")"<<endl;
}

void main(int argc, char ** argv) {

OrderPair pair[] = {
                    OrderPair(-4,4), OrderPair(7,17),
                    OrderPair(19,25), OrderPair(-9,21),
                    OrderPair(37, -93), OrderPair(-15, 72)
                    };

for (int index = 0; index < sizeof(pair)/sizeof(OrderPair);
 index++)
    pair[index].printXY();
}
```

The second C++ example of class `OrderPair` uses strictly C++ techniques and introduces a number of C++ specific keywords. The differences can be summarized as follows:

- The most obvious change to class `OrderPair` is the separation of the implementations of the member functions from the class definition itself. What is left is simply the member function prototypes:

```
class OrderPair {
public:
// member function prototypes
    OrderPair(int x_value, int y_value);
    int getX() const;
    int getY() const;
    void setX(int x_value);
    void setY(int y_value);
    void printXY() const;
```

```
private:
    int x;
    int y;
};

// member function implementations

OrderPair::OrderPair(int x_value = 0, int y_value = 0) :
x(x_value), y(y_value) {
}
```

. . .

Each member function prototype is simply the function name, its signature and the return type.

In C++, there is a very important reason to perform this separation. Typically, you do not want users of your class to see your implementations since you would not want users to write their code to depend on your algorithms. You would want your users to write their code using the interfaces you provide so that you would be free to change the implementations if necessary.

The class definition is normally placed within its own header file with a `.h` or `.hh` extension (or similar convention upon which your project or firm agrees). To prevent multiple declarations that could result from embedded inclusions, the code is also bounded by conditional preprocessor directives:

```
#ifndef  OrderPair_hh
#define  OrderPair_hh

class OrderPair {
public:
// member function prototypes
    OrderPair(int x_value, int y_value);
    int getX() const;
// ...
private:
    int x;
    int y;
};

#endif
```

The member function implementations are kept in a different file with a `.cpp`, `.cc` or `.C` extension (depending on the conventions adopted by your organization). The source is compiled into an object code function library. This source would then be kept in a confidential place, while the header and library files would be provided for others to use.

Note that when the member function implementation is given outside the body of the class, the class name and scope operator (::) must be used:

```
inline int OrderPair::getX() const {
return x;
}
```

Java does not take this C++ approach for organizing code. All of the class method implementations are included as part of the class definition. However, when Java classes are compiled, they can be placed into byte code packages, which is the equivalent to the C++ object library. Information about the method interfaces is provided to the user through hardcopy documentation or through online JavaDoc documents (see *Chapter 2 - Documenting Java Code with JavaDoc*).

- The only constructor for OrderPair in this example was rewritten as follows:

```
OrderPair::OrderPair(int x_value = 0, int y_value = 0) :
x(x_value), y(y_value) { }
```

One difference from the previous implementation is that the formal parameters x_value and y_value are defaulted to zero, meaning that if the user does not pass any explicit values, the default values would be zero for each of data members x and y. For example, in the declaration:

```
OrderPair aPair;
```

The OrderPair object represented by variable aPair would contain zero for x and zero for y.

The constructor also uses an *initializer* list (see bold emphasis above) to set x and y upon object creation. To set each member, the data member is given followed by its formal parameter in parentheses. The idea of the initializer list is to speed object creation by doing resource allocation and initialization in one step (instead of an additional step for assignment in the body of the constructor). This technique is very useful for large composite objects.

Java does not support defaulted arguments, nor initializer lists in its constructors.

- The methods of class OrderPair are all qualified with the keyword inline, such as:

```
inline int OrderPair::getX() const {
return x;
}
```

. . .

```
inline void OrderPair::setX(int x_value) {
x = x_value;
}
```

This keyword is a <u>suggestion</u> to the compiler to create a separate instance of the function's code wherever the function is called. The usage of this keyword is intended to provide efficiency and to avoid the overhead of a function call. The `inline` keyword is strictly in C++ (not C) and it is intended to supersede the traditional use of preprocessor macros masqueraded to look like functions. Macros, unlike inline functions, provide no type checking.

I had mentioned that the keyword `inline` is only a suggestion to the compiler, not a mandate. A function cannot be made inline if it is recursive or if its body is too big (this is dependent on the vendor's implementation). A regular function (with the usual overhead of parameter passing) will be created if it cannot be made inline.

- The signatures of some of the methods of `OrderPair` are also qualified as `const`, as in the following:

```
inline int OrderPair::getX() const {
return x;
}

inline int OrderPair::getY() const {
return y;
}

. . .

inline void OrderPair::printXY() const {
cout<<"("<<getX()<<","<<getY()<<")"<<endl;
}
```

In C++, these are called `const` member functions and, in each case, the data members are read, but not changed. The `const` keyword here is placed after the argument list of the function and before the left brace ({).

The reason these "read only" member functions are qualified as `const` is to notify the compiler that objects declared as `const` can safely call these functions. For example, if we had a slightly different situation where we are given:

```
inline void OrderPair::printXY() { // This became non-const
cout<<"("<<getX()<<","<<getY()<<")"<<endl;
}
. . .
```

```
void main()
{
...
const OrderPair aPair(-5,-9);      // This is a const object
aPair.printXY();   // Compilation error!  This call would be
 illegal!
...
}
```

The variable aPair, which represents a const OrderPair object, would
not be able to call printXY(), since the compiler would believe that the
internal state of aPair may be changed by the call. Restoring
OrderPair::printXY() as a const member function would make the
call legal.

There is no equivalent to const member functions in Java.

A Closer Look at Constructors

The constructor is a special method or member function solely for the purpose
of initializing the instance variables or data members of an object at creation
time. Both Java and C++ have constructors, but there are a few subtle differences between the way they are written and used between the two languages.

Below is a Java class called Student. The class contains two user-defined constructors:

Listing 3–4: Student.java

```
import java.util.*;

public class Student {

    private String name;
    private int    ssn;
    private String birthdate;
    private char   sex;

    public Student() {           // Constructor #1
        name = new String("Nameless");
        ssn  = 0;
        birthdate = new String("01/01/1970");
        sex = 'U';
        }

    public Student(String nm, int id, String bd, char sx) {
    // Constructor #2
        name = nm;
        ssn  = id;
```

```
            birthdate = bd;
            sex = sx;
            }

    public void Display() {
        System.out.println("Student: "+name);
        System.out.println("Social Security Number: "+ssn);
        System.out.println("Birthdate: "+birthdate);
        if (sex == 'M')
            System.out.println("Sex: Male\n");
        else
        if (sex == 'F')
            System.out.println("Sex: Female\n");
        else
            System.out.println("Sex: Unknown\n");
        }

    public static void main(String args[]) {
        Student someone = new Student();
        someone.Display();
        Student fred = new Student(new String("Fred"), 4570,
                new String("03/15/1985"), 'M');
        fred.Display();
    }
}
```

Below is the output from the stand-alone program:

```
Student: Nameless
Social Security Number: 0
Birthdate: 01/01/1970
Sex: Unknown

Student: Fred
Social Security Number: 4570
Birthdate: 03/15/1985
Sex: Male
```

The constructor is always named after the class and returns no value (not even
void). It is qualified with the public access modifier so that it is possible to
instantiate objects of the class from methods of other classes. Furthermore, the
user may define one or more constructors. A constructor may take on zero or
more arguments. The Student class above has two constructors, one with no
arguments (called the *default constructor*) and one with four arguments.

A declaration such as:

```
Student someone;
```

would only create a reference variable called `someone`, which should point to a `Student` object, but the `Student` object has yet to be created. To have the variable refer to a real object, the `new` operator must be used, as in:

```
someone = new Student();
```

or to declare and initialize the variable in one step, we could have:

```
Student someone = new Student();
```

The `new` operator uses heap memory for object creation. Figure 3-1 illustrates these basic concepts.

The `Student` class example above illustrates that it is possible to have two methods of the same name but with different arguments lists. This phenomenom is known as method or function *overloading*. The compiler knows which implementation to call by argument matching. For instance, in the statement:

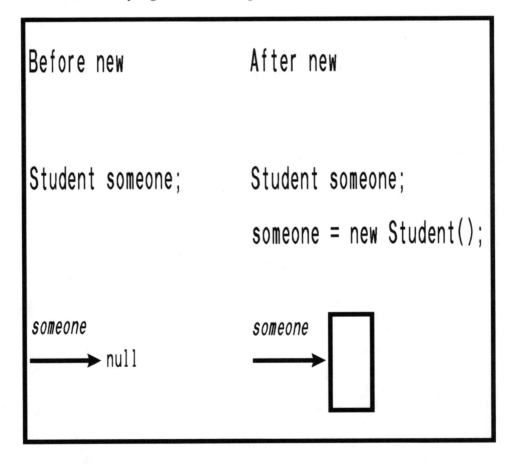

Figure 3-1

```
Student fred = new Student(new String("Fred"), 4570, new
  String("03/15/1985"), 'M');
```

the compiler would determine that there are four parameters and it would go through to match each parameter's type in the proper order against what has been defined for the class. In this case, the compiler chooses constructor #2.

Now, it is possible that the class designer may choose not to define any constructors. In that case, the Java compiler provides the no-argument default constructor for free. With the default constructor, it is still possible to instantiate objects with statements like:

```
Student someone = new Student();
```

The instance variables name, ssn, birthdate and sex would be initialized to null, 0, null and null, respectively. However, it is <u>never</u> a good idea to rely on the compiler to initialize your variables to a predictable state. Besides, when we create objects, we almost always want to initialize the state information to something meaningful. That means you would inevitably define your own constructors.

Almost everything stated about the Java constructor so far is applicable to the C++ constructor. A C++ equivalent to the Java Student class might look like:

Listing 3-5: Student.cpp

```cpp
#include <iostream.h>
#include "String.hh"

class Student {
public:
    Student();                              // Constructor #1
    Student(String, int, String, char);   // Constructor #2
    void Display();
private:
    String name;
    int     ssn;
    String  birthdate;
    char    sex;
};

// Member function implementations

Student::Student() {            // Constructor #1
name = String("Nameless");
ssn  = 0;
birthdate = String("01/01/1970");
sex = 'U';
}
```

```
Student::Student(String nm, int id, String bd, char sx)
 // Constructor #2
: name(String(nm)), ssn(id), birthdate(String(bd)), sex(sx) {
}

void Student::Display() {
cout<<"Student: "<<name<<endl;
cout<<"Social Security Number: "<<ssn<<endl;
cout<<"Birthdate: "<<birthdate<<endl;
if (sex == 'M')
    cout<<"Sex: Male"<<endl;
else
if (sex == 'F')
    cout<<"Sex: Female"<<endl;
else
    cout<<"Sex: Unknown"<<endl;
cout<<endl;
}

void main(String args[]) {
Student someone;
someone.Display();
Student fred(String("Fred"), 4570, String("03/15/1985"), 'M');
fred.Display();
}
```

In the C++ example, the instantiation of Student objects someone and fred in function main is done on the stack (although the sub-objects within Student may be created from the heap). There is no use of the new operator as required in Java.

C++ does have its own new operator for dynamic memory allocation, but its use is not necessary for this example.

Like Java, C++ also has function overloading. The compiler matches the arguments to determine which constructor to call.

Unlike Java, C++ constructors have something called an initializer list. The header of constructor #2 above is written with this feature (illustrated in bold). The initializer list begins with a colon (:) and ends before the left brace ({). It is a comma separated list of data member-value pairs with the value enclosed within parentheses. The initializer list is a mechanism to help improve performance since data members are allocated memory and initialized in one step (instead of an additional step with assignment).

Java has no analog to initializer lists since Java instance variables represent references to objects, not the objects themselves.

Finally, all of the member functions of C++ class Student are implemented outside the body of the class. This style is not possible in Java since Java employs the notion of a package to bundle its code.

Calling a Constructor from a Constructor Using Keyword This

Constructors in Java can be written in such a way that one constructor can call another. If we refer back to the `Student` class of the previous topic (*"A Closer Look at Constructors"*), we can rewrite the implementation of the first Java constructor as:

```
public Student() {
        this(new String("Nameless"),0,new String("01/01/1970"),
        'U');
        }
```

The no-argument default constructor simply calls the second constructor by using the `this` keyword as shown followed by the appropriate parameters enclosed within parentheses.

There is also a second meaning for `this`. The keyword could represent the current object being operated upon by a given method. For instance, if we have some container class (say, `Vector`) that implements a method called `capacity()`, we can have the instance in question call `capacity()` from within another method of the class by writing:

```
this.capacity();
```

C++ also has the `this` keyword. However, the C++ version of `this` means a <u>pointer</u> to the object in question. In C++, the above statement would be written as:

```
this->capacity();
```

In C++ the `this` keyword cannot be used to support the calling of one constructor by another as in Java. If there is code common to two or more C++ constructors, the code could be isolated into a separate member function and called by the constructors. The following is an example of this idea based on the C++ `Student` class of the last section:

```
class Student {
public:
    Student();
    Student(String, int, String, char);
    void Display();
private:
    void setStudent(String &, int, String &, char);
    String name;
    int     ssn;
    String  birthdate;
    char    sex;
};

Student::Student() {
setStudent(String("Nameless"), 0, String("01/01/1970"), 'U');
}

Student::Student(String nm, int id, String bd, char sx) {
```

```
setStudent(nm, id, bd, sx);
}

void Student::setStudent(String & nm, int id, String & bd, char
  sx) {
name = nm;
ssn  = id;
birthdate = bd;
sex  = sx;
}
```

Basically, a special member function called setStudent was added to class Student to deal with the assignment of values or objects to the data members. A design decision was made to prevent setStudent from being used by clients, so it was placed within the private access region of the class.

C++ Destructors and Java Finalizers

When a programmer writes a class in C++ he must be conscientious about the deallocation of resources in the destructor. Typically, these resources are heap memory, file descriptors, database connections, etc. The following code fragment for a C++ class called Publication illustrates this point:

```
class Publication {
public:
    Publication(char *, char *);
    ~Publication();
    // more member functions
private:
    char * title;
    char * subject;
    // more data members
};

Publication::Publication(char * tit, char * sub) {
title = new char[strlen(tit)+1];
subject = new char[strlen(sub)+1];
strcpy(title, tit);
strcpy(subject, sub);
}

Publication::~Publication() {
delete [] title;
delete [] subject;
}
```

For automatic objects, the C++ destructor gets called when the objects go out of scope.

In Java, there are no destructors. The built-in garbage collector takes care of returning memory to the heap for objects that go out of scope. However, what about other resources like file descriptors and database connections?

There is a Java method called `finalize` that the class developer can implement as part of his class. The `finalize` method has the following modifiers and signature:

```
protected void finalize()
```

The developer would perform the resource deallocation within the body of the `finalize` method. This method would be called by the Java runtime environment when the object no longer has any references to it and before the object is garbage collected.

However, there is a potential problem with the *finalize* method. A reference variable to an object may exit scope, but the finalize method on the object may not be called as long as there exists some other reference to the object. This makes the invocation of finalize very unpredictable.

In order to relinquish resources in a timely way, the programmer should implement his own public method (which could be named `dispose()`, as in the case of many of the standard Java classes) and have the object explicitly call this method just before it goes out of scope.

The C++ Copy Constructor

When C++ developers design classes with pointers as data members, they should be aware that they may need to implement their own copy constructor in order to avoid the problem of repetitive deallocation of the same memory. The copy constructor always has the following signature and format:

```
Class_Name::Class_Name(const Class_Name &);
```

where `Class_Name` represents the type. By default, the C++ compiler always provides a default copy constructor if the developer does not provide one. The default implementation is to perform a <u>shallow</u> or <u>bitwise</u> copy of the corresponding data members of the source to the target object.

The notion of the default copy constructor is best illustrated with the help of an example. Suppose we are given a class called `Pair` as follows:

```
#include <iostream.h>
#include <string.h>

class Pair {
public:
    Pair();
    Pair(int, int, char *);
    ~Pair();
    void Display();
```

```cpp
private:
    static int count;
    char * label;
    int x;
    int y;
    int id;    // Used for identifying each unique instance of Pair
};

int Pair::count = 0;

Pair::Pair() : x(0), y(0), id(++count) {
label = new char[strlen("Unknown")+1];
strcpy(label, "Unknown");
}

Pair::Pair(int x_value, int y_value = 0, char * str = "\0") :
x(x_value), y(y_value), id(++count) {
label = new char[strlen(str)+1];
strcpy(label, str);
}

Pair::~Pair() {
delete [] label;
}

void Pair::Display() {
cout<<"("<<x<<", "<<y<<")"<<" is named "<<label<<" with id
"<<id<<'\n';
}

void main()
{   // outer block

    {   // middle block
    Pair pr1(-50, 450, "Mars");
    pr1.Display();

            {   // inner block
            Pair pr2 = pr1;   // copy constructor called here
            pr2.Display();

            // pr2 goes out of scope
            }

    // pr1 goes out of scope
    }

// more executable statements
}
```

In the above example, the developer did not implement his own copy constructor, so the compiler will provide a default that would look like:

```
Pair::Pair(const Pair & pr) {
label = pr.label;
x = pr.x;
y = pr.y;
id = pr.id;
}
```

As things turn out, the `Pair` class as it stands is not safe to use. Within the middle block of function `main()`, a `Pair` object called `pr1` is instantiated with the
help of constructor `Pair(int, int, char *)`. Since `label` is a pointer data
member (`char *`), `pt1.label` points to the beginning of string `"Mars"` (an
array of characters).

Since `pr1` was instantiated within the middle block of `main()`, it is also visible
to the inner block of `main()`. Within the inner block of `main()`, an object called
`pr2` is instantiated with the use of the default copy constructor. When the
instantiation process completes, both `pr1.label` and `pr2.label` point to the
same memory block containing string `"Mars."`

Herein lies the problem, when `Pair` object `pr2` goes out of scope within the
inner block of `main()`, the destructor gets called and the memory previously
pointed to by `pt2.label` is no longer valid. However, when the inner block is
exited, `Pair` object `pr1` still exists, but `pr1.label` no longer points to valid
memory! While `pr1` still exists, the memory pointed to by `pr1.label` may
very well be allocated for use by another object. As `pr1` exits scope from the
middle block, the destructor will be called, thereby resulting in memory corruption for other objects. Unpleasant side effects can result from this scenario (see
figure 3-2).

To remedy this situation, the developer would have to provide his own implementation of the copy constructor. There is certainly more than one way to make
the `Pair` class safe to use. I am going to provide an amended version of class
`Pair` using a technique called *reference counting*:

```
class Pair {
public:
    Pair();
    Pair(int, int, char *);
    Pair(const Pair &);
    ~Pair();
    void Display();
private:
    static int count;
    int  * ref_count_ptr;
    char * label;
```

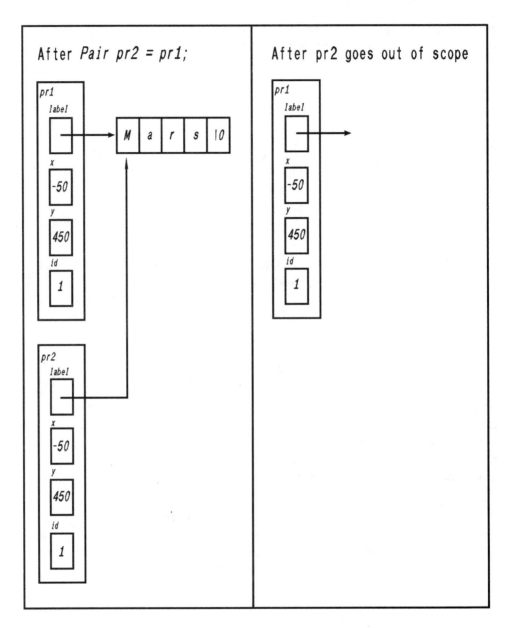

Figure 3-2

```
    int x;
    int y;
    int id;    // Used for identifying each unique instance of
    Pair
};

int Pair::count = 0;
```

```
Pair::Pair() : x(0), y(0), id(++count) {
label = new char[strlen("Unknown")+1];
strcpy(label, "Unknown");
ref_count_ptr = new int;
*ref_count_ptr = 1;
}

Pair::Pair(int x_value, int y_value = 0, char * str = "\0") :
x(x_value), y(y_value), id(++count){
label = new char[strlen(str)+1];
strcpy(label, str);
ref_count_ptr = new int;
*ref_count_ptr = 1;
}

Pair::Pair(const Pair & pr) {
x = pr.x;
y = pr.y;
id = ++count;
label = pr.label;
ref_count_ptr = pr.ref_count_ptr;
++*ref_count_ptr;
}

Pair::~Pair() {
--*ref_count_ptr;
if (*ref_count_ptr <= 0) {
    delete [] label;
    delete ref_count_ptr;
    }
}

void Pair::Display() {
cout<<"("<<x<<", "<<y<<")"<<" is named "<<label<<" with id
"<<id<<'\n';
}

// This example is related to the next topic, "Overloading the
// Assignment Operator in C++". The complete working example
// is contained in the  program, Pair.cpp, which is available
// from the included media - see
// companion Listing 3-6 in the
// next topic.
```

The highlighted code is either new or changed from the original. Basically, these are the main points of the amended class:

- A pointer variable (of type int *), ref_count_ptr, was added to class Pair. It will be used to track the number of references to the character block pointed to by label.

- When an object is created with any non-copy constructor (`Pair::Pair()` and `Pair::Pair(int, int, char *)`, an int will be dynamically allocated for `ref_count_ptr` to point to. Also, `*ref_count_ptr` will be set to 1.

- A user-defined copy constructor (`Pair::Pair(const Pair &)`) is then written. The pointer variable members of the target object are assigned the corresponding pointer variable members of the source object. The reference count (`*ref_count`) is incremented by 1.

- When a `Pair` object goes out of scope, the destructor is called. The reference count (`*ref_count`) is decremented. If the resulting reference count is zero or less, the memory pointed to by `label` and `ref_count_ptr` is deleted.

Figure 3-3 illustrates the new situation with the same client code in function `main()`.

In Java, a developer can provide any number of constructors for a class. However, there is really no notion of a copy constructor in Java, as implemented in C++. C++ developers provide their own copy constructors when they see the need to instantiate clones of existing objects. A clone object carries all of the attribute values as the original object upon creation, but it has an identity of its own. In Java, an object can be cloned if its class has an implementation of the `clone()` method and if its class implements the `Cloneable` interface.

Overloading the Assignment Operator in C++

Just as in the case of the copy constructor, C++ class designers must also take into account the default meaning of assignment (=), especially when the class has pointers as data members. The default meaning of assignment is to perform a shallow copy of the corresponding data members of the source to the destination object. The compiler-provided assignment operator takes on the following signature and format:

```
Class_Name &  Class_Name::operator=(const Class_Name &);
```

The overloaded operator takes a reference to an object of type `Class_Name` and returns a reference to an object of type `Class_Name`. The instance doing the calling (`*this`) is returned so that it is possible to perform cascaded assignments (such as `a = b = c = d;`) on one statement. Now, let us look at a class called `Pair` where the developer relies on the compiler-generated assignment operator:

```
#include <iostream.h>
#include <string.h>

class Pair {
```

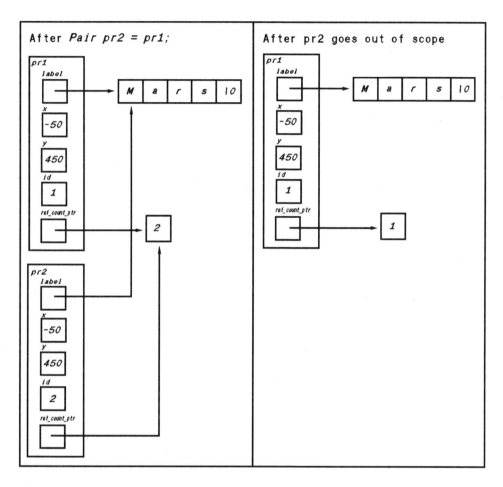

Figure 3-3

```
public:
   Pair();
   Pair(int, int, char *);
   Pair(const Pair &);
   ~Pair();
   void Display();
private:
   static int count;
   char * label;
   int x;
   int y;
   int id;    // Used for identifying each unique instance of Pair
};

int Pair::count = 0;
```

```cpp
Pair::Pair() : x(0), y(0), id(++count) {
label = new char[strlen("Unknown")+1];
strcpy(label, "Unknown");
}

Pair::Pair(int x_value, int y_value = 0, char * str = "\0") :
x(x_value), y(y_value), id(++count){
label = new char[strlen(str)+1];
strcpy(label, str);
}

Pair::Pair(const Pair & pr) {
label = new char[strlen(pr.label) + 1];
strcpy(label, pr.label);
x = pr.x;
y = pr.y;
id = ++count;
}

Pair::~Pair() {
delete [] label;
}

void Pair::Display() {
cout<<"("<<x<<", "<<y<<")"<<" is named "<<label<<" with id
"<<id<<'\n';
}

void main()
{   // outer block

    {   // middle block
    Pair pr1(-50, 450, "Mars");
    pr1.Display();

    {   // inner block
    Pair pr2;
    pr2 = pr1;   // assignment operation performed here
    pr2.Display();

    // pr2 goes out of scope
    }

    // pr1 goes out of scope
    }

// more executable statements
}
```

The `Pair` class as it stands is not safe to use. Within the middle block of function `main()`, a `Pair` object called `pr1` is instantiated with the help of constructor `Pair(int, int, char *)`. Since `label` is a pointer data member (`char *`), `pt1.label` points to the beginning of string `"Mars"` (an array of characters).

Since `pr1` was instantiated within the middle block of `main()`, it is also visible to the inner block of `main()`. Within the inner block of `main()`, an object called `pr2` is instantiated with the use of the no-argument, default copy constructor. When the instantiation completes, `pr2.label` points to the beginning of string `"Unknown."`

On the following line, `pr1` is assigned to `pr2`, meaning that `pr2.x` contains `-50`, `pr2.y` contains `450`, `pr2.id` contains `1` and `pr2.label` points to the beginning of string `"Mars."`

Herein lies the problem, when `Pair` object `pr2` goes out of scope within the inner block of `main()`, the destructor gets called and the memory previously pointed to by `pt2.label` is no longer valid. However, when the inner block is exited, `Pair` object `pr1` still exists, but `pr1.label` no longer points to valid memory! While `pr1` still exists, the memory pointed to by `pr1.label` may very well be allocated for use by another object. As `pr1` exits the scope of the middle block, the destructor will be called, thereby resulting in memory corruption for other objects. On top of this mess, the memory initially pointed to by `pr2.label` (the block containing string `"Unknown"`) is now inaccessible and cannot be freed. We have a situation of dangling pointers and memory leaks: double trouble! Figure 3-4 illustrates these problems.

To remedy this situation, the developer would have to provide his own implementation of the assignment operator. There is certainly more than one way to make the `Pair` class safe to use. The following amended version of class `Pair` will use a technique called *reference counting*:

Listing 3-6: Pair.cpp

```cpp
#include <iostream.h>
#include <string.h>

class Pair {
public:
    Pair();
    Pair(int, int, char *);
    Pair(const Pair &);
    Pair & operator=(const Pair &);
    ~Pair();
    void Display();
```

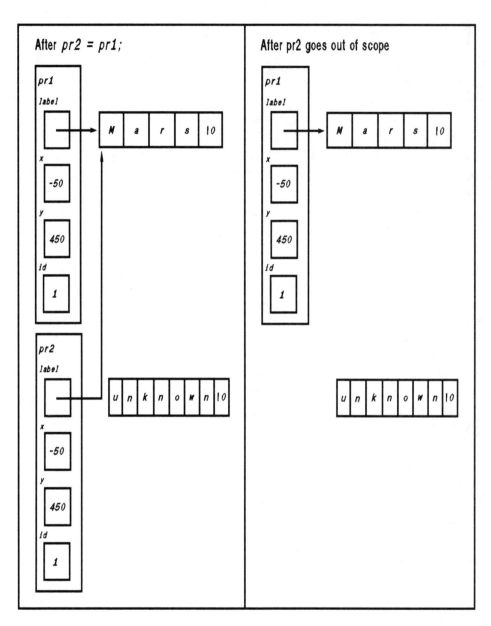

Figure 3-4

```
private:
    static int count;
    int   * ref_count_ptr;
    char * label;
    int x;
```

```
    int y;
    int id;    // Used for identifying each unique instance of Pair
};

int Pair::count = 0;

Pair::Pair() : x(0), y(0), id(++count) {
label = new char[strlen("Unknown")+1];
strcpy(label, "Unknown");
ref_count_ptr = new int;
*ref_count_ptr = 1;
}

Pair::Pair(int x_value, int y_value = 0, char * str = "\0") :
x(x_value), y(y_value), id(++count){
label = new char[strlen(str)+1];
strcpy(label, str);
ref_count_ptr = new int;
*ref_count_ptr = 1;
}

Pair::Pair(const Pair & pr) {
x = pr.x;
y = pr.y;
id = ++count;
label = pr.label;
ref_count_ptr = pr.ref_count_ptr;
++*ref_count_ptr;
}

Pair & Pair::operator=(const Pair & pr) {
if (label != pr.label) {
    - -*ref_count_ptr;
    if (*ref_count_ptr <= 0) {
        delete [] label;
        delete ref_count_ptr;
        }
    label = pr.label;
    ref_count_ptr = pr.ref_count_ptr;
    ++*ref_count_ptr;
    x = pr.x;
    y = pr.y;
    }
return (*this);
}

Pair::~Pair() {
-*ref_count_ptr;
if (*ref_count_ptr <= 0) {
    delete [] label;
```

```
    delete ref_count_ptr;
    }
}

void Pair::Display() {
cout<<"("<<x<<", "<<y<<")"<<" is named "<<label<<" with id
"<<id<<'\n';
}
```

The above example is an enhancement to the second listing of class `Pair` from the topic, *The C++ Copy Constructor*. The lines in bold represent what has been added to the previous version. Refer to the discussions about the role of variable `ref_count_ptr` from the previous topic.

The following is the main point for this enhanced class `Pair`:

The developer has defined his own overloaded assignment operator (`Pair::operator=(const Pair &)`). The implementation will first check to see if there is any attempt at self-assignment (A=A). If there is, simply return the calling object (`*this`). If the target object and the source object are different, then decrement the reference count (`*ref_count_ptr`) for the target object. If the count is zero or less, then the memory pointed to by `label` and `ref_count_ptr` must be deleted. Perform the corresponding assignments for the pointer members of the target and source objects. The target and source objects then belong to the same "community" sharing the same resources. Increment the reference count (`*ref_count_ptr`) by 1.

Since Java does not support operator overloading, this C++ example has no Java equivalent. For that matter, there are no pointers and destructors in Java, either. Memory leaks are not a problem since Java has its own built-in garbage collector.

Cloning Objects in Java

In Java, a declared, uninitialized variable is simply a reference to an object of a particular type. The meaning of assignment (the = sign) is to make the variable on the left-hand side refer to the object referenced by the expression of the right-hand side. For instance, suppose I have a Java class called `StandalonePair` as follows:

Listing 3-7: StandalonePair.java

```
import java.awt.*;

public class StandalonePair {

    public StandalonePair(int x_value, int y_value, String name) {
```

```java
        setX(x_value);
        setY(y_value);
        setLabel(name);
        setId();
    }
    public int getX() {
        return x;
    }
    public int getY() {
        return y;
    }
    public String getLabel() {
        return label;
    }
    public void setX(int x_value) {
        x = x_value;
    }
    public void setY(int y_value) {
        y = y_value;
    }
    public void setLabel(String name) {
    label = name;
    }
    public void setId() {
    id = ++count;
    }
    public void Display() {
    System.out.println("("+getX()+", "+getY()+")"+" is named "+
            getLabel()+" with id "+id+"\n");
    }

    private int x;
    private int y;
    private String label;
    private int id;
    private static int count = 0;

    public static void main(String args[]) {
        // outer block
        StandalonePair pr1 = new StandalonePair(-50, 450,
         Mars");
        pr1.Display();
           {// inner block
           StandalonePair pr2 = pr1;   // initialize pr2 to con-
                                           tents referenced by pr1

           pr2.Display();
           }
    }

}
```

The `StandalonePair` instance referenced by variable `pr1` is instantiated within the outer block of method `main()`. As such, it is accessible to the inner block of `main()` and the variable `pr2` is declared and initialized to the object referenced by `pr1`. In effect, while `pr2` is within scope, both `pr1` and `pr2` refer to the same object. The output would look like:

```
(-50, 450) is named Mars with id 1

(-50, 450) is named Mars with id 1
```

for statements `pr1.Display();` and `pr2.Display();`, respectively.

What must we do if we want variable `pr2` to reference a unique object of its own, but with essentially the same contents as the object referenced by `pr1`? What we would have to do is to implement a method called `clone()` to perform new object instantiation or any deep copies of subobjects. The following class called `CloneablePair` is a modification of the previous `StandalonePair` class:

Listing 3-8: CloneablePair.java

```java
import java.awt.*;

public class CloneablePair implements Cloneable {

    public CloneablePair(int x_value, int y_value, String name) {
        setX(x_value);
        setY(y_value);
        setLabel(name);
        setId();
    }
    public int getX() {
        return x;
    }
    public int getY() {
        return y;
    }
    public String getLabel() {
        return label;
    }
    public void setX(int x_value) {
        x = x_value;
    }
    public void setY(int y_value) {
        y = y_value;
    }
    public void setLabel(String name) {
    label = name;
```

```
    }
    public void setId() {
    id = ++count;
    }
    public void Display() {
    System.out.println("("+getX()+", "+getY()+")"+" is named "+
                        getLabel()+" with id "+id+"\n");
    }
    protected Object clone() {
    String new_label = new String(label);
    CloneablePair pr = new CloneablePair(x, y, new_label);
    return pr;
    }

    private int x;
    private int y;
    private String label;
    private int id;
    private static int count = 0;

    public static void main(String args[]) {   // outer block
        CloneablePair pr1 = new CloneablePair(-50, 450, "Mars");
        pr1.Display();
        { // inner block
        CloneablePair pr2 = (CloneablePair)pr1.clone();
        pr2.Display();
        }
    }

}
```

Note that the declaration of the *CloneablePair* class has a clause called `imple-ments Cloneable`. In Java, there is a predefined interface called `Cloneable` which serves as an indicator to the underlining virtual machine that objects of the class can be cloned. The `implements` keyword is used with interfaces, which are really abstract classes with only method prototypes. This clause is necessary because it will allow unrelated classes to clone `CloneablePair` objects. Interfaces are also part of the inheritance mechanism and will be discussed later.

The `clone()` method is qualified with the `protected` access modifier and it returns an object of type `Object`. This method actually overrides a method of the same name from base class `Object` (whenever a Java class is defined without the `extends` keyword, it is <u>implicitly</u> a subclass or a derived class of `Object`). The `protected` access modifier means that any method of `CloneablePair` or its subclasses or any class within the same package as `CloneablePair` may access method `clone()`. With this summarization, I will defer the details of inheritance until a later chapter.

Note: The `clone()` method must return an object of type `Object`, otherwise the compiler will complain of an attempt at redefining the method with a different type (the dummy `clone()` method of class `Object` returns a type `Object`). Also, within the inner block of method `main()`, `pr2` is initialized to `(CloneablePair)pr1.clone()`. Since `pr1.clone()` returns an object of type `Object`, the result must be casted to a type `CloneablePair` before it can be assigned to `pr2`.

The output for the above would look like:

```
(-50, 450) is named Mars with id 1

(-50, 450) is named Mars with id 2
```

Each of the reference variables `pr1` and `pr2` would refer to unique objects (each with a unique `id` to distinguish the instances from each other).

Comparing References and Objects in Java and C++

Programmers often stumble over the semantics of equality when they work with either Java or C++. In both languages there are mechanisms to support two types of comparisons: *shallow* and *deep*. A shallow comparison is to test whether two variables refer to the same object. A deep comparison tests whether the contents of two potentially different objects contain the same values.

For objects in Java, these two types of comparisons are implemented with the == operator (shallow) and the `equals()` method (deep). The == operator is part of the Java language and the `equals()` method is a public method of base class `Object`. This method is inherited by every other class and may be overridden in the subclasses (whether stated or not, every class in Java is understood to have `Object` as its ancestor).

Let us see an example of both types of comparisons with the standard Java `String` class:

Listing 3-9: CompareDemo.java

```java
import java.awt.*;

public class CompareDemo {

    public static void main(String args[]) {
        String str1 = new String("Tequilla Sunset");
        String str2 = new String("Tequilla Sunset");
        String str3 = new String("Tequilla Sundown");
        String str4 = str1;
        /* (1) */
        if (str1 == str2)
```

```
                System.out.print("Variables str1 and str2 refer to
                   the same object\n");
            else
                System.out.print("Variables str1 and str2 do NOT
                   refer to the same object\n");

            if (str1.equals(str2))
                System.out.println("The objects referred to by str1
                   and str2 are equal in content\n");
            else
                System.out.println("The objects referred to by str1
                   and str2 are NOT equal in content\n");
        /* (2) */
            if (str2 == str3)
                System.out.print("Variables str2 and str3 refer to
                   the same object\n");
            else
                System.out.print("Variables str2 and str3 do NOT
                   refer to the same object\n");

            if (str2.equals(str3))
                System.out.println("The objects referred to by str2
                   and str3 are equal in content\n");
            else
                System.out.println("The objects referred to by str2
                   and str3 are NOT equal in content\n");
        /* (3) */
            if (str1 == str4)
                System.out.print("Variables str1 and str4 refer to
                   the same object\n");
            else
                System.out.print("Variables str1 and str4 do NOT
                   refer to the same object\n");

            if (str1.equals(str4))
                System.out.println("The objects referred to by str1
                   and str4 are equal in content\n");
            else
                System.out.println("The objects referred to by str1 and
                   str4 are NOT equal in content\n");
        }
    }
```

The output generated would be:

```
Variables str1 and str2 do NOT refer to the same object
The objects referred to by str1 and str2 are equal in content

Variables str2 and str3 do NOT refer to the same object
The objects referred to by str2 and str3 are NOT equal in content
```

```
Variables str1 and str4 refer to the same object
The objects referred to by str1 and str4 are equal in content
```

It is apparent that if two variables refer to the same object, the contents referenced by the two variables are also equal.

For built-in types (like `boolean`, `byte`, `char`, `short`, etc.), the `==` operator is understood to mean a content comparison.

The notions of shallow and deep comparisons also apply to C and C++. In C++, shallow comparisons can be done between two pointer variables or two reference variables. The programmer typically has to implement his own function to perform deep comparisons of the objects given the particular type.

Below is a C++ implementation of class `String` with an overloaded `==` operator (for shallow comparisons) and a member function called `Equals()` (for deep comparisons):

Listing 3-10: CompareDemo.cpp

```cpp
#include <iostream.h>
#include <string.h>

class  String {
public:
    enum { FALSE, TRUE };
    String();
    String(const char *);
    String(const String&);
    ~String();
    void DisplayString() const;
    int  ReturnLength() const;
    operator const char * () const;
    String operator+(const String &);
    String& operator=(const String &);
    int operator==(const String &);
    int Equals(const String &);
private:
    int    length;
    char   *text;
};

String::String() : text(0), length(0) {
}

String::String(const char *str) {
```

```
text = new char[strlen(str) + 1];
strcpy(text, str);
length = strlen(str);
}

String::String(const String &str) {
text = new char[strlen(str.text) + 1];
strcpy(text, str.text);
length = strlen(str.text);
}

String::~String() {
delete [] text;
}

String::operator const char * () const {
return text;
}

void String::DisplayString() const {
cout<<"String is "<<text<<'\n';
}

int  String::ReturnLength() const {
return(length);
}

String String::operator+(const String &str) {
int lgth = this->ReturnLength() + str.ReturnLength();
char * temp_text = new char[lgth+1];
strcpy(temp_text, *this);
strcat(temp_text, *this);
String temp_str(temp_text);
return(temp_str);
}

String& String::operator=(const String &str) {
length = str.ReturnLength();
char * temp_text = new char[length+1];
strcpy(temp_text, str);
delete [] text;
text = temp_text;
return(*this);
}

int String::operator==(const String &str) {
if (this == &str)
    return String::TRUE;
else
```

```
        return String::FALSE;
}

int String::Equals(const String &str) {
if (strcmp(*this, str)==0)
    return String::TRUE;
else
    return String::FALSE;
}

void main()
{
String str1("Tequilla Sunset");
String str2("Tequilla Sunset");
String str3("Tequilla Sundown");
String & str4 = str1;

/* (1) */
if (str1 == str2)
    cout<<"Variables str1 and str2 refer to the same object\n";
else
    cout<<"Variables str1 and str2 do NOT refer to the same
     object\n";

if (str1.Equals(str2))
    cout<<"The objects referred to by str1 and str2 are equal in
     content\n\n";
else
    cout<<"The objects referred to by str1 and str2 are NOT equal
     in content\n\n";

/* (2) */
if (str2 == str3)
    cout<<"Variables str2 and str3 refer to the same object\n";
else
    cout<<"Variables str2 and str3 do NOT refer to the same
     object\n";

if (str2.Equals(str3))
    cout<<"The objects referred to by str2 and str3 are equal in
     content\n\n";
else
    cout<<"The objects referred to by str2 and str3 are NOT equal
     in content\n\n";

/* (3) */
if (str1 == str4)
    cout<<"Variables str1 and str4 refer to the same object\n";
else
```

```
    cout<<"Variables str1 and str4 do NOT refer to the same
    object\n";

if (str1.Equals(str4))
    cout<<"The objects referred to by str1 and str4 are equal in
    content\n\n";
else
    cout<<"The objects referred to by str1 and str4 are NOT equal
    in content\n\n";

}
```

The output would appear as follows:

```
Variables str1 and str2 do NOT refer to the same object
The objects referred to by str1 and str2 are equal in content

Variables str2 and str3 do NOT refer to the same object
The objects referred to by str2 and str3 are NOT equal in content

Variables str1 and str4 refer to the same object
The objects referred to by str1 and str4 are equal in content
```

As things turned out, the results are identical. The == operator was implemented to compare the addresses of two `String` objects while the `Equals()` member function utilizes the standard C function `strcmp` to determine if the corresponding bytes contained in each `String` object are identical.

Note: The member function `String::operator const char * () const` is a special member function called a *conversion operator* in C++. Basically, this is a mechanism to allow implicit conversion from a user-defined type like `String` to a built-in type like `char *` (or possibly to another user-defined type). The syntax is rather unusual. No return type (not even `void`) is declared with such special member functions. The `"const char *"` in the function header really represents what is returned, but it is written in place of the function name. In addition, the argument list must always be empty. Java does not support conversion operators. Instead, a Java class must provide an appropriate method for an explicit type conversion to take place.

Using the `String` and `StringBuffer` Classes in Java

String manipulation is one of the most basic activities that programmers perform. Amazingly enough, even though the C++ language has been around since 1979 and even though there is an ANSI draft document for a standard string class, most vendors have yet to include this class with their compilers. Instead, developers have come to rely on their own in-house custom string classes or whatever non-standard implementation a vendor might provide.

Java, on the other hand, does have standard string classes and this has been the case since its official release in the spring of 1996. These classes are called `String` and `StringBuffer` and both are part of the `java.lang` package, which every Java application or applet uses.

Objects of class `String` basically represent strings of characters. The contents of a `String` object are immutable, that is, they cannot be changed. However, new `String` objects can be built easily from other `String` objects. While class `String` has a well-defined set of constructors, it is not always necessary to use a constructor in order to create a `String` object.

Class `String` does offer a host of public methods for reading the contents of a `String` object or altering the contents where the result is a new `String` object. Such methods include finding the character at an index position, content comparisons with other `String` objects, substring extraction and pattern searching.

Class `StringBuffer` is also used for representing strings of characters, except the contents of a `StringBuffer` object is modifiable. The length of a `StringBuffer` object can expand as necessary to accommodate long strings. Its internal buffer may be changed with the `append()`, `insert()` and `setCharAt()` methods.

Between the two classes, `String` and `StringBuffer`, there are enough public methods for the programmer to be effective in practically any situation. In addition, whenever the compiler encounters a string enclosed within double quotes, the string is automatically converted to a `String` object. For instance, we can instantiate `String` objects either as:

```
String str1 = new String("coffee beans");
```

or:

```
String str2 = "coffee beans";
```

Both `str1` and `str2` would be reference variables for different `String` objects, but each object would contain the same value, `"coffee beans"`.

Warning: One thing to be careful about in working with `String` objects is that there is a vast difference between an <u>empty</u> string and a <u>null</u> string. For instance,

```
String str3  =   ""; // This is an empty String with a length of
                zero
```

```
String str4 = null; // This is null since variable str4 does not
                // refer to any instance of String
```

If we inadvertently call the methods of `String` with reference variable `str4`, we will cause a `java.lang.NullPointerException` object to be thrown. In the chapter on exception handling, we will see how to deal with exceptions. However, it is better to test whether `str4` is null and, if so, avoid activities that will cause the exceptions.

Class `String` has a method called `concat()` for string concatenation. However, the Java compiler supports the use of the + operator for this purpose. This is one of the very few instances where an operator is overloaded to mean something different from its original purpose. The Java language does not allow programmers to overload operators with special semantics.

The following is an example of concatenation with `String` objects:

```
String str5 = "Come ";
String str6 = str5 +
"to the Watch Museum, where time is time- less!";
```

Variable `str6` would refer to a `String` object with content, `"Come to the Watch Museum, where time is timeless!"` (without the double quotes).

There is still another operator, +=, which means "concatenate into." For instance,

```
String str7 = "Fly "; // str7 is initialized to refer to a
// String object with content "Fly"
String str8 = " home at half price.";

str7 += str8;
```

After the completion of the above, the `String` object with `"Fly "` was discarded and `str7` is made to refer to a new `String` object with content `"Fly home at half price."`

To change the contents of a `String` object, say, `str6` above, we can do something like:

```
StringBuffer sb6 = new StringBuffer(str6);   // Build a
                                             // StringBuffer
                                             // object from the
                                             // String object
sb6.setCharAt(12, 'C');
sb6.setCharAt(13, 'l');
sb6.setCharAt(14, 'o');
sb6.setCharAt(15, 'c');
sb6.setCharAt(16, 'k');

System.out.println(sb6);
```

The last line would output:

```
Come to the Clock Museum, where time is timeless!
```

We can also insert a string into the middle of an existing string. For example, if we add the following statement:

```
sb6.insert(18, "and Watch ");
```

Variable sb6 would contain `"Come to the Clock and Watch Museum, where time is timeless!"`. The first argument to method `insert()` is the offset. In this example, every character from index 0 through 17 is unaffected and string `"and Watch"` is inserted starting at index 18. The original characters starting at index 18 to the end are simply placed immediately after the inserted block.

Now, suppose we want to extract substrings of the content of sb6. Then, we can do something like:

```
String str9 = sb6.toString();
String str10 = "";
str10 += str9.substring(0,34)
              + str9.substring(str9.length()-1,str9.length());
System.out.println(str10);
```

where the last line will output:

```
Come to the Clock and Watch Museum!
```

Warning: Careful attention must be paid when using the `substring()` method of class `String`. Method `substring()` takes a *start* index and a *stop* index, but the content of the stop index is <u>not</u> extracted. That means the user must go one position beyond the last position to be extracted. Also, keep in mind that counting begins with zero, just as with C-style arrays.

Static Variables and Methods

When the keyword `static` is applied to members of a class, it means that the attribute or behavior applies to the class as a whole and not to just individual instances of the class. Unlike non-static members, static data members are reserved within a global space in memory. Below is a simple Java program with class `Circle` that has a static variable (called a *class variable*) and a static method (called a *class method*):

Listing 3-11: Circle.java

```
import java.awt.Point;

public class Circle {
```

```java
public Circle(Point middle, double rad) {
    center = new Point(middle.x, middle.y);
    radius = rad;
    count++;
    }

public static int Total_Circles() {
    return count;
    }

private static int count = 0;/* (1) */
private Point center;
private double radius;

public static void main(String args[]) {
    Circle circle1 = new Circle(new Point(300,400),10);
    Circle circle2 = new Circle(new Point(400,450),20);
    Circle circle3 = new Circle(new Point(500,300),25);
    Circle circle4 = new Circle(new Point(75,-30),30);

    System.out.println("Total number of circles created: "+
                Circle.Total_Circles()+"\n");
                /* (2)  */
    }
}
```

The above class `Circle` has the following features regarding the `static` keyword:

- A private static variable `count` of type `int` (refer to `/* (1) */`) is part of the definition of class `Circle`. Its purpose is to keep track of the total number of instances of `Circle` ever created. Note that upon definition, `count` is initialized to zero. All static variables are initialized outside of the class constructors.

- A static method called `Total_Circles()` is defined to return whatever value is in `count`. Because static methods are class methods, they can only operate on static variables, never non-static variables.

- In method `main()`, the static method `Total_Circles()` is called by using the class name `Circle` with the dot (`.`) operator (refer to `/* (2) */`). Note that the equivalent syntax in C++ requires the scope (`::`) operator, but there is no scope operator in Java. An instance of `Circle` may also call the static method as in `circle4.Total_Circles()`.

- The sample Java program makes use of class `Point`, which is imported from the standard `java.awt` (*Abstract Window Toolkit*) package.

The C++ equivalent to the above would look something like:

Listing 3-12: Circle.cpp

```cpp
#include <iostream.h>

class Point {// Custom-written class to support class Circle
public:
    Point(int x_value = 0, int y_value = 0);
    int getX();
    int getY();
    void setX(int x_value);
    void setY(int y_value);
private:
    int x;
    int y;
};

Point::Point(int x_value, int y_value) : x(x_value), y(y_value) {
}

int Point::getX() {
return x;
}

int Point::getY() {
return y;
}

void Point::setX(int x_value) {
x = x_value;
}

void Point::setY(int y_value) {
y = y_value;
}

class Circle {
public:
    Circle(Point & middle, double rad);
    static int Total_Circles();
private:
    static int count;
    Point center;
    double radius;
};

int Circle::count = 0;                          /* (1) */

Circle::Circle(Point & middle, double rad) {    /* (2) */
center.setX(middle.getX());
center.setY(middle.getY());
```

```
radius = rad;
count++;
}

int Circle::Total_Circles() {
return count;
}

void main()
{
Circle circle1(Point(300,400),10);                    /* (3) */
Circle circle2(Point(400,450),20);
Circle circle3(Point(500,300),25);
Circle circle4(Point(75,-30),30);

cout<<"Total number of circles created: "
      <<Circle::Total_Circles()<<endl;                /* (4) */
}
```

The C++ version above differs from its Java equivalent in the following ways:

- The static variable `count` must be initialized in a separate statement outside of the body of the class (refer to `/* (1) */`).

- The signature of the only constructor for class `Circle` takes a reference to a `Point` (`Point &`) and a double (refer to `/* (2) */`). This is equivalent to the `Circle` constructor of the Java version (`Circle(Point middle, double rad)`). Remember that objects in Java are always passed by reference and built-in types like double are passed by value (a copy of the variable is passed).

- All of the instances of class `Circle` are created as automatic objects (refer to `/* (3) */`). For this example, there is no need to allocate heap memory with the C++ `new` operator. However, in Java, objects (non-built-in types) are always instantiated from the heap with its `new` operator and the Java garbage collector takes care of clean up when the object no longer has any references to it.

- The static member function `Total_Circles()` can be called by using the class name and scope operator (refer to `/* (4) */`). In addition, an instance can also call the static member function as in the statement:

  ```
  circle4.Total_Circles();
  ```

CHAPTER

4

Inheritance: Up and Down the Class Hierarchy

Inheritance as an "is-a" Relationship

Modern object-oriented programming languages such as C++ and Java include constructs to support the organization of classes into hierarchies. The hierarchy is like a family tree where the classes of the top (the *base* classes or *superclasses*) represent general data abstractions and the classes of the bottom (the *derived* classes or *subclasses*) represent specializations of the base classes. This type of hierarchy is known as an *inheritance* hierarchy, where the derived classes acquire or inherit the attributes and behaviors of their parent (or base) classes. The languages mentioned also allow the derived classes to override whatever they inherit with their own attributes and behaviors.

The relationship that binds any two classes along the same inheritance path of a hierarchy connotes an *"is-a"* relationship. This type of relationship can be found in everyday life. For example, most people will agree that a truck is a vehicle. Furthermore, a produce hauler is a type of truck. The notion of a vehicle might be simply defined as a device with wheels that can move on land. A truck would certainly fit this definition of a vehicle (it is a type of vehicle). In addition, a truck has its own attribute since it contains a rectangular flatbed. The produce hauler certainly has everything the basic truck has. In addition, the produce hauler might carry a refrigeration unit to protect its perishables and require its flatbed to be of a minimum height, width and depth.

Typically, general abstractions like vehicle are located towards the top of a hierarchy while very specific ones like the produce hauler are positioned on the bottom. This approach would permit a class designer to derive other classes from vehicle which are not trucks. For example, an automobile may be considered a vehicle, but not a truck (the automobile has no flatbed).

Traditional procedural languages like C do not have the mechanism to define a class (attributes and behaviors) and do not support inheritance. However, a language like C does permit the definition of data structures (structs) with just attributes. Hence, one can model an automobile as an entity that has a motor, transmission, radiator, wheels, etc. This type of relationship between the whole and the part is called *containment* (or *aggregation)* and it is different from *derivation* (the *"is-a"* relationship). Both C++ and Java support the notions of containment as well as derivation.

To understand how to derive (or subclass) a new class from an existing class, we will look at a preliminary example written in both C++ and Java. The two forms have very similar semantics. Beginning with C++, suppose we have a base class called Person and we derive a subclass called Pupil:

Listing 4-1: InheritanceDemo1.cpp

```cpp
#include <iostream.h>
#include <string.h>
#include "String.hh"

class Person {
public:
    Person(String, String, char, int);
    void DisplayData();
private:
    String name;
    String ssn;
    char gender;
    int age;
};

Person::Person(String nm, String id, char sx, int yrs) :
  name(nm), ssn(id), gender(sx), age(yrs) {
}

void Person::DisplayData() {
cout<<endl;
cout<<"Name = "<<name<<endl;
cout<<"SSN = "<<ssn<<endl;
cout<<"Gender = "<<gender<<endl;
cout<<"Age = "<<age<<endl;
}

class Pupil : public Person {
public:
    Pupil(String nm, String id, char sx, int yrs, String sc,
      int lv);
    void DisplayData();
```

```
private:
    String school;
    int class_level;
};

Pupil::Pupil(String nm, String id, char sx, int yrs, String sc,
 int lv) :
    Person(nm, id, sx, yrs), school(sc), class_level(lv) {
}

void Pupil::DisplayData() {
Person::DisplayData();
cout<<"School = "<<school<<endl;
cout<<"Level = "<<class_level<<endl;
}

void main() {
Person wes("Wes", "570-45-1287", 'M', 17);
wes.DisplayData();

Pupil yvonne("Yvonne", "630-22-0980", 'F', 22,
               "Univ. of Washington", 3);

yvonne.Person::DisplayData();

yvonne.DisplayData();
}
```

When the above is compiled and executed, the following is the output:

```
Name = Wes
SSN = 570-45-1287
Gender = M
Age = 17

Name = Yvonne
SSN = 630-22-0980
Gender = F
Age = 22

Name = Yvonne
SSN = 630-22-0980
Gender = F
Age = 22
School = Univ. of Washington
Level = 3
```

The following observations can be made about the above C++ example:

- To derive Pupil as a subclass from Person, the public keyword must be
  used as part of the declaration of class Pupil:

```
class Pupil : public Person {
...
}
```

The `public` keyword follows a single colon and the name of the base class follows the keyword.

- Within the bodies of both classes `Person` and `Pupil`, the data members (attributes) are placed within a `private` access region and the member functions (behaviors) are placed within a `public` access region. These access regions determine the degree of visibility the members have to the outside world. Private members can only be accessed by member functions of the same class. Since the attributes represent state information about the class, you should keep them private to prevent unauthorized access. On the other hand, public members are typically the behaviors of the class and represent the interfaces into the class. A public member is accessible by member functions of the same class, by member functions of derived classes and by non-member functions (such as in `main()`). Within the member functions of derived classes and within non-member functions, instances of the class or of its derived classes may access those public members (by access, I mean the use of the dot (.) or arrow (->) membership operators). For example, `Person::DisplayData()` is a public member, so in the `main ()` method, it is permissible to execute:

```
wes.DisplayData();
```

where `wes` is an instance of `Person`.

- The class `Pupil` has its own implementation of `DisplayData()` and we say that this implementation overrides the one inherited from class `Person`. In order to override an inherited member function, the same function name, argument list and return type must be used.

- The `Pupil::DisplayData()` shows the name, ssn, gender and age of a `Pupil` object in addition to `school` and `class_level`, which are specific attributes of class `Pupil`. The body of `Pupil::DisplayData()` calls the base class implementation by qualifying the member function with the class name and scope operator:

```
void Pupil::DisplayData() {
Person::DisplayData();
...;
}
```

- Within non-member function `main()`, a `Pupil` object called `yvonne` was instantiated. Since class `Pupil` had overridden the `DisplayData()` member function, a statement such as:

```
yvonne.DisplayData();
```

is understood to call the `Pupil::DisplayData()` implementation since yvonne is of type `Pupil`. If we want yvonne to call `Person::DisplayData()`, we must qualify the member function with the class name and scope operator as follows:

`yvonne.Person::DisplayData();`

If class `Pupil` did not override the `DisplayData()` member function, it would be understood that `yvonne.DisplayData()` would invoke the implementation in class `Person`. In other words, the search for the member function would start from the type represented by yvonne and traverse up the hierarchy. The "closest" implementation to the type represented by yvonne would be the one that is called.

Note: The above scheme for member function resolution is generally true provided no ambiguity arises in a multiple inheritance situation (which C++ supports and Java does not).

A Java equivalent to the C++ sample might look like:

Listing 4-2: InheritanceDemo1.java

```java
import java.awt.*;
import java.io.IOException;

class Person {

    // methods
    public Person(String nm, String id, char sx, int yrs) {
    name = new String(nm);
    ssn = new String(id);
    gender = sx;
    age = yrs;
    }

    public void DisplayData() {
    System.out.print("\n\nName = "+name);
    System.out.print("\nSSN = "+ssn);
    System.out.print("\nGender = "+gender);
    System.out.print("\nAge = "+age);
    System.out.flush();
    }

    // variables
    private String name;
```

```
        private String ssn;
        private char gender;
        private int age;
}

class Pupil extends Person {

    // methods
    public Pupil(String nm, String id, char sx, int yrs, String
      sc, int lv) {
    super(nm, id, sx, yrs);
    school = new String(sc);
    class_level = lv;
    }

    public void DisplayData() {
    super.DisplayData();
    System.out.print("\nSchool = "+school);
    System.out.print("\nLevel = "+class_level);
    System.out.flush();
    }

    // variables
    private String school;
    private int class_level;
}

public class InheritanceDemo1 {

    public static void main(String args[]) {
        Person wes = new Person("Wes", "570-45-1287", 'M', 17);
        wes.DisplayData();

        Pupil yvonne = new Pupil("Yvonne", "630-22-0980", 'F', 22,
                         "Univ. of Washington", 3);
        yvonne.DisplayData();
        }
}
```

The following would be the output from executing the above Java code:

```
Name = Wes
SSN = 570-45-1287
Gender = M
Age = 17

Name = Yvonne
SSN = 630-22-0980
Gender = F
Age = 22
```

```
School = Univ. of Washington
Level = 3
```

The following are essential points about the Java example:

- In Java, the keyword to use for deriving one class from another is `extends`. The following code fragment illustrates how class `Pupil` is derived from class `Person`:

```
class Pupil extends Person {
...
}
```

  The Java `extends` keyword is analogous to the C++ `public` keyword for denoting class derivation.

- Java does have the `public` keyword, which is one of several class *modifiers*. The use of these modifiers is strictly optional. The syntax for declaring a class with modifiers basically follows this format:

```
[modifiers] class ClassName [extends SuperclassName] [imple-
ments InterfaceName]
```

  Java also has an `implements` keyword, which pertains to something called *interfaces*. We will look at interfaces as a separate topic.

  For now, it is sufficient to understand that if a class has the `public` modifier (such as for class `InheritanceDemo1`), then the non-private members of the class are accessible inside and outside the package from where it was originally declared. A *package* is a grouping of related classes (they need not be bounded by inheritance). Membership within a package is determined by the use of the `package` keyword. In this example, there is no use of this keyword, so all of the classes declared are understood to be within the same package and they fall into a no-name, default package maintained by the Java environment.

  If the class has no modifier at all (such as class `Person` and class `Pupil`), then the non-private members of the class are only visible to classes within the same package. We say that such classes are of *package* scope. If Class A is in one package and is of package scope and class B belongs to another package, no method of class B can instantiate an object of class A.

  For example, class `InheritanceDemo1` is within the same package as class `Person` and class `Pupil`. Hence, it is legal for the methods of class `InheritanceDemo1` to instantiate objects of `Person` or `Pupil`.

Warning: Remember that no modifier implies that the visibility of the class is at the package level. Programmers must not only pay attention to keywords, but also to the <u>lack</u> of any keyword!

Other class modifier keywords include `abstract`, `final` and synchro-nizable. These will be introduced in later topics. There are no class mod-ifiers in C++.

- Within the class, the visibility modifiers can also be applied to the individ-ual variables (attributes) and methods (behaviors) of the class. Unlike C++, a modifier (`public` and `private` in this example) must be applied on a field-by-field basis. Typically, the variables should be private since the variables represent state information about the class and you would not want to give outsiders unregulated access to such information. The meth-ods are normally public since the methods represent the interfaces to the outside world. The methods would be used to regulate access to the attributes.

  As in C++, a private field can be accessed only by another method of the same class. A public field can be accessed by any method from any class inside or outside the package (provided the class itself is public).

  Other visibility modifiers for a method may be *private protected*, *protected* or the default. The default uses no keyword. These modifiers will be covered in later topics.

- Java has a keyword called `super`, which can be used by methods of a derived class to refer to variables or methods of a superclass. In this exam-ple there are two distinct uses.

  First, the only constructor for class `Pupil` is implemented as:

```
public Pupil(String nm, String id, char sx, int yrs, String
   sc, int lv) {
      super(nm, id, sx, yrs);
      school = new String(sc);
      class_level = lv;
      }
```

  The statement:

```
super(nm, id, sx, yrs);
```

  is a call to the constructor of base class `Person`. The absence of `super` in the body of a constructor would imply calling `super()`, which represents the no-argument, default constructor of the base class. However, there is no such constructor in class `Person`, so we must use `super` and pass it four arguments that would match constructor `Person(String, String, char, int)`.

  Second, the implementation of `Pupil.DisplayData()` appears as:

```
public void DisplayData() {
      super.DisplayData();
```

```
System.out.print("\nSchool = "+school);
System.out.print("\nLevel = "+class_level);
System.out.flush();
}
```

The statement:

```
super.DisplayData();
```

means to invoke an inherited base class implementation of `DisplayData()`. The search for the "nearest" implementation would begin one class above the class that has the method that uses the keyword `super` and would proceed to the top of the hierarchy until the implementation is found (or an exception thrown). Well, in this case, we do not have to look far. The class above the class that has the method with keyword `super` is `Person`. Class `Person` has an implementation of `DisplayData()` and that is the implementation that gets executed from the statement `super.DisplayData()`. C++ does not have any equivalent to `super`.

- On the other hand, Java does not have any equivalent to the C++ scope operator (`::`). Within the `main()` method of class `InheritanceDemo1` above, variable `yvonne` refers to a `Pupil` object. The statement:

```
yvonne.DisplayData();
```

would call the implementation `Pupil.DisplayData()` for this `Pupil` object. However, there is no syntax to support the calling of `Person.DisplayData()` through reference variable `yvonne`. The use of keyword `super` to call the nearest base class implementation has some slight resemblance to the use of a scope operator. However, `super` can only be used within methods of derived classes. Class `InheritanceDemo1` is essentially a stand-alone class and has no direct relationship to class `Person` or class `Pupil`.

Organizing Java Classes into a Package

The Java package can be thought of as a logical grouping or union of related classes. The classes need not be within the same class hierarchy. It is roughly equivalent to a C function library or a C++ class library.

The main ideas behind the creation of a Java package is 1) to organize your classes for specific purposes and 2) to allow others the benefit of using what already has been developed. In order to re-use an existing class that belongs to a package, the `import` statement is used at the top of the source file, such as:

```
import Animals.Humans.Person;
```

As a logical grouping, the package is actually related to a particular path and directory. All of the classes of the package are stored within that directory. To find the class of interest, Java employs a particular search mechanism to find the package referenced by the import statement. There are three components to locating the packaged class:

- The environment variable CLASSPATH,

- The components comprising the package name, each component being separated by a period:

```
package_component_1.[package_component_2].[package_component_n
].class_name
```

There must be at least one package component name and the final component is the name of the class.

- Finally, the name of the class itself. The asterisk (*) in the last position would mean all classes of the package.

Let us look at each component, beginning with the environment variable, CLASSPATH.

The environment variable CLASSPATH is set in different ways depending on the operating system you are using.

- If you are using Windows 95™ or Windows NT™ 3.5 or higher, CLASS-PATH can be set through the Control Panel utility (see figure 4-1). If you are using Windows 95™, a statement such as the following can be placed inside the AUTOEXEC.BAT file:

```
set  CLASSPATH=.;C:\Java\Lib\classes.zip;C:\JAVAPAKS
```

A semicolon separates each possible path. The single period (.) represents the current directory. The .;C:\Java\Lib\classes.zip portion is actually part of the initial set up of the Java Developer's Kit. (JDK). The classes.zip file is part of the JDK and is a special condensation of all the standard Java packages.

The remaining paths of the CLASSPATH, such as C:\JAVAPAKS, are for the containment of user-defined packages.

The directory and path names are <u>not</u> case sensitive.

- If you are using UNIX or HP-UX with the Bourne or Korn shells, the following line can be placed within the .profile turnkey file (or it can be entered via the command line):

```
CLASSPATH=/Java/Lib/classes.zip:/JAVAPAKS:.;export CLASSPATH
```

Remember that the path delimiters are different between a PC Windows operating system and a UNIX system (backslash versus forward slash). Also, the directory, path and file names on UNIX are case-sensitive.

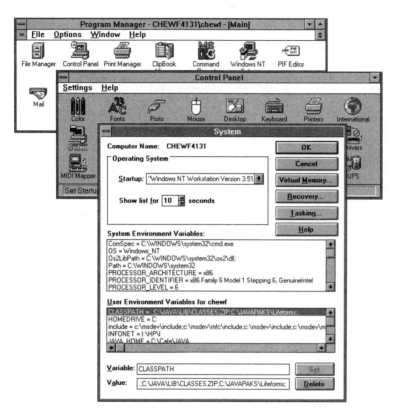

Figure 4-1

• If you are using UNIX or HP-UX with the C shell, the following line can be placed within the `.cshrc` turnkey file (or it can be entered via the command line):

```
setenv  CLASSPATH  /Java/Lib/classes.zip:/JAVAPAKS:.
```

Again, watch for the type of path delimiter being used and case sensitivity.

The complete path to the class to be imported is a concatenation of a path from the CLASSPATH variable and the leading components of the package name. Suppose we are working from a Windows NT™ environment (see Figure 4-2) and our classes are contained within the path:

```
C:\JAVAPAKS\Lifeforms\Animals\Humans\
```

For this example, there are three classes within the package: `Person`, `Pupil` and `Tutor`.

The absolute package name will depend on how we select the paths for the CLASSPATH variable. This will also influence how the programmer will

```
 ─                    C:\JAVAPAKS\Lifeforms\Animals\Humans\*.* -              ▼ ▲
┌ ☐ JAVAPAKS          ↑ 📁..
│  └ ☐ Lifeforms        ☐ Person.class   PERSON~1.CLA      1,416   11/4/96   11:22:38 PM
│     └ ☐ Animals       ☐ Pupil.class    PUPIL~1.CLA       1,518   11/4/96   11:24:46 PM
│        └ 📂 Humans     ☐ Tutor.class    TUTOR~1.CLA       1,938   11/4/96   11:27:40 PM
←                    → ↓ ←                                                        →
```

Figure 4-2

use the `import` statement within his Java source files. Suppose the programmer wanted to import class `Person`. The following chart provides some possible combinations:

CLASSPATH	Package Name	Import Statement
`C:\JAVAPAKS\`	`Lifeforms.Animals.Humans`	`import Lifeforms.Animals.Humans.Person;`
`C:\JAVAPAKS\Lifeforms\`	`Animals.Humans`	`import Animals.Humans.Person;`
`C:\JAVAPAKS\` `Lifeforms\Animals\`	`Humans`	`import Humans.Person;`

Figure 4-3

If the programmer wanted to import all the classes (`Person`, `Pupil` and `Tutor`) of the package, he would use the asterisk (*) in place of a class name:

`import Lifeforms.Animals.Humans.*;`

   or:

`import Animals.Humans.*;`

   or:

`import Humans.*;`

for each of the three cases.

C++ does not have the concept of packages as Java does. Rather, C++ developers take the traditional approach of providing class header files (`.h` or `.hh` files) and class member function implementations bundled as an object code library to be linked with the C++ sources.

Resolving Name Collisions with C++ Namespaces and Java Packages

Actually, C++ has a mechanism that resembles a Java package. There is a relatively new feature incorporated into the C++ language called *namespace*. At the time of this writing, not all compiler vendors have implemented this feature.

The C++ program has only one global namespace. As such it becomes difficult at times to incorporate libraries from different vendors without name collisions. Historically programmers have used workarounds like wrapping the classes or functions with macros or other classes, but these approaches are tedious and troublesome to maintain. The namespace feature allows the programmer to partition the global namespace. The programmer can specify which members of which namespace may be used at any given time. Furthermore, he can also mix and match members from different namespaces, provided there is no ambiguity.

This topic will demonstrate the namespace feature and introduce the new C++ keywords: `namespace` and `using`.

The `namespace` keyword is somewhat like the `class` keyword, but it can only be used at the global level of a translation unit. Its basic syntax looks like:

```
namespace   identifier {
                        // members
                        }
```

where `identifier` is the user-defined name of the namespace. The members are placed within the enclosing braces and there is no semicolon after the right brace. The members may be class names, non-member functions or global variables.

As an example, suppose I am engaged in doing business in the pet industry. I might have a class called `Bird` that is part of a namespace called `Pets`:

```
namespace Pets {

class Bird {
public:
    enum { FEMALE, MALE };
    Bird(String, int, double);
    void getData();
    double  getSalesPrice();
private:
    String name;
    int     gender;
    int     coat;
    double sales_price;
};

Bird::Bird(String nm, int sx, double cost)  :
name(nm), gender(sx), sales_price(cost) {
}

void Bird::getData() {
cout<<"Pet Data:"<<endl;
cout<<"Species = "<<name<<endl;
cout<<"Gender = "<<((gender==FEMALE)?"Female":"Male")<<endl;
```

```
cout<<"Price = "<<sales_price<<endl;
cout<<endl;
}

double Bird::getSalesPrice() {
return sales_price;
}
```

} // End of namespace Pets

In the above, the header and member function implementations of class `Bird` are declared as part of namespace `Pets`. The header and function implementations can be separated into two separate files, `PetsBird.hh` and `PetsBird.cpp`, and the compiler will still recognize the contents as belonging to one namespace:

Listing 4-3: PetsBird.hh

```
// PetsBird.hh

#ifndef PETS_BIRD_HH
#define PETS_BIRD_HH

namespace Pets {

class Bird {
public:
   enum { FEMALE, MALE };
   Bird(String, int, double);
   void getData();
   double  getSalesPrice();
private:
   String name;
   int    gender;
   int    coat;
   double sales_price;
};

} // End of namespace Pets

#endif
```

Listing 4-4: PetsBird.cpp

```
// PetsBird.cpp

#include <iostream.h>
#include <string.h>
#include "String.hh"
```

```
#include "PetsBird.hh"

Pets::Bird::Bird(String nm, int sx, double cost) :
name(nm), gender(sx), sales_price(cost) {
}

void Pets::Bird::getData() {
cout<<"Pet Data:"<<endl;
cout<<"Species = "<<name<<endl;
cout<<"Gender = "<<((gender==FEMALE)?"Female":"Male")<<endl;
cout<<"Price = "<<sales_price<<endl;
cout<<endl;
}

double Pets::Bird::getSalesPrice() {
return sales_price;
}
```

The contents of file `PetsBird.cpp` would be compiled into a translation unit and placed into an object code library. To tell the compiler that the constructor and member functions of `Bird` are part of the `Pets` namespace, it is necessary to qualify all of the function names with the scope resolution operator. In other words, all the names must be prefixed with `Pets::`.

Using the namespace name and scope resolution operator can get tedious, so it is possible to take a shortcut by specifying a `using namespace` directive. The following is equivalent to the above:

```
// PetsBird.cpp

#include <iostream.h>
#include <string.h>
#include "String.hh"
#include "PetsBird.hh"

using namespace Pets;

Bird::Bird(String nm, int sx, double cost) :
name(nm), gender(sx), sales_price(cost) {
}

void Bird::getData() {
cout<<"Pet Data:"<<endl;
cout<<"Species = "<<name<<endl;
cout<<"Gender = "<<((gender==FEMALE)?"Female":"Male")<<endl;
cout<<"Price = "<<sales_price<<endl;
cout<<endl;
}

double Bird::getSalesPrice() {
```

```
    return sales_price;
}
```

Within the scope where the using directive is specified, it is understood that `Bird::Bird` is `Pets::Bird::Bird` and similarly for the other functions.

It is also possible to specify other classes, functions and variables as members of a namespace, but have them reside in different files. For instance, I can add a class `Dog` into namespace `Pets`:

Listing 4-5: PetsDog.hh

```cpp
// PetsDog.hh

#ifndef PETS_DOG_HH
#define PETS_DOG_HH

namespace Pets {

class Dog {
public:
    enum { FEMALE, MALE };
    enum { SMOOTH, SHORT_HAIR, LONG_HAIR, SHAGGY };
    Dog(String, int, int, double);
    void getData();
    int  getCoat();
private:
    String name;
    int    gender;
    int    coat;
    double sales_price;
};

} // Namespace Pets

#endif
```

Listing 4-6: PetsDog.cpp

```cpp
// PetsDog.cpp

#include <iostream.h>
#include <string.h>
#include "String.hh"
#include "PetsDog.hh"

using namespace Pets;

Dog::Dog(String nm, int sx, int fur, double cost) :
```

```
name(nm), gender(sx), coat(fur), sales_price(cost) {
}

void Dog::getData() {
cout<<"Pet Data:"<<endl;
cout<<"Species = "<<name<<endl;
cout<<"Gender = "<<((gender==FEMALE)?"Female":"Male")<<endl;
cout<<"Coat = ";
switch (coat) {
    case SMOOTH:
        cout<<"Smooth"<<endl;
      break;
    case SHAGGY:
      cout<<"Shaggy"<<endl;
      break;
    case SHORT_HAIR:
      cout<<"Short hair"<<endl;
      break;
    case LONG_HAIR:
      cout<<"Long hair"<<endl;
      break;
    }
cout<<"Price = "<<sales_price<<endl;
cout<<endl;
}

int Dog::getCoat() {
return coat;
}
```

In the above, each of the translation units representing class `Bird` and class `Dog`
would belong to namespace `Pets`. It is also possible to have multiple namespace
blocks for the same namespace in the same source file. The compiler will not
view the repeating of the namespace identifier as a redeclaration.

The main point about having namespaces is to avoid name contention. For
instance, I may also be interested in the anatomy of birds, which is defined in
another class `Bird` in namespace `Zoology`:

Listing 4-7: ZoologyBird.hh

```
// ZoologyBird.hh

#ifndef ZOOLOGY_BIRD_HH
#define ZOOLOGY_BIRD_HH

namespace Zoology {

class Bird {
```

```
public:
    Bird(String, String, double, long);
    void getData();
    long getSpeed();
private:
    String name;
    String family;
    double wing_span;
    long   speed;
};

}  // Namespace Zoology

#endif
```

Listing 4-8: ZoologyBird.cpp

```
// ZoologyBird.cpp

#include <iostream.h>
#include <string.h>
#include "String.hh"
#include "ZoologyBird.hh"

using namespace Zoology;

Bird::Bird(String nm, String fm, double sn, long sp) :
      name(nm), family(fm), wing_span(sn), speed(sp) {
}

void Bird::getData() {
cout<<"Animal Data:"<<endl;
cout<<"Species = "<<name<<endl;
cout<<"Family = "<<family<<endl;
cout<<"Wing span = "<<wing_span<<" feet"<<endl;
cout<<"Speed in flight = "<<speed<<" miles per hour"<<endl;
cout<<endl;
}

long Bird::getSpeed() {
return speed;
}
```

Now, I have two different classes for Bird, each within its own namespace. As a user of these classes, I can now write client code, such as:

Listing 4-9: NamespaceDemo.cpp

```
#include <iostream.h>
#include <string.h>
#include "String.hh"
```

```
#include "ZoologyBird.hh"
#include "PetsBird.hh"
#include "PetsDog.hh"

void main() {

Pets::Bird macaw1("Macaw", Pets::Bird::FEMALE, 249.98);
macaw1.getData();
...
}
```

where I can explicitly specify which `Bird` class I want to use with the scope resolution operator. Or the alternative is to use the `using namespace` directive:

```
void main() {
using namespace Pets;

Bird macaw1("Macaw", Bird::FEMALE, 249.98);
macaw1.getData();
...
}
```

The `using namespace` directive imports the definitions of namespace `Pets` into the enclosing block. The use of the definitions is understood to emanate from namespace `Pets`.

It is also possible to employ the `using` keyword as a `using` declaration. A `using` declaration is a selective import of a namespace member into the local scope. Take, for example:

```
void CreateAnimals() {
using namespace Zoology;
using Pets::Dog;
Bird cockatoo("Cockatoo", "Parrot", 0.80, 6);
cockatoo.getData();
Dog collie("Collie", Dog::FEMALE, Dog::LONG_HAIR, 539.50);
collie.getData();
}
```

The `using namespace Zoology` directive makes available all members of `Zoology`, which has its class `Bird`. On the other hand, the `using Pets::Dog` declaration is the importing of the class `Dog` from the namespace `Pets` into the local scope. From these `using` statements, it is understood that cockatoo is of type `Zoology::Bird` while collie is of type `Pets::Dog`.

It is also possible to employ `using namespace` directives and `using` declarations multiple times. However, care must be taken to avoid ambiguity conflicts. For instance, the compiler will flag an error if it sees:

```
void CreateHawk() {
using namespace Zoology;
using namespace Pets;
```

```
Bird hawk("Hawk", "Flying Predators", 5.0, 25);
...
}
```

The using statements are fine. However the attempt to instantiate a Bird object called hawk raises a problem. Do we want Zoology::Bird or Pets::Bird? The compiler is unable to choose.

The namespace keyword also has another use: it can be used to specify alias names to namespace names. This feature would be very helpful to avoid typing long namespace names. For instance, if we have:

```
namespace Zoo = Zoology;
```

then we can write statements like:

```
Zoo::Bird  macaw("Macaw", "Parrot", 2.0, 10);
macaw.getData();
```

The alias name Zoo must refer to an official namespace name like Zoology. Wherever Zoo is used, it is understood to mean Zoology.

Finally, it is possible to have an unnamed or an anonymous namespace. The members of an anonymous namespace are guaranteed to be unique within the translation unit. It is equivalent to applying the static keyword to all of the members (everything is of file scope). Since the namespace is unnamed, the use of the members naturally requires no qualification:

```
namespace {   // Anonymous namespace

class Cat {
public:
    Cat(String, String);
    void getData();
private:
    String name;
    String family;
};

Cat::Cat(String nm, String fm) : name(nm), family(fm) {
}

void Cat::getData() {
cout<<"Cat Data:"<<endl;
cout<<"Species = "<<name<<endl;
cout<<"Family = "<<family<<endl;
cout<<endl;
}

}   // End of anonymous namespace
```

```
void  main()
{
...
Cat kitty("House Cat", "Tabby");      // Cat is unique to this
                                      // translation unit
kitty.getData();
}
```

The code samples above are part of the C++ NamespaceDemo program, which is on the included media. The reader is encouraged to compile and execute this sample program to get a feel for how namespaces work.

Summary: C++ namespaces not only help the developer avoid name collisions, but are also a mechanism to logically group related classes and functions. In many ways, it is equivalent to the Java package.

In Java, it is also possible to have inherently different classes with the same name. In this case, such classes would be placed into different packages. In the case of two different Bird classes, one would be in package Pets and the other in package Zoology. To use both Bird classes within the same program we must explicitly qualify the class name with the package name and membership operator (.):

Listing 4-10: NamespaceDemo.java

```
import Pets.*;
import Zoology.*

public class NamespaceDemo {

    public static void main(String args[]) {

    Pets.Bird macaw1 =
              new Pets.Bird("Macaw", Pets.Bird.FEMALE, 249.98);
    macaw1.getData();
    ...
    Zoology.Bird macaw2 =
              new Zoology.Bird("Macaw", "Parrot", 2.0, 10);
    macaw2.getData();
    ...
    }
}
```

The above is from the Java equivalent of the NamespaceDemo program on the supplied media. For more on Java packages, refer to the previous topic, *Organizing Java Classes into a Package.*

Visibility for the Subclasses: C++ `protected` and Java `private protected`

Both C++ and Java have keywords to regulate the visibility of the methods and fields of a class. A class designer may want to give subclasses of a class access to certain members, but prohibit non-subclasses from such privileges. In many respects, the rules regulating class member access are somewhat more complicated in Java than C++, as there are more cases to consider. In this section, I am going to compare the use of `protected` in C++ versus `private protected` (two keywords used as one) in Java.

Note: The `private protected` members for methods only applies to Java 1.0 and has been dropped from the language specification for Java 1.1 (possibly to reduce the complexity of the language). At the time of this writing, many software tool vendors have yet to upgrade their products to support Java 1.1. Nevertheless, a discussion of Java's `private protected` to similar semantics in C++ will provide a useful foundation to understand the other access modes of Java.

Starting with C++, suppose we modify the previous `Person-Pupil` class hierarchy (see the topic, *Inheritance as an "is-a" Relationship*) as follows:

Listing 4-11: InheritanceDemo2.cpp

```cpp
#include <iostream.h>
#include <string.h>
#include "String.hh"

class Person {
public:
    Person(String, String, char, int);
    void DisplayData();
protected:
    int getAge();
    void setAge(int);
private:
    String name;
    String ssn;
    char gender;
    int age;
};

Person::Person(String nm, String id, char sx, int yrs) :
            name(nm), ssn(id), gender(sx), age(yrs) {
}

void Person::DisplayData() {
```

```
cout<<endl;
cout<<"Name = "<<name<<endl;
cout<<"SSN = "<<ssn<<endl;
cout<<"Gender = "<<gender<<endl;
cout<<"Age = "<<age<<endl;
}

int Person::getAge() {
return age;
}

void Person::setAge(int yrs) {
age = yrs;
}

class Pupil : public Person {
public:
    Pupil(String nm, String id, char sx, int yrs, String sc, int
    lv);
    void DisplayData();
    void incrementAge();
private:
    String school;
    int class_level;
};

Pupil::Pupil(String nm, String id, char sx, int yrs, String sc,
 int lv) :
            Person(nm, id, sx, yrs), school(sc), class_level(lv) {
}

void Pupil::DisplayData() {
Person::DisplayData();
cout<<"School = "<<school<<endl;
cout<<"Level = "<<class_level<<endl;
}

void Pupil::incrementAge() {
int curr_age = getAge();
setAge(++curr_age);
}

void main() {
Person wes("Wes", "570-45-1287", 'M', 17);
wes.DisplayData();

Pupil yvonne("Yvonne", "630-22-0980", 'F', 22, "Univ. of
 Washington", 3);
yvonne.DisplayData();
```

```
yvonne.incrementAge();
yvonne.DisplayData();
}
```

The highlighted lines of code are additions over the previous version. The execution of the above code would yield:

```
Name = Wes
SSN = 570-45-1287
Gender = M
Age = 17

Name = Yvonne
SSN = 630-22-0980
Gender = F
Age = 22
School = Univ. of Washington
Level = 3

Name = Yvonne
SSN = 630-22-0980
Gender = F
Age = 23
School = Univ. of Washington
Level = 3
```

This sample program introduces the `protected` keyword. The following is a discussion of its use with C++:

- Within the body of the class, the `protected` keyword denotes a particular access region. Basically, protected members, whether they are data members or member functions, are only accessible to member functions of the same class or to member functions of derived classes. In the example shown, `Person::getAge()` and `Person::setAge()` are protected member functions. Derived class `Pupil` inherits these members of `Person` and a member function like `Pupil::incrementAge()` can access these members:

```
void Pupil::incrementAge() {
int curr_age = getAge();        // Person::getAge()
setAge(++curr_age);             // Person::setAge(int);
}
```

Data members (attributes) can also be made protected. However, this is not a good idea since other developers can derive subclasses with methods to directly access those base class attributes. It is better to provide protected member functions and regulate access to such state information.

- Client code, such as the `main()` function, cannot access any protected member of a class through instances of the class. For instance, if the following statement had appeared in `main()`:

```
yvonne.setAge(24);     // Illegal!  Cannot access a protected
                       member
```

the statement would be flagged as a compilation error.

However, given the design of class `Pupil`, there is a limited ability to change a pupil's age and that is through the public `Pupil::incrementAge()` member function:

```
yvonne.incrementAge();      // Instances of Pupil can call
                            // incrementAge()
```

Class `Pupil` inherits `Person::getAge()` and `Person::setAge()` and hence, `Pupil::incrementAge()` may access these protected members.

- The previous point that instances cannot access protected members also applies to member functions of derived classes. For instance, suppose we enhance class `Pupil` as follows:

```
class Pupil : public Person {
public:
    ...
    void adjustAge(Person &, int);
private:
    String school;
    int class_level;
};
...
void Pupil::adjustAge(Person & individual, int new_age) {
individual.setAge(new_age);          // Illegal!
}
```

A new member function called `adjustAge()` is added to class `Pupil`. Within its argument list, one of the arguments is a reference to type `Person`, variable `individual`. As a C++ reference variable, `individual` refers to an instance of `Person`. Since `setAge()` is a protected member within class `Person`, the statement:

```
individual.setAge(new_age);
```

is considered illegal. The methods of a subclass are not allowed to access the protected members of a superclass through instances of the superclass. However, the methods of a subclass can access the protected members of a superclass through instances of the subclass or through instances of the subclasses of the subclass.

There is an equivalent to this example in Java. It would look something like the following:

Listing 4-12: Person.java

```java
// Source file: Person.java
package Humans;
import java.awt.*;
import java.io.IOException;

public class Person {

    public Person(String nm, String id, char sx, int yrs) {
    name = new String(nm);
    ssn = new String(id);
    gender = sx;
    age = yrs;
    }

    public void DisplayData() {
    System.out.print("\n\nName = "+name);
    System.out.print("\nSSN = "+ssn);
    System.out.print("\nGender = "+gender);
    System.out.print("\nAge = "+age);
    System.out.flush();
    }

    private protected int getAge() {
    return age;
    }

    private protected void setAge(int yrs) {
    age = yrs;
    }

    private String name;
    private String ssn;
    private char gender;
    private int age;
}
```

Listing 4-13: Pupil.java

```java
// Source file: Pupil.java
package Humans;
import java.awt.*;
import java.io.IOException;

public class Pupil extends Person {
```

```
public Pupil(String nm, String id, char sx, int yrs, String
  sc, int lv) {
super(nm, id, sx, yrs);
school = new String(sc);
class_level = lv;
}

public void DisplayData() {
super.DisplayData();
System.out.print("\nSchool = "+school);
System.out.print("\nLevel = "+class_level);
System.out.flush();
}

public void incrementAge() {
int curr_age = getAge();
setAge(++curr_age);
}

private String school;
private int class_level;
}
```

Listing 4-14: InheritanceDemo2.java

```
// Source file: InheritanceDemo2.java
import java.awt.*;
import java.io.IOException;
import Humans.*;

public class InheritanceDemo2 {

    public static void main(String args[]) {
        Person wes = new Person("Wes", "570-45-1287", 'M', 17);
        wes.DisplayData();

        Pupil yvonne = new Pupil("Yvonne", "630-22-0980", 'F',
         22, "Univ. of Washington", 3);
        yvonne.DisplayData();

        yvonne.incrementAge();
        yvonne.DisplayData();
    }
}
```

The execution of the above Java code would produce:

```
Name = Wes
SSN = 570-45-1287
Gender = M
Age = 17

Name = Yvonne
SSN = 630-22-0980
Gender = F
Age = 22
School = Univ. of Washington
Level = 3

Name = Yvonne
SSN = 630-22-0980
Gender = F
Age = 23
School = Univ. of Washington
Level = 3
```

The output from the Java sample is identical to the output from the C++ sample. The Java example has the following distinctive features:

- The Java `private protected` members, whether they are fields or methods, are only accessible to methods of the same class or to methods of subclasses. The subclasses may be in a package different from the package containing the parent class.

  In the example, class `Pupil` inherits methods `getAge()` and `setAge()` from class `Person` and accesses these methods in the body of its `incrementAge()` method:

  ```java
  public void incrementAge() {
  int curr_age = getAge();
  setAge(++curr_age);
  }
  ```

- Like C++ `protected` members, Java `private protected` members cannot be accessed through client code. For instance, class `InheritanceDemo2` has no direct relationship to the `Person-Pupil` hierarchy. If its `public static main()` method contained the statement:

  ```java
  yvonne.setAge(30);      // Illegal!  Person.setAge() is
                          // private protected.
  ```

  the compiler would flag this as an error.

- In addition, the methods of a derived class cannot access the `private protected` members of the superclass through instances of the superclass. For example, if class `Pupil` had included the following method:

  ```java
  void adjustAge(Person  individual, int new_age) {
  ```

```
        individual.setAge(new_age);                    // Illegal!
    }
```

the compiler would flag the statement, `individual.setAge(yrs);` as an error because `individual` is a reference to a `Person` object. However, if `individual` had represented a `Pupil` or a subclass of `Pupil`, then the statement would be legal. In summary, this behavior is equivalent to a protected `Pupil::adjustAge(Person &, int)` counterpart in C++.

• It is possible that the subclass may be in a package different from its superclass. In this situation, the subclass will still continue to inherit the `private protected` members of the superclass. As an extension of this example, suppose we have a class called `Tutor`, which is a subclass of `Pupil`:

```java
import java.io.IOException;
import Humans.*;

public class Tutor extends Pupil {

    public Tutor(String nm, String id, char sx, int yrs,
                String sc, int lv, String sj, String prof) {
    super(nm, id, sx, yrs, sc, lv);
    subject = new String(sj);
    professor = new String(prof);
    }

    public void DisplayData() {
    super.DisplayData();
    System.out.print("\nSubject = "+subject);
    System.out.print("\nProfessor = "+professor);
    System.out.flush();
    }

    public void decrementAge() {
    int curr_age = getAge();
    setAge(-curr_age);
    }

    private String subject;
    private String professor;

    public static void main(String args[]) {

    Tutor veronica= new Tutor("Veronica", "630-22-0980", 'F', 27,
                            "Monroe Community College", 4,
                            "Mathematics", "Dr. R. Thompson");
    veronica.DisplayData();
```

```
        veronica.setAge(23);
        veronica.DisplayData();

        veronica.decrementAge();
        veronica.DisplayData();
        }
}
```

Class `Tutor` belongs to the no-name, default package and not to package `Humans`, where class `Person` and class `Pupil` reside. Nevertheless, `Tutor` is a subclass of `Pupil` and `Tutor` does inherit `getAge()` and `setAge()` from `Person`. These inherited methods are used by method `decrementAge()` in `Tutor`.

Widening the Visibility: the Java `protected` Keyword

The `protected` keyword by itself is a legal field modifier in Java. However, it is semantically different from the C++ `protected` keyword (which is actually equivalent to Java's `private protected` keyword). Protected members are actually accessible to classes via instances of the class, provided the classes doing the accessing are within the <u>same</u> package as the class with the protected fields. The following is an enhancement to the previous Java example with the `Person-Pupil` hierarchy:

Listing 4-15: Person.java

```
// Source file: Person.java
package Humans;
import java.awt.*;
import java.io.IOException;

public class Person {

    public Person(String nm, String id, char sx, int yrs) {
    name = new String(nm);
    ssn = new String(id);
    gender = sx;
    age = yrs;
    }

    public void DisplayData() {
    System.out.print("\n\nName = "+name);
    System.out.print("\nSSN = "+ssn);
    System.out.print("\nGender = "+gender);
    System.out.print("\nAge = "+age);
    System.out.flush();
    }
```

```
protected int getAge() {           // Formerly private protected
return age;
}

protected void setAge(int yrs) {   // Formerly private
                                   // protected
age = yrs;
}

private String name;
private String ssn;
private char gender;
private int age;
}
```

Listing 4-16: Pupil.java

```
// Source file: Pupil.java
package Humans;
import java.awt.*;
import java.io.IOException;

public class Pupil extends Person {

    public Pupil(String nm, String id, char sx, int yrs, String
     sc, int lv) {
    super(nm, id, sx, yrs);
    school = new String(sc);
    class_level = lv;
    }

    public void DisplayData() {
    super.DisplayData();
    System.out.print("\nSchool = "+school);
    System.out.print("\nLevel = "+class_level);
    System.out.flush();
    }

    public void incrementAge() {
    int curr_age = getAge();
    setAge(++curr_age);
    }

    public void adjustAge(Person individual, int new_age) {
    individual.setAge(new_age);         /* (1) */
    }
```

```
        private String school;
        private int class_level;
}
```

Listing 4-17: InheritanceDemo3.java

```java
// Source file: InheritanceDemo3.java
package Humans;
import java.awt.*;
import java.io.IOException;

public class InheritanceDemo3 {

    public static void main(String args[]) {
    Person wes = new Person("Wes", "570-45-1287", 'M', 17);
    wes.DisplayData();

    wes.setAge(20);                        /* (2) */

    wes.DisplayData();

    Pupil yvonne = new Pupil("Yvonne", "630-22-0980", 'F', 22,
                         "Univ. of Washington", 3);
    yvonne.DisplayData();

    yvonne.setAge(30);                     /* (3) */
    yvonne.DisplayData();
    }

}
```

Listing 4-18: RunInheritanceDemo3.java

```java
// Source file: RunInheritanceDemo3.java
import java.awt.*;
import java.io.IOException;
import Humans.*;

public class RunInheritanceDemo3 {

    public static void main(String args[]) {
        InheritanceDemo3.main(null);
        }
}
```

The lines of code in bold are either additions or changes to the previous Java example. The execution of RunInheritanceDemo3.main() would display the following:

```
Name = Wes
SSN = 570-45-1287
```

```
Gender = M
Age = 17

Name = Wes
SSN = 570-45-1287
Gender = M
Age = 20

Name = Yvonne
SSN = 630-22-0980
Gender = F
Age = 22
School = Univ. of Washington
Level = 3

Name = Yvonne
SSN = 630-22-0980
Gender = F
Age = 30
School = Univ. of Washington
Level = 3
```

Unlike the Java `private protected` modifier (see the previous topic, *Visibility for the Subclasses: C++ protected and Java private protected*), the `protected` methods of class `Person` are accessible to classes derived from `Person` and to classes that belong to the same package as `Person`. Those classes may access the protected members through instances of `Person` (see /* (1) */ and /* (2) */) or through instances of subclasses of `Person` (see /* (3) */).

As in the case for `private protected` members, a subclass can belong to a package different from the package of its superclass and still inherit the `protected` members of the superclass. These superclass protected members may be used by the methods of the subclass.

Summary: Obviously, the use of the Java `protected` modifier is far less restrictive than `private protected` and minimizes the concealment of such members of a class. To prevent unrestricted access to the state information of a class, neither modifier should be used with variable fields. When the `protected` modifier is applied to a method, that method can be accessed through instances of the class, within subclasses or non-subclasses within the same package.

The Default Visibility Modifier for the Java Method

When it comes to visibility modifiers, the Java class designer and programmer certainly must be aware of the semantics of `private`, `private protected`, `protected` and `public`. In addition, he has to pay attention to the <u>lack</u> of a modifier, the default, for this also carries a particular meaning. Suppose the

Person class of an earlier Java example (see the topic, *Visibility for the Subclasses: C++ protected and Java private protected*) did not have a modifier for method getAge():

```
package Humans;
import java.awt.*;
import java.io.IOException;

public class Person {

    public Person(String nm, String id, char sx, int yrs) {
    ...
    }
    ...
    int getAge() {                          // No modifier keyword
    return age;
    }
    ...
    private int age;
}
```

In this situation, the derived class, Pupil, will continue to inherit method getAge() from superclass Person because Pupil co-resides with Person within the same package, Humans. The incrementAge() method, which is specific to Pupil, is able to use getAge() within its implementation:

```
package Humans;
import java.awt.*;
import java.io.IOException;

public class Pupil extends Person {

    public Pupil(String nm, String id, char sx, int yrs, String
     sc, int lv) {
    ...
    }
    ...
    public void incrementAge() {
    int curr_age = getAge();
    setAge(++curr_age);
    }

    private String school;
    private int class_level;
}
```

However, a problem arises when class Tutor is subclassed from class Pupil. If Tutor resides in a different package (not within package Humans), class Tutor will not inherit getAge() from base class Person. This is evident during an attempt to compile class Tutor:

```
import java.io.IOException;
import Humans.*;

public class Tutor extends Pupil {

    public Tutor(String nm, String id, char sx, int yrs, String sc,
                 int lv, String sj, String prof) {
    ...
    }
    ...
    public void decrementAge() {
    int curr_age = getAge();      // Compilation error!
    setAge(-curr_age);
    }
    ...
}
```

The compiler will not recognize `getAge()` and will report `"No method matching getAge() found in Tutor."`

Summary: The default modifier for a variable or method has all of the capabilities of the `protected` modifier, except subclasses belonging to different packages cannot inherit such members. If the intent is to give a subclass the ability to inherit such members, then either move the subclass into the same package as the superclass or make the superclass method `private protected`, `protected` or `public`.

Final Methods and Final Classes in Java

Earlier, we had learned that `final` variables in Java are similar to `const` variables in C++. The `final` variable is intended to be used as a named constant. It is initialized once and holds information that is not supposed to change regardless of the circumstances.

The `final` keyword can also be applied as a modifier to a method or to a class. If a superclass method is declared as final, its subclasses may not override the method. For example, if we return to the previous `Person-Pupil-Tutor` class hierarchy and made an adjustment to method `incrementAge()` in `Pupil`:

```
public class Pupil extends Person {
    ...
    public final void incrementAge() {      // method is now final
    int curr_age = getAge();
    setAge(++curr_age);
    }
    ...
}
```

and an attempt is made by class `Tutor` to override the method:

```
public class Tutor extends Pupil {
    ...
    public void incrementAge() {
        ...
    }
    ...
}
```

the compiler will point to `incrementAge()` and inform the user that `"Final methods cannot be overridden."`

Basically, methods are made `final` to force derived classes to use the implementations of the base class.

A class can also be marked `final`. When a class has been declared `final` no class may subclass from it. In other words, the class must be used "as is" through its public variables and public methods. The `Math` class in the standard Java package, `java.lang`, is a good example of a final class.

A `private` method or a `static` method is understood to be final, as are all the members of a `final` class. Final methods and `final` classes have no equivalents in C++.

Dynamic Method Lookup and Virtual Functions

Polymorphism is the ability of an object to respond appropriately to a message based upon its type and position on a class hierarchy. By responding appropriately, we mean the ability of the object to choose the method implementation that best suits its capabilities. In C++, polymorphism must be designed into the classes. In Java, polymorphism is a default feature of classes.

Polymorphic behavior is best understood with an example. Suppose we are in the supermarket business. We will need to track food costs and calculate what to charge the customer to make a reasonable profit. Domestic candy may require us to add a percentage of local tax. On the other hand, imported candy may require a percentage of local tax and a percentage of import tax. Below is a C++ example based on a `Food-Candy-ForeignCandy` class hierarchy:

```
#include <iostream.h>
#include <string.h>
#include <iomanip.h>
#include "String.hh"

class Food {
public:
    Food(String, double, double);
    String getName();
    double calculatePayment();
```

```
private:
    String name;
    double unit_cost;
    double percent_profit;
};

Food::Food(String nm, double cost, double gain) :
            name(nm), unit_cost(cost), percent_profit(gain) {
}

String Food::getName() {
return name;
}

double Food::calculatePayment() {
return unit_cost + unit_cost * percent_profit;
}

class Candy : public Food {
public:
    Candy(String, double, double, double);
    double calculatePayment();
protected:
    double getLocalTax();
private:
    double local_tax;
};

Candy::Candy(String nm, double cost, double gain, double ltax) :
    Food(nm, cost, gain), local_tax(ltax) {
}

double Candy::getLocalTax() {
return local_tax;
}

double Candy::calculatePayment() {
double sales_price = Food::calculatePayment();
return sales_price + sales_price * local_tax;
}

class ForeignCandy : public Candy {
public:
    ForeignCandy(String, double, double, double, double);
    double calculatePayment();
private:
    double import_tax;
};

ForeignCandy::ForeignCandy(String nm, double cost, double gain,
```

```
                        double ltax, double itax) :
            Candy(nm, cost, gain, ltax), import_tax(itax) {
}

double ForeignCandy::calculatePayment() {
double sales_price = Food::calculatePayment();
return   sales_price+sales_price*getLocalTax()+sales_price*
 import_tax;
}

void main() {
ForeignCandy biscotti("Mocha au Lait", 3.00, 0.25, 0.10, 0.05);
cout<<biscotti.getName()<<" will cost the consumer $"
    <<biscotti.calculatePayment()<<endl;
Food & edible = biscotti;
cout<<edible.getName()<<" will cost the consumer $"
    <<edible.calculatePayment()<<endl;
}
```

The above would produce the following output:

```
Mocha au Lait will cost the consumer $4.3125
Mocha au Lait will cost the consumer $3.75
```

Basically, the following is observed about the example:

- The base class is `Food`. Class `Candy` is derived from `Food` and class `ForeignCandy` is derived from `Candy`. Each of these classes has its own implementation of member function `calculatePayment()`, which is used to determine what to charge the customer per unit of the item.

- Within `main()`, an instance of `ForeignCandy` is represented by variable `biscotti`. Its cost to the customer is correctly calculated as $4.3125.

- A reference variable, `edible`, is initialized to `biscotti`. However,

    `edible.calculatePayment()`

    returns $3.75, not $4.3125. It is apparent that even though `edible` really refers to an object of type `ForeignCandy`, the implementation of `calculatePayment` that is called is `Food::calculatePayment`, since `edible` is a reference variable of type `Food`. The results are not consistent.

To correct the situation, one would need to make `calculatePayment()` a `virtual` member function:

Listing 4-19: VirtualFunctionDemo.cpp

```
class Food {
public:
    Food(String, double, double);
    String getName();
```

```
        virtual double calculatePayment();
private:
        String name;
        double unit_cost;
        double percent_profit;
};
...
class Candy : public Food {
public:
        Candy(String, double, double, double);
        virtual double calculatePayment();
protected:
        double getLocalTax();
private:
        double local_tax;
};
...
class ForeignCandy : public Candy {
public:
        ForeignCandy(String, double, double, double, double);
        virtual double calculatePayment();
private:
        double import_tax;
};
...
```

With the above enhancement, the output would then appear as:

```
Mocha au Lait will cost the consumer $4.3125
Mocha au Lait will cost the consumer $4.3125
```

When the C++ `virtual` keyword is used, the compiler creates a hidden data member in each class called the *virtual function table pointer*. This pointer points to a *virtual function table*, which is an array of addresses to the various member function implementations. Each member function declared virtual in the hierarchy has an entry in the virtual function table.

The `virtual` keyword is typically used with the member function in the base class. Its use there will generate the *virtual function table pointer* and the *virtual function table* (see Figure 4-4) for the base class and subsequent derived classes. The `virtual` keyword is not required for the derived classes, but it is used anyway to document that the member function can be called dynamically.

The use of base class reference variables (or base class pointer variables) to refer to an object within a particular hierarchy is very powerful feature. We are not obligated to check the object's type with lengthy `if` or `switch` statements to determine the proper course of action. During run time, the object simply looks up its implementation in the *virtual function table* and calls it.

Java does <u>not</u> use the `virtual` keyword. There is no need since dynamic

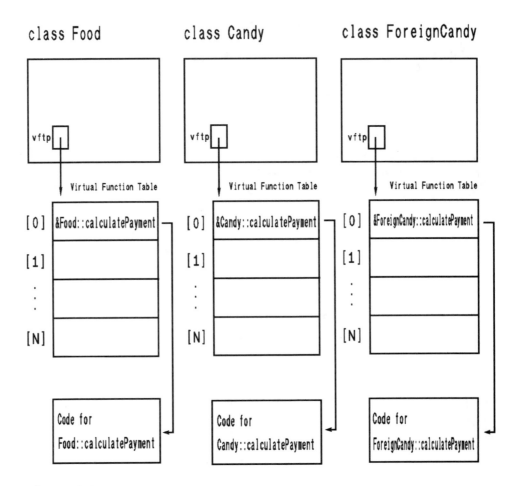

Figure 4-4

method lookup is built into each class. The equivalent to the C++ example with virtual functions would be the following Java sample:

Listing 4-20: DynamicMethodDemo.java

```java
import java.awt.*;

class Food {

    Food(String nm, double cost, double gain) {
    name = new String(nm);
    unit_cost = cost;
```

```
      percent_profit = gain;
       }

    String getName() {
    return name;
    }

    private protected double calculateSalesPrice() {
    return unit_cost + unit_cost * percent_profit;
    }

    double calculatePayment() {
    return calculateSalesPrice();
    }

  private String name;
  private double unit_cost;
  private double percent_profit;

}

class Candy extends Food {

    Candy(String nm, double cost, double gain, double ltax) {
    super(nm, cost, gain);
    local_tax = ltax;
    }

    double calculatePayment() {
    double sales_price = calculateSalesPrice();
    return sales_price + sales_price * local_tax;
    }

    private protected double getLocalTax() {
    return local_tax;
    }

  private double local_tax;

}

class ForeignCandy extends Candy {

    ForeignCandy(String nm, double cost, double gain,
                double ltax, double itax) {
    super(nm, cost, gain, ltax);
    import_tax = itax;
    }

    double calculatePayment() {
    double sales_price = calculateSalesPrice();
```

```
        return   sales_price + sales_price * getLocalTax()
                             + sales_price * import_tax;

    }

    private double import_tax;

}


public class DynamicMethodDemo {

    public static void main(String args[]) {
        ForeignCandy biscotti = new ForeignCandy("Mocha au
                Lait", 3.00, 0.25, 0.10, 0.05);
        System.out.println(biscotti.getName()+" will cost the
                consumer $"+biscotti.calculatePayment());
        Food edible = biscotti;
        System.out.println(edible.getName()+" will cost the
                consumer $"+edible.calculatePayment());

    }
}
```

The output is identical to the C++ example with virtual functions:

```
Mocha au Lait will cost the consumer $4.3125
Mocha au Lait will cost the consumer $4.3125
```

 Summary: Unlike C++, the Java classes of any class hierarchy are inherently polymorphic, i.e., all of the methods are virtual. Java methods cannot be made nonvirtual.

Abstract Classes in Java and C++

All of the previous classes we have seen are *concrete* classes, meaning that it is possible to create instances of the classes. There is another type of class called an *abstract* class. An abstract class is a class that contains the names of behaviors without the implementations to execute those behaviors. Objects cannot be instantiated from an abstract class.

One of the objectives of good object-oriented programming is to recognize the elements that are in common and to group those elements into general abstractions. For instance, if I were to construct a framework of classes for geometric shapes, I might start with the general notion of a "shape" as the base class. From this base class, I would derive specific shape classes, such as Circle or Rectangle (see figure 4-5).

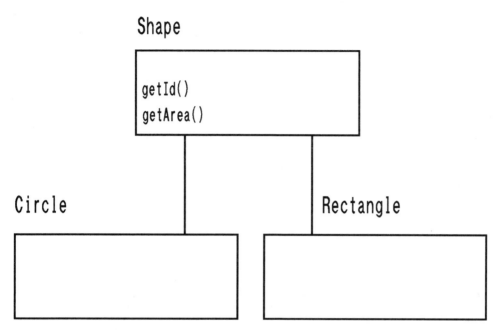

Figure 4-5

One of the things I might do in the design of the framework is to have a unique id assigned to each shape upon instantiation. At times, I would need to get the shape object's id, so a method such as getId() would be specified for Shape and its implementation would be very straightforward.

In addition, there is the notion of an area that can be calculated from any shape object. However, the calculation or formula to derive an area varies from one specific shape to another. In this case, a method prototype, such as getArea(), would be included in the body of class Shape and it would be up to the derived classes, such as Circle and Rectangle, to provide the specific implementations. We will examine how this is done in C++ and Java.

In C++, abstract classes are directly tied to the use of the virtual keyword and the notion of *pure virtual functions*. Below is an implementation of the shape hierarchy:

Listing 4-21: ShapeDemo.cpp

```
#include <iostream.h>
#include <stdlib.h>
#include <math.h>
#include "Point.hh"
```

```cpp
class Shape {
public:
   Shape();
   int getId();
   virtual double getArea() = 0;                    /* (1) */
private:
   static int count;
   int id;
};

int Shape::count = 0;

Shape::Shape() : id(++count) {
}

int Shape::getId() {
return id;
}

class Circle : public Shape {
public:
   Circle(int, int, int);
   virtual double getArea();                        /* (2) */
private:
   int radius;
   Point center;
};

Circle::Circle(int x, int y, int rad) :
            center(Point(x,y)), radius(rad) {
}

double Circle::getArea() {
return 4 * atan(1.0) * radius * radius;    // pi == 4 * atan(1.0)
}

class Rectangle : public Shape {
public:
   Rectangle(int, int, int, int);
   virtual double getArea();                        /* (3) */
private:
   Point upperLeft;
   Point lowerRight;
};

Rectangle::Rectangle(int ul_x, int ul_y, int lr_x, int lr_y) :
   upperLeft(Point(ul_x, ul_y)), lowerRight(Point(lr_x, lr_y)) {
}

double Rectangle::getArea() {
```

```
double result = abs(upperLeft.getX() - lowerRight.getX()) *
                abs(upperLeft.getY() - lowerRight.getY());
return result;
}


void main() {
Circle cir1(7, 9, 15);
cout<<" cir1has id = "<<cir1.getId()
    <<", area = "<<cir1.getArea()<<endl;

Rectangle rect1(-50,70,150,180);
cout<<" rect1has id = "<<rect1.getId()
    <<", area = "<<rect1.getArea()<<endl;

Shape * shape1 = &cir1;                      /* (4) */
cout<<"shape1 has id = "<<shape1->getId()
    <<", area = "<<shape1->getArea()<<endl;

shape1 = &rect1;                             /* (5) */
cout<<"shape1 has id = "<<shape1->getId()
    <<", area = "<<shape1->getArea()<<endl;
}
```

The execution of the above would yield:

```
cir1 has id = 1, area = 706.858
rect1 has id = 2, area = 22000
shape1 has id = 1, area = 706.858
shape1 has id = 2, area = 22000
```

The following are the main points of this C++ example:

- Class `Shape` is defined with member function `getArea()` as a pure virtual function:

  ```
  virtual double getArea() = 0;
  ```

  A pure virtual function must use the keyword `virtual` and be tagged with the `= 0` designation. Whenever a C++ class contains at least one pure virtual function, it becomes an abstract class, which means that clients cannot instantiate objects of the class. For example,

  ```
  Shape some_shape;    // Error!
  ```

  would be illegal. However, declaring pointers to abstract classes is fine:

  ```
  Shape * shape1;
  ```

- Making a member function `virtual` will tell the compiler to establish a virtual function dispatch mechanism. This mechanism allows an object of a given type to execute the method implementation appropriate to it. This is called *late binding* or *dynamic binding*. In C++, a base class pointer (see

/* (4) */ and /* (5) */ above) is used to represent some object from a particular class hierarchy. At any given point during execution, we may not know the type of the object to which the pointer variable actually points. However, with the virtual function dispatch mechanism, we are assured that the implementation corresponding to the object's type will be called.

The ability of different objects to respond differently to the same message is called *polymorphism*. When an object is capable of responding, it does so with an implementation of its own or with an implementation inherited from a superclass.

- When a derived class overrides an inherited pure virtual function and provides an implementation, it must do so with the same function name, argument list and return type. The function prototype in the derived class can also be qualified with the `virtual` keyword (see /* (2) */ and /* (3) */), although it is not mandatory. It is nevertheless a good idea to continue to use the `virtual` keyword as a way of documenting the fact that such functions were declared `virtual` in some superclass. A derived class that does not provide an implementation to an inherited pure virtual function will become an abstract class.

- The presence of at least one pure virtual function will make the class an abstract class, such as the case with `Shape`. However, abstract classes can also have member functions with implementations. `Shape::getId()` is such a function.

The Java equivalent to the above C++ example would look something like the following:

Listing 4-22: ShapeDemo.java

```java
import java.awt.Point;

abstract class Shape {
    public Shape() {
    id = ++count;
    }

    public int getId() {
    return id;
    }

    public abstract double getArea();                    /* (1) */

    private static int count = 0;
```

```
    private int id;
}

class Circle extends Shape {

    public Circle(int x, int y, int rad) {
    center =  new Point(x, y);
    radius = rad;
    }

    public double getArea() {
    return 4 * Math.atan(1.0) * radius * radius;
    // pi == 4 * atan(1.0)
    }

    private int radius;
    private Point center;
}

class Rectangle extends Shape {

    public Rectangle(int ul_x, int ul_y, int lr_x, int lr_y) {
    upperLeft  = new Point(ul_x, ul_y);
    lowerRight = new Point(lr_x, lr_y);
    }

    public double getArea() {
    double result = Math.abs(upperLeft.x - lowerRight.x) *
                    Math.abs(upperLeft.y - lowerRight.y);
    return result;
    }

    private Point upperLeft;
    private Point lowerRight;
}

public class ShapeDemo {

    public static void main(String args[]) {
        Circle cir1 = new Circle(7, 9, 15);
        System.out.println("cir1 has id = "+cir1.getId()
                        +", area = "+cir1.getArea());

        Rectangle rect1 = new Rectangle(-50,70,150,180);
        System.out.println("rect1 has id = "+rect1.getId()
                        +", area = "+rect1.getArea());

        Shape shape1 = cir1;                        /* (2) */
        System.out.println("shape1 has id = "+shape1.getId()
                        +", area = "+shape1.getArea());
```

```
        shape1 = rect1;                              /* (3) */
        System.out.println("shape1 has id = "+shape1.getId()
                          +", area = "+shape1.getArea());
    }
}
```

The execution of the above Java code would output:

```
cir1 has id = 1, area = 706.858
rect1 has id = 2, area = 22000
shape1 has id = 1, area = 706.858
shape1 has id = 2, area = 22000
```

The following are the main points about the Java equivalent:

- Instead of the C++ `virtual` keyword, Java uses the keyword `abstract`:

  ```
  public abstract double getArea();
  ```

  In this case, the keyword `abstract` serves as a modifier to method `getArea()`. As in C++ classes, the presence of at least one abstract method will make the whole class abstract. When a class contains at least one abstract method, the `abstract` modifier must also be applied to the class declaration:

  ```
  abstract class Shape
  ```

  One may not create instances of abstract classes. For example, the following would be illegal:

  ```
  Shape some_shape = new Shape();    // Error!
  ```

- One fundamental difference between C++ methods and Java methods is that Java methods are *virtual* by default. In other words, Java automatically provides the virtual dispatch mechanism with every class hierarchy so that an object, based on its type and position on the hierarchy, will be able to invoke the correct implementation of a method. In the above (see `/* (2) */` and `/* (3) */`), reference variable `shape1` may refer to any subclass of `Shape` at any given time. However, because of dynamic binding, `shape1` will exhibit the correct behavior when message `getArea()` is sent to it.

- When a derived class overrides an abstract method and provides an implementation, it must do so with the same method name, argument list and return type. A derived class that does not provide an implementation to an inherited abstract method will become an abstract class and must be declared as such.

- As in C++, the presence of at least one abstract method will make the class abstract, such as with class `Shape`. However, abstract classes can also have non-abstract methods. The `getId()` method of class `Shape` is such a method.

Multiple Inheritance and Interfaces

One of the major differences between C++ and Java is how inheritance is supported. C++ supports multiple inheritance while Java does not. The designers of Java had realized that multiple inheritance as implemented by C++ is too controversial and too complicated to be used safely and hence decided to refrain from putting these features into Java. Instead, Java has a feature called *interfaces*, which permits the inheritance of method prototypes from multiple sources. We will see how each language uses its respective scheme to arrive at a result.

Starting with a C++ example, suppose we have two base classes: `Employee` and `Transportation` (which describes a means of travel). We might derive a class called `TravelingEmployee`, which inherits the non-private members of both superclasses:

Listing 4-23: MultipleInheritanceDemo.cpp

```cpp
#include <iostream.h>
#include <string.h>
#include "String.hh"

class Transportation {
public:
    Transportation(long);
    long getDistance();
    void travel(long);
private:
    long distance;
};

Transportation::Transportation(long dist) : distance(dist) {
}

long Transportation::getDistance() {
return distance;
}

void Transportation::travel(long dist) {
distance += dist;
}

class Employee {
public:
    Employee(String, long, char);
    String getName();
private:
    String name;
    long ssn;
```

```
        char gender;
};


Employee::Employee(String nm, long id, char sx) :
    name(nm), ssn(id), gender(sx) {
}


String Employee::getName() {
return name;
}


class TravelingEmployee : public Employee, public Transportation {
public:
    TravelingEmployee(String, long, char, long);
};


TravelingEmployee::TravelingEmployee(String nm, long id, char sx,
    long dist) : Employee(nm, id, sx), Transportation(dist) {
 }


void main()
{
TravelingEmployee emp("Bob", 45900, 'M', 10000);
cout<<emp.getName()<<"'s transportation has accumulated "
                    <<emp.getDistance()<<" miles."<<endl;
emp.travel(225);
cout<<emp.getName()<<"'s transportation has accumulated "
                    <<emp.getDistance()<<" miles."<<endl;
}
```

The execution of the above will produce the following output:

```
Bob's transportation has accumulated 10000 miles.
Bob's transportation has accumulated 10225 miles.
```

The following are the main points of this C++ example:

- The syntax for designating `TravelingEmployee` as a subclass of both class `Employee` and class `Transportation` is:

  ```
  class TravelingEmployee : public Employee, public
   Transportation
  ```

  Each superclass is preceded by the `public` keyword and is comma delimited.

- Class `TravelingEmployee` inherits `getName()` from `Employee` and `getDistance()` from `Transportation`.
  `Transportation::getDistance()` basically returns the total number of miles the transportation vehicle has accumulated.

- One of the things developers must avoid when using multiple inheritance is the problem of ambiguity when inheriting members with the same name from different subobjects. For instance, if base class `Transportation` is enhanced with:

```
class Transportation {
public:
   ...
   String getName();
private:
   String name;
   ...
};


String Transportation::getName() {
return name;
}
```

The compiler would flag the line:

```
cout<<emp.getName()<<"'s transportation has accumulated "
    <<emp.getDistance()<<" miles."<<endl;
```

as an error because it would not know whether to call:

```
Employee::getName()  or  Transportation::getName().
```

The above C++ example has no Java equivalent. However, something close to the above can be achieved with the help of the interface. The interface is like an abstract class, except the body of the interface consists of method prototypes. Each method prototype consists of the method's signature and return type (no implementation code). Variable fields are allowed only if they are `final` and <u>not</u> `private` nor `protected` (i.e., they must be `public` or the default—no modifier). Furthermore, `final` variables must be initialized.

Like the abstract class, one cannot instantiate an object of an interface. However, one may declare a reference variable of an interface type and such variables may be fields inside a class. Whenever a class *implements* an interface, the class must provide the implementations for the method prototypes of the interface. If the class does not implement every method, then the class must be qualified as `abstract`.

Below is a rough Java equivalent to the C++ example using the Java interface:

Listing 4-24: InterfaceDemo.java

```
import java.io.IOException;

interface Transportation {
    public long getDistance();
```

```java
        public void travel(long dist);
}

class Employee {

    Employee(String nm, long id, char sx) {
        name = new String(nm);
        ssn  = id;
        gender = sx;
    }

    public String getName() {
        return name;
    }

    private String name;
    private long ssn;
    private char gender;
}

class TravelingEmployee extends Employee implements Transportation {

    TravelingEmployee(String nm, long id, char sx, long dist) {
        super(nm, id, sx);
        distance = dist;
    }

    public long getDistance() {
        return distance;
    }

    public void travel(long dist) {
        distance += dist;
    }

    private long distance;
}

public class InterfaceDemo {

    public static void main(String args[]) {

        TravelingEmployee emp = new TravelingEmployee("Bob",
                                        45900, 'M', 10000);
        System.out.println(emp.getName()
                        +"'s transportation has accumulated "
                        +emp.getDistance()+" miles.");
        emp.travel(225);
        System.out.println(emp.getName()
                        +"'s transportation has accumulated "
```

```
                              +emp.getDistance()+" miles.");
    }
}
```

The above example will output:

```
Bob's transportation has accumulated 10000 miles.
Bob's transportation has accumulated 10225 miles.
```

The following are the key points of the Java example:

- Defining an interface is very similar to defining a class:

```
interface Transportation {
    public long getDistance();
    public void travel(long dist);
}
```

Like the class, the interface cannot be `private` or `protected`. If the interface is qualified with the `public` modifier, then it can be placed within its own package. The body of the interface encloses the method prototypes.

- The inheriting class, `TravelingEmployee`, is subclassed from one class, but it can implement any number of interfaces:

```
class TravelingEmployee extends Employee implements
 Transportation
```

The name following keyword `extends` is the superclass and the name following keyword `implements` is the interface. If there is more than one interface being implemented, then the entire list follows the `implements` keyword with the names delimited by commas (`implements A1, A2, A3`).

- The class, `TravelingEmployee`, actually implements the method prototypes inherited from the interface. In other words, the implementing class actually provides the logic behind the methods:

```
public long getDistance() {
    return distance;
 }

public void travel(long dist) {
    distance += dist;
}

private long distance;
```

- If the interface is redefined to be:

```
interface Transportation {
    public long getDistance();
    public void travel(long dist);
    public String getName();
}
```

would there be an ambiguity problem for subclass `TravelingEmployee`? After all, the name, `getName()`, appears in both interface `Transportation` and class `Employee`. As it turns out, the answer is no because `TravelingEmployee` does provide an implementation for `getName()` by inheriting the implementation of the same name from class `Employee`. Certainly, if the class designer chooses to do so, he may override the implementation from `Employee` with an implementation specific to class `TravelingEmployee`. Nevertheless, there is no conflict in terms of which implementation to choose because there is at most one.

Summary: The Java interface provides a way to organize generic behaviors into very high level abstractions. The method prototypes only describe what is to be done. It is up to the specific classes to determine how the behaviors are to be implemented. This scheme of separating the interface from implementation provides a nice way for developers to respond to changes without impacting their clients who work with the interfaces. The interface is a way to establish a common protocol of communication among objects, while giving objects of different types freedom to respond to the messages in their own way.

CHAPTER
5

- An Overview of Run-Time Type Information
- The Java `instanceof` Operator
- The C++ `dynamic_cast` Operator
- Creating Objects Dynamically in Java

Run-Time Type Information

An Overview of Run-Time Type Information

On occasion, there will be a need to determine the exact type of an object so that diagnostic messages about the object's properties can be recorded. Also, if we know the exact type of the object, then we know which methods the object can call. Given a particular hierarchy of classes, it is not uncommon for a subclass to have methods that are unique to itself, i.e., methods that are not inherited from superclasses.

Both C++ and Java have standard classes, methods or operators that facilitate the determination of an object's type or subtype. In this section, we will examine certain run-time type information (RTTI) features that are common to both languages.

We will begin with C++. In C++ there is an operator called `typeid` that takes a type name or expression and returns a *reference* to a `type_info` object. The `type_info` object contains the information about the object's type and the type name. Let us look at the following example:

Listing 5-1: RunTimeTypeInfoDemo.cpp

```cpp
#include <iostream.h>
#include <typeinfo.h>
#include "String.hh"

class Publication {
public:
    Publication(String, String, String);
    String getTitle();
```

```cpp
    String getSubject();
    String getPublisher();
private:
    String title;
    String subject;
    String publisher;
};

Publication::Publication(String tit, String sub, String pub) :
title(tit), subject(sub), publisher(pub) {
}

String Publication::getTitle() {
return title;
}

String Publication::getSubject() {
return subject;
}

String Publication::getPublisher() {
return publisher;
}

class Book : public Publication {
public:
    Book(String, String, String, String);
    String getAuthor();
private:
    String author;
};

Book::Book(String tit, String sub, String pub, String aut) :
          Publication(tit, sub, pub), author(aut) {
}

String Book::getAuthor() {
return author;
}

class Manual : public Book {
public:
    Manual(String, String, String, String, String);
    String getProduct();
private:
    String product;
};

Manual::Manual(String tit, String sub, String pub, String aut,
String prod) : Book(tit, sub, pub, aut), product(prod) {
```

```
}

String Manual::getProduct() {
return product;
}

void main()
{
Book book1("Sunrise over Saratoga", "Fiction", "Story Tellers,
Ltd.", "Vern Goodman");

if (typeid(book1) == typeid(Publication))
    cout<<"book1 is of type Publication"<<endl;
else
    cout<<"book1 is NOT of type Publication"<<endl;

if (typeid(book1) == typeid(Book)) {
    cout<<"book1 is of type Book"<<endl;
    cout<<"book1 is authored by "<<book1.getAuthor()<<endl;
    }
else
    cout<<"book1 is NOT of type Book"<<endl;

if (typeid(book1) == typeid(Manual))
    cout<<"book1 is of type Manual"<<endl;
else
    cout<<"book1 is NOT of type Manual"<<endl;

cout<<"Variable book1 represents an instance of"
    <<typeid(book1).name()<<endl;
}
```

When the program is executed, the output looks like:

```
book1 is NOT of type Publication
book1 is of type Book
book1 is authored by Vern Goodman
book1 is NOT of type Manual
Variable book1 represents an instance of class Book
```

In the above, we are given a simple hierarchy of three classes. This simple framework might represent the beginning of an attempt to categorize the inventory of, say, a public library. The base class is called Publication, which consists of title, subject and publisher as the attributes with corresponding accessor methods. Class Book is derived from Publication with its own private attribute author. Finally, class Manual is derived from Publication with its own private attribute product.

Within function main(), a Book object represented by variable book1 is instantiated and the typeid operator is applied to determine its type. The following are the key points about this example:

- The use of operator `typeid` requires the inclusion of the file, `typeinfo.h`. This header file has the definition for class `type_info` and its function prototypes.

- The expression, `typeid(book1)` will return a reference to class `type_info` (`type_info &`). Comparison to a target type would require an expression such as:

```
typeid(book1) == typeid(Book)
```

- The `typeid` operator is used to find the <u>exact</u> type of an object. In the example, `book1` is determined to be of type `Book` and even though `Book` objects are also `Publication` objects, `book1` is not merely of type `Publication`.

- Very often, we want to know the name of the type. We would then use the member function called `name()` from class `type_info` and use it as follows:

```
typeid(book1).name()
```

The result is a `const char *` type, which can be manipulated as a string. The above statement would return `"class Book."`

Note: The usage of `typeid` in the example was to determine whether `book1` is of type `Book`, so that we could find the author if the condition is true. Over-reliance on `typeid` is not a good practice, since it encourages frequent changes to existing code with multi-branch conditionals (`if` and `switch` statements). Rather, if you are the class designer, it is better to provide virtual functions with perhaps dummy implementations in the base classes so that the virtual dispatch mechanism can be invoked automatically during run-time to determine the type of the object.

An equivalent Java example to the above might look like:

Listing 5-2: Publication.java

```java
// Source file: Publication.java
package Publications;
import java.awt.*;

public class Publication {
    private String title;
    private String subject;
    private String publisher;

    public Publication(String tit, String sub, String pub) {
    title = new String(tit);
    subject = new String(sub);
```

```
publisher = new String(pub);
}

public String getTitle() {
return title;
}

public String getSubject() {
return subject;
}

public String getPublisher() {
return publisher;
}

public void Display() {
System.out.println("Title: "+getTitle()+", Subject:
 "+getSubject()+", Publisher: "+getPublisher());
}

}
```

Listing 5-3: Book.java

```
// Source file: Book.java
package Publications;
import java.awt.*;

public class Book extends Publication {
private String author;

public Book() {
this("some title", "some subject", "some publisher", "some
 author");
}

public Book(String tit, String sub, String pub, String aut) {
super(tit, sub, pub);
author = new String(aut);
}

public String getAuthor() {
return author;
}

public void Display() {
System.out.println("Title: "+getTitle()+", Subject:
 "+getSubject()
+", Publisher: "+getPublisher()+", Author: "+getAuthor());
```

```
    }

}
```

Listing 5-4: Manual.java

```java
// Source file: Manual.java
package Publications;
import java.awt.*;

public class Manual extends Book {
    private String product;

    public Manual(String tit, String sub, String pub, String aut,
        String prod)
        {
        super(tit, sub, pub, aut);
        product = new String(prod);
        }

    public String getProduct() {
    return product;
    }

    public void Display() {
    System.out.println("Title: "+getTitle()+", Subject:
     "+getSubject()
        +", Publisher: "+getPublisher()+", Author: "+getAuthor()
        +", Product: "+getProduct());
    }

}
```

Listing 5-5: RunTimeTypeInfoDemo.java

```java
// Source file: RuntimeTypeInfoDemo.java
import java.awt.*;
import java.io.IOException;
import Publications.*;

public class RuntimeTypeInfoDemo {

    public static void main(String args[]) {
    Book book1 = new Book("Sunrise over Saratoga", "Fiction",
                          "Story Tellers, Ltd.", "Vern Goodman");

    if (book1.getClass().getName().equals("Publications.
     Publication"))
        System.out.println("book1 is of type Publication");
    else
```

```
    System.out.println("book1 is NOT of type Publication");

if (book1.getClass().getName().equals("Publications.Book")) {
    System.out.println("book1 is of type Book");
    System.out.println("book1 is authored by
     "+book1.getAuthor());
    }
else
    System.out.println("book1 is NOT of type Book");

if (book1.getClass().getName().equals("Publications.Manual"))
    System.out.println("book1 is of type Manual");
else
    System.out.println("book1 is NOT of type Manual");

System.out.println("Variable book1 represents an instance
of "
                    +book1.getClass().getName());

}
```

The output would appear as:

```
book1 is NOT of type Publication
book1 is of type Book
book1 is authored by Vern Goodman
book1 is NOT of type Manual
Variable book1 represents an instance of Publications.Book
```

The Java example above shows the equivalent classes for `Publication`, `Book` and `Manual`. Each of these classes has its own source file and all of the resulting bytecode files are bundled into a package called `Publications` (plural). Example class `RunTimeTypeInfoDemo` uses the classes contained in package `Publications`. All of the sample client code is within the `main()` method of `RunTimeTypeInfoDemo`. The following are the key points of the example:

- In Java, there is a special class called `Class`, which has all of the run-time information about a loaded class, such as its type, its name or its parent base class. The Java class `Class` is roughly equivalent to the C++ `type_info` class. The class `Class` is part of the standard Java language package (`java.lang`).

- As I had mentioned earlier, every user-defined class in Java ultimately is derived from the base class called *Object*. As such, every class inherits a method called `getClass()`, which allows one to find the type of the object. This method is equivalent to the C++ `typeid` operator. The statement:

```
book1.getClass()
```

will return the `Class` object associated with the object referenced by variable `book1`.

- After getting the above result, we can then apply the method `getName()` to get the class name as a `String` object. The `getName()` method belongs to class `Class` and can be used in an expression for string comparison:

```
book1.getClass().getName().equals("Publications.Book")
```

The expression `book1.getClass().getName()` will return the name of the class qualified by the package name (`Publications.Book`). In Java, it is possible to use the same class name in different packages. The Java `getName()` method is basically equivalent to the C++ `name()` function that is used with operator `typeid`.

The Java `instanceof` Operator

The Java language has an operator called `instanceof` that can be used to determine the type of a given object. The following `InstanceofDemo` example is based on the `Publication`, `Book` and `Manual` classes of package `Publications` (these classes are listed under the topic, *An Overview of Run-Time Type Information* of this chapter):

Listing 5-6: InstanceofDemo.java

```java
import java.awt.*;
import Publications.*;
import java.io.IOException;

public class InstanceofDemo {

    public static void main(String args[]) {
    Publication pub1 = new Publication("The Handyman Journal",
        "Home Repairs", "Easy Publications");
Book book1 = new Book("Sunrise over Saratoga", "Fiction",
 "Story Tellers, Ltd.", "Vern Goodman");
    Manual manual1 = new Manual("Steller C++ User's Guide",
                                "Programming Languages",
                                "Star Publishers",
                                "Roberta Soo", "Steller C++");

    if (pub1 instanceof Book)
        System.out.println("pub1 is a Book with author "
                        +((Book)pub1).getAuthor());
    else
        System.out.println("pub1 is NOT a Book");

    if (book1 instanceof Book)
        System.out.println("book1 is a Book with author "
```

```
                            +((Book)book1).getAuthor());
    else
        System.out.println("book1 is NOT a Book");

    if (manual1 instanceof Book)
        System.out.println("manual1 is a Book with author "
                            +((Book)manual1).getAuthor());
    else
        System.out.println("manual1 is NOT a Book");
    }
}
```

The output from the execution of the above program would appear as:

```
pub1 is NOT a Book
book1 is a Book with author Vern Goodman
manual1 is a Book with author Vern Goodman
```

An examination of the code and the results reveals the following points:

- Unlike the `Object.getClass()` method (see the topic, *An Overview of Run-Time Type Information*), the `instanceof` operator checks to see if the expression of the left operand is a <u>type</u> or <u>subtype</u> of the right operand. Within the `main()` method of `InstanceofDemo`, a `Manual` object called `manual1` was instantiated. A `Manual` is also a `Book`, hence the expression:

  ```
  manual1  instanceof  Book
  ```

  is true.

- If the reference variable does refer to an object of the type of interest, we usually want to call some method supported by that type. However, before we call that method, we must be certain that the type of the reference variable matches what it is referring to. For instance, `pub1` was originally declared as a reference variable to a `Publication`. If, in the course of program execution, `pub1` later refers to a `Book` and if we wish to find the author, then we must cast `pub1` to refer to a `Book`:

  ```
  ((Book)pub1).getAuthor()
  ```

Explicit casting is necessary if we are going from a base type to a derived type (called *downcasting* or *narrowing*). Downcasting means the object will take on more characteristics or becomes more specialized. Using the `instanceof` operator is a way of insuring that such casts can be done safely. If such casts cannot be done safely, a run-time exception will be thrown.

The opposite of downcasting is *upcasting* or *widening*. This is where the object goes from a derived type to a base type. Within the class hierarchy, this conversion happens automatically and does not require any explicit casting. For instance, the expression:

```
String Manual::getProduct() {
return product;
}

void Manual::Display() {
cout<<"Title: "<<getTitle()<<", Subject: "<<getSubject()
    <<", Publisher: "<<getPublisher()<<", Author:
     "<<getAuthor()
    <<", Product: "<<getProduct()<<endl;
}

void main()
{
Publication pub1("The Handyman Journal", "Home Repairs",
               "Easy Publications");
Book book1("Sunrise over Saratoga", "Fiction", "Story Tellers,
         Ltd.", "Vern Goodman");
Manual manual1("Steller C++ User's Guide",
             "Programming Languages", "Star Publishers",
             "Roberta Soo", "Steller C++");
Publication * pSomething1 = &pub1;
Book * pSomething2 = &book1;
Manual * pSomething3 = &manual1;/* (2) */

Book * pBook;

pBook = dynamic_cast<Book *>(pSomething1);

if (pBook == 0)
    cout<<"pBook does NOT point to a Book"<<endl;
else
    cout<<"pBook points to a Book with author "
        <<pBook->getAuthor()<<endl;

pBook = dynamic_cast<Book *>(pSomething2);

if (pBook == 0)
    cout<<"pBook does NOT point to a Book"<<endl;
else
    cout<<"pBook points to a Book with author "
        <<pBook->getAuthor()<<endl;

pBook = dynamic_cast<Book *>(pSomething3);

if (pBook == 0)
    cout<<"pBook does NOT point to a Book"<<endl;
else
    cout<<"pBook points to a Book with author "
        <<pBook->getAuthor()<<endl;
}
```

The execution of the above program would yield the following output:

```
pBook does NOT point to a Book
pBook points to a Book with author Vern Goodman
pBook points to a Book with author Roberta Soo
```

The structure of this sample C++ program and its results are quite similar to the sample Java program regarding the instanceof operator (see the topic, *The Java* instanceof *Operator*). However, the C++ dynamic_cast operator works in a different way. The following points summarize its main features.

- The basic notation of dynamic_cast looks like:

  ```
  dynamic_cast<type-id>( expression )
  ```

  where type-id is a pointer to a type and expression is a pointer. The target type, type-id, must be within angled brackets. Furthermore, type-id could be a void *.

  In the following statement:

  ```
  pBook = dynamic_cast<Book *>(pSomething1);
  ```

  an attempt is made to cast pointer variable pSomething1 into a pointer to a Book (Book *). If the cast is successful, pointer variable pBook would point to some Book object. Otherwise, if the cast is unsuccessful, pBook would point to null (zero).

- The class hierarchy must be polymorphic. That is, the base class, Publication in this example, must have at least one virtual function (Display() and the destructor for base class Publication (refer to /* (1) */). A virtual dispatch mechanism is created by the compiler when there are virtual functions and the dynamic_cast operator relies on this mechanism to work.

- Note that pSomething3 is a pointer to a Manual object and happens to point to a Manual object (refer to /* (2) */). In this case, when the statement completes:

  ```
  pBook = dynamic_cast<Book *>(pSomething3);
  ```

  pBook will point to a Book object since a Manual object is a Book object.

In this simple example, it is visually apparent what types of objects each of pSomething1, pSomething2 and pSomething3 points to. However, there will be situations during run-time when such things are not obvious. That is the whole purpose of the dynamic_cast operator. It is used to check what kind of object the pointer really points to before an attempt is made to call a member function specific to a particular class.

Creating Objects Dynamically in Java

The Java environment has a way to keep track of classes that are loaded during run-time. It does this by creating a `Class` object for every loaded class. The `Class` object supports methods that allow ad-hoc instantiation of objects during execution. These features provide great flexibility, provided certain conditions are met. The following is an example based on the `Book` class of the `Publications` package (this class is listed under the topic, *An Overview of Run-Time Type Information* of this chapter):

Listing 5-8: NewInstanceDemo1.java

```java
import java.awt.*;
import java.io.*;
import java.util.*;
import Publications.*;
import java.io.IOException;

public class NewInstanceDemo1 {

  public static void main(String args[]) {
     Publication book1 = new Book("Sunrise over Saratoga",
      "Fiction",
         "Story Tellers, Ltd.", "Vern Goodman");
     Object obj1;
     try {
         obj1 = book1.getClass().newInstance();/* (1) */

         if (obj1.getClass().getName().equals
          ("Publications.Book")) {
            System.out.println("obj1 is of type Book");
            System.out.println("obj1 is authored by "+
                              ((Book)obj1).getAuthor());
            }
         else
            System.out.println("obj1 is NOT of type Book");

         System.out.println("Variable obj1 represents an instance
          of "+
                              obj1.getClass().getName());
         }
     catch (Exception error) {
         System.out.println("General Exception!");
         System.exit(1);
         }
}
```

The execution of the above will produce the following output:

```
obj1 is of type Book
```

```
obj1 is authored by some author
Variable obj1 represents an instance of Publications.Book
```

In order for the above code to compile and execute as shown, the following points must be understood:

- The getClass() method is a method in class Object. Since all other classes are either explicitly or implicitly derived from class Object, such classes inherit the getClass() method. The expression:

  ```
  book1.getClass()
  ```

  will return the Class object of the type referred to by book1. Even though book1 is declared as a reference variable of type Publication, book1 refers to an object of type Book. Since newInstance() is a method of Class, the expression:

  ```
  book1.getClass().newInstance()
  ```

  will return a new instance that has the same type as the object referred to by book1. The newInstance() method itself will return a reference to an object of type Object. If the result is assigned to a non-Object reference variable, the result must be casted to that non-Object type.

- In order for book1.getClass().newInstance() to execute successfully, the class of the object referred to by book1 (which is class Book) must support a no-argument default constructor. Below is a fragment of class Book with the default constructor:

  ```
  public class Book extends Publication {
  private String author;

  public Book() { // no-argument default constructor
  this("some title", "some subject", "some publisher", "some
   author");
  }

  public Book(String tit, String sub, String pub, String aut) {
  super(tit, sub, pub);
  author = new String(aut);
  }
  ...
  }
  ```

  If a no-argument default constructor does not exist for the class of interest, then an exception called NoSuchMethodError will be thrown.

  In addition to the NoSuchMethodError exception, the newInstance() method is also defined to throw other exceptions, such as InstantiationException or IllegalAccessException. Note that the following code is bound by what is known as a try block:

```
try {
        obj1 = book1.getClass().newInstance();

        if (obj1.getClass().getName().equals
         ("Publications.Book")) {
           System.out.println("obj1 is of type Book");
           System.out.println("obj1 is authored by "+
                            ((Book)obj1).getAuthor());
        }
        else
           System.out.println("obj1 is NOT of type Book");

        System.out.println("Variable obj1 represents an instance
         of "+
                        obj1.getClass().getName());
        }
```

The `try` block is followed by a `catch` handler:

```
catch (Exception error) {
       System.out.println("General Exception!");
       System.exit(1);
       }
```

The exception object called `Exception` is the base type of all other exception types. This catch handler acts as a "catch all" handler. In other words, regardless of the type of exception object thrown, processing will always resume in this handler. The catch handler is intended to deal with any recovery or clean-up activities.

This discussion is just a very brief introduction to Java exception handling. The reader is encouraged to refer to the chapter devoted to this subject.

The sample program `NewInstanceDemo1` demonstrated how to instantiate a new object based on what a reference variable actually refers to. It is also possible to instantiate an object of some type if we are given the string name of the class. Suppose the statement labeled with `/* (1) */` of `NewInstanceDemo1` was changed to be the following:

```
obj1 = Class.forName("Publications.Book").newInstance();
```

The execution of the amended program will generate the same output as seen earlier:

```
obj1 is of type Book
obj1 is authored by some author
Variable obj1 represents an instance of Publications.Book
```

These are the main points of this modified example:

- The `forName()` method is a method of class `Class`. The string name of the desired class is passed as an argument into this method. The string name must include the full package name. If the class name cannot be found, then method `forName()` will throw a `ClassNotFoundException` object.

- A no-argument default constructor must have been defined for the class of interest. Otherwise, a `NoSuchMethodError` object will be thrown.

The code for the modified example is from the Java example, `NewInstanceDemo2`, which can be found on the supplied media.

Summary: The use of the Java `new` operator is the traditional, static way to instantiate objects of a given type (during compile time). The methods offered by class `Class` provide a dynamic means to create objects of different types from different run-time invocations. These particular features have no equivalent in the C++ language.

CHAPTER
6

- The Case for Defensive Programming
- The `throw`, `throws`, `try` and `catch` Keywords
- Ordering the Catch Handlers
- C++ Destructors and the Unwinding of the Stack
- Rethrowing an Exception for Further Processing
- Cleaning Up with the Java `finally` Block
- Redirecting the Flow of Control with C++ `set_unexpected`
- Using C++ `set_terminate` to Dispose of Resources
- A Useful Java Method for Debugging: `printStackTrace()`
- Uses and Misuses of Exception Handling

Dealing with the Unexpected: Exception Handling

The Case for Defensive Programming

An exception is basically an unexpected error condition, such as division by zero or attempting to access an array element that is out of bounds. In the early 1990s, the ISO/ANSI C++ standards committee adopted a scheme to deal with exceptions in C++, largely because traditional ways of dealing with errors in C are insufficient. The Java programming language follows the C++ exception handling model with a few additional features.

As a veteran of numerous software projects over the years, I can testify that far too little attention is paid to dealing with negative circumstances. Either programmers are too lazy or project managers do not make it a point to make exception handling a critical part of software design. The end result is not surprising: the software simply does not work and it is often painful to diagnose and fix. To top things off, when the software is in production among hundreds or even thousands of users, the lost productivity plus the support costs become astronomical.

The exception handling mechanism for C++ is still a fairly recent addition to the language. It is not a feature that programmers are obligated to use. In many respects, the exception handling mechanism of C++ is somewhat of a mixed blessing. If not used correctly, it can cause problems rather than prevent them. As in pre-exception handling days, the dynamic allocation and deallocation of resources remains a tricky problem due to many possible programming scenarios.

On the other hand, the Java language was born with exception handling. With automatic garbage collection, exception handling in Java is much easier and safer to use than the equivalent from C++. Many of the Java classes of the standard packages have methods that throw exception objects of various types. The notion of throwing is to embark on an alternate flow of control. We will see how exceptions are thrown as well as how they are caught.

It is also possible, to some extent, to avoid using exception handling in Java. However, chances are you will make use of the standard Java classes and the compiler will remind you to deal with certain exception objects that might be thrown. The whole intent of exception handling is to produce better and more reliable code. I strongly encourage developers to make good use of this feature.

The `throw`, `throws`, `try` and `catch` Keywords

Overall, the exception handling mechanisms of C++ and Java are so similar that they share most of the relevant keywords: `throw`, `try` and `catch`. Java has an additional keyword called `throws` (note the 's'), which is not in C++. In this section, we will see how all four keywords are used for both languages.

We will start with a C++ class called `Glossary`, which is constructed from some conventional C file input-output routines:

Listing 6-1: ExceptionDemo1.cpp

```cpp
#include <stdio.h>
#include <iostream.h>
#include <iomanip.h>
#include <fstream.h>
#include <string.h>
#include <fcntl.h>
#include <io.h>

class Glossary {
public:
    Glossary(char *)  throw(char *);                /* (1) */
    ~Glossary();
    void Display();
    enum { MAX_WORD_LENGTH = 161 };
private:
    char * filename;
    Glossary(const Glossary &);
    Glossary & operator=(const Glossary &);
};

Glossary::Glossary(char * name) {
int descriptor = _open(name, _O_RDONLY);
if (descriptor == -1) {
    char errmsg[80];
    sprintf(errmsg, "Unable to open file %s", name);
    throw(errmsg);
    }
else {
```

```
    filename = new char[strlen(name)+1];
    strcpy(filename, name);
    _close(descriptor);
    }
}

Glossary::~Glossary() {
delete [] filename;
}

void Glossary::Display() {
fstream filestream(filename, ios::in);
char word[MAX_WORD_LENGTH];
while (!filestream.eof()) {
    filestream>>setw(MAX_WORD_LENGTH)>>word;
    cout<<word<<endl;
    }
filestream.close();
}

void main()
{
try {
    Glossary gloss("TERMS.TXT");
    gloss.Display();
    }
catch (char * msg) {
    cout<<msg<<endl;
    }
}
```

The throw, try and catch keywords are highlighted to emphasize where they are used in the code. The Glossary class is quite straightforward. Its only constructor, Glossary::Glossary(char *), is used to test whether a file exists and if so, whether it can be opened for read only mode. If everything is fine, the file name is retained in the private member, filename. Class Glossary also has a regular member function called Display() that opens the file, outputs each record and closes the file. If the file exists ("TERMS.TXT" in this example), then everything would proceed normally and we would see something like:

```
vintage
emerge
station
shelf
continent
reef
walrus
periodical
```

```
shoes
painting
```

However, what happens when things do not go well? For this example, here is how things work:

- Within the body of constructor `Glossary::Glossary(char *)`, if the attempt to open the file (represented by formal parameter `name`) fails, an exception is thrown. The exception object can be of a built-in type or a user-defined type. In this case, a type of `char *` is thrown:

```
int descriptor = _open(name, _O_RDONLY);
if (descriptor == -1) {
    char errmsg[80];
    sprintf(errmsg, "Unable to open file %s", name);
    throw(errmsg);
    }
```

  Since the constructor is definitely known to possibly throw a `char *`, the function prototype (refer to comment `/* (1) */`) should be decorated with a `throw specification list`. This list is not mandatory in C++, but it will inform other users what each member function is capable of throwing. If the body of the function can throw more than one type of exception object, then the specification list would look like:

```
return_type  function_name(arg1, arg2, ..., argN)  throw (e1,
    e2, ..., eN);
```

  where e1 through eN are types of exceptions.

- When the client code is written, the developer needs to anticipate which functions may throw exceptions and what those exception types might be. Within `main()`, we know that the attempt to instantiate a `Glossary` object from:

```
Glossary gloss("TERMS.TXT");
```

  may fail, so the statement is surrounded within a `try` block:

```
try {
    Glossary gloss("TERMS.TXT");
    gloss.Display();
    }
```

  followed by one or more suitable `catch` handlers:

```
catch (char * msg) {
    cout<<msg<<endl;
    }
```

  If the attempt to open file `"TERMS.TXT"` fails, a `char *` is thrown and processing immediately leaves the try block. The search begins to find a suitable catch handler with a matching signature of a `char *`. In this case, there is such a handler and the body of the catch handler simply displays:

```
Unable to open file TERMS.TXT
```

If the search for a matching catch handler fails, the object thrown percolates up the stack to the immediate calling function and the search resumes for a catch handler from there and so on. If it cannot be caught whatsoever in the program, then an abnormal termination will occur. We will see a little later how to catch exceptions of unknown type.

Note: The purpose of the catch handler is to deal with the exception. In serious cases, like memory and disc space exhaustion, the only course of action is to clean up any lingering resources and terminate the application gracefully. In other cases, it may be possible to "repair" the problem and retry the operation. The flow of control can never resume from where the object was originally thrown.

We will now look at a roughly equivalent Java example. I say "roughly" because the underlining classes and methods for Java are somewhat different from those of C and C++. The Java example follows:

Listing 6-2: ExceptionDemo1.java

```java
import java.awt.*;
import java.io.*;

class Glossary {
    Glossary(String name) throws FileNotFoundException,
     IOException {
        FileInputStream inStream = new FileInputStream(name);
        filename = new String(name);
        inStream.close();
        }
    void Display() throws FileNotFoundException, IOException {
        String line = null;
        FileInputStream inStream = new FileInputStream(filename);
        DataInputStream inDataStream = new
         DataInputStream(inStream);
        while ((line = inDataStream.readLine()) != null)
            System.out.println(line);
        inDataStream.close();
        inStream.close();
        }
    private String filename;
    final int MAX_WORD_LENGTH = 161;
}

public class ExceptionDemo1 {

    public static void main(String args[]) {
        try {
            Glossary gloss = new Glossary("TERMS.TXT");
```

```
        gloss.Display();
        }
    catch (FileNotFoundException err) {
        System.out.println(err.toString());
        }
    catch (IOException err) {
        System.out.println(err.toString());
        }
    }

}
```

Under normal conditions where file `"TERMS.TXT"` exists, running the above program will yield the same output as the C++ equivalent:

```
vintage
emerge
station
shelf
continent
reef
walrus
periodical
shoes
painting
```

However, there are some notable differences in the way the Java exception handling mechanism is used. The following are the main points:

- To open a file for reading bytes, we need to create a `FileInputStream` object associated with the physical file. `FileInputStream` has some fairly low-level, public interfaces for reading bytes from a file:

  ```
  FileInputStream instream = new FileInputStream(name);
  ```

- Now, certain public constructors and public methods of class `FileInputStream` are designed to be capable of throwing certain types of exception objects. The following lists the method prototypes of `FileInputStream` used in the example:

  - `public FileInputStream(String name) throws FileNotFoundException`

  - `public void close() throws IOException`

  Within method `Display()`, there is another class used to help display each line of the file and that is `DataInputStream`. This class has all of the public interfaces to read any built-in data type (Boolean, char, float, etc.). `DataInput Stream` has a constructor that accepts a `FileInputStream` object. The following method of `DataInputStream` is capable of throwing an exception:

- `public final String readLine() throws IOException`

`DataInputStream` also inherits the `close()` method from its superclass, `FilterInputStream`:

- `public void close() throws IOException`

Now, here is an interesting aspect about the `Glossary(String)` constructor and the `Display()` method. The bodies of each of these `Glossary` methods uses one or more of the above methods from class `FileInputStream` or `DataInputStream`. I could have chosen to handle any exceptions raised by enclosing the methods in `try` blocks and supporting these blocks with suitable `catch` handlers. However, to mimic the C++ example, I had chosen to allow such exceptions to propagate to the outer level. I do that by decorating the method headers with a `throw` `specification list` using the Java `throws` (not `throw`) keyword:

```
Glossary(String name)  throws  FileNotFoundException,
 IOException

void Display()  throws  FileNotFoundException, IOException
```

Note that the exception types of the specification list are delimited by commas but the entire list is not enclosed in parentheses.

- Within method `Display()`, a `DataInputStream` object is created from a `FileInputStream` object. The `DataInputStream` class has a method called `readLine()`, which will read a stream of characters up to an '\n', '\r', "\r\n" or end-of-file. When the end-of-file is encountered, the various stream objects are closed.

- The client code is provided in the `main()` method of class `ExceptionDemo1`. The `try` block encloses the attempt to instantiate a `Glossary` object for reference variable `gloss` and the call to the `Glossary` method `Display()`:

```
try {
     Glossary gloss = new Glossary("TERMS.TXT");
     gloss.Display();
     }
catch (FileNotFoundException err) {
    System.out.println(err.toString());
    }
catch (IOException err) {
    System.out.println(err.toString());
    }
```

A catch handler to accommodate each possible exception type thrown follows the try block. All exception types are ultimately derived from superclass `Throwable` and all inherit a method called `toString()`, which will return the contents of the exception object to a `String` object. For this example, the body of each catch handler simply displays information about the exception object. If the `"TERMS.TXT"` file did not exist, the output would be:

```
java.io.FileNotFoundException:  TERMS.TXT
```

Note: Unlike most C++ compilers, the Java compiler will actually sense what exception types might be thrown and flag errors if certain catch handlers are missing. It is obvious that the designers of Java are very serious about promoting better practices to produce reliable code. Putting executable statements within try blocks and writing catch handlers requires more effort than conventional C programming, but the proactive efforts will be worth it when problems do arise.

Ordering the Catch Handlers

Even though the catch handler appears to be a function, it is not. There is no return type associated with a catch handler (not even `void`) and its argument list takes exactly one parameter. The whole purpose of a catch handler is to determine the nature of the exception and perform any recovery, clean up or termination.

From the previous topic, we have seen that the statements within a try block can potentially throw exception objects of various types, including any of the built-in types. That being the case, we must understand how to arrange the catch handlers properly after the try block. The fundamental idea behind the proper ordering of the catch handlers applies to both C++ and Java.

Starting with C++, suppose C is a subclass of B and B is a subclass of A. Now, suppose we have the following catch handlers appearing after some try block:

```
catch(...)  {  }
catch(void *)  {  }
catch(char *)  {  }
catch(A)  {  }
catch(B)  {  }
catch(A *)  {  }
catch(C *)  {  }
```

The above order of the catch handlers presents a few problems to say the least. Basically,

- `catch(...)` means to catch an exception object of any type. The other handlers would never be reached.

- `catch(void *)` means to catch any pointer, including A *, B * and C *. The other catch handlers with non-void pointer types will never be reached.

- `catch(A)` will catch exception objects of type A or any subtype of A, including B and C. The catch handler for B will never be reached.

- `catch(A *)` will catch exception objects of type A *. Since C is a remote subclass of A, the catch handler for C * will never be reached.

A correct way to rearrange the catch handlers would be something like:

```
catch(B) { }
catch(A) { }
catch(C *) { }
catch(A *) { }
catch(char *) { }
catch(void *) { }
catch(...){ }
```

The basic rule of thumb is to put the catch handlers with the most derived class types first and the catch handlers with the base class types last. If used, the "catch-all" handler (`catch(...)`) is always the very last.

Note: Some compilers, like the HP-UX C++ compiler (version 3.0 or higher) will actually flag an error that certain catch handlers are unreachable. However, do not rely on every C++ compiler to be smart enough to tell you such things!

The rule of thumb concluded from above basically applies to Java as well, except Java does not have the "catch-all" handler with the (. . .) signature and Java has no pointer types.

However, Java does have a predefined hierarchy of exception classes. The uppermost base class of the hierarchy is a class called `Throwable`. Class `Throwable` is important because it has all of the public methods for analyzing an exception object. All exception classes are subclasses of `Throwable` and inherit these methods.

The first real exception class is class `Exception`, which is an immediate sub-class of class `Throwable`. A Java catch handler for type `Exception` would act as the "catch-all" handler.

Both `Throwable` and `Exception` are classes of package `java.lang`.

If we refer back to the previous topic, *The throw, throws, try and catch Keywords* and examine method `main()` of class `ExceptionDemo1`:

```
public static void main(String args[]) {
        try {
```

```
        Glossary gloss = new Glossary("TERMS.TXT");
        gloss.Display();
        }
    catch (FileNotFoundException err) {
        System.out.println(err.toString());
        }
    catch (IOException err) {
        System.out.println(err.toString());
        }
    }
```

Would it be possible to put catch(IOException) before
catch(FileNotFoundException)? The answer is no, because class
FileNotFoundException is a subclass of class IOException. If we attempt
to reorder the catch handlers, the Java compiler will actually flag an error and
declare catch(FileNotFoundException) to be unreachable.

If we want to add a catch handler for type Exception, we would put this handler at the very last:

```
    catch (FileNotFoundException err) {
        // statements
        }
    catch (IOException err) {
        // statements
        }
    catch (Exception err) {
        // statements
        }
```

As with C++, catch handlers with the most derived types come first and catch
handlers with the base types come last.

C++ Destructors and the Unwinding of the Stack

If you use exception handling in your C++ code, it is important to understand
what goes on when something fails and an exception is thrown. More than
likely, when the exception is thrown there are completely instantiated objects
already in existence. If the objects are automatic, they are removed from the call
stack and a destructor is called for each. This activity, called the "unwinding of
the stack," can best be visualized with the following example:

Listing 6-3: StackUnwindDemo1.cpp

```
#include <iostream.h>
#include <string.h>

class Pair {
public:
```

```cpp
    Pair(int, int);
    virtual ~Pair();
    void Display() const;
protected:
    int getX() const;
    int getY() const;
    int getId() const;
private:
    static int count;
    int x;
    int y;
    int id;         // Used for identifying each unique instance
};

int Pair::count = 0;

Pair::Pair(int x_value, int y_value) : x(x_value), y(y_value),
 id(++count){
}

void Pair::Display() const {
cout<<"("<<getX()<<", "<<getY()<<")"<<" has id
 "<<getId()<<endl;
}

int Pair::getX() const {
return x;
}

int Pair::getY() const {
return y;
}

int Pair::getId() const {
return id;
}

Pair::~Pair() {
cout<<"~Pair() called for "<<"("<<getX()<<", "<<getY()
    <<")"<<" with id "<<getId()<<'\n';
}

class Triplet : public Pair {
public:
    Triplet(int, int, int);
    Triplet operator+(Triplet &);
    virtual ~Triplet();
    void Display() const;
private:
    int z;
};
```

```
Triplet::Triplet(int x_value, int y_value, int z_value) :
    Pair(x_value, y_value), z(z_value) {
//   Intentionally set up this way to cause a throw
if ((x_value == 0) && (y_value == 0) && (z_value == 0))
    throw("Cannot instantiate a Triplet with all zero
    components");
}

Triplet Triplet::operator+(Triplet & tr) {
return Triplet(getX()+tr.getX(), getY()+tr.getY(), z+tr.z);
}

void Triplet::Display() const {
cout<<"("<<getX()<<", "<<getY()<<", "<<z<<")"
    <<" has id "<<getId()<<endl;
}

Triplet::~Triplet() {
cout<<"~Triplet() called for "<<"("<<getX()<<", "<<getY()
    <<", "<<z<<")"<<" with id "<<getId()<<endl;
}

void main()
{
Pair * tr1 = new Triplet(-10, -90, 85);
try {
    Triplet tr2(-5, -34, 45);
     tr2.Display();

    Triplet tr3(5, 34, -45);
    tr3.Display();

    Triplet tr4 = tr2+tr3;
    tr4.Display();             // This statement is never reached
    }
catch(char * errmsg) {
    cout<<errmsg<<endl;
     delete tr1;
     cout<<"Exiting program"<<endl;
    return;
    }
delete tr1;
}
```

The output generated would appear as:

```
(-5, -34, 45) has id 2
(5, 34, -45) has id 3
~Pair() called for (0, 0) with id 4
```

```
~Triplet() called for (5, 34, -45) with id 3
~Pair() called for (5, 34) with id 3
~Triplet() called for (-5, -34, 45) with id 2
~Pair() called for (-5, -34) with id 2
Cannot instantiate a Triplet with all zero components
~Triplet() called for (-10, -90, 85) with id 1
~Pair() called for (-10, -90) with id 1
Exiting program
```

The following is a discussion of the key points of the example:

- Class `Pair` represents an ordered pair (x, y). Class `Triplet` is derived from `Pair` and represents a triplet (x, y, z). The only constructor for `Triplet` is written in such a way that if the user attempts to instantiate `(0, 0, 0)`, the constructor will throw an exception of a `char *` type.

- The bodies of the destructors for `Pair` and `Triplet` contain `cout` statements to help trace the flow of control.

- An important point to understand about objects of derived classes is that the base class portion of a derived class object is instantiated first and then the derived class portion. When a derived class object goes out of scope, the reverse happens: the derived class portion is destructed first and then the base class portion.

  As complete automatic objects go out of scope within an enclosed block of code (bounded by { and }), the last to be instantiated is the first to be destructed.

- Within function `main()`, one `Triplet` object is dynamically instantiated (pointed to by pointer `tr1`) and two `Triplet` objects are automatically instantiated. An attempt is made to instantiate a third automatic object, `tr4`. This attempt is made with the statement:

  ```
  Triplet tr4 = tr2+tr3;
  ```

  through the use of the overloaded + operator and implicit use of the default copy constructor of `Triplet` to initialize `tr4`. The result of the addition is `(0, 0, 0)`, which will cause an exception to be thrown from the constructor of `Triplet`. Any statements following `Triplet tr4 = tr2+tr3;` will not be executed.

- Before the exception object is actually thrown, any partially instantiated objects are destructed. We see this for `tr4`, where the base class destructor for `Pair` is called.

- After the partially constructed object is removed, the fully instantiated, automatic objects represented by `tr2` and `tr3` are each removed from the call stack. The destructor for `Triplet` is called for each.

- The exception object is then caught by the matching catch handler. In this case, the decision was made to simply display the exception message and exit the program. However, before exiting, there is the need to use `delete` on pointer variable `tr1`, since `tr1` points to a dynamically instantiated object. This object was created on the heap and could not be affected by the stack unwinding process. The use of `delete` will invoke all derived class and base class destructors on the dynamically instantiated object.

 Warning: Observe that `tr1` is a `Pair *`, not a `Triplet *`. That being the case, it is important that the destructor for base class `Pair` be declared `virtual`. If it were otherwise, then the compiler would only see the base class portion of the object pointed to by `tr1`. The result would be that only the destructor of `Pair` would be called when `delete` is applied to `tr1`. It is always a good idea to make the base class destructors `virtual` for situations of this sort.

Now, what would happen if a throw occurs during an attempt to instantiate an array element? Suppose we make the following enhancements and changes to the above example:

Listing 6-4: StackUnwindDemo2.cpp

```cpp
#include <iostream.h>
#include <string.h>

class Pair {
// same as above
};

// member functions of Pair remain unchanged

class Triplet : public Pair {
public:
    Triplet();                      // added
    Triplet(int, int, int);
    Triplet operator+(Triplet &);
    virtual ~Triplet();
    void Display() const;
private:
    static int trigger;             // added
    int z;
};

int Triplet:: trigger = 0;
```

```
Triplet::Triplet() : Pair(0,0), z(0) {
                              // no-argument default constructor
if (++trigger == 7)       // intentionally set up to cause a throw
    throw("Cannot instantiate a seventh Triplet object!");
}


Triplet::Triplet(int x_value, int y_value, int z_value) :
        Pair(x_value, y_value), z(z_value) {
// previous throw statement removed
}


// other member functions of Triplet remain unchanged

void main()                          // new example
{
try {
    Triplet tr[9];
    }
catch(char * errmsg) {
    cout<<errmsg<<endl;
    }

}
```

Running the amended program, the following output would be generated:

```
~Pair() called for (0, 0) with id 7
~Triplet() called for (0, 0, 0) with id 6
~Pair() called for (0, 0) with id 6
~Triplet() called for (0, 0, 0) with id 5
~Pair() called for (0, 0) with id 5
~Triplet() called for (0, 0, 0) with id 4
~Pair() called for (0, 0) with id 4
~Triplet() called for (0, 0, 0) with id 3
~Pair() called for (0, 0) with id 3
~Triplet() called for (0, 0, 0) with id 2
~Pair() called for (0, 0) with id 2
~Triplet() called for (0, 0, 0) with id 1
~Pair() called for (0, 0) with id 1
Cannot instantiate a seventh Triplet object!
```

This example differs slightly from the previous in that an attempt was made to instantiate an array of nine `Triplet` objects. It is set up so that an exception is thrown during the attempt to instantiate the seventh object. These are the main features of the example:

- A private, `static int` variable `trigger` is initialized to zero and added to class `Triplet`. It is used to track how many elements are instantiated.

- In order to instantiate an array of `Triplet`, the class requires a no-argument, default constructor. This was added and the constructor's body has a conditional statement to check for the seventh attempt at instantiation. A throw would occur if the condition is met.

- Within function `main()`, an attempt is made to instantiate an array of nine `Triplet` objects. As anticipated, a throw occurs during the attempt to instantiate the seventh object.

- Before the exception object is actually thrown, any partially constructed objects are cleaned up. Such is the case with element `tr[6]` (with id 7), whose base class destructor for `Pair` is called.

- After the partially constructed object is removed, the fully instantiated objects already created (elements `tr[0]` through `tr[5]`) are also removed from the call stack.

- The exception object is then thrown and caught by the matching catch handler. In this example, an exception message is simply displayed. The processing proceeds to the outer level of `main()` and the program terminates normally.

The stack unwinding process for C++ exception handling does not apply to Java since Java has no destructors. In Java, objects of non-primitive types are instantiated from the heap and the Java garbage collector manages the destruction of such objects.

Rethrowing an Exception for Further Processing

Both Java and C++ allow an exception object to be rethrown from a catch handler. This may be important in order to perform clean-up activities at a higher level before the program is exited. This type of action can also provide a trace of where the exception is thrown so that the source of the problem can be pinpointed more easily.

For this topic I will demonstrate with two roughly equivalent samples, one in Java and one in C++. The goal of the sample program is very straightforward: two existing input files, each with a word on a separate line terminated by a newline character, are merged together into a third file. For example, one file (`"TERMS1.TXT"`) may contain:

```
apricot
blue
ale
cheetah
whisper
```

and the other ("TERMS2.TXT") may contain:

```
lemon
auto
fan
restaurant
company
```

which would result in a file ("TERMS3.TXT") containing:

```
apricot
blue
ale
cheetah
whisper
lemon
auto
fan
restaurant
company
```

During execution, if any of the three files experience an input-output problem (like trying to open the file when it does not exist), an exception object would be thrown, clean-up activities would be performed and the program would exit gracefully.

I will first start with a Java example. The example makes use of standard file stream classes and standard exception classes.

Listing 6-5: ExceptionDemo2.java

```java
import java.awt.*;
import java.io.*;

public class ExceptionDemo2 {

    static void MergeStreams(FileInputStream in1, FileInputStream
    in2, String outfile)
                    throws IOException, FileNotFoundException {
        FileOutputStream outStream = null;
        try {
            byte [] buffer = new byte[1];
            outStream = new FileOutputStream(outfile);

            // The following statements of this try block
            // are ignored if an exception is thrown from
```

```java
            // the previous statement

            while ((in1.read(buffer) != -1))
               outStream.write(buffer);

            while ((in2.read(buffer) != -1))
               outStream.write(buffer);

            outStream.close();
            }
        catch (IOException err) {
           System.out.println(err.toString());
           System.out.println("Closing the output stream...\n");
           if (outStream != null)
              outStream.close();
            throw new FileNotFoundException(outfile);
            }
        catch (Exception err) {
            System.out.println(err.toString());
            System.out.println("Closing the output stream.\n");
            if (outStream != null)
               outStream.close();
            throw new FileNotFoundException(outfile);
            }
        }

   static void OpenSecondInputStream(FileInputStream input1,
  String infile2)
                 throws IOException, FileNotFoundException {
      FileInputStream inStream2 = null;
      try {
         inStream2 = new FileInputStream("TERMS2.TXT");
         MergeStreams(input1, inStream2, "TERMS3.TXT");
         inStream2.close();
         }
      catch (FileNotFoundException err) {
         System.out.println(err.toString());
         System.out.println("Closing second input stream...\n");
         if (inStream2 != null)
            inStream2.close();
         throw err;
         }
      catch (IOException err) {
         System.out.println(err.toString());
         System.out.println("Closing second input stream.\n");
         if (inStream2 != null)
             inStream2.close();
         throw err;
         }
      }
```

```java
public static void main(String args[]) {
    FileInputStream inStream1 = null;
    try {
        inStream1 = new FileInputStream("TERMS1.TXT");
        OpenSecondInputStream(inStream1, "TERMS2.TXT");
        inStream1.close();
        }
    catch (Exception err) {
        System.out.println(err.toString());
        System.out.println("Closing first input stream.\n");
        if (inStream1 != null)
            try {
                inStream1.close();
                }
            catch (IOException e) {
                System.out.println(e.toString());
                }
            System.out.println("At least one input or output
                    stream failed to open...");
            System.out.println("Exiting program...");
        }
    }
}
```

There are a number of different scenarios that can happen with the above example. For this discussion, we are interested in the worst case scenario. Suppose the two input files "TERMS1.TXT" and "TERMS2.TXT" exist and FileInputStream objects can be constructed from these files. Now, suppose there is a problem with creating a FileOutputStream object from "TERMS3.TXT." The following output would be displayed:

```
java.io.IOException: TERMS3.TXT
Closing the output stream...

java.io.FileNotFoundException: TERMS3.TXT
Closing second input stream...

java.io.FileNotFoundException: TERMS3.TXT
Closing first input stream...

At least one input or output stream failed to open...
Exiting program...
```

The following are the main points of the example:

*   The three static methods of class ExceptionDemo2 constitute the entire example. The main() method first attempts to create a FileInputStream for "TERMS1.TXT." If it is successful,

OpenSecondInputStream() is called and a reference to the first FileInputStream is passed to it. The objective of OpenSecondInputStream() is to create a FileInputStream object for "TERMS2.TXT." If that is successful, MergeStreams() is called and is given references to both FileInputStream objects. The objective of MergeStreams() is to create a FileOutputStream for "TERMS3.TXT." If successful, the contents of both input streams are merged into the output stream. If the attempt to open any file stream is unsuccessful, an exception object is thrown, clean-up is performed and the program exits gracefully.

Each of the three static methods has a distinct objective and is organized so that each contains one try block followed by catch handlers. In addition, each method is responsible for disposing of the resources it creates. This keeps the example as simple and as straightforward as possible.

- Within method MergeStreams(), the first observation about the failed attempt to create a FileOutputStream is that the constructor, FileOutputStream(String), will throw an IOException object. That being the case, the exception will be caught by:

```
catch (IOException err) {
    System.out.println(err.toString());
    System.out.println("Closing the output stream...\n");
    if (outStream != null)
        outStream.close();
    throw new FileNotFoundException(outfile);
    }
```

Within the body of the catch handler, the information contained within the IOException object is displayed with the help of method toString(). Now, there is the possibility that the read() and write() calls within the static method could have thrown the exception, instead of the constructor for FileOutputStream. With that in mind, we must close the output stream if variable outStream is not null. From there, we will throw a new exception object, a FileNotFoundException, to the caller.

- The caller is OpenSecondInputStream() and the rethrown FileNotFoundException object will search for a matching catch handler within the body of this method. The handler that it finds is:

```
catch (FileNotFoundException err) {
    System.out.println(err.toString());
    System.out.println("Closing second input stream.\n");
    if (inStream2 != null)
        inStream2.close();
```

```
    throw err;
    }
```

Once again, the contents of the exception object are displayed to the standard output device and the second `FileInputStream` object is closed. The same object is then rethrown to the caller of `OpenSecondInputStream()`.

• That caller is none other than `main()`. Since the object rethrown from `OpenSecondInputStream()` is of type `FileNotFoundException`, again, a search is conducted to find a matching catch handler. Within `main()`, there is only one catch handler:

```
catch (Exception err) {
   System.out.println(err.toString());
   System.out.println("Closing first input stream...\n");
   if (inStream1 != null)
     try {
         inStream1.close();
         }
     catch (IOException e) {
         System.out.println(e.toString());
         }
 System.out.println("At least one input or output stream
  failed to open...");
 System.out.println("Exiting program...");
 }
```

This handler does accept the exception object since the `FileNotFoundException` type is a subtype of `Exception`. The formal parameter in the handler, `err`, is a reference to an `Exception`. Nevertheless, because of the dynamic method look-up that is built into Java, the statement:

```
System.out.println(err.toString());
```

still correctly indicates that the exception object is of type `FileNotFoundException`. The first `FileInputStream` object is then closed and the program exits in the normal way.

The significance of this example is that one's code can be arranged in such a manner that if it becomes necessary to exit, all of the previously allocated resources can be relinquished in a systematic way. It is also possible to direct the rethrow of an exception object to a particular catch handler of the calling method by throwing an object of a particular type. The whole exception handling mechanism is really based on the notion of throwing objects, but catching types.

Note: An observation is that if the error handling does not differ significantly from one exception type to another, a single catch handler to catch an `Exception` type would suffice. This would reduce the need for writing many catch handlers per try block.

The fundamental ideas discussed so far for exception handling in Java also apply to C++. Providing a rough equivalent to the Java example is not quite so simple, since C++ does not have exact equivalents to the Java stream and exception classes. The C++ listing that follows uses a simulation of the Java `FileInputStream`, `FileOutputStream` and exception classes.

Listing 6-6: ExceptionDemo2.cpp

```cpp
#include <stdio.h>
#include <iostream.h>
#include <iomanip.h>
#include <fstream.h>
#include <string.h>
#include <fcntl.h>
#include <io.h>
#include <sys/types.h>
#include <sys/stat.h>

// Xception class hierarchy

class Xception {
public:
    Xception(char *);
    virtual void Display() const;
protected:
    const char * getMessage() const;
private:
    char message[80];
};

Xception::Xception(char * msg) {
strcpy(message, msg);
}

const char * Xception::getMessage() const {
return message;
}

void Xception::Display() const {
cout<<"Xception: "<<getMessage()<<endl;
}
```

```
class IOException : public Xception {
public:
    IOException(char *);
    virtual void Display() const;
};

IOException::IOException(char * msg) : Xception(msg) {
}

void IOException::Display() const {
cout<<"IOException: "<<getMessage()<<endl;
}

class FileNotFoundException : public IOException {
public:
    FileNotFoundException(char *);
    virtual void Display() const;
};

FileNotFoundException::FileNotFoundException(char * msg) :
 IOException(msg) {
}

void FileNotFoundException::Display() const {
cout<<"FileNotFoundException: "<<getMessage()<<endl;
}

// FileInputStream and FileOutputStream classes

class FileInputStream {
public:
    FileInputStream(char *);
    ~FileInputStream();
    int read(char *, int);
    int getDescriptor();
private:
    int     descriptor;
    char * filename;
    FileInputStream(const FileInputStream &);
    FileInputStream & operator=(const FileInputStream &);
};

FileInputStream::FileInputStream(char * name) {
descriptor = _open(name, _O_RDONLY);
if (descriptor == -1) {
    char errmsg[80];
    sprintf(errmsg, "Unable to open file %s", name);
    throw FileNotFoundException(name);
    }
else {
```

```
      filename = new char[strlen(name)+1];
      strcpy(filename, name);
      }
}

FileInputStream::~FileInputStream() {
close(descriptor);
delete [] filename;
}

int FileInputStream::read(char * buffer, int num_of_chars) {
int bytes_read;
if ( (bytes_read = _read(descriptor, buffer, num_of_chars)) <= 0 )
   return -1;
else
   return  bytes_read;
}

int FileInputStream::getDescriptor() {
return descriptor;
}

class FileOutputStream {
public:
   FileOutputStream(char *);
   ~FileOutputStream();
   int write(char *, int);
private:
   int     descriptor;
   char * filename;
   FileOutputStream(const FileOutputStream &);
   FileOutputStream & operator=(const FileOutputStream &);
};

FileOutputStream::FileOutputStream(char * name) {
descriptor = _open(name, _O_WRONLY, _S_IREAD | _S_IWRITE);
                         // Exception if file does not exist
if (descriptor == -1) {
   char errmsg[80];
   sprintf(errmsg, "Unable to open file %s", name);
   throw IOException(name);
   }
else {
   filename = new char[strlen(name)+1];
   strcpy(filename, name);
   }
}

FileOutputStream::~FileOutputStream() {
close(descriptor);
```

```cpp
delete [] filename;
}


int FileOutputStream::write(char * buffer, int num_bytes) {
if ( _write(descriptor, buffer, num_bytes) != num_bytes )
    return -1;
else
    return  0;
}


// Start of main example in C++

void MergeStreams(FileInputStream * in1, FileInputStream * in2,
 char * outfile) {
FileOutputStream * outStream = NULL;
try {
    int nbytes;
    char buffer[1];
    outStream = new FileOutputStream(outfile);

    while ((nbytes = (in1->read(buffer, 1)) != -1)) {
        outStream->write(buffer, nbytes);
        }

    while ((nbytes = (in2->read(buffer, 1)) != -1)) {
        outStream->write(buffer, nbytes);
        }

    delete outStream;
    }
catch (IOException & err) {
    err.Display();
    cout<<"Deleting dynamic outStream object"<<endl;
    delete outStream;
    throw FileNotFoundException(outfile);
    }
catch (Xception & err) {
    err.Display();
    cout<<"Deleting dynamic FileOutputStream object"<<endl;
    delete outStream;
    throw FileNotFoundException(outfile);
    }
}


void OpenSecondInputStream(FileInputStream * input1, char *
 infile2) {
FileInputStream * inStream2 = NULL;
try {
    inStream2 = new FileInputStream(infile2);
```

```
        MergeStreams(input1, inStream2, "TERMS3.TXT");
        delete inStream2;
        }
catch (FileNotFoundException & err) {
        err.Display();
        cout<<"Deleting second dynamic FileInputStream
         object"<<endl;
        delete inStream2;
        throw err;
        }
catch (IOException & err) {
        err.Display();
        cout<<"Deleting second dynamic FileInputStream
         object"<<endl;
      delete inStream2;
      throw err;
        }
}

void main()
{
FileInputStream * inStream1 = NULL;
try {
        inStream1 = new FileInputStream("TERMS1.TXT");
        OpenSecondInputStream(inStream1, "TERMS2.TXT");
        delete inStream1;
        }
catch (Xception & err) {
        err.Display();
        cout<<"Deleting first dynamic FileInputStream object"<<endl;
        delete inStream1;
        cout<<"At least one input or output stream failed to
         open..."<<endl;
        cout<<"Exiting program..."<<endl;
        }
}
```

Once again, we have the scenario where the processing of the input files,
"TERMS1.TXT" and "TERMS2.TXT," turn out fine, but there is a problem with
output file, "TERMS3.TXT." The result is the following output:

```
IOException: TERMS3.TXT
Deleting dynamic outStream object
FileNotFoundException: TERMS3.TXT
Deleting second dynamic FileInputStream object
FileNotFoundException: TERMS3.TXT
Deleting first dynamic FileInputStream object
At least one input or output stream failed to open...
Exiting program...
```

The overall structure and organization of the C++ equivalent mimics the Java example very closely. For that reason, I will leave it to the reader to study the details of the code. The C++ example differs from the Java version in these respects:

- The `FileInputStream` and `FileOutputStream` objects are instantiated from the heap. The clean-up that will need to be done, whether processing is successful or not, is to call `delete` on these objects. In the Java example, the clean-up was to have the objects close their streams.

- Each of the `FileInputStream` and `FileOutputStream` classes stores the file name and the file descriptor. Each of these classes also has a destructor that calls `delete` on the file name and closes the file descriptor. The destructors are automatically invoked when the `delete` operator is applied to the `FileInputStream` and `FileOutputStream` objects.

- The `Xception` class hierarchy mimics the exception classes used in the Java example. The base class was not called `"Exception"` because this term is a reserved word in C++.

- When an exception object is caught by a handler, the contents of the exception object are output with member function `Display()`. This is an overridden member function that is implemented in each of the exception classes. Furthermore, it is declared `virtual` so that the appropriate implementation will be called based on the object's type and its position in the exception class hierarchy.

Note: Each of the C++ catch handlers takes a reference to some type. For instance:

```
catch (Xception & err) {
    err.Display();
    cout<<"Deleting first dynamic FileInputStream object"<<endl;
    delete inStream1;
    cout<<"At least one input or output stream failed to
     open..."<<endl;
    cout<<"Exiting program..."<<endl;
    }
```

The header of the catch handler could have been written as:

```
catch (Xception err)
```

and that would also be correct. However, it would mean passing the exception object by value and that would incur the overhead of the copy constructor. Using a reference variable as the formal parameter is simply more efficient.

Cleaning Up with the Java `finally` Block

The technique of doing rethrows of exceptions so that all resources can be disposed of properly can become a little tiring. In Java, there is a way to put all of the clean-up code in one place and that is within a `finally` block. The `finally` block <u>always</u> gets executed, regardless of whether exceptions are thrown or not.

The use of finally blocks does introduce new complexities to the flow of control of a Java program. In this section we will examine these different flows if an exception is thrown, rethrown or not thrown. Furthermore, we will see how finally blocks can help simplify coding.

I will begin the discussion by adding finally blocks to a previous Java example (refer to the earlier topic, *Rethrowing an Exception for Further Processing*). At various places inside and outside the blocks, statements were added to provide an audit trail of the flow at different locations of the processing. The first version with `finally` blocks is as follows:

Listing 6-7: FinallyDemo.java

```java
import java.awt.*;
import java.io.*;

public class FinallyDemo {

    static void MergeStreams(FileInputStream in1, FileInputStream
    in2, String outfile)
                    throws IOException, FileNotFoundException {
        FileOutputStream outStream = null;
        try {
            byte [] buffer = new byte[1];
            outStream = new FileOutputStream(outfile);

            // The following statements of this try block
            // are ignored if an exception is thrown from
            // the previous statement

            while ((in1.read(buffer) != -1))
                outStream.write(buffer);

            while ((in2.read(buffer) != -1))
                outStream.write(buffer);
        }
        catch (IOException err) {
            System.out.println("In catch(IOException) block of
             MergeStreams");
            System.out.println(err.toString());
            throw new FileNotFoundException(outfile);
```

```
                }
        catch (Exception err) {
             System.out.println("In catch(Exception) block of
              MergeStreams");
             System.out.println(err.toString());
             throw new FileNotFoundException(outfile);
             }
        finally {
             System.out.println("In finally block of
              MergeStreams");
             System.out.println("Closing the output stream...");
             if (outStream != null)
                outStream.close();
                }
        // Executable statements after the try-catch-finally
         blocks
        System.out.println("First statement after finally block
         of MergeStreams");
        }

    static void OpenSecondInputStream(FileInputStream input1,
     String infile2)
          throws IOException, FileNotFoundException {
        FileInputStream inStream2 = null;
        try {
            inStream2 = new FileInputStream("TERMS2.TXT");
            MergeStreams(input1, inStream2, "TERMS3.TXT");
            }
        catch (FileNotFoundException err) {
           System.out.println("In catch(FileNotFoundException)
            block of OpenSecondInputStream");
           System.out.println(err.toString());
           throw err;
           }
        catch (IOException err) {
            System.out.println("In catch(IOException) block of
             OpenSecondInputStream");
            System.out.println(err.toString());
            throw err;
            }
        finally {
           System.out.println("In finally block of
            OpenSecondInputStream");
           System.out.println("Closing the second input
            stream...");
           if (inStream2 != null)
              inStream2.close();
           }
         // Executable statements after the try-catch-finally
          // blocks
```

```java
        System.out.println("First statement after finally block
         of OpenSecondInputStream");
        }

    public static void main(String args[]) {
        FileInputStream inStream1 = null;
        try {
            inStream1 = new FileInputStream("TERMS1.TXT");
            OpenSecondInputStream(inStream1, "TERMS2.TXT");
            }
        catch (Exception err) {
            System.out.println("In catch(Exception) block of main");
            System.out.println(err.toString());
            }
        finally {
            System.out.println("In finally block of main");
            System.out.println("Closing the first input
             stream...");
            try {
                if (inStream1 != null)
                    inStream1.close();
                }
            catch (IOException e) {
                System.out.println(e.toString());
                }
        System.out.println("Leaving finally block of main");
            }
            // The flow of control proceeds to the following
            // statement
        System.out.println("First and last statement after
         finally block of main");
            }

}
```

Assuming the worst case scenario where the input files (`"TERMS1.TXT"` and `"TERMS2.TXT"`) can be opened successfully and the output file (`"TERMS3.TXT"`) cannot be opened, the following diagnostics will be displayed on the standard output device:

```
In catch(IOException) block of MergeStreams
java.io.IOException: TERMS3.TXT
In finally block of MergeStreams
Closing the output stream...

In catch(FileNotFoundException) block of OpenSecondInputStream
java.io.FileNotFoundException: TERMS3.TXT
In finally block of OpenSecondInputStream
Closing the second input stream...
```

```
In catch(Exception) block of main
java.io.FileNotFoundException: TERMS3.TXT
In finally block of main
Closing the first input stream...
Leaving finally block of main
First and last statement after finally block of main
```

The following is a discussion of the essential aspects of the above program:

- The three static methods of class `FinallyDemo` comprise the example. The `main()` method first attempts to create a `FileInputStream` for `"TERMS1.TXT."` If it is successful, `OpenSecondInputStream()` is called and a reference to the first `FileInputStream` is passed to it. The objective of `OpenSecondInputStream()` is to create a `FileInputStream` object for `"TERMS2.TXT."` If that is successful, `MergeStreams()` is called and is given references to both `FileInputStream` objects. The objective of `MergeStreams()` is to create a `FileOutputStream` for `"TERMS3.TXT."` If successful, the contents of both input streams are merged into the output stream. If the attempt to open any file stream is unsuccessful, an exception object is thrown, clean-up is performed and the program exits gracefully.

  Each of the three static methods has a distinct objective and is organized so that each contains one try block followed by one or more catch handlers followed by a single finally block. The finally block contains clean-up code, which is to have the `FileInputStream` and `FileOutputStream` objects close their streams.

- The first throw of an exception object occurs in method `MergeStreams()`. For this example, we assume that the attempt to call constructor `FileOutputSteam(String)` fails and an exception object of `IOException` type is thrown. The following catch handler in `MergeStreams()` will deal with the exception:

```
catch (IOException err) {
    System.out.println("In catch(IOException) block of
    MergeStreams");
    System.out.println(err.toString());
    throw new FileNotFoundException(outfile);
    }
...
finally {
    System.out.println("In finally block of
    MergeStreams");
    System.out.println("Closing the output stream...");
    if (outStream != null)
        outStream.close();
        }
```

```
// Executable statements after the try-catch-finally blocks
System.out.println("First statement after finally
 block of MergeStreams");
```

- When the exception occurs, the following events take place:

  - All of the statements following the statement that caused the exception within the try block are ignored.
  - The exception object is caught by a catch handler, namely the one with signature `catch (IOException)`.
  - All of the statements of the body of the catch handler are executed. The last statement is a request to throw another exception object, which is of type `FileNotFoundException`. The request is noted, but the statement is not executed immediately since there is a `finally` block.
  - All of the statements in the finally block are then executed, where any open `FileOutputStream` object is closed. The last request to throw the exception of type `FileNotFoundException` is then performed. Processing proceeds to the caller method, which is `OpenSecondInputStream()`. The statements following the finally block are ignored.

- The flow of control percolates to `OpenSecondInputStream()` where the following catch handler deals with the exception object:

```
catch (FileNotFoundException err) {
    System.out.println("In catch(FileNotFoundException)
     block of OpenSecondInputStream");
    System.out.println(err.toString());
    throw err;
    }
...
finally {
    System.out.println("In finally block of
     OpenSecondInputStream");
    System.out.println("Closing the second input
     stream...");
     if (inStream2 != null)
        inStream2.close();
    }
    // Executable statements after the try-catch-
     finally blocks
    System.out.println("First statement after finally
     block of OpenSecondInputStream");
```

Like the method `MergeStreams()`, the same series of steps takes place within `OpenSecondInputStream()`: the statements in the body of the catch handler are executed, the request to do another throw is noted, the statements within the finally block are executed and the throw is actually performed. Processing proceeds to the caller, which is `main()`. Once again, the statements following the finally block of `OpenSecondInputStream()` are ignored.

- The flow of control elevates to the `main()` method. The object thrown is of type `FileNotFoundException`, which is a subtype of `Exception`. Hence, the only catch handler in `main()` will deal with the exception:

```
catch (Exception err) {
    System.out.println("In catch(Exception) block of
     main");
    System.out.println(err.toString());
    }
finally {
    System.out.println("In finally block of main");
    System.out.println("Closing the first input
     stream...");
    try {
        if (inStream1 != null)
            inStream1.close();
        }
    catch (IOException e) {
        System.out.println(e.toString());
        }
    System.out.println("Leaving finally block of main");
    }
    // The flow of control proceeds to the following
     statement
    System.out.println("First and last statement after
     finally block of main");
```

The processing proceeds in a similar fashion as in the cases for `OpenSecondInputStream()` and `MergeStreams()`. However, the notable difference this time is that there is no rethrow of any exception from the catch handler. Given this situation, all of the statements of the catch handler are executed, all of the statements of the finally block are executed and any statements after the finally block are also executed.

The whole idea of using finally blocks is to rid yourself of the need to rethrow exception objects. I had intentionally left the throw statements within the catch handlers of the `OpenSecondInputStream()` and `MergeStreams()` methods because it is important to understand the flow of control when all three types of blocks are present.

Now, suppose the throw statements of the catch handlers of `OpenSecondInputStream()` and `MergeStreams()` are commented out:

```
// In OpenSecondInputStream
catch (IOException err) {
```

```
System.out.println("In catch(IOException) block of
 MergeStreams");
System.out.println(err.toString());
//  throw new FileNotFoundException(outfile);
}
```

and:

```
// In MergeStreams
catch (FileNotFoundException err) {
    System.out.println("In catch(FileNotFoundException) block of
     OpenSecondInputStream");
    System.out.println(err.toString());
//  throw err;
    }
```

If we maintain the previous worst-case scenario, then we would see the following on the standard output device:

```
In catch(IOException) block of MergeStreams
java.io.IOException: TERMS3.TXT
In finally block of MergeStreams
Closing the output stream...
First statement after finally block of MergeStreams

In finally block of OpenSecondInputStream
Closing the second input stream...
First statement after finally block of OpenSecondInputStream

In finally block of main
Closing the first input stream...
Leaving finally block of main
First and last statement after finally block of main
```

- In this situation, the original exception object thrown is dealt with by the catch handler within method `MergeStreams()`. The statements within the catch handler are executed, followed by the statements within the finally block and followed by any statements <u>after</u> the finally block.

- After processing has been exhausted within method `MergeStreams()`, control returns to the caller, which is method `OpenSecondInputStream()`. Within this method, the statements within the finally block are executed, followed by any statements <u>after</u> the finally block.

- Control then returns to the highest level, which is method `main()`. Within `main()`, the statements within the finally block are executed, followed by any statements <u>after</u> the finally block. The program then terminates normally.

As a conclusion to this discussion, let us see what the output would be if every-thing proceeds normally <u>without</u> any exceptions thrown:

```
In finally block of MergeStreams
Closing the output stream...
First statement after finally block of MergeStreams

In finally block of OpenSecondInputStream
Closing the second input stream...
First statement after finally block of OpenSecondInputStream

In finally block of main
Closing the first input stream...
Leaving finally block of main
First and last statement after finally block of main
```

As stated earlier, the statements of the finally blocks will be executed whether or not any exceptions are thrown.

Conclusion: The code to relinquish resources should be placed within finally blocks. That includes the closing of network port connections, database connec-tions and disposing of graphics contexts.

Unlike Java, the C++ language does not have the `finally` keyword. The sys-tematic relinquishing of resources would have to employ the technique of rethrowing exception objects to the calling functions and having the callers han-dle them.

Redirecting the Flow of Control with C++ `set_unexpected`

This topic will discuss a standard C++ only function called `set_unex-pected()`. Basically, this function is used to help alter the flow of control of an exception thrown from a function whose type is not listed in the function's exception specification list. The `set_unexpected()` function adds additional complexity to the usual try block and catch handler architecture. Its impact on C++ programs that use exception handling is best understood with some exam-ples.

Let us first examine a C++ program that does not use the `set_unexpected()` function. The heart of this example is a class called `Vector`. Basically this is a special array class for integers that incorporates certain restrictions: exceptions are thrown if the total number of elements is non-positive or exceeds a certain maximum, if the element indexed is out-of-bounds or if heap memory gets exhausted. A simple exception class hierarchy was constructed to support the specific types of exceptions that can be thrown. The first version of the example is as follows:

Listing 6-8: SetUnexpectedDemo.cpp

```cpp
#include <stdio.h>
#include <iostream.h>
#include <string.h>
#include <fcntl.h>
#include <io.h>
#include <except.h>

// Beginning of exception class framework

class Xception {
public:
    Xception(long);
    virtual void Display() const;
protected:
     long getValue() const;
private:
    long actual_value;
};

Xception::Xception(long some_value) : actual_value(some_value) {
}

long Xception::getValue() const {
return actual_value;
}

void Xception::Display() const {
cout<<"Xception: "<<"illegal value = "<<getValue()<<endl;
}

class Out_of_Memory : public Xception {
public:
    Out_of_Memory(long);
    virtual void Display() const;
};

Out_of_Memory::Out_of_Memory(long some_value) :
            Xception(some_value) {
}

void Out_of_Memory::Display() const {
cout<<"Out_of_Memory: "<<"heap exhausted during attempt to
                          allocate "
                    <<getValue()<<" elements"<<endl;
}

class Illegal_Size : public Xception {
public:
```

```
      Illegal_Size(long);
      virtual void Display() const;
};

Illegal_Size::Illegal_Size(long some_value) : Xception(some_value) {
}

void Illegal_Size::Display() const {
cout<<"Illegal_Size: "<<"requested array size of "
                      <<getValue()<<" is illegal"<<endl;
}

class Out_of_Bounds : public Xception {
public:
   Out_of_Bounds(long, long, long);
   virtual void Display() const;
private:
   long lower_bounds;
   long upper_bounds;
};

Out_of_Bounds::Out_of_Bounds(long some_value, long lbounds,
                  long ubounds) : Xception(some_value),
                  lower_bounds(lbounds), upper_bounds(ubounds) {
}

void Out_of_Bounds::Display() const {
cout<<"Out_of_Bounds: "<<"attempt to index element at "
                      <<getValue()<<" is illegal"<<endl;
}

// End of the exception class framework

// Beginning of the mainstream of the example

class Vector {
public:
   Vector(int) throw(Out_of_Memory, Illegal_Size);
   int & operator[](int) const throw(Out_of_Bounds);
   void Traverse() const;
   ~Vector();
private:
   Vector(const Vector &);
   void operator=(const Vector &);
   enum { MAXSIZE = 100 };
   static int count;   // Used only for identifying the instance
   int id;             // Used only for identifying the instance
   int * vector_ptr;
   int    size;
};
```

```cpp
int Vector::count = 0;

Vector::Vector(int init_size) throw(Out_of_Memory, Illegal_Size) {
id = ++count;
if (!((0 < init_size) && (init_size <= MAXSIZE))) {
    throw Illegal_Size(init_size);
    }
size = init_size;
vector_ptr = new int[init_size];
if (!vector_ptr) {
    throw Out_of_Memory(init_size);
    }
}

int & Vector::operator[](int index) const throw(Out_of_Bounds) {
if ( (0 <= index) && (index < size) )
    return(vector_ptr[index]);
else {
    throw Out_of_Bounds(index, 0, size - 1);
    }
}

void Vector::Traverse() const {
for (int i = 0; i < size; i++)
   cout<<vector_ptr[i]<<endl;
}

Vector::Vector(const Vector &) { }

void Vector::operator=(const Vector &) { }

Vector::~Vector() {
delete [] vector_ptr;
}

void Create_New_Vector() {

try {
    Vector vec2(-6);          // An exception is thrown here

    for (int index = 0; index < 6; index++) vec2[index] = 6.0 *
     index;
    cout<<"Elements of vec2: "<<endl;
    vec2.Traverse();
    }

catch(char * err) {
cout<<"Inside catch(char *) of Create_New_Vector..."<<endl;
cout<<err<<endl;
}
```

```
catch(Xception & err) {
cout<<"Inside catch(Xception &) of Create_New_Vector..."<<endl;
err.Display();
}

catch(...) {
cout<<"Inside the catch all handler of Create_New_Vector..."
 <<endl;
}

cout<<"First line after the catch handlers of Create_New_Vector"
 <<endl;
}

void main()
{
int fd;

if ((fd = open("TERMS1.TXT", O_RDONLY | O_CREAT)) == -1 )  {
    cout<<"Unable to open file TERMS1.TXT"<<endl;
    return;
    }

try {
    Vector vec1(4);

    for (int index = 0; index < 4; index++) vec1[index] = 4.0 *
     index;
    cout<<"Elements of vec1: "<<endl;
    vec1.Traverse();

    Create_New_Vector();
    }

catch(char * err) {
cout<<"Inside catch(char *) of main..."<<endl;
cout<<err<<endl;
}

catch(Xception & err) {
cout<<"Inside catch(Xception &) of main..."<<endl;
err.Display();
}

catch(...) {
cout<<"Inside the catch all handler of main..."<<endl;
}

cout<<"Closing file descriptor..."<<endl;
```

```
close(fd);

cout<<"Exiting main - program completed..."<<'\n';
}
```

The above sample centers on two non-member functions: `main()` and `Create_New_Vector()`. Each function basically instantiates a `Vector` object, uses a `for` loop to assign values to each member and displays the members on the standard output device with the `Vector::Traverse()` member function.

The function `Create_New_Vector()` is called by `main()`. Within `Create_New_Vector()`, the attempt to create a `Vector` object of negative size:

```
Vector vec2(-6);
```

will cause an exception of type `Illegal_Size` to be thrown. This will result in the following output:

```
Elements of vec1:
0
4
8
12
Inside catch(Xception &) of Create_New_Vector...
Illegal_Size: requested array size of -6 is illegal
First line after the catch handlers of Create_New_Vector
Closing file descriptor...
Exiting main - program completed...
```

Basically, the following are the main points with respect to the flow of control:

- Within `main()`, the `Vector` object represented by variable `vec1` is successfully created, its members are assigned values and the contents of the members are displayed.

- The function, `Create_New_Vector()`, is called by `main()`. Its first statement is to create a `Vector` object (`vec2`) of size `-6`. This causes an exception object of type `Illegal_Size` to be thrown.

- The exception object is caught by a matching handler with signature `(Xception &)`, since class `Xception` is the superclass of class `Illegal_Size`. The contents of the exception object are displayed.

- With processing completed in the body of `catch(Xception &)`, the remaining catch blocks are ignored and the flow of control goes to the first statement after the last catch block. A single line ("`First line after the catch handlers of Create_New_Vector`") is displayed. The flow of control then returns to the caller, `main()`.

- Within `main()`, the last line within the try block is `Create_New_Vector()`. Since the exception was thrown and handled within `Create_New_Vector()`, the catch handlers of `main()` are ignored and processing proceeds to the first statement after the last catch block. The user is notified that the previously opened resources (a file descriptor) will be closed and the program exits.

As things stand, all of the code above will handle the known exceptions in a predictable way. However, what would happen if a developer has difficulty anticipating what types of exceptions might be thrown from a function? For the sake of an example, let us take the constructor `Vector(int)` and remove `Illegal_Size` from its exception specification list. The resulting code would look like:

```
class Vector {
public:
    Vector(int)  throw(Out_of_Memory);      // exception specification
                                            list

    . . .
private:
    . . .
};


. . .


Vector::Vector(int init_size)  throw(Out_of_Memory) {
id = ++count;
if (!((0 < init_size) && (init_size <= MAXSIZE))) {
    throw Illegal_Size(init_size);
    }
size = init_size;
vector_ptr = new int[init_size];
if (!vector_ptr) {
    throw Out_of_Memory(init_size);
    }
}
```

One of the problems with the exception specification list is that a C++ class developer is not obligated to use it. The reasons are basically historical since C++ exception handling is relatively new and there is a lot of existing C++ code without exception handling. However, if a developer is going to use exception handling it is a good idea to use the specification list because there is the need to inform users of your classes which member functions may throw what types of exceptions.

Even for the conscientious developer, there may be another problem that arises. He may be using functions that are capable of throwing exception types that are not documented. This may very well be the case if he buys or uses class libraries from another source.

Since the `Illegal_Size` type is no longer on the exception specification list for constructor `Vector(int)`, what would happen with the same scenario when the statement:

```
Vector vec2(-6);
```

fails?

In this case, the user would simply see a message similar to:

```
Program Aborted
```

when the exception is thrown.

Internally, this is what happens:

The throw of an exception of type `Illegal_Size` is about to take place and the compiler checks the specification list. Since this type is not on the list, the compiler calls an internal function called `unexpected()`, which by default calls `terminate()`, which aborts the program.

To avert this situation, the user can provide and register his own version of `unexpected()` and have the processing proceed in the manner he wants. He would first write his own version of `unexpected()` such as:

```
void unexpected_routine() {
cout<<"unexpected_routine called..."<<endl;
throw "Message from unexpected_routine...";
}
```

He may call this non-member function any name he wishes. The requirements are that the argument list is empty and the return type is `void`.

After that, he needs to register his `unexpected_routine()` by using `set_unexpected ()`, which takes a pointer to a function that takes no arguments and returns `void` (which is how `unexpected_routine ()` is declared):

```
void main()
{
int fd;

set_unexpected(unexpected_routine);          // This was added

if ((fd = open("TERMS1.TXT", O_RDONLY | O_CREAT)) == -1 )   {
    cout<<"Unable to open file TERMS1.TXT"<<endl;
    return;
    }
...

}
```

After incorporating the additions, recompiling and running the program, the following would be displayed:

```
Elements of vec1:
0
4
8
12
unexpected_routine called...
Inside catch(char *) of Create_New_Vector...
Message from unexpected_routine...
First line after the catch handlers of Create_New_Vector
Closing file descriptor...
Exiting main - program completed...
```

Basically, these are the key aspects of the amended program:

When the throw of an `Illegal_Size` object results from statement:

```
Vector vec2(-6);
```

the compiler would call the user's version of `unexpected()`, which is unexpected_routine(). The statements within this function are executed. The last statement is a throw of a string (`char *`) message.

The flow of control returns to function `Create_New_Vector()` and a search begins to find a suitable catch handler. The exception object is caught by the following handler:

```
catch(char * err) {
cout<<"Inside catch(char *) of Create_New_Vector..."<<endl;
cout<<err<<endl;
}
```

The statements within the handler are executed and the string message thrown from `unexpected_routine ()` is displayed.

After the statements of the catch handler are processed, the remaining catch handlers of `Create_New_Vector()` are ignored and any statements following the last catch block are processed. Processing then returns to the caller, which is `main()`.

Within `main()`, processing starts after the call to `Create_New_Vector()`. Again, since the exception was thrown and handled within `Create_New_Vector()`, all the catch handlers of `main()` are ignored and the flow of control goes to the first statement after the last catch block. The user is notified that the previously opened resources (a file descriptor) will be closed and the program exits.

Conclusion: Creating and registering a user-defined version of `unexpected()` can put predictability back into the flow of control if exceptions of unknown type are thrown. The user-defined `unexpected()` function should throw an object of a known type so that clean-up of local and global resources can proceed in a systematic manner.

Java does not have functions like `unexpected()` and `set_unexpected()`. Furthermore, Java does not support pointers or pointers to functions.

Using C++ `set_terminate` to Dispose of Resources

I had mentioned in the earlier topic, *Redirecting the Flow of Control with set_unexpected,* that the built-in `unexpected()` function will call `terminate()` by default. The built-in `terminate()` function in turn calls `abort()`, which abnormally exits the program, regardless of the state of the conditions. All of these functions are strictly C++ features.

The `terminate()` function also will be called if an exception is thrown and no matching catch handler can be found as the exception traverses up the program stack. The user, however, can provide his own `terminate()` function and divert the program flow to his function with `set_terminate()`. This is useful for disposing of any global program resources, such as locks on database tables.

We will now look at how to use `set_terminate()` for our own `terminate()` function. The example below is an adaptation of the one from *Redirecting the Flow of Control with set_unexpected.* In order to focus on the subject at hand, the code for the `Xception` class framework and for the `Vector` class have been omitted. The reader may refer to this code from the earlier topic.

Listing 6-9: SetTerminateDemo.cpp

```
void Create_New_Vector() {

try {
    Vector vec2(-6);          // An exception is thrown here

    for (int index = 0; index < 6; index++) vec2[index] = 6.0 *
     index;
    cout<<"Elements of vec2: "<<endl;
    vec2.Traverse();
    }

catch(char * err) {
cout<<"Inside catch(char *) of Create_New_Vector..."<<endl;
cout<<err<<endl;
}

catch(Out_of_Bounds & err) {
```

```
cout<<"Inside catch(Out_of_Bounds &) of Create_New_Vector..."
    <<endl;
err.Display();
}

cout<<"First line after the catch handlers of Create_New_Vector"
    <<endl;
}

int fd;

void terminate_routine() {
cout<<"terminate_routine called..."<<endl;
cout<<"An exception object of unknown type was not caught..."
 <<endl;
cout<<"Closing file descriptor..."<<endl;
close(fd);
exit(-1);
}

void main()
{

set_terminate(terminate_routine);

if ((fd = open("TERMS1.TXT", O_RDONLY | O_CREAT)) == -1 )  {
    cout<<"Unable to open file TERMS1.TXT"<<endl;
    return;
    }

try {
    Vector vec1(4);

    for (int index = 0; index < 4; index++) vec1[index] = 4.0 *
     index;
    cout<<"Elements of vec1: "<<endl;
    vec1.Traverse();

    Create_New_Vector();
    }

catch(char * err) {
cout<<"Inside catch(char *) of main..."<<endl;
cout<<err<<endl;
}

catch(Out_of_Bounds & err) {
cout<<"Inside catch(Out_of_Bounds &) of main..."<<endl;
err.Display();
}
```

```
cout<<"Closing file descriptor..."<<endl;

close(fd);

cout<<"Exiting main - program completed..."<<'\n';
}
```

Running the above example will yield the following output:

```
Elements of vec1:
0
4
8
12
terminate_routine called...
An exception object of unknown type was not caught...
Closing file descriptor...
```

Basically, this is the sequence of events that takes place:

- Within function `main()`, the `set_terminate()` function is used to register the user's termination function, which is called `terminate_routine()`. The `set_terminate()` function takes a single argument, which is a pointer to a function that takes no arguments and returns `void` (which is how `terminate_routine()` is declared).

- Next, within `main()`, a `Vector` object called `vec1` was successfully created. The `Vector` object is assigned integral values to each of its members and the contents are then displayed. From there, the non-member function, `Create_New_Vector()` is called.

- The first statement of `Create_New_Vector()` is to instantiate another `Vector` object, represented by variable `vec2`. However, the size is negative and this causes an exception to be thrown. The exception object is of type `Illegal_Size`.

- A search begins to find a matching catch handler within `Create_New_Vector()`, but none is found. Processing then exits to the caller function, which is `main()`.

- The catch handlers of `main()` are examined to see if there is a match. There is no match. The `terminate_routine()`, which had overridden the default `terminate()` function, is then called.

- The `terminate_routine()` notifies the user that it was called. The only global resource, a file descriptor, is closed and the program exits normally.

Using `set_terminate()` in order to use one's own termination function has a rather limited benefit. Unlike the user-defined `unexpected()` routine, a user-defined `terminate()` routine cannot throw an exception object with the hope that the flow of control will reenter the mainstream of the program. If any such attempt is made, the program will abnormally terminate. Therefore, the only purpose of a user-defined termination function is to get rid of any lingering global resources and exit the program normally.

With that said, the best way to deal with this situation is to incorporate a catch handler with a base class signature such as (Xception &) or the "catch-all" signature (...) at the end of every series of catch blocks:

```cpp
void Create_New_Vector() {

try {
    ...
    }

catch(char * err) {
...
}

catch(Out_of_Bounds & err) {
...
}

catch(Xception & err) {
...
}

catch(...) {
...
}

...
}

void main()
{
...
try {
    ...
    }

catch(char * err) {
...
}

catch(Out_of_Bounds & err) {
...
}

catch(Xception & err) {
```

```
...
}

catch(...) {
...
}


...
}
```

Conclusion: The best way to prevent abnormal termination is to handle the exception object within the body of the function. In doing so, resources owned by the function can be disposed of. If necessary, the resources of the callers can also be disposed of through a series of well-planned returns. For this situation, the best policy is a preventive one.

Java does not have functions like `terminate()` and `set_terminate()`. Furthermore, Java does not support pointers or pointers to functions. However, the lessons of handling the exceptions within the functions where they may be thrown still applies to Java. If an exception is not caught and handled within the program, it will also terminate abnormally as in C++.

A Useful Java Method for Debugging: `printStackTrace()`

I had mentioned earlier that the Java `Exception` class is a subclass of class `Throwable`. Class `Throwable` has a very valuable method called `printStackTrace()` which will display the name of the method that originally threw the exception plus the entire lineage of calling methods. Since `Throwable` is a rudimentary base class, all exception classes inherit `printStackTrace()`. If we modify the `main()` method of `ExceptionDemo2` from one of the previous topics (see *Rethrowing an Exception for Further Processing*) as follows (highlighting added for emphasis):

```java
public static void main(String args[]) {
        FileInputStream inStream1 = null;
        try {
            inStream1 = new FileInputStream("TERMS1.TXT");
            OpenSecondInputStream(inStream1, "TERMS2.TXT");
                inStream1.close();
            }
        catch (Exception err) {
            err.printStackTrace();    // was System.out.
                                       // println(err.toString());
            System.out.println("Closing first input stream...\n");
            if (inStream1 != null)
               try {
                   inStream1.close();
                   }
```

```
                 catch (IOException e) {
                     System.out.println(e.toString());
                     }
                 System.out.println("At least one input or output
                  stream failed to open...");
                 System.out.println("Exiting program...");
             }
         }
```

and then rerun the program with an exception being thrown because file
"TERMS3.TXT" cannot be created, then we will obtain the following output:

```
java.io.IOException: TERMS3.TXT
Closing the output stream...

java.io.FileNotFoundException: TERMS3.TXT
Closing second input stream...

java.io.FileNotFoundException: TERMS3.TXT
        at ExceptionDemo3.MergeStreams(ExceptionDemo3.java:36)
        at ExceptionDemo3.OpenSecondInputStream(Exception
         Demo3.java:52)
        at ExceptionDemo3.main(ExceptionDemo3.java:75)
Closing first input stream...

At least one input or output stream failed to open...
Exiting program...
```

The highlighted output above is the result of statement:

```
err.printStackTrace();
```

With methods of various objects being called from many nested levels, the
printStackTrace() is indeed valuable for locating a problem quickly
(even source file line numbers are given!). A sample Java program called
ExceptionDemo3 on the supplied media illustrates what has been discussed.

Uses and Misuses of Exception Handling

Exception handling in both Java and C++ are mechanisms to help the developer write more reliable and supportable programs. The use of exception handling does introduce a form of non-linear programming and it requires a good
understanding of the flow of control when an exception object is thrown.
However, using exception handling for the wrong purposes can result in the
opposite of what it was intended for. The following guidelines will help the
developer stay on track.

⇒Do Not Use Exception Handling in Place of Normal Program Flow

Exception handling is intended for exceptional situations. It is not meant for things like exiting loops. For example, if someone had written:

```
try {
    while (true) {
        System.out.println(count++);
        if (count > 100) throw(new Throwable());
        }
    }

catch(Throwable msg)   { }
```

simply to output 1 to 100, then that is clearly overkill. A single `for` loop would have sufficed. Keep things simple!

Along the same lines, if you write a method or function where status information can either be a return value or an exception, the preference is to use the return value. In the case of a no-argument, default constructor, the only alternative is to throw an exception.

These recommendations apply to both Java and C++.

⇒Dispose of Any Allocated Resources When a Constructor Throws an Exception

A constructor normally does not handle exceptions thrown within its body. If an object cannot be instantiated, it is due to some irreconcilable resource problem where one or more of its components cannot be created. As such, the constructor usually propagates the exception object to the caller and it is the caller's responsibility to handle the exception.

Now, the body of a constructor may perform many activities, including allocating heap memory (in C++) or accessing other resources (like securing network port connections). If an exception is encountered along the way, it is important that those resources that are already secured be relinquished. Otherwise, the handles to those resources will be lost and other processes in need of those resources will suffer. The following is a short C++ example:

```
class Publication {
public:
    Publication(char *, char *)   throw(char *);
    ...
private:
```

```
    char * title;
    char * date;
};

Publication::Publication(char * caption, char * curr_date)
throw(char *) {
title = new char[strlen(caption)+1];
if  (title == 0)
    throw("Unable to allocate heap memory for title");
else
    strcpy(title, caption);
date = new char[strlen(curr_date)+1];
if  (date == 0) {
    delete [] title;         // Clean up before doing the throw
    throw("Unable to allocate heap memory for date");
    }
else
    strcpy(date, curr_date);
}
```

The main ideas of this point apply to both Java and C++. Of course, manual deallocation of heap memory is not a worry in Java due to garbage collection.

⇒Do Not Throw Exceptions from the Destructor

This advice only applies to C++ since there are no destructors in Java.

The role of a destructor is to relinquish resources and nothing else. As much as possible, it is a good idea to <u>avoid</u> using functions that are capable of throwing exceptions within the body of the destructor. If the destructor gets called as a result of the stack unwinding process and the destructor itself throws an exception, it is a sure way to cause an abnormal termination of the program. The exception thrown from the destructor will mask the original exception and will make it very difficult to pinpoint the source of the original problem.

If there is the unusual need to use a function that can throw an exception within the destructor, then that exception must be handled within the destructor.

⇒Determine the Number of Catch Handlers You Need

The reader who is accustomed to procedural language programming may have noticed that there is some additional effort to trapping exceptions. Another form of overkill is to write try, catch and finally blocks for every single line of mainstream application code. That is a lot of work and is not necessary. The recommendation is to 1) write your mainstream statements of the function, 2) enclose those statements into a try block, 3) determine what exception types might be thrown from all those statements and 4) write a suitable number of catch handlers to deal with those exception types.

In many cases, the exception types thrown will belong to a particular hierarchy and a catch handler with the signature of a base class type may suffice. However, you would want a catch handler with the signature of a specific sub-class type if there is special processing to be done. The important point here is to use discretion on the number of catch handlers that are really necessary to get the job done.

It is also a good idea to set up "catch-all" handlers at various places in the code so that unanticipated exceptions will be caught. The most generic catch handler for Java would have the `catch(Exception)` signature while the one for C++ would have `catch(...)`.

Last, but not least, for Java, all resource disposal statements should be grouped within `finally` blocks. This will guarantee that the resources will be disposed whether or not any exceptions are thrown.

The spirit of these recommendations applies to both Java and C++.

CHAPTER

7

The Land of Streams: Input and Output

An Overview of the C++ and Java Stream Classes

One of the biggest challenges a programmer faces as he learns a new programming language is to find the services that are already in existence. For languages, these services are either in the form of standard function libraries or, in the case of C++ and Java, standard class libraries. These class libraries, which are also known as `frameworks`, can span quite a number of service categories, such as support for common data structures, networking and user interface components. In this chapter, we will do a comparison of the standard stream classes between C++ and Java.

A user who is adept at using the class libraries of one language may find himself initially floundering before he is comfortable with the libraries of the other. This is especially the case with C++ and Java since these languages appear so similar. Each category of services for each language is represented by a hierarchy of classes. Within each hierarchy, classes that do similar things between two languages often have different names and each class will have different sets of methods and different protocols for usage. In addition, it is not uncommon to find services for one language that are missing from the frameworks of the other language.

Both C++ and Java support the fundamental notion of a stream. A stream is basically a linear progression of information. We do not care so much about the sources of the data. The sources may be files, pipes or network sockets. What matters is that once the data is incorporated into a stream, it may be manipulated in the same manner. By starting with the high-level abstraction of a stream, both C++ and Java provide class frameworks with services that are useful in many situations.

The purpose of the overview of the C++ and Java I/O frameworks is to give us a macroscopic picture of how each framework is organized. I will not be dwelling on the details of each class since there are simply too many. Instead, the idea is to help the reader locate the essentials of what he needs when he needs it. The end of this section includes references to sources where he can find the details of the classes and their public methods.

Starting with C++, its collection of stream classes is called `iostreams`. Figure 7-1 is an illustration of the major classes and their interrelationships. The classes are connected by single arrow lines. The class that is being pointed to represents the superclass of the other.

Below is a brief description of the purposes of each class:

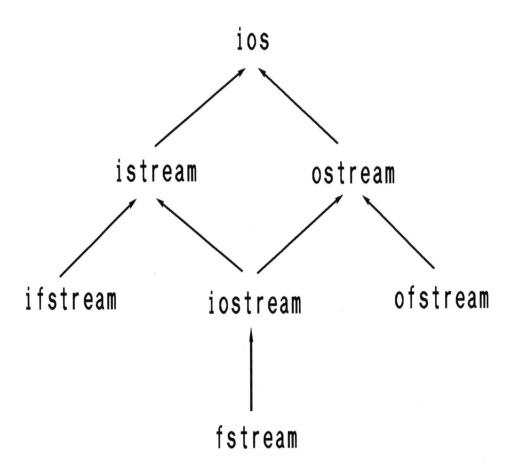

Figure 7-1

- **ios:** This class is the great ancestor of all the stream classes. Class ios includes a number of bit masks for tracking the state of an object, for controlling the opening of files and for format control. The class has a number of public accessor and mutator functions for reading and setting of the bits.

- **istream:** This class is a base class strictly for input functions. Its public interface includes member functions for the unformatted extraction (reading) of data. Here is where the right shift operator (>>) is defined to support the extraction of all of the built-in types.

- **ostream:** This class is a base class strictly for output functions. Its public interface includes member functions for the unformatted insertion (writing) of data. Here is where the left shift operator (<<) is defined to support the insertion of all of the built-in types.

- **ifstream:** This class is derived from istream and is specialized to work with files in read mode. Class ifstream has constructors that will allow the user to associate a file name or file descriptor with the object.

- **iostream:** This class is a subclass of both istream and ostream and has a public interface that is the union of the public interfaces of ios, istream and ostream. This class allows for bidirectional input and output.

- **ofstream:** This class is derived from ostream and is specialized to work with files in write mode. Class ofstream has constructors that will allow the user to associate a file name or file descriptor with the object.

- **fstream:** This class is basically intended for bidirectional file input and output and possesses the capabilities of both ifstream and ofstream. Its public interface matches very closely with the public interfaces of either ifstream or ofstream.

The succeeding topics in this chapter will provide examples of frequently used classes and public member functions.

Now, we will get an overview of the stream classes of Java. The Java input-output classes are contained in the standard package java.io. Figure 7-2 is an illustration of the class hierarchy.

Except for class Object, which is the ancestor to all classes, every class or interface is contained in package java.io. Below is a brief description of each class or interface:

- **FilenameFilter:** An interface for specifying which files in a directory should be selected.

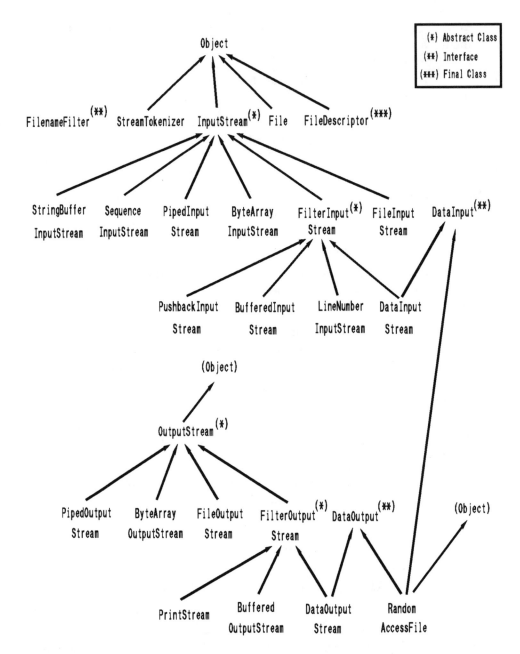

Figure 7-2

- **StreamTokenizer:** This class will turn an input stream into a stream of tokens. The class has methods to specify word characters and white space characters.

- **InputStream:** An abstract class representing an input stream of bytes. It has abstract methods for reading bytes from a stream and for the positioning of the stream pointer.

- **File:** This class encapsulates a file name so that activities with the file can be performed in a platform-independent way. Basic methods include testing for existence, testing for type (file or directory) and determining the permissions (read and write).

- **FileDescriptor:** A platform-independent way to obtain a file descriptor from an operating system. This class has no public constructor. Instances of FileDescriptor are obtained through the getFD() method of class FileInputStream, FileOutputStream or RandomAccessFile.

- **StringBufferInputStream:** A subclass of InputStream, this class uses a string buffer as an input stream.

- **SequenceInputStream:** This class can be used to concatenate the data from one input stream with the data of another input stream.

- **PipedInputStream:** This class must be used with PipedOutputStream since it implements one-half of a pipe. This class is used for communication between threads. A thread would read from a PipedInputStream object.

- **ByteArrayInputStream:** This class implements an array of bytes to serve as an input stream. This class is similar to StringBufferInputStream.

- **FilterInputStream:** An abstract class for the filtering of input streams. It allows multiple input streams to be chained together so that the data can migrate through stages of processing. Objects of this class are not instantiated directly. Rather, input classes that do the special processing are subclassed from this class.

- **FileInputStream:** As a subclass of class InputStream, a FileInputStream is constructed from a File or FileDescriptor object with the purpose of reading data from a file. This class is only capable of reading data into individual bytes or arrays of bytes.

- **DataInput:** This interface has a collection of public abstract methods for reading Java built-in data types in a platform-independent way. This interface is implemented by the DataInputStream and RandomAccessFile classes.

- **PushbackInputStream:** As a subclass of FilterInputStream, this class has a one-byte buffer for "look ahead" reads. It has an unread() method for "pushing" the read character back into the input stream.

- **BufferedInputStream:** As a subclass of FilterInputStream, this class provides buffering for large blocks of data. Instead of constantly reading from streams that are associated with slow devices, BufferedInputStream objects cache the data in an internal buffer for quicker access.

- **LineNumberInputStream:** As a subclass of FilterInputStream, this class keeps track of the number of lines read from an input stream.

- **DataInputStream:** This class is probably the most popular class for doing input. It has methods for reading lines of text and all of the Java built-in types in a platform-independent way.

- **OutputStream:** An abstract class representing an output stream of bytes. It has abstract methods for writing bytes to a stream and for flushing the stream.

- **PipedOutputStream:** This class must be used with PipedInputStream since it implements one-half of a pipe. This class is used for communication between threads. A thread would write to a PipedOutputStream object.

- **ByteArrayOutputStream:** This class uses an internal array of bytes to serve as an output stream.

- **FileOutputStream:** As a subclass of class OutputStream, a FileOutputStream is constructed from a File or FileDescriptor object with the purpose of writing data to a file. This class is only capable of writing data from individual bytes or from arrays of bytes.

- **FilterOutputStream:** An abstract class for the filtering of output streams. It allows multiple output streams to be chained together so that the data can migrate through stages of processing. Objects of this class are not instantiated directly. Rather, output classes that do the special processing are subclassed from this class.

- **DataOutput:** This interface has a collection of public abstract methods for writing Java built-in data types in a platform-independent way. This interface is implemented by the DataOutputStream and RandomAccessFile classes.

- **PrintStream:** This class is probably the most popular class for doing output. This class has a series of overloaded print() and println() methods for displaying Java built-in types as text.

- **BufferedOutputStream:** As a subclass of `FilterOutputStream`, this class provides buffering for large blocks of data. Instead of writing to the stream every time, information is collected into the buffer until it is full or until a `flush()` is called to do the actual write.

- **DataOutputStream:** As a subclass of `FilterOutputStream`, this class has methods to write Java built-in types in a platform-independent way. All of the built-in types are written in a binary representation, not in an ASCII representation.

- **RandomAccessFile:** This class implements the `DataInput` and `DataOutput` interfaces. This class is not descended from either `InputStream` or `OutputStream` since it provides random instead of sequential access to files. The public interface for `RandomAccessFile` is essentially the union of the public interfaces for the `DataInputStream` and `DataOutputStream` classes.

One important thing to note about these classes is that they cannot be used within applets in ways that would violate security. Popular browsers like Netscape Navigator will check the retrieved applets to make sure that they cannot read and write to local files, delete files, execute local programs, make network connections to hosts (other than the host the applet originated from) and load libraries.

That completes the overview of the C++ and Java frameworks for streams. In the following topics, we will examine specific applications of some of the classes and their methods.

For more details on these frameworks, please refer to the following:

- *C++ IOStreams Handbook*
  by Steve Teale
  Addison-Wesley Publishing Company
  ISBN 0–201–59641–5

  This excellent book gives a very detailed account of the C++ iostreams framework, including implementation classes that are used by the main classes presented in the overview.

- *Java in a Nutshell: A Desktop Quick Reference for Java Programmers*
  David Flanagan
  O'Reilly & Associates, Inc.
  ISBN 1–56592–183–6

  This book is a very convenient reference guide covering all of the Java classes, interfaces and methods. Each of the standard Java packages is well illustrated with structured diagrams.

Getting Input with C++ `ifstream` and Java `DataInputStream`

The class frameworks for handling streams between C++ and Java have fairly equivalent capabilities. However, between the two languages, the frameworks are different by design. In this section, we are going to focus on the input of character data from the standard input device or from a text file.

The sample program that follows is a utility called `CatDemo`, which is based on the `cat` utility of UNIX or the `type` command of MSDOS. If the program is started without any command line arguments, then the program will immediately echo whatever the user had entered after the entry has been terminated by a return. The interaction stops after the user inputs an end-of-file (`ctrl-Z` in MSDOS or `ctrl-D` in UNIX). If the program has a number of command line arguments, each of which is a text file, then the contents of each will be displayed on the standard output device. If any file does not exist, then the user will be notified.

Below is the C++ version of the `CatDemo` program:

Listing 7-1: CatDemo.cpp

```cpp
#include <iostream.h>
#include <iomanip.h>
#include <fstream.h>
#include <io.h>
#include <fcntl.h>

const int MAX_SIZE = 81;

void GetAndDisplayKeyboardInput () {
char buffer[MAX_SIZE];
int input_status = 1;

while (input_status) {
   cin.getline(buffer, MAX_SIZE);
   if (cin.eof())
      break;
   cout<<buffer<<endl;
   }
}

void GetAndDisplayLines(const char * filename) {
char buffer[MAX_SIZE];
int input_status = 1;

ifstream infile(filename, ios::in | ios::nocreate);
if (!infile) {
```

```
      cout<<"File "<<filename<<" not found!"<<endl;
      cout<<endl;
      return;
      }

cout<<filename<<":"<<endl;
while (input_status) {
    infile.getline(buffer, MAX_SIZE);
    if (infile.eof())
       break;
    cout<<buffer<<endl;
    }
cout<<endl;
}

void main(int argc, char ** argv)
{

if (argc == 1)
   GetAndDisplayKeyboardInput();
else
if (argc > 1)
    for (int index = 1; index < argc; index++)
      GetAndDisplayLines(argv[index]);

}
```

If the above is executed without arguments from the command line:

```
CatDemo
```

there would be an interactive session until the user presses `ctrl-Z` (under MSDOS, Windows 95™ or Windows NT™). The non-italicized text is what the user enters and the italicized text is the output.

His clothes made him appear taller than his actual height.
His clothes made him appear taller than his actual height.
The cat curiously gazed into the mirror.
The cat curiously gazed into the mirror.
^Z

If the program is executed with command line parameters:

```
CatDemo   TERMS1.TXT   TERMS2.TXT   SLANG.TXT   TERMS3.TXT
```

then we can expect to see something like:

```
TERMS1.TXT:
apricot
blue
ale
cheetah
```

```
whisper

TERMS2.TXT:
lemon
auto
fan
restaurant
company

File SLANG.TXT not found!

TERMS3.TXT:
heavens
photography
cable
audio
mocha
```

The following is a discussion of the key points of this C++ example:

- Within function `main()`, the number of arguments is checked. When `CatDemo` is executed, there is a minimum of one argument, the first being the name of the program itself (`argv[0]`). If there is exactly one argument, processing goes to `GetAndDisplayKeyboardInput()`. If there is more than one, then there is at least one file name being passed. If that is the case, then a for loop will call `GetAndDisplayLines()` for each file name parameter.

- The function `GetAndDisplayKeyboardInput()` uses `cin`, a special, global `istream` variable that is associated with the standard input device. The `cin` object uses an `istream` member function called `getline()` to extract character data entered from the keyboard. The `getline()` function will extract up to `MAX_SIZE - 1` characters from the input stream buffer. The last position is reserved for the terminating character, which, by default, is the newline character (this can also be changed by specifying a different terminating character as the optional third argument to `getline()`).

  When the user finishes his keyboard entry by pressing `ctrl-Z`, the `ios::eofbit` within `cin` will be set. This bit is part of a bit mask that is used to control various states of the `istream` object. Class `ios` has a number of bits and bit masks and it is the ancestor class to all stream classes, including class `istream`. To check the `ios::eofbit`, `cin` would use the public accessor function `ios::eof()`.

  As we have seen many times before, variable `cout` is the special, global `ostream` variable associated with the standard output device.

- If function `GetAndDisplayLines()` is called, the first order of business is to see if the file with the given name can be opened. An attempt is made to instantiate an `ifstream` object `infile` by using constructor `ifstream::ifstream(const char *, int)`. The first argument is the file name and the second argument is the mode (open the <u>existing</u> file for reading). The second argument is specified by setting certain `ios` bits (`ios::in | ios::nocreate`).

    If the `ifstream::ifstream(const char *, int)` constructor fails, variable `infile` will be null, which basically means the file does not exist or it could not be opened for reading (lack of permissions). If the constructor succeeds, a `while` loop will have the `ifstream` object `infile` use `getline()` to extract blocks of data from its input file. As each block is extracted, it is written to the standard output device, which is represented by `cout`. The object `infile` can call `getline()` because `ifstream` is a subclass of `istream`. The `istream::getline()` function works the same way for `infile` as it did for `cin`.

Now, we will examine an equivalent `CatDemo` program written in Java:

Listing 7-2: CatDemo.java

```
import java.awt.*;
import java.io.*;

public class CatDemo {

    static void GetAndDisplayKeyboardInput(DataInputStream
     dataIn) {
    try {
        String inBuffer = null;
        while ((inBuffer = dataIn.readLine()) != null)
           System.out.println(inBuffer);
        }
    catch (IOException err) {
        System.out.println(err.toString());
        System.exit(1);
        }
    }

    static void GetAndDisplayLines(String filename,
                                    DataInputStream dataIn) {
    try {
        String inBuffer = null;
        System.out.println(filename+":");
        while ((inBuffer = dataIn.readLine()) != null)
           System.out.println(inBuffer);
        System.out.println();
```

```
            }
    catch (IOException err) {
        System.out.println(err.toString());
        System.exit(1);
        }
    }

    public static void main(String args[]) {

    DataInputStream dataInputStream = null;

    if (args.length == 0) {
        dataInputStream = new DataInputStream(System.in);
        GetAndDisplayKeyboardInput(dataInputStream);
        }
    else
    if (args.length > 0) {
        int index = 0;
        for (index = 0; index < args.length; index++) {
            try {
                dataInputStream =
                    new DataInputStream(new FileInputStream
                    (args[index]));
                GetAndDisplayLines(args[index], dataInputStream);
                try {
                    dataInputStream.close();
                    }
                catch(IOException err) {
                    System.err.println(err.toString());
                    System.exit(1);
                    }

                }
            catch(FileNotFoundException err) {
                System.out.println("File "+args[index]+" not
                found!");
                System.out.println();
                }
            }  // for
        }  // if (args.length > 0)
    }  // main

}
```

The stand-alone Java program above acts and behaves in the same manner as its C++ counterpart. The only difference is how the Java program would be started. In interactive mode (no parameters), the command line would look like:

```
java  CatDemo
```

The CatDemo parameter is understood to represent file CatDemo.class. If the program is intended to display the contents of files, then the command line would look something like:

```
java  CatDemo TERMS1.TXT  TERMS2.TXT  SLANG.TXT  TERMS3.TXT
```

The following is a summary of the main points of the Java sample:

- Like the C++ equivalent, the `main()` method is the starting point of the execution. In the case of Java, command line arguments are captured in an array of `String` objects. Furthermore, the counting of the arguments begins after the `.class` name entry. For the example above, there are four command line arguments (beginning with `TERMS1.TXT`) and the first one would be contained in `args[0]`.

- The `main()` method checks for the number of arguments and then determines the course of action. If the number of arguments is zero, a `DataInputStream` object is created from `System.in`, which represents the standard input device. The `DataInputStream` class is very useful because all primitive data types can be read from a stream in a platform-independent way. If the `DataInputStream` object (represented by variable `dataInputStream`) is successfully instantiated, the reference to the `DataInputStream` object is passed to method `GetAndDisplayKeyboardInput()`.

  Within `main()`, if the number of arguments is positive, a `for` loop will create a `FileInputStream` object from each file name. Each `FileInputStream` object represents the input file, which is to be opened for reading (`FileInputStream` has no write methods). If the file does not already exist, an `IOException` will be thrown. A `DataInputStream` object in turn is created with the `FileInputStream` object. If these instantiations are successful, then the file name and the reference to the `DataInputStream` object are passed to `GetAndDisplayLines()`.

- Within method `GetAndDisplayKeyboardInput()`, the primary way to read keyboard input is a method called `readLine()`. The `readLine()` method, which is part of the public interface of class `DataInputStream`, will extract input terminated by `\n`, `\r`, `\r\n` or the end-of-file character. The `readLine()` method will return a `String` object (which is referenced by variable `inBuffer`) and when the user presses `ctrl-Z` (for MSDOS systems), a null will be returned and the loop will exit.

- The `GetAndDisplayLines()` method works in a manner very similar to `GetAndDisplayKeyboardInput()`, except the file name associated with the `DataInputStream` object is also displayed.

Both the C++ and Java programs were written to be as similar as possible. Obviously, the differences lie in the way the stream classes and their public interfaces are used. For file input, one would create `DataInputStream` objects from `FileInputStream` objects in Java, whereas in C++, one would instantiate `ifstream` objects with the desired modes.

Generating Output with C++ `ofstream` and Java `PrintStream`

Earlier, we saw an example of how to create input streams from files for reading. For this section, we will focus on outputting to a file.

One of the observations that the reader will discover is that the support for input streams is balanced with complementary support for output streams. This is true whether the developer uses C++ or Java. Even the names of the classes and the methods are complementary.

For this topic, I will provide an example program called `SortFileDemo` to accept an input file of text data and have the contents sorted into an output file. The input file will consist of words, where each word is terminated with a new-line character.

Below is the C++ version of `SortFileDemo`:

Listing 7-3: SortFileDemo.cpp

```cpp
#include <iostream.h>
#include <iomanip.h>
#include <fstream.h>
#include <stdlib.h>
#include <string.h>
#include <io.h>
#include <fcntl.h>

typedef char * char_ptr;

const int MAX_SIZE = 256;

void Partition(char ** str, int left, int right) {
int index1;
int index2;
char * curr_str = 0;
char * temp_str = 0;

index1 = left;
index2 = right;

curr_str = str[(left+right)/2];

do {
    while ( (strcmp(str[index1], curr_str)<0) && (index1 <
    right) ) index1++;
    while ( (strcmp(curr_str, str[index2])<0) && (index2 > left) )
    index2-;
```

```
   if (index1 <= index2) {
     temp_str    = str[index1];
     str[index1] = str[index2];
     str[index2] = temp_str;
     index1++;
     index2-;
     }
   } while (index1 <= index2);

if (left < index2)  Partition(str, left, index2);
if (index1 < right) Partition(str, index1, right);
}

void Quicksort(char ** str, int num_recs) {
Partition(str, 0, num_recs-1);
}

void ReadAndSortFile(const char * source_file, const char *
 target_file) {
char buffer[MAX_SIZE];
char ** record = 0;
int count = 0;
int input_status = 1;
int index;

ifstream infile(source_file, ios::in | ios::nocreate);
if (!infile) {
    cout<<"File "<<source_file<<" not found!"<<endl;
    cout<<endl;
    return;
    }

ofstream outfile(target_file, ios::out);
if (!outfile) {
    cout<<"File "<<target_file<<" not found!"<<endl;
    cout<<endl;
    return;
    }

while (input_status) {
   infile.getline(buffer, MAX_SIZE);
   if (infile.eof())
      break;
   count++;
   }

record = new char_ptr[count];

infile.clear();    // Reset the ios::eofbit
```

```
infile.seekg(0);   // Put the file pointer to the beginning of the
  file

index = 0;

while (input_status) {
    infile.getline(buffer, MAX_SIZE);
    if (infile.eof())
        break;
    record[index] = new char[strlen(buffer)+1];
    strcpy(record[index++], buffer);
    }

Quicksort(record, count);

for (index = 0; index < count; index++)
    outfile<<record[index]<<endl;

delete [] record;

infile.close();
outfile.close();
}

void main(int argc, char ** argv)
{

if (argc != 3) {
    cout<<"Usage: SortFileDemo <source file> <target
     file>"<<endl;
    return;
    }
ReadAndSortFile(argv[1], argv[2]);

}
```

The program above would be executed from the command line as:

```
SortFileDemo   TERMS1.TXT   TERMS2.TXT
```

where "TERMS1.TXT" is an existing input file and "TERMS2.TXT" is the target
output file. The contents of "TERMS1.TXT" might contain the following:

```
x-ray
mill
silo
painting
ceiling
shallow
deep
```

```
errand
generous
thoughtful
verify
epilog
```

and the contents of `"TERMS2.TXT"` would contain:

```
ceiling
deep
epilog
errand
generous
mill
painting
shallow
silo
thoughtful
verify
x-ray
```

Below is a summary of the main points about the sample program:

- The execution starts with function `main()`, where the number of command line arguments is checked. The program name must be given exactly two file names, one for reading and the other for writing. If the command line entry is good, the file names are passed to function `ReadAndSortFile()`.

- `ReadAndSortFile()` will take the file names and attempt to create an `ifstream` object (for input) and an `ofstream` object (for output). Each of the stream objects will create file descriptors for the file names and store the descriptors internally. The mode (second parameter) of the `ifstream` object, `infile`, is set to read-only (`ios::in`, the default) and the input file must already exist (`ios::nocreate`). The mode of the `ofstream` object, `outfile`, is set to write-only (`ios::out`, the default). The output file need not already exist (if it does, then it will be overridden). The mode for each of the stream objects is set by enabling certain bits in a bit mask contained in class `ios`, which is the ancestor of `ifstream` and `ofstream`.

  If the attempt to open either file fails, `ReadAndSortFile()` exits and the program terminates.

  If the file streams are successfully created, the lines of the input file stream will be read into an array of strings (`char *`). However, before the array is allocated, the input file stream is first read to determine the number of lines. An array of (`char *`) is then allocated with:

```
record = new char_ptr[count];
```

After that, the input file stream's `ios:eofbit` is cleared and the stream's file pointer is reset to the beginning of the file:

```
infile.clear();        // Reset the ios::eofbit
infile.seekg(0);       // Put the file pointer to the beginning
                       // of the file
```

The input file stream is then read until the end-of-file and each line is stored as an array element. The storage for each element is dynamically allocated from the heap.

When the input file has been read, the array of strings and the number of elements is sent to function `Quicksort()` to put the strings into ascending order.

When the sort completes, each element of the sorted array is written to the output file stream.

The `ReadAndSortFile()` completes with the deallocation of the array of strings with:

```
delete [] record;
```

which will perform a cascaded deallocation of all elements and the initial storage for the element pointers. The input and output file streams are also closed.

- The Quicksort algorithm is considered one of the most efficient means of sorting large amounts of data. While the standard C library provides a Quicksort function called `qsort()`, there is no such equivalent in Java, so the decision was made to provide a custom `Quicksort()` function just to be consistent. Besides, this is a good way to illustrate that functions can be recursive in either C++ or Java.

  The heart of the `Quicksort()` function is actually the `Partition()` function. The `Partition()` function would begin by taking a range of array elements and first recording the endpoint index values (`left` and `right`). Within the middle of the range, an element is selected as the model for comparison. The whole idea is to try to find the model's permanent location within the range. Ideally, the elements to the left of the model should be less than the model (lexically speaking) and the elements to the right of the model should be greater than the model.

  Two indexes, `index1` and `index2`, serve as iterators. The `index1` iterator starts from the left and determines if the string it is currently pointing to is less than the model and will continue to traverse to the right until it finds a string that is greater than or equal to the model. The index2 iterator works in a similar fashion, except it traverses from the right and stops at the first string that is less than or equal to the model.

When both iterators stop traversing and index1 is less than index2, then the addresses contained within str[index1] and str[index2] are swapped. Iterator index1 is incremented by one and iterator index2 is decremented by one.

If index1 is less than or equal to index2, the traversing will start again at the top of the do loop. If index1 is greater than index2, then the iterators have passed each other. At this point if [left, index2] is a valid range or [index1, right] is a valid range, the Partition() function will be called recursively for these sub-ranges. These recursive calls continue until there are ranges of two elements and there can no longer be any calls because the elements are already in order.

Now, let us look at a Java equivalent to the above C++ example:

Listing 7-4: SortFileDemo.java

```java
import java.awt.*;
import java.io.*;

public class SortFileDemo {

    static void Partition(String [] str, int left, int right) {
    int index1;
    int index2;
    String curr_str = null;
    String temp_str = null;

    index1 = left;
    index2 = right;

    curr_str = str[(left+right)/2];

    do {
        while ( (str[index1].compareTo(curr_str) < 0) && (index1
           < right) ) index1++;
        while ( (curr_str.compareTo(str[index2]) < 0) && (index2
           > left)  ) index2-;

    if (index1 < index2) {
        temp_str     = str[index1];
        str[index1] = str[index2];
        str[index2] = temp_str;
        index1++;
```

```
            index2−;
            }
    else
    if (index1 == index2) {
        index1++;
        index2−;
        }

    } while (index1 <= index2);

if (left < index2)  Partition(str, left,  index2);
if (index1 < right) Partition(str, index1, right);
}

static void Quicksort(String [] str, int num_recs) {
Partition(str, 0, num_recs−1);
}

static void ReadAndSortFile(String source_file, String
 target_file) throws IOException {
String line = null;

int count = 0;
int index;

RandomAccessFile ins = new RandomAccessFile(source_file,
 "r");
PrintStream ps = new PrintStream(new FileOutputStream
 (target_file));

while ((line = ins.readLine()) != null) {
    count++;
    }

String record[] = new String[count];

ins.seek(0);

index = 0;

while ((line = ins.readLine()) != null) {
    record[index++] = line;
    }

Quicksort(record, count);

for (index = 0; index < count; index++)
    ps.println(record[index]);
```

```
    ins.close();
    ps.close();
    }

    public static void main(String args[]) {

    if (args.length != 2) {
       System.err.println
          ("Usage: java SortFileDemo <source file> <target
          file>");
       return;
       }
    try {
        ReadAndSortFile(args[0], args[1]);
        }
    catch(IOException err) {
        System.err.println(err.toString());
        System.exit(1);
        }
    }

}
```

Execution of the Java version with the same file parameters will yield the same results as those for the C++ example. The only difference is in the way the Java program is executed from the command line:

```
java   SortFileDemo   TERMS1.TXT   TERMS2.TXT
```

Structurally, the Java program is very close to its C++ counterpart. The following summary discusses the differences between the two versions.

- Within the `main()` method, we once again check for the number of parameters. In this case we look for exactly two arguments (whatever is after `SortFileDemo` on the command line). Since many of the methods of the `java.io` package are capable of throwing exceptions, we must use `try` and `catch` blocks to deal with possible exceptions. In the C++ version, we had relied on the traditional approach of checking return codes or checking the state of the stream object.

- If there are exactly two arguments, method `main()` will call method `ReadAndSortFile()`. Here is where there are a few differences from the protocols used in C++ and even earlier Java examples. The input file name is used to create a `RandomAccessFile` object in read-only mode (ins). The reason `RandomAccessFile` was chosen and not `DataInputStream` is because this class has all the methods necessary to rewind the file pointer back to the beginning of the file (as we will see shortly).

Similarly, the output file name is used to create a `PrintStream` object for collecting output (ps).

The first order of business is to have the `RandomAccessFile` object count how many lines there are in its input file by doing reads until the end-of-file. This is accomplished with the help of the `readLine()` method, which will look for the newline character or the end-of-file character as the terminator.

An array of `String` object references (record) is then instantiated to accommodate the number of lines in the input file. The file pointer within the `RandomAccessFile` object is then reset to the beginning of the file with:

```
ins.seek(0);
```

Now, when `ins` reads its input file a second time, each line read is assigned to an element of the array `record`.

When the input file has been read, the array of `String` references, record, and the number of elements, count, are passed to the `Quicksort()` method.

When the sorting has completed, the elements of `record` are written to the output stream with:

```
for (index = 0; index < count; index++)
    ps.println(record[index]);
```

The `ReadAndSortFile()` method then concludes with the closing of the `RandomAccessFile` object and the `PrintStream` object.

- The implementations of the `Quicksort()` and `Partition()` methods are nearly identical to their C++ counterparts. Like C++, recursion is also supported in Java. I will not describe the Quicksort algorithm again, since this has been done earlier with the summarization of the C++ version.

A minor difference between the versions of `Partition()` is the way the contents of `String` objects are compared. In C and C++, the standard library function for string comparison is `strcmp()`. Here is the function prototype and the meaning of the various return values:

```
int strcmp( const char * string1, const char * string2 );
```

Return Value	Relationship
< 0	string1 is less than string2
0	string1 is equal to string2
> 0	string1 is greater than string2

In Java, the method to perform string comparisons is `compareTo()`, which is part of the public interface of class `String`. If `string1` and `string2` were Java `String` objects, the `compareTo()` method might be used as:

```
int  value = string1.compareTo(string2);
```

The Java `compareTo()` method also returns an `int` with the same semantics as the table above for `strcmp()` from C.

Finding the Attributes of a File

Determining the attributes of a file, like its permissions, size and location, is one of the most basic and useful services for the application developer. However, the means for finding such information varies from one operating system to another, not to mention that some operating systems have more than one underlining file system. This could present some tacky problems in the area of portability.

In this section, I will present an interactive, command line program where the user enters a file name and the program returns information about the file, provided that it exists. The example will be presented in both C++ and Java. The C++ version runs on Microsoft Windows NT™ and was written with the help of applications programming interface (API) functions from Microsoft Visual C++ 4.0™.

Let us first examine the C++ version. The following is the listing of the source:

Listing 7-5: FileAttributesDemo.cpp

```
#include <iostream.h>
#include <iomanip.h>
#include <fstream.h>
#include <io.h>
#include <fcntl.h>
#include <string.h>
#include <sys/types.h>
#include <sys/stat.h>
#include <stdio.h>
#include <conio.h>
#include <stdlib.h>
#include <direct.h>

const int MAX_SIZE = 256;

enum FTYPE { FILE_TYPE, DIR_TYPE };

void DisplayFileAttributes(const char * filename, int fd,
                           enum FTYPE ftype) {
```

```cpp
int not_readable  = _access(filename, 4);
int not_writeable = _access(filename, 2);

char fpath[_MAX_PATH];
if( _fullpath( fpath, filename, _MAX_PATH ) == NULL ) {
   cerr<<"Absolute path cannot be found for file
    "<<filename<<endl;
   return;
   }

// Display all of the information collected

cout<<endl;
if (ftype == FILE_TYPE)
   cout<<"Attributes of File: "<<filename<<endl;
if (ftype == DIR_TYPE)
   cout<<"Attributes of Directory: "<<filename<<endl;

cout<<"Absolute path: "<<fpath<<endl;
cout<<"Readable: "<<(!not_readable?"Yes":"No")<<endl;
cout<<"Writeable: "<<(!not_writeable?"Yes":"No")<<endl;

if (ftype == FILE_TYPE) {
   struct _stat sbuffer;
   int ret_val = _fstat(fd, &sbuffer);
   if (ret_val) {
      cerr<<"Invalid file descriptor"<<endl;
      return;
      }
   cout<<"Length of file: "<<sbuffer.st_size<<endl;
   }
if (ftype == DIR_TYPE) {
   char * cmd = new char[strlen("dir /b ")+strlen(filename)+1];
   strcpy(cmd, "dir /b ");
   strcat(cmd, filename);
   cout<<endl;
   cout<<filename<<" contains:"<<endl;
   system(cmd);
   delete [] cmd;
   }
}

void EditFileName(const char * filename) {
int fd;
char curr_dir[_MAX_PATH];

// Get the current working directory
if( _getcwd(curr_dir, _MAX_PATH ) == NULL ) {
   cout<<"Unable to get current directory"<<endl;
```

```
        return;
        }

if ((fd = _open(filename, _O_RDONLY)) != -1)
    DisplayFileAttributes(filename, fd, FILE_TYPE);
else
if (!_chdir(filename)) {  // If filename is a directory, this
    // should work
    _chdir(curr_dir);       // Change the current directory back to
        // the original
    DisplayFileAttributes(filename, fd, DIR_TYPE);
    }
else {
    cerr<<"File "<<filename<<" does not exist!"<<endl;
    return;
    }

}

void main(int argc, char ** argv)
{
char line[MAX_SIZE];
int done = 0;

do {
    cout<<"\nEnter the name of a file or directory or press EOF
     to exit: " <<flush;

    if (!cin.eof()) {
       cin.getline(line, MAX_SIZE);
       if (strlen(line) != 0)
         EditFileName(line);
       }

    } while(!cin.eof());
}
```

An interactive session of the above program might yield something like the following. The non-italicized text is entered by the user and the italicized text is the output.

Enter the name of a file or directory or press EOF to exit:
 TERMS1.TXT

Attributes of File: TERMS1.TXT
Absolute path: C:\MSDEV\Projects\FileAttributesDemo\TERMS1.TXT
Readable: Yes
Writeable: Yes
Length of file: 99

```
Enter the name of a file or directory or press EOF to exit:
 TERMS2.TXT

Attributes of File: TERMS2.TXT
Absolute path: C:\MSDEV\Projects\FileAttributesDemo\TERMS2.TXT
Readable: Yes
Writeable: No
Length of file: 99

Enter the name of a file or directory or press EOF to exit:
 TERMS3.TXT
File TERMS3.TXT does not exist!

Enter the name of a file or directory or press EOF to exit:
Document

Attributes of Directory: Documents
Absolute path: C:\MSDEV\Projects\FileAttributesDemo\Documents
Readable: Yes
Writeable: Yes

Documents contains:
ADDR01.DOC
ADDR02.DOC
TOPICS.DOC
GRAPH1.GIF

Enter the name of a file or directory or press EOF to exit: Memos

Attributes of Directory: Memos
Absolute path: C:\MSDEV\Projects\FileAttributesDemo\Memos
Readable: Yes
Writeable: No

Memos contains:
LETTER1.DOC
LETTER2.DOC
TASKS.DOC

Enter the name of a file or directory or press EOF to exit:
 C:\UTIL

Attributes of Directory: C:\UTIL
Absolute path: C:\UTIL
Readable: Yes
Writeable: Yes

C:\UTIL contains:
PKUNZIP.EXE
```

```
PKZIP.EXE
PKZIPFIX.EXE
ZIP2EXE.EXE
```

Enter the name of a file or directory or press EOF to exit: ^Z

Now, we will walk through the code to get a basic understanding of the utility functions that were used.

- Starting from function `main()`, the processing enters a loop where the user is prompted to enter the name of a file or directory. On the first line with `cout`, the statement ends with a C++ manipulator called `flush`, which is a call to empty everything from the internal buffer onto the screen. Unlike `endl`, `flush` does not write a newline character, so the blinking cursor will immediately follow the text prompt.

  If the user enters at least one character, the `EditFileName()` function will be called. If he enters the end-of-file (`ctrl-Z` on MSDOS, `ctrl-D` on UNIX), the program exits.

- The `EditFileName()` function basically has the responsibility to determine whether the file name entered represents an existing file, an existing directory or something non-existent. There is a rather curious approach to determine whether an existing name represents a file or a directory. There is no system function in Windows 95™ or Windows NT™ to simply query whether the name is a directory. Rather, an attempt must be made to change the current directory (using `_chdir()`) to the supposed directory represented by the name. If the call is successful, then we know the name is a directory.

  When `EditFileName()` begins, its first task is to find the current working directory and save it. It does that with the API `_getcwd()` function. Next, an attempt is made to open the file name as an existing file. If that is not successful, then the file name may be an existing directory. The API `_chdir()` is applied to the name. If that call is not successful, then we know the name does not represent either a file or directory.

  If the file name does represent a file or directory, function `DisplayFileAttributes()` is called and passed the file name, the file descriptor and the file type (regular file or directory).

- The `DisplayFileAttributes()` function does the busy work of using a number of API functions to gather attribute information about the file or directory. Some attributes are only relevant to certain file types, like the size in bytes for a file or the contents of a directory. After all of the data has been gathered, the data is neatly displayed on the standard output device.

`DisplayFileAttributes()` first uses the API function `_access()` to find whether the file or directory is readable or writeable. The second argument of `_access()` is the mode. The value 2 is used to check the write bit while the value 4 is used to check the read bit.

The API function, `_fullpath()`, is used to find and construct the absolute path name from the given file name.

The `_fstat()` API function is similar to the traditional UNIX `stat()` function, except `_fstat()` is used only after a file has been successfully opened. It uses a predefined data structure (`struct _stat`) to store information about the file. One such piece of information is the length or size of the file in bytes (`sbuffer.st_size`).

Finally, if the file type is a directory, the `system()` API function is used to perform a directory listing. Under MSDOS, Windows 95™ and Windows NT™, the interactive command is `dir` and a complete command line string is constructed before calling `system()`. For simplicity, only the file and directory names contained within the directory are listed.

After displaying all of the information about the file or directory, the `DisplayFileAttributes()` function returns back to the caller and the flow of control eventually returns to `main()`, where the user is prompted to enter another entry.

One observation about the C++ example is that there are quite a number of individual API functions to remember in order to gather what one needs. Furthermore, there are API functions that are not available on every operating system. System directory functions like `opendir()`, `closedir()` and `readdir()` from UNIX are non-existent in Microsoft Visual C++ 4.0™.

Another problem is that a traditional API function may not necessarily be used in the manner that it was originally intended. Visual C++ does have a `_stat()` function that parallels the UNIX `stat()` function and even has the same data structure (`struct _stat`) to capture the results of the call. However, the `st_ino` member of `struct _stat` represents the `inode`, which is used to find file permissions in UNIX. For PC file systems like FAT, HPFS and NTFS, the `st_ino` member is meaningless.

One further point about the C++ example is that the API functions are all C-style functions. The C++ `iostreams` and `fstreams` class libraries do not provide any classes or methods for determining file attributes.

On the other hand, Java has a standard class called `File`, which provides a number of methods for finding file attributes. The following is the source listing of the Java equivalent to the C++ program:

Listing 7-6: FileAttributesDemo.java

```java
import java.awt.*;
import java.io.*;

public class FileAttributeDemo {

    static void DisplayFileAttributes(File fobj) {

    System.out.println();
    System.out.println("Attributes of File: "+fobj.getName());
    System.out.println("Absolute path: "+fobj.getAbsolutePath());
    System.out.println("Readable: "+ (fobj.canRead()?
     "Yes":"No"));
    System.out.println("Writeable: "+ (fobj.canWrite()?
     "Yes":"No"));
    if (fobj.isFile())
       System.out.println("Length of file: "+fobj.length());
    if (fobj.isDirectory()) {
       System.out.println();
       System.out.println(fobj.getName()+" contains:");
       String [] element = fobj.list();
       for (int index=0; index<element.length; index++)
          System.out.println(element[index]);
       }
    }

    static void EditFileName(String filename) {

    try {
        File file_obj = new File(filename);
        if (file_obj.exists())
           DisplayFileAttributes(file_obj);
        else
           System.out.println(file_obj.getName()+" does not
            exist!");
        }
    catch (NullPointerException err) {
        System.err.println(err.toString());
        }
    }

    public static void main(String args[]) {

    try {
        String line = null;

        DataInputStream ins = new DataInputStream(System.in);
        do {
```

```
        System.out.print
          ("\nEnter the name of a file or directory or press
            EOF to exit: ");
        System.out.flush();

        if ((line = ins.readLine()) != null)
            if (line.length() != 0)
                EditFileName(line);

        } while (line != null);

    }
catch (IOException err) {
    System.err.println(err.toString());
    }
}

}
```

The execution of the Java equivalent with the same input data will produce the same results. The look and feel is also identical except for the initial execution of the application from the command line:

```
java  FileAttributesDemo
```

One observation the reader may have noticed is that the Java source is much shorter and more concise than the C++ version. That is because all of the public methods that one needs are contained within class `File`. Below is a summarization of the Java version.

- Within method `main()`, a `DataInputStream` object (`ins`) is first created from the standard input device (represented by `System.in`). By doing this, the programmer has access to method `readLine()`, which provides a convenient way to enter individual lines of text terminated by the newline character. Whenever the user enters at least one character, the method `EditFileName()` will be called. This interaction continues until the user enters the end-of-file character (`ctrl-Z` on MSDOS and `ctrl-D` on UNIX).

- Within `EditFileName()`, a `File` object (`file_obj`) is created from the file name that was passed to it by caller `EditFileName()`. The main task of the `EditFileName()` method is to determine whether the file name really represents an existing entity (file or directory) or not. The `File` object does this by calling method `exists()`. If the method returns true, then method `DisplayFileAttributes()` is called. No special effort is required to determine whether the object is a file or a directory since this information is kept within the `File` object itself.

- The `DisplayFileAttributes()` method simply displays the attributes contained with the `File` object that was passed to it from `EditFileName()`. The `File` class has a number of public methods to retrieve the attributes: `getName()`, `getAbsolutePath()`, `canRead()`, `canWrite()`, `length()`, `list()`, `isFile()` and `isDirectory()`. If the `File` object really represents a directory, then the `list()` method will return an array of `String` objects, where each element is either a file name or a sub-directory name.

Summary: Unlike the collection of C API functions, the Java `File` class provides a nice, consistent and portable interface to get a file's attributes from operating systems that have Java support. With the `File` class, the developer is spared from dealing with the details of the operating system.

Formatting Output in C++

Currently, C++ enjoys an advantage over Java in that the C++ `iostreams` class libraries provide a lot of support for formatted output. With these libraries, the programmer can display data within fields, control left and right justification of text, set the precision of floating point numbers, select fixed or scientific notations, etc. On the other hand, the standard Java streams library (version 1.0.x) does not provide any of this support.

Nevertheless, despite these shortcomings of Java, I have provided the reader with a special class called `IOS` to deal with the formatting of output. We will first concentrate on understanding how the formatting functions work in C++ and then I will provide an overview of the custom Java `IOS` class in the next section. The latter has been designed to mimic most of the C++ formatting functions given the rules and constraints of the Java language.

Within the C++ `iostreams` hierarchy is the very important base class called `ios`. Class `ios` contains a series of bit masks that determine what sort of controls should be performed on the output. For instance, there is a bit mask for left and right justification of text. There is another to choose the radix (decimal, octal or hexadecimal) of an integer. Furthermore, there is still another for choosing numerical representation (fixed or scientific notation) for floating point numbers. The setting or unsetting of these formatting bits is done through a series of public `ios` member functions. In many instances, there is more than one way to set these bits. In short, there are numerous ways to arrive at a desired result.

The C++ `ios` class also has public member functions for the programmer to set output field sizes, choose fill characters and set precision for numerical output. There are also some control features that are a bit more uncommon and obscure.

We will examine how these formatting functions are used through a series of examples.

The first example deals with field widths and selecting a fill character:

```
char * bird = "penguin";
char * fish = "rock cod";
char * tree = "maple";

cout.fill('~');
cout.width(12);
cout <<bird<<endl;
cout.width(12);
cout <<fish<<endl;
cout <<tree<<endl;
```

The output would appear as:

```
~~~~~penguin
~~~~rock cod
maple
```

In all of the examples, `cout`, the global `ofstream` object attached to the standard output device, is modified with the desired formatting characteristics. However, whatever applies to `cout` can also be applied to any instance of `ofstream`. The sample C++ program that demonstrates all of these scenarios, IOSDemo, uses unique instances of `ofstream` and has the output written to files. IOSDemo can be found on the supplied media.

Before the code executes, there are certain default formatting characteristics of `cout`. By default, right justification and a fill character of a space is the norm. <u>Furthermore, the default for a text field size is zero, which means that the field should exactly accommodate whatever the size of the text should be.</u>

In the example above, we use the member function `fill()` to choose the tilde (~) as the fill character and use member function `width()` to set the field size to 12 characters. Each of `fill()` and `width()` will return the previous fill character and field size, respectively. The first line of output (with `"penguin"`) is displayed as anticipated.

One thing about the field width specification is that the setting for the size is only good for one write invocation. If the same or different field size is desired for subsequent write invocations, then `width()` must be applied to the `ofstream` object again. Except for field width, all formatting characteristics are maintained by the `ofstream` object for all write invocations until the programmer sets the attribute to a different value. This phenomenon is demonstrated by the last two lines of output. Note that the default field width of zero is applied to variable tree in statement `cout <<tree<<endl;`.

The above code sample can also be rewritten with the use of C++ manipulators. The same output would be produced:

```
char * bird = "penguin";
```

```
char * fish = "rock cod";
char * tree = "maple";

cout<<setfill('~')<<setw(12)<<bird<<endl;
cout <<setw(12)<<fish<<endl;
cout <<tree<<endl;
```

A manipulator is basically a special function that is used to filter or alter an input or output stream. The inset, *How C++ Manipulators Work*, describes manipulators in greater detail. Manipulators are not in Java because they require operator overloading, a feature omitted from Java.

Some of the `ofstream` member functions have manipulators. For instance, function `fill()` corresponds to manipulator `setfill()` and function `width()` corresponds to `setw()`. The usage and syntax of `ofstream` variables with the insertion operator and manipulators is somewhat similar to the use of UNIX pipes from the command line.

How C++ Manipulators Work

Programmers who are new to C++ may be baffled by how manipulators seem to work. Manipulators take on the appearance of being special key-words, but in reality they are functions designed to massage a data input stream or a data output stream. In addition to manipulators such as `dec`, `oct` and `hex`, which are part of the standard C++ library (defined in header file `iostream.h`), the programmer is free to write manipulators of his own. For instance, suppose the developer wants a more convenient way to set justification within a field. He can write a `left` justification manipulator as:

```
ostream &  left(ostream & os) {
return  os<<resetiosflags(ios::right)<<setiosflags(ios::left);
}
```

or a `right` justification manipulator as:

```
ostream &  right(ostream & os) {
return  os<<resetiosflags(ios::left)<<setiosflags(ios::right);
}
```

With these custom-written `left` and `right` manipulators, a developer can simply set the field justification with statements like:

```
char * feline = "bob cat";
cout<<left<<setfill('#')<<setw(12)<<feline<<endl;
cout<<right<<setfill('*')<<setw(12)<<feline<<endl;
```

and the output would appear as:

```
bob cat#####
*****bob cat
```

This is much easier than using the `setf()`/`unsetf()` combination of functions or the `setiosflags()`/`resetiosflags()` combination of manipulators.

Now, the question arises: what makes this work? These custom-written manipulators work because of a predefined dispatcher function in `iostream.h`. The dispatcher function might be defined as:

```
ostream & operator<<(ostream & os, ostream & (*func)
 (ostream &)) {
return (*func)(os);
}
```

The actual implementation details may vary from vendor to vendor. However, this is the gist of what the dispatcher function would look like.

The dispatcher function is actually an overloading of the << operator as a non-member function. The second argument, `ostream & (*func) (ostream &)`, actually represents a pointer to a function, which is expressed as `(*func)`. The signature of `(*func)` has an argument list that takes a single type, `(ostream &)` and returns an `ostream &` (a reference to an ostream object). Also, note that within the implementation of the dispatcher function, the first argument, `os`, is also an argument to `(*func)`.

Now, let us take a simple statement like:

```
cout<<left;
```

and see what happens when it is executed. First of all, the statement can be rewritten as:

```
operator<<(cout, left);
```

which is the equivalent prefix notation in C++ (`operator<<` could very well be replaced by a name, hence underscoring the point that operators are really functions with syntactically convenient symbols).

Now, the signature of `operator<<(cout, left)` matches the signature of the dispatcher function. The global variable `cout` is an existing `ostream` object and `left` is a pointer to a function (a function name by itself represents the pointer to the function). Furthermore, `left` does take exactly one argument, a `(ostream &)` and returns `ostream &`. Hence, the compiler will call the dispatcher function.

Variable `cout` and pointer to function `left` are passed as parameters into the dispatcher function. Within the dispatcher function, `cout` is passed as an argument to `left`, as we can see from:

```
return (*func)(os);        // implementation of the dispatcher
                           function
```

The above statement will invoke left(ostream & os), which will disable the ios::right bit, enable the ios::left bit and return an ostream &. The flow of control would then go back to the return statement of the dispatcher function. The dispatcher function then returns an ostream &, which completes the execution of the original statement cout<<left;.

The next example has to do with precision or the display of significant digits from floating point numbers.

```
double num1 = 17.7875678;
cout.precision(8);
cout<<num1<<endl;
```

The output would appear as:

```
17.787568
```

Without specifying a precision, the default precision is up to six. If the number exceeds the precision value, a potential rounding up is performed before the number is displayed. If the floating point number is very small with respect to the precision, then the compiler will resort to scientific notation.

The precision() member function also has a manipulator equivalent, setprecision(). Below is the equivalent code:

```
double num1 = 17.7875678;
cout<<setprecision(8)<<num1<<endl;
```

Integral types can also be displayed as octal or hexadecimal. Below is an example:

```
int num1 = 160;

cout.setf(ios::oct, ios::basefield);
cout<<"Octal = "<<num1<<endl;
cout.setf(ios::showbase);
cout<<"Octal = "<<num1<<endl;
cout.setf(ios::hex, ios::basefield);
cout<<"Hexadecimal = "<<num1<<endl;
cout.setf(ios::uppercase);
cout<<"Hexadecimal = "<<num1<<endl;
cout.setf(ios::dec, ios::basefield);
cout<<"Decimal = "<<num1<<endl;
```

An execution of the above would yield the following output:

```
Octal = 240
Octal = 0240
Hexadecimal = 0xa0
Hexadecimal = 0XA0
Decimal = 160
```

Without an explicit setting of the radix, the default is decimal. The main `ios` member functions used for toggling the bits are `setf()` and `unsetf()`. As you will see, these two functions can be used in a variety of situations.

For radix selection, the `setf()` function is used above. The first argument to `setf()` is either `ios::dec, ios::oct` or `ios::hex`. Each of these are values of an enumerated type defined within class `ios`. The second argument, `ios::basefield`, is used to clear the bit mask before setting the radix bit of interest.

 Warning: `setf()` is an overloaded function with either one argument (`setf(long)`) or two arguments (`setf(long, long)`). The two-argument implementation is the preferred one to use since the second argument is for clearing the bit mask (which is the justification mask, radix mask or numerical representation mask). For radix selection, each radix has its own bit and if more than one of these bits is set, the outcome is really undefined (actually, each vendor provides some default, but you cannot rely on these defaults if portability is a concern). Using the two-argument implementation will assure you that only the bits you want set will be set.

The above example also illustrates two other bits: `ios::showbase` and `ios::uppercase`. The setting of the `ios::showbase` bit will display `"0"` for octal and `"0x"` for hexadecimal. If the `ios::uppercase` bit is enabled, then all hexadecimal-related alphabets (`X, A, B, C, D, E, F`) will be in upper case. In addition, displays in scientific notation will use `"E,"` instead of `"e."`

There are also manipulators for setting the bits of a bit mask. An equivalent to the above radix example would be:

```
int num1 = 160;

cout<<setiosflags(ios::oct)<<"Octal = "<<num1<<endl;
cout<<setiosflags(ios::showbase)<<"Octal = "<<num1<<endl;
cout<<resetiosflags(ios::oct)<<setiosflags(ios::hex)
    <<"Hexadecimal =" <<num1<<endl;
cout<<setiosflags(ios::uppercase)<<"Hexadecimal ="
    <<num1<<endl;
cout<<resetiosflags(ios::hex)<<setiosflags(ios::dec) <<"Decimal ="
    <<num1<<endl;
```

The `setiosflags()` and `resetiosflags()` manipulators are analogous to the `setf()` and `unsetf()` functions, respectively. The enabling or disabling of bits can be done with either set of routines. There is one exception: the `setiosflags()` manipulator only comes with a one-argument implementation. Hence, its use should be complemented with `resetiosflags()` for disabling bits.

The setting of the radix is a fairly common necessity, so the use of either of the two schemes above can get pretty tedious. Fortunately, there is a more straight-forward way:

```
int num1 = 160;

cout<<oct<<"Octal = "<<num1<<endl;
cout <<setiosflags(ios::showbase)<<"Octal = "<<num1<<endl;
cout <<hex<<"Hexadecimal = "<<num1<<endl;
cout <<setiosflags(ios::uppercase)<<"Hexadecimal =
  "<<num1<<endl;
cout <<dec<<"Decimal = "<<num1<<endl;
```

The special manipulators, dec, oct and hex are a convenient, abbreviated way to perform a resetiosflags() with a setiosflags() on the radix bit of interest.

The next example illustrates how output can be justified within a field of a particular size:

```
char * feline = "bob cat";
long    lnum   = 757905;
double dnum    = 2345070.00915756;

cout.setf(ios::left, ios::adjustfield);
cout.fill('#');
cout.width(12);
cout.precision(14);
cout<<feline<<endl;
cout.width(12);
cout<<lnum<<endl;
cout.width(12);
cout<<dnum<<endl;

cout.unsetf(ios::left);
cout.fill('*');
cout.width(12);
cout.precision(14);
cout<<feline<<endl;
cout.width(12);
cout<<lnum<<endl;
cout.width(12);
cout<<dnum<<endl;
```

The results of the execution would be:

```
bob cat#####
757905######
2345070.0091576
*****bob cat
******757905
2345070.0091576
```

As mentioned earlier, right justification is the default. Hence, there must be an explicit effort to request left justification. For this example, a non-space was chosen as the fill character so that the entire width of the field can be seen. One interesting thing about this example is that the precision value takes precedence over the width of the field. The double in this example has 15 significant digits, so a round-up is performed in order to display 14 of the digits, which goes beyond the field size.

Returning to right justification mode is done by using unsetf(ios::left) or by using setf(ios::right, ios::adjustfield).

The ios::left and ios::right bits can also be enabled or disabled using the setiosflags() and resetiosflags() manipulators. Unfortunately, there are no convenience manipulators called left or right, as in the case for radix control. However, it is not difficult to write custom manipulators (see the discussion within the inset).

There is another bit called ios::internal that can be used to determine if fill character padding is desired between the sign and the rest of a floating point number. Below is an example:

```
int    int1 = 34950;
int    int2 = -int1;
float flt1 = 17.5829f;
float flt2 = -flt1;

cout.setf(ios::internal, ios::adjustfield);
cout.fill('^');
cout.width(16);
cout<<int1<<endl;
cout.width(16);
cout<<int2<<endl;
cout.width(16);
cout<<flt1<<endl;
cout.width(16);
cout<<flt2<<endl;

cout.unsetf(ios::internal);
cout.width(16);
cout<<flt2<<endl;
```

The above would display:

```
^^^^^^^^^^^34950
^^^^^^^^^^-34950
^^^^^^^^^^17.5829
-^^^^^^^^^17.5829
^^^^^^^^-17.5829
```

One observation about setting the `ios::internal` bit is that the separation of the sign from the digits only applies to floating point numbers. This bit can also be enabled or disabled using the `setiosflags()` and `resetiosflags()` manipulators.

Finally, there is a way to choose the numerical representation of a floating point number:

```
long    lng1 = 875090406;
double dbl1 = 395.0;
double dbl2 = 7693.8356;
double dbl3 = 3409.958;

cout<<dbl1<<endl;

cout.setf(ios::showpos | ios::showpoint);
cout<<dbl1<<endl;

cout. setf(ios::scientific, ios::floatfield);
cout<<lng1<<endl;
cout<<dbl2<<endl;
cout<<dbl3<<endl;

cout.unsetf(ios::showpos | ios::showpoint | ios::scientific);
cout<<lng1<<endl;
cout<<dbl1<<endl;
cout<<dbl2<<endl;
cout<<dbl3<<endl;
```

The execution of the above would yield:

```
395
+395.000
+875090406
+7.693836e+003
+3.409958e+003
875090406
395
7693.84
3409.96
```

For this example, the default width (as wide as necessary) is used. For positive numbers, the plus sign can be made to appear by setting the `ios::showpos` bit. For floating point numbers, insignificant zeros after a decimal point can be displayed by setting the `ios::showpoint` bit.

By default, floating point numbers are displayed in fixed format. Scientific notation can be requested by enabling the `ios::scientific` bit. The `ios::floatfield` parameter of `setf()` is a request to clear the bit mask before setting the `ios::scientific` bit.

Both the setf() and unsetf() functions will accept parameters constructed with the bitwise OR operator (|). This would allow the enabling or disabling of multiple ios bits at one time. This use of the bitwise OR operator is also applicable to the setiosflags() and resetiosflags() manipulators.

The test samples of all the scenarios discussed (using the setf()/unsetf() approach or the setiosflags()/resetiosflags() approach) are enclosed within a C++ driver program called IOSDemo, which is on the supplied media. The execution of each scenario will put the results into individual output files (instead of to the standard output).

Formatting Output in Java with Class IOS

I had mentioned from the previous topic that the current version of Java has no methods to manipulate and format output. Without such routines, it takes considerable work to arrange data that is pleasant to the eye or even to write data in fixed blocks so that random access would be possible. That being the case, I had decided to compose a Java equivalent of the C++ ios class to give the serious developer a jump start in this area. The Java class is called IOS, which includes services for setting precision, setting field widths, text justification and selection of numerical formats.

By design, Java only provides a precision of up to six significant digits for floating point numbers. If there are more than six significant digits, the compiler will resort to scientific notation. Furthermore, there is no way to force scientific notation on floating point numbers of less than six significant digits.

Before I provide the source listing of the code, I will first give the reader a description of the services that class IOS provides as well as the limitations. The main idea behind class IOS is that individual IOS objects keep track of formatting specifications and serve as filters to massage data output streams. I will assume the reader has read the last topic (*Formatting Output in C++*) or already has a firm understanding of the C++ ios functions for setting the formatting attributes.

- In any attempt to mimic features that something else has, one must always consider the rules and constraints from which one must work. That is true whether one works with Java or with any other host language. Certainly, one cannot mimic features where the underlying support is not there. Since Java does not support the overloading of operators, it is not possible to construct C++ style manipulators.

- From the previous topic, we have seen that many related attributes, such as the selection of text justification, numerical representations and radix, are regulated by the enabling or disabling of bits within a bit mask. I had pointed out that since each value has its own bit, this can lead to situations of ambiguity, where bits representing opposing values may be set. This can present many baffling and bizarre results for the programmer. Hence, the bit mask approach is avoided for class IOS. Values that represent a particular functional domain, such as justification, are mapped to exactly one private variable field.

- Two constructors for the IOS class are provided. A no-argument, default constructor will set default values for nine formatting attributes. The second constructor will allow the programmer to instantiate an IOS object with values of his choice. The no-argument, default constructor is the easier one to use since most of the defaults should be applicable to most situations.

- Each of the private variable fields has a public mutator method to allow the changing of the attribute's value. Each of the mutator methods returns the previous value of the attribute, which allows the programmer to retain the original information. The C++ ios::fill() and ios::width() functions behave in exactly the same manner. The mutator methods complement the use of the no-argument, default constructor.

- One difference between the Java IOS class and the C++ ios class is that the field width specification is maintained until the programmer explicitly changes it. In C++, this specification is only good for one write invocation.

- The IOS class has public print() and println() methods that are overloaded to support the outputting of most of the built-in types. The first argument to these methods is of type PrintStream, which will allow either output to a file or to the standard output device.

- There are a number of private methods in class IOS that deal with the details of string parsing given the desired attributes. That includes the location of any signs, placement of the decimal point, padding with the fill character, construction of the scientific notation string, etc.

- With the help of the IOS class, a floating point number can be made to display up to 12 significant digits. If the floating point number provided exceeds 12 significant digits, the Java compiler will resort to presenting in scientific notation. That being the case, the decision was made to accept the compiler defaults for such situations. Hence, even though a fixed numerical representation is requested, the results may still be presented in scientific notation.

- The Java IOS class attempts to implement all of the formatting features that can be found from the equivalent C++ ios class except for two items.

With IOS, the base is always displayed for octal and hexadecimal numbers and cannot be disabled (equivalent to the C++ `ios::showbase` bit). Furthermore, there is no mechanism to request that a floating point number be padded with insignificant zeros after a decimal point (equivalent to the C++ `ios::showpoint` bit). These are left as challenges for the daring reader.

Here is an overview of the public contents of class IOS:

- **Variable Index**

```
public static final int DEC;
public static final int OCT;
public static final int HEX;
public static final boolean RIGHT;
public static final boolean LEFT;
public static final boolean FIXED;
public static final boolean SCIENTIFIC;
```

- **Constructor Index**

```
public IOS();
public IOS(int base, int size, char fill, boolean just, int
           significant, boolean cap,  boolean sign, boolean
           pad, boolean format);
```

- **Method Index**

```
public int setRadix(int base);
public int setWidth(int size);
public char setFill(char fill);
public boolean setJustify(boolean just);
public int setPrecision(int prec);
public boolean setUpperCase(boolean cap);
public boolean setShowSign(boolean sign);
public boolean setInternalPad(boolean pad);
public boolean setNumericalFormat(boolean format);

public void print(PrintStream ps, char aChar);
public void print(PrintStream ps, char [] aCharArray);
public void print(PrintStream ps, int anInt);
public void print(PrintStream ps, long aLong);
public void print(PrintStream ps, float aFlt);
public void print(PrintStream ps, double aDbl);
public void print(PrintStream ps, String aStr);
public void println(PrintStream ps, char aChar);
public void println(PrintStream ps, char [] aCharArray);
public void println(PrintStream ps, int anInt);
public void println(PrintStream ps, long aLong);
public void println(PrintStream ps, float aFlt);
```

```
public void println(PrintStream ps, double aDbl);
public void println(PrintStream ps, String aStr);
```

Now, we will apply the methods of IOS to a few examples. The first example deals with setting the field size and the fill character. The default field size is zero, which means make the field as wide as necessary to fit the string. The default fill character is the space character. These defaults conform to the C++ iostreams approach:

```
IOS os1A = new IOS();

String bird = "penguin";
String fish = "rock cod";
String tree = "maple";

os1A.setFill('~');
os1A.setWidth(12);
os1A.println(System.out, bird);
os1A.println(System.out, fish);
os1A.setWidth(0);
os1A.println(System.out, tree);
```

The output would go to the standard output device and would look like:

```
~~~~~penguin
~~~~rock cod
maple
```

The System.out variable could be replaced with a PrintStream object that is attached to an output file. In fact, all of the test scenarios from the media actually output to individual files. This is done to insure the uniqueness of each test case.

For the benefit of the reader, the output file names for the corresponding test scenarios of the C++ and Java samples are identical. This will help the reader make comparisons more easily.

The next example deals with the setting of precision:

```
IOS os2A = new IOS();

double num1 = 17.7875678;
os2A.setPrecision(8);
os2A.println(System.out, num1);
```

The information displayed would appear as:

```
17.787568
```

As the reader can see, the default numerical presentation is the fixed format.

We can also set the radix for integral types:

```
IOS os3A = new IOS();
int num2 = 160;

os3A.setRadix(IOS.OCT);
os3A.print(System.out, "Octal = ");
os3A.println(System.out, num2);
os3A.setRadix(IOS.HEX);
os3A.print(System.out, "Hexadecimal = ");
os3A.println(System.out, num2);
os3A.setUpperCase(true);
os3A.print(System.out, "Hexadecimal = ");
os3A.println(System.out, num2);
os3A.setRadix(IOS.DEC);
os3A.print(System.out, "Decimal = ");
os3A.println(System.out, num2);
```

The output would be displayed as:

```
Octal = 0240
Hexadecimal = 0xa0
Hexadecimal = 0XA0
Decimal = 160
```

After examining the above code, there may be a temptation to concatenate the prompt string with the int variable, num2. However, this would not allow the proper radix to be displayed. An expression such as:

```
os3A.print(System.out, "Hexadecimal = "+num2);
```

would yield:

```
Hexadecimal = 160
```

because one of the first evaluations would be "Hexadecimal = "+num2, which will result in a String object. Hence, the print(PrintStream, String) implementation would be called. This method has no way of knowing that a substring of the string it contains really originated from a numerical type.

Then, we have text justification:

```
IOS os5A = new IOS();

os5A.setJustify(IOS.LEFT);
os5A.setFill('*');
os5A.setWidth(12);
os5A.println(System.out, bird);
os5A.println(System.out, fish);
os5A.setJustify(IOS.RIGHT);
os5A.println(System.out, tree);
```

which would produce the following:

```
penguin*****
rock cod****
******maple
```

As with C++, right justification is the default, so an explicit effort must be made to request left justification. The static, final variables IOS.LEFT and IOS.RIGHT are equivalent to const variables in C++. They simulate the use of ios::left and ios::right for the C++ ios functions.

The IOS class will also allow us to specify any internal padding of floating point numbers:

```
IOS os6A = new IOS();

int    int1 = 34950;
int    int2 = -int1;
float flt1 = 17.5829f;
float flt2 = -flt1;

os6A.setInternalPad(true);
os6A.setFill('^');
os6A.setWidth(16);
os6A.println(System.out,  int1);
os6A.println(System.out,  int2);
os6A.println(System.out,  flt1);
os6A.println(System.out,  flt2);
os6A.setInternalPad(false);
os6A.println(System.out,  flt2);
```

The data displayed would be:

```
^^^^^^^^^^^34950
^^^^^^^^^^-34950
^^^^^^^^^17.5829
-^^^^^^^^17.5829
^^^^^^^^-17.5829
```

As in C++, the request to pad the area of the field between the sign and the digits only applies to floating point numbers. Integral types are not affected.

Finally, the IOS class offers some control over the selection of fixed or scientific format for floating point numbers. The following is an example:

```
IOS os7A = new IOS();

long    long1 = 875090406;
double doub1 = 395.0;
double doub2 = 7693.8356;
double doub3 = 3409.958;
```

```
os7A.println(System.out, doub1);
os7A.setShowSign(true);
os7A.println(System.out, doub1);
os7A.setNumericalFormat(IOS.SCIENTIFIC);
os7A.println(System.out, long1);
os7A.println(System.out, doub2);
os7A.println(System.out, doub3);
os7A.setShowSign(false);
os7A.setNumericalFormat(IOS.FIXED);
os7A.println(System.out, long1);
os7A.println(System.out, doub1);
os7A.println(System.out, doub2);
os7A.println(System.out, doub3);
```

The output would appear as:

```
395
+395
+875090406
+7.69384e+003
+3.40996e+003
875090406
395
7693.84
3409.96
```

Similar to text justification, two static final variables, IOS.FIXED and IOS.SCIENTIFIC, are used to select the numerical presentation. As in C++, scientific format only applies to floating point numbers.

The example uses the default precision of six significant digits. Since each of doub2 and doub3 exceeds six significant digits, a round off is performed in each case before the results are displayed in fixed format.

In addition, the default for displaying positive numbers is not to show the plus sign. This can be changed by using the setShowSign() method.

The following sample compares the output of PrintStream.println() versus IOS.println():

```
double [] dbl4 = {
                1.1,    12.12,   123.123,   1234.1234,   12345.12345,
                123456.123456,   1234567.1234567
                };

IOS os11A = new IOS();

os11A.setPrecision(20);
os11A.setWidth(30);
os11A.setJustify(IOS.RIGHT);
```

```
os11A.println(System.out, "Default System.out.println()");
for(int index = 0; index < dbl4.length; index++)
   System.out.println(dbl4[index]);

os11A.println(System.out, "IOS Fixed Format");
for(int index = 0; index < dbl4.length; index++)
   os11A.println(System.out, dbl4[index]);

os11A.setNumericalFormat(IOS.SCIENTIFIC);

os11A.println(System.out, "IOS Scientific Format");
for(int index = 0; index < dbl4.length; index++)
   os11A.println(System.out, dbl4[index]);
```

The execution of the above would yield the following:

```
Default System.out.println()
1.1
12.12
123.123
1234.12
12345.1
123456
1.23457e+006
                        IOS Fixed Format

                          12.12
                         123.123
                        1234.1234
                       12345.12345
                      123456.123456
                       1.23457e+006
              IOS Scientific Format
                        1.1e+000
                       1.212e+001
                      1.23123e+002
                     1.2341234e+003
                    1.234512345e+004
                   1.23456123456e+005
                       1.23457e+006
```

Class IOS will attempt to provide a precision of up to 12 significant digits. It does this by attempting to expand the precision of the whole and fractional components of the floating point number. Since the implementation relies on the compiler's ability to present each component as a string, each of the components is limited to a precision of six.

Now, we have finally arrived at the point where the definitions of class IOS and its methods are presented. Overall, there is a considerable amount of detail and the reader may choose to skip this portion of the topic. However, if the reader is really interested in the nitty-gritty of how the formatting mechanism works, all of the internal logic is concentrated around the private methods.

All of the examples regarding usage of the `IOS` class can be found in the `main()` method of the class.

Listing 7-7: IOS.java

```java
import java.awt.*;
import java.io.*;

public class IOS {

public IOS() {
radix = DEC;
width = 0;
fillchar = ' ';
justify_right = RIGHT;
precision = 6;
upper_case = false;
show_sign = false;
internal_pad = false;
fixed_format = FIXED;
}

public IOS(int base, int size, char fill, boolean just,
           int significant, boolean cap, boolean sign,
           boolean pad, boolean format) {

if ((base < 0) || (base > 2))
    base = DEC;
if (size < 0)
    size = 0;
radix = base;
width = size;
fillchar = fill;
justify_right = just;
precision = significant;
upper_case = cap;
show_sign = sign;
internal_pad = pad;
fixed_format = format;
}

// public mutator methods for IOS attributes

public int setRadix(int base) {
int org_radix = radix;
if ((base < 0) || (base > 2))
    base = DEC;
```

```
radix = base;
return org_radix;
}

public int setWidth(int size) {
int org_width = width;
if (size < 0)
    size = 0;
width = size;
return org_width;
}

public char setFill(char fill) {
char org_fillchar = fillchar;
fillchar = fill;
return org_fillchar;
}

public boolean setJustify(boolean just) {
boolean org_just = justify_right;
justify_right = just;
return org_just;
}

public int setPrecision(int prec) {
int org_precision = precision;
precision = prec;
return org_precision;
}

public boolean setUpperCase(boolean cap) {
boolean org_upper_case = upper_case;
upper_case = cap;
return org_upper_case;
}

public boolean setShowSign(boolean sign) {
boolean org_show_sign = show_sign;
show_sign = sign;
return org_show_sign;
}

public boolean setInternalPad(boolean pad) {
boolean org_internal_pad = pad;
internal_pad = pad;
return org_internal_pad;
}
public boolean setNumericalFormat(boolean format) {
boolean org_fixed_format = fixed_format;
fixed_format = format;
return org_fixed_format;
}
```

```java
// Methods used for development and debugging

void showState(PrintStream ps) {
String radix_str = "";
String width_str = "";
String just_str = "";
String fillchar_str = "";
String format_str = "";

switch (radix) {
    case DEC: radix_str += "Decimal";
              break;
    case OCT: radix_str += "Octal";
              break;
    case HEX: radix_str += "Hexadecimal";
              break;
    }

if (width == 0)
    width_str += "Default";
else
    width_str += width;

if (justify_right)
    just_str += "RIGHT";
else
    just_str += "LEFT";

if (fillchar == ' ')
    fillchar_str += "Space";
else
    fillchar_str += fillchar;

if (fixed_format)
    format_str += "Fixed";
else
    format_str += "Scientific";

ps.println();
ps.println("Radix = "+radix_str);
ps.println("Width = "+width_str);
ps.println("Fill Character = "+fillchar_str);
ps.println("Justification = "+just_str);
ps.println("Precision = "+precision);
ps.println("Upper case = "+upper_case);
ps.println("Show sign = "+show_sign);
ps.println("Internal pad = "+internal_pad);
ps.println("Numerical format = "+format_str);
ps.println();
}
```

```
// public methods for print() and println()

public void println(PrintStream ps, char aChar) {
String newStr = "";
newStr += aChar;
print(ps, newStr);
ps.println();
}

public void println(PrintStream ps, char [] aCharArray) {
String newStr = "";
newStr += aCharArray;
print(ps, newStr);
ps.println();
}

public void println(PrintStream ps, int anInt) {
println(ps, (long)anInt);
}

public void println(PrintStream ps, long aLong) {
print(ps, aLong);
ps.println();
}

public void println(PrintStream ps, float aFlt) {
println(ps, (double) aFlt);
}

public void println(PrintStream ps, double aDbl) {
print(ps, aDbl);
ps.println();
}

public void println(PrintStream ps, String aStr) {
print(ps, aStr);
ps.println();
}

public void print(PrintStream ps, char aChar) {
String newStr = "";
newStr += aChar;
print(ps, newStr);
}

public void print(PrintStream ps, char [] aCharArray) {
String newStr = "";
newStr += aCharArray;
print(ps, newStr);
}
```

```java
public void print(PrintStream ps, int anInt) {
print(ps, (long)anInt);
}

public void print(PrintStream ps, long aLong) {
String newStr = "";
if ((show_sign) && (aLong > 0))
    newStr += "+";
switch (radix) {
    case DEC: newStr += aLong;
            break;
    case OCT: newStr += "0"  + newBase(aLong, 3, 7, "01234567");
            break;
    case HEX: if (upper_case)
                newStr += "0X" + newBase(aLong, 4, 15,
                    "0123456789ABCDEF");
            else
                newStr += "0x" + newBase(aLong, 4, 15,
                    "0123456789abcdef");
            break;
    }
print(ps, newStr);
}

public void print(PrintStream ps, float aFlt) {
print(ps, (double)aFlt);
}

public void print(PrintStream ps, double aDbl) {
String newStr = "";
String tmpStr = "";
if (fixed_format)
    tmpStr += prepareFixedFormat(aDbl);
else
    tmpStr += prepareScientificFormat(aDbl);
newStr += padString(tmpStr, aDbl);
print(ps, newStr);
}

public void print(PrintStream ps, String aStr) {
ps.print(prepareField(aStr));
ps.flush();
}

// private helper methods

private void drawRuler(PrintStream ps) {
    String interval = new String("1234567890");
    String ruler = "";
    for (int index = 0; index < 6; index++)
```

```
        ruler += interval;
    ps.println();
    ps.println(ruler);
    ps.println();
}

private String newBase(long value, int no_of_bits, int one_bits,
 String digits) {
String result = "";
if (value == 0) {
    result += "0";
    }
else {
    while (value != 0) {
        result = digits.charAt((int)(value & one_bits)) + result;
        value = value >>> no_of_bits;
        }
    }
return result;
}

private String prepareField(String aStr) {
if (width == 0) {
    return aStr;
    }

if (width <= aStr.length()) {
    return aStr;
    }

String newStr = "";
int delta = width - aStr.length();
if (justify_right) {          // RIGHT
    for (int index = 0; index < delta; index++)
        newStr += fillchar;
    newStr += aStr;
    }
else {                        // LEFT
    StringBuffer sbuffer = new StringBuffer(aStr);
    char [] cbuffer = new char[delta];
    sbuffer.append(cbuffer);
    for (int index = 0; index < delta; index++)
        sbuffer.setCharAt(aStr.length()+index, fillchar);
    newStr += new String(sbuffer);
    }

return newStr;
}

private String eNotation(char sign, long exponent) {
```

```java
String expStr = new Long(exponent).toString();
int leading_zeros = 3 - (expStr.length());
String result = "";
result += (upper_case)?"E":"e";
result += sign;
for (int index = 0; index < leading_zeros; index++)
    result += "0";
result += expStr;
return result;
}

private String moveDecimalLeft(long aLong) {
String result = "";
String str = "";
str += aLong;
result += str.substring(0, 1) + "." + str.substring(1,
str.length());
return result;
}

private String moveDecimalRight(String str) {
char ch;
long pwr = 0;
int index2 = 0;
String result = "";
String newStr = "";

for (int index1 = 0; index1 < str.length(); index1++) {
    if ((ch = str.charAt(index1)) == '0')
        pwr++;
    else
        newStr += ch;
    }

pwr++;

if ((newStr.substring(1, newStr.length())).length() != 0)
    result += newStr.substring(0, 1) + "."
            + newStr.substring(1, newStr.length()) + eNotation
            ('-', pwr);
else
    result += newStr.substring(0, 1) + "." + "0" + eNotation
    ('-', pwr);

return result;
}

private boolean alreadyScientific(String str) {
boolean flag = false;
```

```java
for(int index=0; index < str.length(); index++) {
    if ( (str.charAt(index) == 'e') || (str.charAt(index) == 'E') )
        flag = true;
    }
return flag;
}

private String improveDefault(String str) {
boolean decimal_pt = false;
int e_index = 0;
for (int index = 0; index < str.length(); index++) {
    if (str.charAt(index) == '.')
        decimal_pt = true;
    else
    if ( (str.charAt(index) == 'e') || (str.charAt(index) == 'E') )
        e_index = index;
    }

String result = "";

if (decimal_pt) {
    result += str.substring(0, e_index) + (upper_case?"E":"e")
            + str.substring(e_index+1, str.length());
    }
else {
    result += str.substring(0, e_index) + ".0" +
    (upper_case?"E":"e")
            + str.substring(e_index+1, str.length());
    }

return result;
}

private String padString(String str, double num) {
int lgth = width - str.length();

if (((show_sign) || (num < 0.0)) && (lgth > 0) && (internal_pad)) {
    String result = "";
    result += str.substring(0, 1);
    for (int index = 0; index < lgth; index++) result +=
     fillchar;
    result += str.substring(1, str.length());
    return result;
    }

return str;
}

private String prepareScientificFormat(double aDbl) {
```

```java
String result = "";

// The double may already be in scientific format

String dblStr = "";
dblStr += aDbl;

if (alreadyScientific(dblStr)) {
   String newStr = "";
   if ((show_sign) && (aDbl > 0))
      newStr += "+";
   newStr += improveDefault(dblStr);
   return newStr;
   }

// Include the sign if necessary

if (aDbl < 0.0) {
   result += "-";
   aDbl = -1 * aDbl;
   }
else
if (show_sign)
   result += "+";

// Find the whole part and the fractional part

long whole = (long) aDbl;
double fraction = aDbl - whole;

String wholeStr = "";
wholeStr += whole;

if (wholeStr.length() >= precision) {
   if (fraction >= 0.5) whole++;
   long pwr = wholeStr.length() - 1;
   result += moveDecimalLeft(whole) + eNotation('+', pwr);
   }
else {
   int frac_prec = precision - wholeStr.length();
   if (fraction == 0.0) {
      long pwr = wholeStr.length() - 1;
      result += moveDecimalLeft(whole) + ((whole==0)?"0":"")
            + eNotation('+', pwr);
      }
   else
      result += determineFraction(frac_prec, fraction, whole);
   }
```

```
return result;
}

private String determineFraction(int prec, double aDbl, long
 org_whole) {

String result = "";
String aDblStr = "";
aDblStr += aDbl;
int lgth = aDblStr.length()-2;
String frac_str = "";

if (prec < lgth) {
   double newDbl = aDbl;
   for (int index = 0; index < prec; index++)
      newDbl *= 10.0;
   long sub_whole = (long)newDbl;
   double sub_fraction = newDbl - sub_whole;
   if (sub_fraction >= 0.5) sub_whole++;
   frac_str += sub_whole;
   }
else
   frac_str += aDblStr.substring(2, aDblStr.length());

String orgWholeStr = "";
orgWholeStr += org_whole;

if (org_whole > 0) {
   long pwr = orgWholeStr.length() - 1;
   result += moveDecimalLeft(org_whole) + frac_str
            + eNotation('+', pwr);
   }
else {
   result += moveDecimalRight(frac_str);
   }

return result;
}

private String prepareFixedFormat(double aDbl) {
String result = "";
// The double may already be in scientific format

String dblStr = "";
dblStr += aDbl;

if (alreadyScientific(dblStr)) {
   String newStr = "";
```

```
    if ((show_sign) && (aDbl > 0))
        newStr += "+";
    newStr += improveDefault(dblStr);
    return newStr;
    }

// Include the sign if necessary

if (aDbl < 0.0) {
    result += "-";
    aDbl = -1 * aDbl;
    }
else
if (show_sign)
    result += "+";

// Find the whole part and the fractional part

long whole = (long) aDbl;
double fraction = aDbl - whole;

String wholeStr = "";
wholeStr += whole;

if (wholeStr.length() >= precision) {
    if (fraction >= 0.5) whole++;
    result += whole;
    }
else {
    int frac_prec = precision - wholeStr.length();
    if (fraction == 0.0)
        result += whole;
    else
        result += whole + "." + findFraction(frac_prec, fraction);
    }

return result;
}

private String findFraction(int prec, double aDbl) {

String result = "";
String aDblStr = "";
aDblStr += aDbl;
int lgth = aDblStr.length()-2;

if (prec < lgth) {
    double newDbl = aDbl;
    for (int index = 0; index < prec; index++)
```

```
        newDbl *= 10.0;
    long sub_whole = (long)newDbl;
    double sub_fraction = newDbl - sub_whole;
    if (sub_fraction >= 0.5) sub_whole++;
    result += sub_whole;
    }
else
    result += aDblStr.substring(2, aDblStr.length());

return result;
}

// public final fields

public static final int DEC = 0;
public static final int OCT = 1;
public static final int HEX = 2;
public static final boolean RIGHT = true;
public static final boolean LEFT  = false;
public static final boolean FIXED = true;
public static final boolean SCIENTIFIC  = false;

// private variable fields

private int  precision;
private int  radix;
private int  width;
private char fillchar;
private boolean justify_right;
private boolean upper_case;
private boolean show_sign;
private boolean internal_pad;
private boolean fixed_format;

public static void main(String args[]) throws IOException {

// Test cases: see the file on the media

// All of the test cases are the individual samples
// already discussed in this chapter
}

}  // end of class IOS
```

CHAPTER

8

- Processes, Threads and Java

- The Java Thread Class

- The Java `Runnable` Interface

- Contention for Resources and the Java `synchronized` Keyword

- Waiting for Conditions to Change with `wait()` and `notify()`

- Organizing Java Threads into a `ThreadGroup`

Threads:
Charting
Multiple
Courses

Processes, Threads and Java

The act of performing multiple activities at almost the same time is a given part of everyday life. It is not uncommon for a human to rapidly toggle his attention among activities like eating breakfast, speaking on the phone, watching television and browsing a newspaper. Modern computers can also multitask, but computers can shift contexts so quickly that all activities appear to progress together.

A computer program is a series of instructions to achieve a goal. However, a process, which is an instance of the program, is simply the setting or backdrop for the execution of the instructions. The process would own resources like the code in a memory address space, global data, a stack, file descriptor tables, directory information, environment variables, etc. In UNIX, these resources would be recorded into a complex data structure called a process table.

The process itself does not execute a program's instructions. Rather, an object called a thread is what carries out the instructions. In short, each thread is a computational unit with its own flow of control. In order for any work to be done, a process must have at least one thread. In multithreaded operating systems like Microsoft Windows NT™, the thread of a process that is capable of creating other threads is called the main or primary thread.

In many areas of business, data processing is still being performed by machines with operating systems that are only capable of creating single-threaded processes. While programmers have made good use of the limitations of such older operating systems, the overhead of achieving an objective without threads can be quite high. For instance, in UNIX it is not uncommon to spawn child processes with the `fork()` intrinsic so that time-consuming activities can be handled in the background. However, `fork()` is not an ordinary function call.

297

This function will cause a context switch from user mode to kernel mode, which will create a new process table on behalf of the child process. The process table of the child would be a copy of the parent's process table, which would include a copy of the code, a copy of the global data, a copy of the stack, a copy of virtual memory, etc. In short, that is a lot of duplication.

A C programming example with the UNIX system call `fork()` can be found under the topic, *A File Retrieval Service in C* from Chapter 10, *Networking the Java Environment*.

It is also more difficult to share data among multiple processes, since each process owns its own address space. In a multithreaded environment, all threads of a process share the same address space and can access global variables.

With this said, the trend of the software industry is to go towards multithreaded environments for efficiency. Sun Solaris OS™, Microsoft Windows NT™ and POSIX 1003.4a™ are clearly influences in this direction. As a programming tool, Java is also making an impact on this type of technology.

The Java language was conceived to support multithreaded programming and it has a `Thread` class that is part of the standard language package (`java.lang`). Other languages, including C++, do not have such support, either with language constructs or with standard class libraries. Thread support for such languages must be purchased from software vendors and each product would have proprietary classes and interfaces.

The beauty of Java is that the language presents a common set of classes, interfaces and protocols for doing object-oriented, multithreaded programming on a variety of platforms. Until recently, this capability in a programming language was unprecedented.

In addition, the Java approach to writing multithreaded applications or applets is not quite as complicated as programming with other application programming interfaces (APIs). These APIs typically have many functions, each with long argument lists and with numerous rules about how they should be used. Struggling to use them correctly is often a frustrating, time-consuming, error-prone process.

With Java gaining influence in the software industry, I expect many developers to take advantage of Java's multithreading capabilities. In the topics to follow, I will elaborate on how a Java application should be structured to harness these capabilities.

The Java **Thread** Class

For interactive programs, spawning a thread to handle long activities is often a good way to avoid annoying a user with long waits. Sorting large amounts of data, for instance, is often a time-consuming activity. In my first example, I have a sample program called `ThreadDemo1`, which sorts data from three input streams and has the results written to three corresponding output streams. To help me to do this, I had taken the Quicksort routines I had presented in chapter 7 (`SortFileDemo`) and created a `QSort` helper class. The `QSort` object is basically a "factory" that converts raw, unsorted data from an input file into sorted data for an output file.

The driver program, `ThreadDemo1`, basically instantiates three `QSort` objects and has a thread manage each `QSort` object.

I will first present the classes and their methods and then discuss the essential points. The `QSort` class is placed within its own package called `Sort`. The listings are as follows:

Listing 8-1: QSort.java

```java
// Class QSort

package Sort;
import java.awt.*;
import java.io.*;

public class QSort extends Thread {

    private void Partition(String [] str, int left, int right) {
    int index1;
    int index2;
    String curr_str = null;
    String temp_str = null;

    index1 = left;
    index2 = right;

    curr_str = str[(left+right)/2];

    do {
        while ( (str[index1].compareTo(curr_str) < 0) && (index1
         < right) )
          index1++;
        while ( (curr_str.compareTo(str[index2]) < 0) && (index2
         > left) )
          index2—;

        if (index1 < index2) {
          temp_str    = str[index1];
          str[index1] = str[index2];
          str[index2] = temp_str;
          index1++;
          index2—;
          }
```

```
        else
        if (index1 == index2) {
          index1++;
          index2-;
          }

        } while (index1 <= index2);

try {
    System.out.println(getName()+" is going to sleep...");
    sleep(100);                  // Sleep for 100 milliseconds
    }
catch(InterruptedException err) {
    System.out.println(err.toString());
    }

if (left < index2)  Partition(str, left,  index2);
if (index1 < right) Partition(str, index1, right);
}

private void Quicksort(String [] str, int num_recs) {
Partition(str, 0, num_recs-1);
}

public void run() {

String line = null;
int count = 0;
int index;

try {
    RandomAccessFile ins = new RandomAccessFile(source_file,
    "r");
    PrintStream ps =
          new PrintStream(new FileOutputStream(target_file));

    while ((line = ins.readLine()) != null) {
      count++;
      }

    String record[] = new String[count];

    ins.seek(0);

    index = 0;

    while ((line = ins.readLine()) != null) {
      record[index++] = line;
      }
```

```
        Quicksort(record, count);

        for (index = 0; index < count; index++)
            ps.println(record[index]);

        ins.close();
        ps.close();
        }
    catch(IOException err) {
        System.out.println(err.toString());
        }
    }

    public QSort(String sfile, String tfile, String name) {
    super(name);
    source_file = sfile;
    target_file = tfile;
    }

    private String source_file;
    private String target_file;

}
```

Listing 8-2: ThreadDemo1.java

```java
// Class ThreadDemo1

import java.awt.*;
import java.io.*;
import Sort.QSort;

public class ThreadDemo1 {

    public static void main(String args[]) {
    QSort qs1 = new QSort("TERMS1.TXT", "TERMS2.TXT", "qs1");
    QSort qs2 = new QSort("TERMS3.TXT", "TERMS4.TXT", "qs2");
    QSort qs3 = new QSort("TERMS5.TXT", "TERMS6.TXT", "qs3");

    qs1.start();
    qs2.start();
    qs3.start();

    while ((qs1.isAlive()) || (qs2.isAlive()) || (qs3.isAlive()));
    }

}
```

Each of the original input files (the odd numbered file names) contains a list of words, each word on a separate line. For instance, file TERMS5.TXT would look like:

```
material
pony
patience
crash
barricade
ruthless
unfold
miscellaneous
deodorant
color
spiral
transcribe
employee
corrections
authentic
skirmish
philosophical
leisure
tarnish
factory
```

The sorted results would be written to file TERMS6.TXT:

```
authentic
barricade
color
corrections
crash
deodorant
employee
factory
leisure
material
miscellaneous
patience
philosophical
pony
ruthless
skirmish
spiral
tarnish
transcribe
unfold
```

In an effort to illustrate a thread running when it owns the CPU and the context switching, a System.out.println() statement was inserted into the Partition() method of class QSort. On a command line window, the user would see something like:

```
qs2 is going to sleep...
qs1 is going to sleep...
qs2 is going to sleep...
qs3 is going to sleep...
qs1 is going to sleep...
qs2 is going to sleep...
qs3 is going to sleep...
qs1 is going to sleep...
qs2 is going to sleep...
qs3 is going to sleep...
```

Now, let us discuss the essential points of the example. The code in bold highlights key points of the discussion. One aspect I will not discuss is the Quicksort algorithm itself since this has been covered in chapter 7 (refer to the topic, *Generating Output with C++ ofstream and Java PrintStream*).

- The methods pertaining to the Quicksort algorithm were taken from the SortFileDemo class of chapter 7. The methods of the algorithm, Quicksort() and Partition(), were converted to instance methods and made private. These methods mainly serve as helper methods to class QSort and there is no need for clients to access them directly.

- The QSort class is made a subclass of class Thread. We are not doing this because a sorting process is necessarily a thread. Rather, we are using inheritance from a technical perspective so that we can access the public methods of class Thread. Class Thread has a number of important methods that will allow us to regulate the life cycle of an execution process.

- The QSort class is given a constructor so that the names of the input and output files can be retained in private variable fields. The constructor of QSort also takes a name of type String, which is passed to one of the constructors of class Thread through the call:

  ```
  super(name);
  ```

- One method that class QSort inherits from superclass Thread is the public run() method. The inheriting class must override this method so that the desired work gets done. The run() method is transparently called by another method called start() (which is also inherited from class Thread). For our example, the run() method establishes the file streams, counts the number of records in the input stream, reads the input records into an array of appropriate size, calls method Quicksort(), writes the sorted records into the output stream and closes the streams.

- The heart of the sorting mechanism is within the recursive, private method called `Partition()` of class `QSort`. Here is where the work is done to locate the permanent index location of each array element. It is within this method that we put a call to the static `Thread` method, `sleep()`, to force the currently active thread to suspend itself and give another thread the opportunity to run. The `sleep()` method takes a single `int` argument, which represents the time in milliseconds that the thread will be in a blocked state.

  After the elapse of so many milliseconds, the thread reenters the runnable state, which means that it is a candidate to become active. If its priority is higher than the currently active thread, then it becomes the active thread and its predecessor will be placed into a wait queue. Otherwise, the formerly blocked thread will enter the wait queue.

  The inset entitled, *The Thread States of Java,* summarizes the four states of a thread.

- Finally, there is the `main()` method of the `ThreadDemo1` class, which creates three instances of `QSort`, each with the name of an existing input file and the name of an output file. When an instance of `Thread` (and `QSort` is a `Thread`) is first created, it is in the <u>new</u> state, since it has never been active. When each of these instances is delivered a `start()` message, each `Thread` object enters the runnable state. The scheduler then decides whether to make the `Thread` object active or to let it wait in a queue, where it will eventually get its turn. As mentioned earlier, the `start()` method, which is inherited from class `Thread`, will call the appropriate `run()` method of the instance. In this case, instance method `run()` from subclass `QSort` will be called.

  The primary thread is the thread responsible for creating other threads. In this example, the primary thread puts itself into an indefinite loop to wait for the secondary threads to finish. The `isAlive()` method of class `Thread` returns a value of `true` if the `Thread` object is either runnable or blocked. In the context that this method is used, if the return value is `false`, then it either has completed normal processing or it has been terminated by another thread (which this example does not demonstrate, nor is such action recommended).

 Summary: The `QSort` objects were all started with the default thread priority of 5 (it can be as low as 1 or as high as 10). As the console output had indicated, the amount of time granted to each `Thread` object turned out to be fairly even. Each thread represented a unique sort process and each was able to achieve its goals without disruption.

In the next topic, we will see how to achieve the same thing with a slightly different approach.

The Thread States of Java

The Java language defines four states for a thread. They are:

- `New`: This is a newly instantiated `Thread` object that has <u>not</u> been sent the `start()` message. None of the code inside the `Thread` object has ever been executed.

- `Runnable`: The `start()` message has been sent to the `Thread` object and certain bookkeeping is established for the object. It is in the runnable state, but it may not actually be running. It is up to the scheduler to determine when the thread gets the CPU and is allowed to run. By runnable, we mean that the thread is <u>capable</u> of running and is a candidate to be chosen by the scheduler.

- `Blocked`: A thread enters the blocked state if the `sleep()`, `suspend()` or `wait()` messages are sent to the thread. The thread can also enter this state if it is waiting on input or output. In this state, the `Thread` object is certainly alive, but it is not runnable. The thread will reenter the runnable state if the time for `sleep()` has expired, if `resume()` is called in response to `suspend()` or if `notify()` (or `notifyAll()`) is called in response to `wait()`. It will also become runnable if the input-output operation has finished.

- `Dead`: A thread becomes dead either because it has completed execution of its `run()` method in a normal manner or if it is killed by a `stop()` message from another source. The death of the thread becomes complete when the `Thread` superclass receives a `ThreadDeath` object (which is thrown by `stop()`).

The Java `Runnable` Interface

You might recall that Java supports single inheritance and hence a class can only `extend` one superclass. However, a Java class may `implement` any number of `interfaces`. The interface is treated like an abstract class because the interface only has method prototypes. The interface has no method implementations nor any nonfinal variable fields. It is up to the inheriting class to provide the implementations for the methods.

In the previous example, class `QSort` extended class `Thread` so that the subclass could take advantage of the public methods of `Thread`. However, there will be times when it will be impossible to subclass from `Thread` because there is the greater need to inherit the methods of a different class. That is certainly the case with applet programming, as we will see later.

We still want to incorporate threads into our program and yet we cannot sub-class from `Thread`. To get around this problem, we would have our subclass implement a predefined interface called `Runnable`. This interface is very straightforward. It is defined as:

```
public interface Runnable extends Object {
public abstract void run();
}
```

Interface `Runnable` only has one method prototype and that is `run()`. Method `run()` takes no arguments and returns `void`. The inheriting class must provide an implementation for `run()` with this signature and return type.

We will now look at `ThreadDemo2`, which uses an amended version of class `QSort` from the previous topic ("The Java Thread Class"). Only the changes and amendments to the previous version are listed. The amendments are highlighted in bold:

Listing 8-3: QSort.java

```
// Class QSort

package RunnableSort;        // Put this class into a different
                            // package
import java.awt.*;
import java.io.*;

public class QSort implements Runnable {

    private void Partition(String [] str, int left, int right) {
    int index1;
    int index2;
    String curr_str = null;
    String temp_str = null;

    index1 = left;
    index2 = right;

    curr_str = str[(left+right)/2];

    do {
        while ( (str[index1].compareTo(curr_str) < 0) && (index1
         < right) )
          index1++;
        while ( (curr_str.compareTo(str[index2]) < 0) && (index2
         > left)  )
          index2-;

        if (index1 < index2) {
```

```
            temp_str     = str[index1];
            str[index1] = str[index2];
            str[index2] = temp_str;
            index1++;
            index2-;
            }
         else
         if (index1 == index2) {
            index1++;
            index2-;
            }

         } while (index1 <= index2);

   System.out.println(Thread.currentThread().getName()+"
    yielding...");
   Thread.yield();

   if (left < index2)  Partition(str, left,  index2);
   if (index1 < right) Partition(str, index1, right);
   }

   private void Quicksort(String [] str, int num_recs) {
   Partition(str, 0, num_recs-1);
   }

   public void run() {

  // No changes to this code

  }

   public QSort(String sfile, String tfile) {
   source_file = sfile;
   target_file = tfile;
   }

   private String source_file;
   private String target_file;

}
```

Listing 8-4: ThreadDemo2.java

```
// Class ThreadDemo2

import java.awt.*;
import java.io.*;
```

```
import RunnableSort.QSort;

public class ThreadDemo2 {

    public static void main(String args[]) {
    QSort qs1 = new QSort("TERMS1.TXT", "TERMS2.TXT");
    QSort qs2 = new QSort("TERMS3.TXT", "TERMS4.TXT");
    QSort qs3 = new QSort("TERMS5.TXT", "TERMS6.TXT");

    Thread td1 = new Thread(qs1, "td1");
    Thread td2 = new Thread(qs2, "td2");
    Thread td3 = new Thread(qs3, "td3");

    td1.setPriority(Thread.NORM_PRIORITY);
    td2.setPriority(Thread.NORM_PRIORITY+1);
    td3.setPriority(Thread.NORM_PRIORITY+2);

    td1.start();
    td2.start();
    td3.start();

    while ((td1.isAlive()) || (td2.isAlive()) || (td3.isAlive()));
    }

}
```

For ThreadDemo2, the sorting of the original input files will generate results identical to ThreadDemo1 of the previous topic The informational line that is displayed on the standard output device for the purposes of illustrating a thread's state is a little different, since I had chosen to use a different method to do suspension:

```
td3 yielding...
td3 yielding...
td3 yielding...
td3 yielding...
td3 yielding...
td1 yielding...
td2 yielding...
td1 yielding...
td2 yielding...
td1 yielding...
td2 yielding...
td1 yielding...
td2 yielding...
td1 yielding...
td2 yielding...
```

Now, we will take a closer look at how this example is different from the previous.

- The first change is quite simple. To keep the different versions of QSort distinct and unique within the global name space, the amended version is placed within its own package called RunnableSort.

- Instead of subclassing QSort from class Thread as was the case earlier, QSort would implement interface Runnable:

```
public class QSort implements Runnable
```

- The QSort class still has its own implementation of method run() and that is unchanged from the previous version. Since interface Runnable has run() as its method prototype, class QSort must provide an implementation for run().

- The core logic of method Partition() is also unchanged from the prior version. The try-catch block for method sleep() of the previous version is replaced with statements:

```
System.out.println(Thread.currentThread().getName()+"
 yielding...");
Thread.yield();
```

The static method yield() is similar to static method sleep() except there is no time-out value. Method yield() will simply suspend the currently active thread and put it into the runnable wait queue.

The static method currentThread() will return a reference to the currently active thread. The non-static method getName() will return the name of the Thread object.

- Since QSort is no longer derived from class Thread, the signature of the only QSort constructor is modified slightly. The third argument, which had represented the thread's name, is dropped.

- The main() method of ThreadDemo2, which drives the example, contains a few changes. After the instantiation of three QSort objects is the instantiation of three Thread objects. This time, a QSort object, which is a Runnable object, is passed into a constructor of Thread. The signature of that constructor looks like:

```
Thread(Runnable, String);
```

where the second argument is the user-assigned name for the Thread object.

- Within method main() of ThreadDemo2, a thread priority is assigned to each of the Thread objects before it is started. The assigning of priorities is done with the setPriority() method of class Thread. This method can accept values from 1 (MIN_PRIORITY) to 10 (MAX_PRIORITY). The default priority is 5 (NORM_PRIORITY).

High priority threads are given preference by the scheduler over those of low priority. In the example, the `Thread` object represented by variable `td3` was given the highest priority of the three threads. From the sample output displayed on the console, `Thread` object `td3` tended to be reactivated after it had yield. Consequently, `td3` was the first to finish processing.

If all the runnable threads have equal priority, the scheduler will activate each thread in a round-robin fashion. Each thread is given an opportunity to run.

• Finally, each of the `Thread` objects of `main()` will call `start()`. This method will set up bookkeeping for each thread and then call the `run()` method of the `Runnable` object that was passed to it in the constructor. In this case, the `Runnable` object is a `QSort` object. All three input files are sorted into three output files as in the previous example.

Note: The results demonstrate another important difference between `yield()` and `sleep()`. The `yield()` method will cause the scheduler to activate a runnable thread that has a priority greater than or equal to the priority of the thread being displaced. Since the thread represented by `td3` has the highest priority, naturally the scheduler would select it to replace itself as the active thread. For a situation where there are many threads of different priorities and the tasks are long, the use of `yield()` may not be suitable since low-priority threads will never execute. Use the `sleep()` method instead.

Contention for Resources and the Java synchronized Keyword

The next example is going to show what happens when several threads have unbridled access to a common resource. The example uses the Java implementation for pipes (`PipedInputStream` and `PipedOutputStream` classes) as the means to foster interthread communication. A number of objects from a user-defined class called `Transmitter` would write to one end of the pipe (the `PipedOutputStream`) and a single object of a user-defined class called `Receiver` would read from the pipe (the `PipedInputStream`). The data to be sent is generated from a pseudo-random number generator, `public static` method `random()` from `final` class `Math` (part of the `java.lang` package). Method `random()` generates a `double` between 0 and 1 (0 inclusive and 1 exclusive).

The following is the listing of the example. I will first discuss the key classes and methods of the example, the possible outcomes from the execution of the code and the inherent problem of the example.

Listing 8-5: ThreadDemo3.java

```java
import java.io.*;

class FullPipe {

    FullPipe() {                                            /* (1) */
    try {
        inPipe  = new PipedInputStream();
        outPipe = new PipedOutputStream(inPipe);
        send_count = 0;
        recv_count = 0;
        }
    catch(IOException err) {
        System.out.println(err.toString());
        System.exit(-1);
        }
    }

    PipedOutputStream getOutPipe() {
    return outPipe;
    }

    PipedInputStream getInPipe() {
    return inPipe;
    }

    long getSendCount () {
    return send_count;
    }

    void updateSendCount(long value) {
    send_count += value;
    }

    long getRecvCount () {
    return recv_count;
    }

    void updateRecvCount(long value) {
    recv_count += value;
    }

    public void close() {
    try {
        inPipe.close();
        outPipe.close();
        }
    catch(IOException err) {
        }
    }
```

```java
    private PipedOutputStream outPipe;
    private PipedInputStream  inPipe;
    private long                 recv_count;
    private long                 send_count;
}


class Transmitter extends Thread {                      /* (2) */

    Transmitter(int times, FullPipe fp) {
    fullPipe = fp;
    iterations = times;
    }

    public void run() {                                 /* (3) */
    int ivalue;
    byte buffer = 0;
    try {
        for (int index = 0; index < iterations; index++) {
            buffer = (byte)(100 * Math.random());
            fullPipe.getOutPipe().write(buffer);
            fullPipe.updateSendCount(1);
            try {
                sleep(1);
                }
            catch(InterruptedException err) {
                System.out.println(err.toString());
                System.exit(-1);
                }
            }
        buffer = (byte) -1;
        fullPipe.getOutPipe().write(buffer);
        }
    catch(IOException err) {
        System.out.println(err.toString());
        System.exit(-1);
        }
    }

    private FullPipe            fullPipe;
    private int                iterations;
}

class Receiver extends Thread {                         /* (4) */

    Receiver(int count, FullPipe fp) {
    fullPipe = fp;
    no_of_senders = count;
    }
```

```
    public void run() {                              /* (5) */
    int   ivalue;
    int count = 0;
    byte [] buffer = new byte[1];
    PipedInputStream dis = fullPipe.getInPipe();
    try {
        while ((ivalue = dis.read(buffer, 0, 1)) != -1){
            if (buffer[0] == -1) {
                count++;
                if (count==no_of_senders)
                    break;
                }
            else {
                fullPipe.updateRecvCount(1);
                if (fullPipe.getRecvCount() % 500 == 0)
                    System.out.println("Send count ="+fullPipe.
                     getSendCount()
                    +", receive count = "+fullPipe.getRecvCount());
                }
            try {
                sleep(1);
                }
            catch(InterruptedException err) {
                System.out.println(err.toString());
                System.exit(-1);
                }
            }  // while
        }
    catch(IOException err) {
        System.out.println(err.toString());
        System.exit(-1);
        }
    }

    private int             no_of_senders;
    private FullPipe    fullPipe;
}

public class ThreadDemo3                    { /* (6) */

    public static void main(String args[]) {
    FullPipe pipe = new FullPipe();
    Transmitter tran1  = new Transmitter(3000, pipe);
    Transmitter tran2  = new Transmitter(3000, pipe);
    Transmitter tran3  = new Transmitter(3000, pipe);
    Transmitter tran4  = new Transmitter(3000, pipe);
    Transmitter tran5  = new Transmitter(3000, pipe);
    Transmitter tran6  = new Transmitter(3000, pipe);
```

```
Transmitter tran7  = new Transmitter(3000, pipe);
Transmitter tran8  = new Transmitter(3000, pipe);
Transmitter tran9  = new Transmitter(3000, pipe);
Transmitter tran10 = new Transmitter(3000, pipe);

Receiver    recv   = new Receiver(10, pipe);

tran1.setPriority(Thread.NORM_PRIORITY + 1);
tran2.setPriority(Thread.NORM_PRIORITY + 1);
tran3.setPriority(Thread.NORM_PRIORITY + 1);
tran4.setPriority(Thread.NORM_PRIORITY + 1);
tran5.setPriority(Thread.NORM_PRIORITY + 1);
tran6.setPriority(Thread.NORM_PRIORITY + 1);
tran7.setPriority(Thread.NORM_PRIORITY + 1);
tran8.setPriority(Thread.NORM_PRIORITY + 1);
tran9.setPriority(Thread.NORM_PRIORITY + 1);
tran10.setPriority(Thread.NORM_PRIORITY + 1);
recv.setPriority(Thread.NORM_PRIORITY + 3);

tran1.start();
tran2.start();
tran3.start();
tran4.start();
tran5.start();
tran6.start();
tran7.start();
tran8.start();
tran9.start();
tran10.start();
recv.start();

while ((tran1.isAlive()) || (tran2.isAlive()) ||
       (tran3.isAlive()) ||
       (tran4.isAlive()) || (tran5.isAlive()) ||
        (tran6.isAlive()) ||
       (tran7.isAlive()) || (tran8.isAlive()) ||
        (tran9.isAlive()) ||
       (tran10.isAlive()) || (recv.isAlive()));

System.out.println("Total number of bytes sent = "
                    + pipe.getSendCount());
System.out.println("Total number of bytes received = "
                    + pipe.getRecvCount());

pipe.close();

System.out.println("(press Enter to exit)");
try {
    System.in.read();
    }
```

```
catch (IOException e) {
    return;
    }
}

}
```

Now, we will examine the key points of the sample program.

- The pipe is a very well-known "first in, first out" (FIFO) data structure that is used for interprocess communication, especially in UNIX. In Java, the utility of the pipe goes a step further: it is for interthread communication. The Java pipe is constructed with the help of two standard classes from the java.io package: PipedInputStream and PipedOutputStream. Each of these classes represents an endpoint of the pipe. Furthermore, both these classes must be used together to build the pipe. The PipedInputStream class represents the end for reading, while the PipedOutputStream class represents the end for writing.

  The ThreadDemo3 example uses a single pipe as the shared resource between the multiple Transmitter objects and the Receiver object. To make this sharing easier, a class called FullPipe (comment /* (1) */) was created.

  The constructor FullPipe() instantiates a PipedInputStream object and a PipedOutputStream object and makes a connection between them with:

  ```
  outPipe = new PipedOutputStream(inPipe);
  ```

  The PipedInputStream and the PipedOutputStream instances are retained in private variable fields, inPipe and outPipe.

  The FullPipe class also has two private long variables, send_count and recv_count, that are used to track and verify how many bytes are transmitted and how many bytes are received. Both these private variables have associated accessor and mutator methods.

- The Transmitter class (comment /* (2) */) represents objects that perform the sending of data to the pipe. The constructor Transmitter(int, FullPipe) takes the number of bytes to be generated and a reference to the already instantiated FullPipe object.

  The Transmitter class is subclassed from class Thread so that such object can share the CPU. That being the case, class Transmitter must override and provide its own run() method (comment /* (3) */). This method has a loop to generate a byte of data and writes the data into the pipe. The Transmitter object would signal completion by sending a byte value of -1.

After the `Transmitter` has written its data to the pipe, it performs a:

```
fullPipe.updateSendCount(1);
```

to increment the actual number of bytes sent. This information is retained in the private `send_count` variable of the `FullPipe` object.

- The `Receiver` class (comment `/* (4) */`) is also subclassed from class `Thread`. The constructor, `Receiver(int, FullPipe)` takes an argument for the number of `Transmitter` objects and the reference to the `FullPipe` object.

Within its `run()` method (`/* (5) */`), the `Receiver` object reads the pipe to collect the data sent to it from the `Transmitter` objects. Executing in its own thread, the `Receiver` reads a byte at a time from the pipe.

Since the data from the pipe comes from multiple sources, the `Receiver` object must track the number of senders who have sent the end-of-data indicator. Once all of the senders have completed transmission, the `Receiver` object disengages from reading the pipe:

```
if (buffer[0] == -1) {
    count++;
    if (count==no_of_senders)
        break;
}
```

While the `Transmitter` objects record the number of bytes sent, the `Receiver` object records the number of bytes received. It does that with:

```
fullPipe.updateRecvCount(1);
```

- Finally, we come to the demonstration class, `ThreadDemo3`. The `main()` method (comment `/* (6) */`) of `ThreadDemo3` instantiates ten `Transmitter` objects and one `Receiver` object. Since all of these objects are really `Thread` objects, each is put into the runnable state by sending each object the `start()` message. Meanwhile, the main thread waits until all of these secondary threads are done. As the program executes, messages are displayed periodically to indicate data being written and read from the pipe. When the secondary threads finish, the main thread will display the total number of bytes sent and the total number of bytes received. The program exits after the `FullPipe` object is closed (which is the closing of its `PipedInputStream` and `PipedOutputStream` components).

Now that we have a basic understanding of what the program does, we can execute it and inspect the output. We are only interested in the final results: the total number of bytes sent versus the total number of bytes received. If each `Transmitter` object does 3000 iterations, we might see something like:

```
...
Send count  =  24000,  receive count  =  24000
Send count  =  24540,  receive count  =  24500
Send count  =  25070,  receive count  =  25000
Send count  =  25500,  receive count  =  25500
Send count  =  26030,  receive count  =  26000
Send count  =  26560,  receive count  =  26500
Send count  =  27100,  receive count  =  27000
Send count  =  27520,  receive count  =  27500
Send count  =  28060,  receive count  =  28000
Send count  =  28590,  receive count  =  28500
Send count  =  29020,  receive count  =  29000
Send count  =  29550,  receive count  =  29500
Send count  =  30000,  receive count  =  30000
Total number of bytes sent = 30000
Total number of bytes received = 30000
```

where the total sent equals the total received. However, if the program is executed a number of times, there will be instances where the total sent will be less than the total received, such as:

```
Total number of bytes sent = 29991
Total number of bytes received = 30000
```

Apparently, something is not quite right!

In the example, there is only one `Receiver` object doing updates to the private `recv_count` field of `FullPipe`, so we can be certain that the number of bytes received is accurate. However, there are ten `Transmitter` objects doing updates to the private `send_count` field of `FullPipe` and this is the essence of the problem.

Each of the `Transmitter` objects updates the private `send_count` field via the `updateSendCount()` method of class `FullPipe`. There is only one statement to this method:

```
send_count += value;
```

but the operations represented by the statement are <u>not</u> atomic. The quantity in variable `value` is not added into variable `send_count` directly. The sequence of steps that really takes place within the underlining byte codes is:

1. make a copy of the contents of `send_count` and put it into a working register,

2. add the contents of `value` to the contents of the register,

3. load the result from the register into variable `send_count`, thus overlaying the previous contents.

A `Transmitter` thread that is about to perform step 3 can be interrupted by the scheduler and placed on the wait queue. Meanwhile another `Transmitter` thread comes along and performs all three steps without interruption. Later, the former thread regains active status to complete step 3. Each of the two `Transmitter` objects had sought to increment `send_count` by one, but the result of both operations is only an increase of one, not two. This sort of activity is potentially repeated many times over the life of the program. Figure 8-1 illustrates this problem.

The solution to resolving this phenomenon is to use the `synchronized` keyword modifier on the `updateSendCount()` method of class `FullPipe`:

```
synchronized void updateSendCount(long value) {
    send_count += value;
    }
```

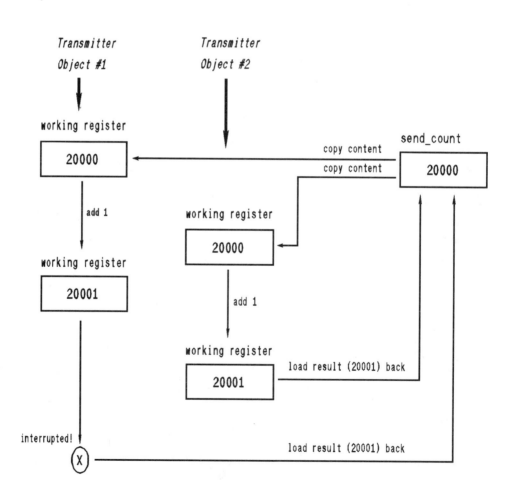

Figure 8-1

The `synchronized` keyword essentially puts a lock on the method so that if one thread is executing the code, another thread cannot come along and do the same.

With synchronized methods, Java will set up a wait queue for threads desiring to execute the method. When the active thread is finished with the method, the scheduler will select the next highest priority thread in the queue to access the method.

Now, the total number of bytes sent will always equal the total number of bytes received.

Summary: Whenever two or more threads perform updates to a shared resource, care must be taken to insure that their efforts do not corrupt each other. Using the `synchronized` modifier on critical methods is a way to avoid such contention. This modifier does not need to be applied to methods that only read data.

Warning: If there are two or more synchronized methods being used, a deadlock situation can arise and hang the system. This can happen if one synchronized method calls another. Thread X owns synchronized method A and waits for access to synchronized method B. Meanwhile, Thread Y has possession of method B and is waiting for method A. Java has no mechanism to avoid these situations. A program must be carefully designed to avoid these circular conditions and provide a means for every waiting thread to eventually become active.

Waiting for Conditions to Change with `wait()` and `notify()`

When a thread gains ownership of a synchronized method, it is possible that conditions may not be suitable for the thread to execute the code. Java has methods for an active thread to suspend itself in hopes that another active thread might change the situation. The suspended thread would proceed once it regains active status.

The `ThreadDemo4` example is a contest among several competing threads to see who can "draw" and display the first integer that is a multiple of 20. The example uses the static method called `random()`, which is the pseudo-random number generator from the `public final Math` class (part of package `java.lang`). The `Math.random()` method returns a `double` value between 0 and 1 (0 inclusive and 1 exclusive).

The following is a listing of `ThreadDemo4`:

Listing 8-6: ThreadDemo4.java

```java
import java.io.IOException;

class Player extends Thread {

    Player(String name, int value) {
    super(name);
    key = value;
    }

    public void run() {
    play();
    try {
        sleep(5);
        }
    catch(InterruptedException err) {
        System.out.println(err.toString());
        System.exit(-1);
        }
    }

    private synchronized void play() {

    while (((key % 20) != 0) && (pause)) {
        try {
            System.out.println(getName()+" has key = "+key);
            wait(5);
            key = (int)(100 * Math.random());
            }
        catch(InterruptedException err) {
            System.out.println(err.toString());
            System.exit(-1);
            }
        }

    System.out.println(getName()+" has finished with "+"key =
     "+key);
    setPause(false);
    notify();
    }

    public static void setPause(boolean value) {
    pause = value;
    }

private int key;
private static boolean pause = true;
}
```

```
public class ThreadDemo4 {

    public static void main(String args[]) {
        int num1 = (int)(100 * Math.random());
        int num2 = (int)(100 * Math.random());
        int num3 = (int)(100 * Math.random());
        int num4 = (int)(100 * Math.random());
        int num5 = (int)(100 * Math.random());

        Player p1 = new Player("p1", num1);
        Player p2 = new Player("p2", num2);
        Player p3 = new Player("p3", num3);
        Player p4 = new Player("p4", num4);
        Player p5 = new Player("p5", num5);

        p1.start();
        p2.start();
        p3.start();
        p4.start();
        p5.start();

        while ((p1.isAlive()) || (p2.isAlive()) || (p3.isAlive()) ||
               (p4.isAlive()) || (p5.isAlive()));
    }
}
```

The results generated on the standard output device would look something like the following (results vary with each run):

```
p5 has key = 12
p2 has key = 15
p2 has key = 5
p5 has key = 86
p2 has key = 52
p1 has key = 50
p5 has key = 54
p2 has key = 95
p1 has key = 27
p5 has finished with key = 40
p3 has key = 85
p4 has key = 74
p1 has key = 57
p2 has key = 47
p4 has finished with key = 3
p3 has finished with key = 37
p1 has finished with key = 36
p2 has finished with key = 82
```

The following are the essentials of the example:

- A `Player` class was subclassed from class `Thread` to represent the participant in the contest. The `Player` object is assigned a name and an initial random number.

- The `Player` class uses a private static Boolean field, `pause`, as a signal to all `Player` instances when the game is over. The field is initialized to `true`.

- Like all classes derived from class `Thread`, the `run()` method must be overridden and implemented. The main method called from `run()` is the private synchronized method `play()`.

- Within method `play()`, the active `Player` object enters a loop if it does not have an integer that is a multiple of 20 and `pause` is `true`. Within the loop, the object would call `wait(long)` with a time-out value. After being blocked for so many milliseconds, it would try to escape the loop by obtaining another random number. Another way the thread escapes is by another thread setting `pause` to `false` and doing a call to method `notify()`. The `notify()` method will notify one thread waiting for conditions to change (whereas `notifyAll()` will notify all waiting threads). Both `wait(long)` and `notify()` can only be used within synchronized methods.

- The first `Player` object with a multiple of 20 will output that fact, set the variable `pause` to `false` and perform a `notify()` for a waiting thread.

- The `main()` method of class `ThreadDemo4` is what drives the example. Five `Player` objects are instantiated with initial values from the `Math.random()` method and all of them are placed into the runnable state with the `start()` message. The main thread then waits until all of the `Player` threads have completed.

Organizing Java Threads into a `ThreadGroup`

Java has a special container class called the `ThreadGroup` which is used to group threads of similar functions. By organizing threads into a `ThreadGroup` object, it becomes easier to suspend, resume or stop an entire set of threads. In addition, one can also set certain properties, such as priorities, that can apply to the whole group.

For this topic, we will look at how to place threads into a `ThreadGroup` object and demonstrate certain methods from the `ThreadGroup` class. `ThreadDemo5` will feature a dialog box with four buttons. The user will have a chance to `start`, `suspend`, `resume` or `stop` all the threads placed into a `ThreadGroup`. `ThreadDemo5` is similar to `ThreadDemo3` (see the earlier topic, *Contention for Resources and the Java synchronized Keyword*) and uses the user-defined

FullPipe, Transmitter and Receiver classes. The only differences are that ThreadDemo5 uses a dialog box built with the Java Abstract Window Toolkit (AWT) and the program displays the results and status in read-only text fields. Since a later chapter will explain the components of the AWT, I will not be dwelling too much on this aspect for this topic. Rather, I will focus on Threads and ThreadGroups. Figure 8-2 shows what the dialog box looks like.

Like the earlier ThreadDemo3, TheadDemo5 instantiates ten Transmitter objects that generate and write data to a pipe while a single Receiver object reads from the pipe. I will not discuss the roles of these classes in detail and leave it to the reader to refer to the discussions around ThreadDemo3. Both the Transmitter and Receiver classes are only slightly changed for ThreadDemo5. The Receiver class for ThreadDemo5 no longer has responsibility for periodically displaying the results. A user-defined Monitor object, which is a subclassed from Thread, is given this task. I will explain the work of the Monitor object very shortly.

Below is a listing of the relevant code behind ThreadDemo5. Code unchanged from ThreadDemo3 has been omitted and substituted with simple comments. The complete source is on the supplied media.

Listing 8-7: ThreadDemo5.java

```java
import java.awt.*;
import java.io.*;

class FullPipe {
```

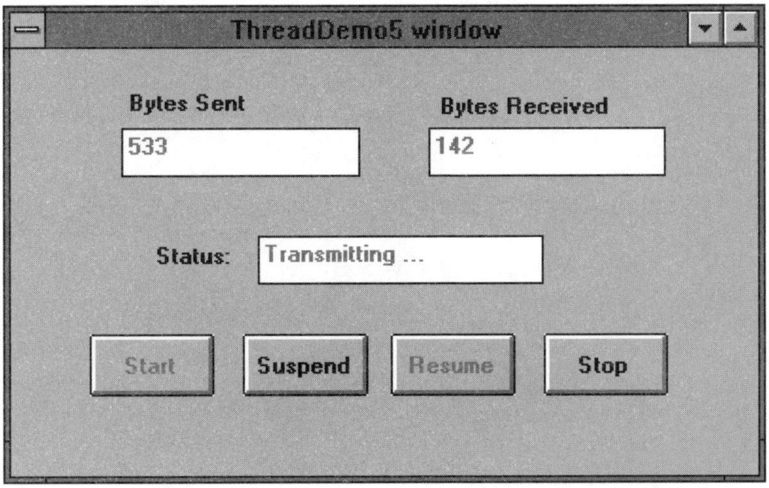

Figure 8-2

```
// Unchanged from ThreadDemo3

}

class Transmitter extends Thread {

Transmitter(ThreadGroup group, String name, int times, FullPipe
 fp) {
    super(group, name);                              /* (1) */
    fullPipe = fp;
    iterations = times;
    }

// The rest  is unchanged from ThreadDemo3

}

class Receiver extends Thread {

    Receiver(ThreadGroup group, String name, int count, FullPipe
     fp) {
    super(group, name);                              /* (1) */
    fullPipe = fp;
    no_of_senders = count;
    }

    public void run() {

    // This portion is unchanged

    try {
        while ( ((ivalue = dis.read(buffer, 0, 1)) != -1) &&
        (not_done) ){
          if (buffer[0] == -1) {

        // This portion is unchanged

            }
          else {
            fullPipe.updateRecvCount(1); // No more displaying
                                         of the
            }                            // send_count and
                                         recv_count
          try {                          // to the standard
                                         output device
            sleep(1);
            }
        catch(InterruptedException err) {
            System.out.println(err.toString());
            System.exit(-1);
            }
```

```
                } // while
            }
    catch(IOException err) {
        System.out.println(err.toString());
        System.exit(-1);
        }
    }

    private int              no_of_senders;
    private FullPipe    fullPipe;
}

class Monitor extends Thread {                              /* (2) */
    Monitor(ThreadGroup group, String name, FullPipe fp,
            TextField send, TextField receive, TextField status,
            Thread recvThread, Button beginButton, Button
             endButton,
            Button continueButton, Button pauseButton) {
    super(group, name);
    fullPipe             = fp;
    sendField          = send;
    recvField          = receive;
    statusField        = status;
    receiveThread = recvThread;
    startButton        = beginButton;
    stopButton         = endButton;
    resumeButton   = continueButton;
    suspendButton = pauseButton;
    }

    public void run()
    while (true) {
        if (fullPipe.getRecvCount() % 20 == 0) {
            sendField.setText(new
             Long(fullPipe.getSendCount()).toString());
            recvField.setText(new
             Long(fullPipe.getRecvCount()).toString());
            statusField.setText("Transmitting ...");
            }
        if (!receiveThread.isAlive()) {
            statusField.setText("Transfer Completed");
            startButton.enable();
            stopButton.disable();
            resumeButton.disable();
            suspendButton.disable();
            break;
            }
        try {
            sleep(10);
            }
        catch (InterruptedException err) {
```

```
                }
            }
        }

        private FullPipe   fullPipe;
        private TextField sendField;
        private TextField recvField;
        private TextField statusField;
        private Thread     receiveThread;
        private Button     startButton;
        private Button     stopButton;
        private Button     resumeButton;
        private Button     suspendButton;

}

public class ThreadDemo5 extends Frame {

    public ThreadDemo5() {

        super("ThreadDemo5 window");
        threadGroup = null;

        setLayout(null);
        addNotify();
        resize(insets().left + insets().right + 396, insets().top
                + insets().bottom + 227);
        sendField=new TextField(15);
        sendField.setFont(new Font("Dialog",Font.BOLD,12));
        sendField.disable();
        add(sendField);
        sendField.reshape(insets().left + 59,insets().top +
         42,126,26);
        recvField=new TextField(15);
        recvField.setFont(new Font("Dialog",Font.BOLD,12));
        recvField.disable();
        add(recvField);
        recvField.reshape(insets().left + 221,insets().top +
         42,126,26);
        startButton=new Button("Start");
        startButton.setFont(new Font("Dialog",Font.BOLD,12));
        add(startButton);
        startButton.reshape(insets().left + 42,insets().top +
         151,66,33);
        suspendButton=new Button("Suspend");
        suspendButton.setFont(new Font("Dialog",Font.BOLD,12));
        suspendButton.disable();
        add(suspendButton);
        suspendButton.reshape(insets().left + 123,insets().top +
         151,66,33);
```

```
        resumeButton=new Button("Resume");
        resumeButton.setFont(new Font("Dialog",Font.BOLD,12));
        resumeButton.disable();
        add(resumeButton);
        resumeButton.reshape(insets().left + 201,insets().top +
         151,66,33);
        stopButton=new Button("Stop");
        stopButton.setFont(new Font("Dialog",Font.BOLD,12));
        stopButton.disable();
        add(stopButton);
        stopButton.reshape(insets().left + 282,insets().top +
         151,66,33);
        statusField=new TextField(18);
        statusField.setFont(new Font("Dialog",Font.BOLD,12));
        statusField.disable();
        add(statusField);
        statusField.reshape(insets().left + 131,insets().top +
         99,151,26);
        statusLabel=new Label("Status:");
        statusLabel.setFont(new Font("Dialog",Font.BOLD,12));
        add(statusLabel);
        statusLabel.reshape(insets().left + 65,insets().top +
         101,55,18);
        sendLabel=new Label("Bytes Sent");
        sendLabel.setFont(new Font("Dialog",Font.BOLD,12));
        add(sendLabel);
        sendLabel.reshape(insets().left + 51,insets().top +
         21,95,16);
        recvLabel=new Label("Bytes Received");
        recvLabel.setFont(new Font("Dialog",Font.BOLD,12));
        add(recvLabel);
        recvLabel.reshape(insets().left + 215,insets().top +
         21,108,20);

        show();
    }

public synchronized void show() {
    move(50, 50);
    super.show();
}

public boolean handleEvent(Event event) {          /* (6) */

    if (event.id == Event.WINDOW_DESTROY) {
        if (threadGroup != null) {
            threadGroup.stop();
            threadGroup.destroy();
            }
          hide();
```

```java
        dispose();
        System.exit(0);
        return true;
    }
    return super.handleEvent(event);
}

public boolean action(Event event, Object arg)     {/* (3) */
    if (event.target instanceof Button) {
        String label = (String) arg;
        if (label.equalsIgnoreCase("Start")) {
            startThreads();
            startButton.disable();
            stopButton.enable();
            suspendButton.enable();
            resumeButton.disable();
            return true;
            }
        else
        if (label.equalsIgnoreCase("Suspend")) {
            suspendThreads();
            suspendButton.disable();
            resumeButton.enable();
            return true;
            }
        else
        if (label.equalsIgnoreCase("Resume")) {
            resumeThreads();
            resumeButton.disable();
            suspendButton.enable();
            return true;
            }
        else
        if (label.equalsIgnoreCase("Stop")) {
            stopThreads();
            stopButton.disable();
            startButton.enable();
            suspendButton.disable();
            resumeButton.disable();
            return true;
            }
    }
    return super.action(event, arg);
}

public void startThreads() {                        /* (4) */
FullPipe pipe = new FullPipe();

threadGroup = new ThreadGroup("ThreadDemo5");
```

```
Transmitter tran1   = new Transmitter(threadGroup,  "tran1",
  200, pipe);
Transmitter tran2   = new Transmitter(threadGroup,  "tran2",
  200, pipe);
Transmitter tran3   = new Transmitter(threadGroup,  "tran3",
  200, pipe);
Transmitter tran4   = new Transmitter(threadGroup,  "tran4",
  200, pipe);
Transmitter tran5   = new Transmitter(threadGroup,  "tran5",
  200, pipe);
Transmitter tran6   = new Transmitter(threadGroup,  "tran6",
  200, pipe);
Transmitter tran7   = new Transmitter(threadGroup,  "tran7",
  200, pipe);
Transmitter tran8   = new Transmitter(threadGroup,  "tran8",
  200, pipe);
Transmitter tran9   = new Transmitter(threadGroup,  "tran9",
  200, pipe);
Transmitter tran10 = new Transmitter(threadGroup,  "tran10",
  200, pipe);
Receiver    recv     = new Receiver(threadGroup,  "recv",
  10, pipe);
Monitor     watch    = new Monitor(threadGroup,  "watch",
                   pipe,
                   sendField, recvField, statusField,
                   recv, startButton, stopButton,
                   resumeButton, suspendButton);

threadGroup.setMaxPriority(Thread.NORM_PRIORITY-1);
recv.setPriority(Thread.NORM_PRIORITY+2);
watch.setPriority(Thread.NORM_PRIORITY+2);

tran1.start();
tran2.start();
tran3.start();
tran4.start();
tran5.start();
tran6.start();
tran7.start();
tran8.start();
tran9.start();
tran10.start();
recv.start();
watch.start();

sendField.setText("0");
recvField.setText("0");
statusField.setText("Started...");
```

```
        }

        public void suspendThreads() {                    /* (5) */
        threadGroup.suspend();
        statusField.setText("Suspended...");
        }

        public void resumeThreads() {                     /* (5) */
        threadGroup.resume();
        statusField.setText("Resumed...");
        }

        public void stopThreads() {                       /* (5) */
        threadGroup.stop();
        statusField.setText("Stopped...");
        }

        public static void main(String args[]) {
            new ThreadDemo5();
        }

        private ThreadGroup threadGroup;
        private TextField sendField;
        private TextField recvField;
        private Button startButton;
        private Button suspendButton;
        private Button resumeButton;
        private Button stopButton;
        private TextField statusField;
        private Label statusLabel;
        private Label sendLabel;
        private Label recvLabel;

}
```

Now, let us take a look at the essential points of the above example.

- The constructors for class `Transmitter` and class `Receiver` (comment
  `/* (1) */`) had undergone minor changes. The signatures were
  expanded to accept a `ThreadGroup` and a `String`. The `Thread` class has
  a constructor with signature `Thread(ThreadGroup thread_group,
  String thread_name)` and since both `Transmitter` and `Receiver`
  are subclasses of `Thread`, we must provide constructors so that
  `Transmitter` and `Receiver` objects can become members of a
  `ThreadGroup`. Within the bodies of each of the constructors, the statement:

  ```
  super(group, name);
  ```

  is a call to base constructor `Thread(ThreadGroup, String)`.

- As mentioned earlier, class `Receiver` no longer has responsibility for periodically displaying the count statistics. A new subclass of `Thread`, class `Monitor`, has that responsibility (comment `/* (2) */`). In fact, class `Monitor` is in charge of updating the text fields and buttons of class `ThreadDemo5` while the data transfer is in progress.

  Like all subclasses of `Thread`, a `run()` method is implemented for class `Monitor`. Whenever the total number of bytes received is a multiple of 20, the `sent_count` and `recv_count` fields of `FullPipe` are read and displayed on the screen. It is important to note that the display of the total bytes received may not show a multiple of 20 because the `Monitor` object may become inactive from the time the condition is tested and the time the `recv_count` field is read again for display in the text field.

  Since the single `Receiver` object would be the last important `ThreadGroup` object to be active, the `Monitor` object would test its state with the `isActive()` method to determine when the data transfer is complete. When the process does complete, the `Monitor` object will display that fact in the status text field and exit the run loop.

- The demonstration class, `ThreadDemo5`, is a standard application using the AWT. It is <u>not</u> an applet. As such, the class is subclassed from class `Frame` and it has the typical `public static main()` method.

  The constructor for `ThreadDemo5` has the responsibility for creating and initializing instances of all the necessary window controls (`Label`, `Button` and `TextField` objects).

- The windowing environment of Java is a message-driven environment. As such, any subclass of class `Frame` that has window controls is most likely to have an `action()` method of its own (comment `/* (3) */`). The `action()` method is where the event is analyzed for its origin and a determination is made for a course of action (such the user clicking on a particular button for a service).

  Basically, the `action()` method of `ThreadDemo5` tests to see if the event object had originated from a `Button` object. If so, further tests are conducted to see which button so the correct activity can be performed (start the threads, suspend the thread group, resume the thread group or stop the thread group).

  The `action()` method also insures that only certain buttons would be enabled depending on the state of the whole program. For instance, if the threads have yet to be started, the `Stop` button is disabled.

- The `startThreads()` method (comment `/* (4) */`) is a major action method of `ThreadDemo5`. Here is where all the `Transmitter` objects,

Receiver object and Monitor object are created and associated with the ThreadGroup object.

One interesting point is that a maximum priority can be established for the ThreadGroup:

```
threadGroup.setMaxPriority(Thread.NORM_PRIORITY-1);
```

However, even after the Thread objects acquire membership in this group, individual Thread objects can still have their priorities adjusted beyond the maximum for the group. Such is the case for the single Receiver and single Monitor objects:

```
recv.setPriority(Thread.NORM_PRIORITY+2);
watch.setPriority(Thread.NORM_PRIORITY+2);
```

- The remaining action methods, suspendThreads(), resumeThreads() and stopThreads() (comment /* (5) */) are tied to the Suspend, Resume and Stop buttons, respectively.

  Each of these methods is very straightforward since each button action has a method that applies to the entire thread group. For instance, one statement will suspend all threads of the thread group:

  ```
  threadGroup.suspend();
  ```

  Likewise for the resumption and stopping all the threads.

  Suspending a thread means to temporarily halt it and put it into the blocked state. Resuming a thread is to make it runnable again so that it can become active. Stopping a thread is to kill it or put it into the dead state.

- Finally, when the user is done with the program, there is the handleEvent() method (comment /* (6) */) which deals with clean-up before the main window is destroyed.

  When the user closes the window, one of the last messages to come to the main window is Event.WINDOW_DESTROY. Method handleEvent() tests for this message and if true, the threads of the ThreadGroup object are stopped and the ThreadGroup object itself is destroyed as part of the clean-up process:

  ```
  if (threadGroup != null) {
      threadGroup.stop();
      threadGroup.destroy();
      }
  ```

Summary: The ThreadGroup class of Java provides a handy way to group threads of similar functionality so that they can be manipulated as a unit.

CHAPTER
9

- The Quest for a Common Denominator

- The Java AWT Event-Driven Environment

- Events in a Microsoft Foundation Class Environment

- Converting a Stand-Alone Java Application to an Applet

- Simple Layout Managers

- Stacking the Deck: The CardLayout Manager of Java

- Optimizing Flexibility with the Java `GridBagLayout` Manager

The Java AWT: Windows to Many Worlds

The Quest for a Common Denominator

In today's world, it is impossible to be successful with an interactive, commercial software product unless you make your product easy to use for your customer (often referred to as "user friendliness"). Ease of use means that the product must be straightforward, intuitive and does not require a lot of new learning. For interactive software, it means making good use of graphical user interface components such as text fields, list boxes, buttons and menus and organizing these components in such a way that the user will be successful with the program's functions.

In order to give the customer this friendly, graphical user interface, you or your development team must be familiar with at least one of the many popular user interface libraries (Microsoft Windows 95™ or NT, OSF Motif™, Macintosh, etc.) dominant in the industry today. All of these user interface systems are highly sophisticated and require considerable training and experience in order to program correctly. Without the help of expensive third party code generators, the creation, placement, sizing, coloring and management of a single window component (also called widget) could require many lines of code. Worst of all, an investment with one of these technologies means that the product only runs on the machine or operating system that supports that user interface library.

The quest for a common set of "look and feel" specifications has come a long way over the years and this has certainly influenced all of the windowing systems mentioned. Everyone offers the standard window with similar menus, similar text fields, similar list boxes, similar check boxes, etc. Many of the functions ("Open , " "Save As...") have common semantics and widget behavior is very similar (such as mutual exclusiveness for a group of radio buttons).

However, the effort to forge a common applications programming interface (API) behind the widgets has not made much progress and is an area that still leaves much to be desired.

The release of the Java language with its Abstract Window Toolkit (AWT) is the latest of several steps to unify the industry on a single windowing system. Java and its AWT is a layer that uses the native windowing system and provides a common API for user interface development. It means that a windows-based Java application can be developed once and it can be expected to behave in the same manner, whether the underlining windows system is OSF Motif™, Windows NT or Macintosh. Portability is the single most important advantage offered by the AWT.

Since the Java Abstract Window Toolkit™ is intended to be portable across platforms, it is only a subset of the features of each of the native windowing systems. The first release of the AWT only offers basic features found in all of the native user interface toolkits. For example, if you compare AWT to the Microsoft Windows Visual C++ 4.0™ development package, you will not find controls like track bars, spin buttons and progress meters. If your application must use these sophisticated controls, then you must design your own with Java and the AWT, buy a vendor's package or use a native toolkit that offers the features.

None of the native user interface libraries is considered part of any programming language standard, even though all of the libraries have C language bindings. Their popularity and influence mostly stems from the marketing power of various corporations and the efforts of standards committees representing various segments of the industry.

The release of the AWT is a bold move to promote a new protocol for user interface development as well as the Java programming language. Obtaining a basic understanding of this protocol would be a major advantage for any software developer.

However, it must be recognized that the current AWT is far from perfect. This is to be expected of any new product with such lofty goals. As of this writing, it is undergoing major enhancements and changes for the upcoming Java 1.1 release.

In this chapter, the focus will be on the basics of the AWT for user interface development. Wherever applicable, comparisons will be made to native window systems in order to demonstrate equivalent features or functionality. A major area of discussion in this chapter is a comparison of the layout management schemes offered by Java versus traditional, equivalent schemes offered by OSF Motif™. In addition, the chapter will discuss the fundamental programmatic differences between a Java application and a Java applet.

The Java AWT Event-Driven Environment

Java programs that are built with the Abstract Window Toolkit run in an event-driven environment. Unlike conventional procedural language programs where the flow of control is sequential, a Java AWT application or applet is asynchronous. The AWT code waits for user input: keystrokes, mouse movements, mouse clicks, button selections, menu selections, etc. Each event of interest is trapped by your code and processed by a method called a message handler.

For programs with graphical user interfaces (GUI), the object-oriented and event-driven approaches work very well together. For class frameworks like the Java AWT or the Microsoft Foundation Classes™ (for Microsoft Windows 95™ or NT), a default set of classes is provided for the developer to mix, match and customize. To be proficient with these toolkits is a matter of understanding the predefined protocols and rules for working with the various classes.

To become successful with any of these toolkits, a developer must learn the types of messages that are routed to the GUI application, the order of the messages and what default methods must be overridden in order to provide custom processing. Both the Java and the Microsoft Windows environments send numerous messages of various types to their respective client applications. In normal everyday practice, a developer would only be interested in a small subset of all the message types.

In this section, I will demonstrate where all the incoming messages can be trapped within a typical Java AWT application (which applies to applets as well). An understanding of the order of the events is essential for synchronizing the activities of an application (you do not put on your shoes before your socks!). In the next section, I will demonstrate an equivalent example written with the Microsoft Foundation Classes™ (MFC).

The sample Java AWT program is called `EventDemo`. It is a window with a few AWT window controls. The program produces an ASCII text file called "MESSAGES.TXT," which contains an assortment of incoming messages generated either by the user working with the controls or by the Java environment itself. Below is a listing of the relevant source (the highlighted code represent key points of the example):

Listing 9-1: EventDemo.java

```
import java.awt.*;
import java.io.*;

public class EventDemo extends Frame {          /* (1) */

    public EventDemo() {                         /* (2) */
```

```java
super("EventDemo window");

try {
   ps =
      new PrintStream(new FileOutputStream("MESSAGES.TXT"));
   }
catch(IOException err) {
   System.out.println(err.toString());
   System.exit(-1);
   }

 setLayout(null);
 addNotify();
 resize(insets().left + insets().right + 279,
        insets().top + insets().bottom + 530);
 choice1= new Choice();
 choice1= new Choice();
 choice1.addItem("Chocolate");
 choice1.addItem("Peach");
 choice1.addItem("Pumpkin");
 choice1.addItem("Vanilla");
 choice1.addItem("Spumoni");
 choice1.addItem("Rocky Road");
 choice1.addItem("Strawberry");
 choice1.addItem("French Vanilla");
 choice1.addItem("Dutch Apple");
 choice1.addItem("Mocha");
 choice1.addItem("Cookies 'n Cream");
 choice1.addItem("Mandarin Orange");
 add(choice1);
 choice1.reshape(insets().left + 30,insets().top +
  156,222,150);

 // more statements to create the other window controls

 show();
}

public synchronized void show() {
  move(50, 50);
  super.show();
}

public boolean handleEvent(Event event) {          /* (4) */
   if (event.id == Event.MOUSE_MOVE)
     return super.handleEvent(event);
   else
   if (event.id == Event.WINDOW_DESTROY) {
      ps.println(event.toString());
      ps.close();
```

```
                    hide();
                    dispose();
                    System.exit(0);
                    return true;
                }
            else
              ps.println(event.toString());

            return super.handleEvent(event);
            }

            public boolean action(Event event, Object arg) {   /* (3) */
                return super.action(event, arg);
            }

            public static void main(String args[]) {
                new EventDemo();
            }

        private CheckboxGroup group1;
        private Choice choice1;
        private Button OKButton;
        private Button cancelButton;
        private Label typeLabel;
        private Label flavorLabel;
        private Label dessertLabel;
        private Checkbox iceCreamButton;
        private Checkbox frozenYogartButton;
        private Checkbox caramelToppingCheckBox;
        private Checkbox cherriesCheckBox;
        private Checkbox nutsCheckBox;
        private TextField additionalTextField;
        private Label additionalLabel;
        private PrintStream ps;

}
```

The above is a stand-alone AWT application, which is executed from the command line:

```
java    EventDemo
```

As the user tracks the mouse and clicks on the check boxes, buttons and text field, a series of messages would be collected into file MESSAGES.TXT. The contents would look something like:

```
java.awt.Event[id=504,x=265,y=144,target=EventDemo[50,50,287x557,
 resizable,title=EventDemo window]]
java.awt.Event[id=1001,x=166,y=114,target=java.awt.Checkbox[166,1
 14,120x26,label=Frozen Yogurt,state=true],arg=true]
```

The window that appears would look like:

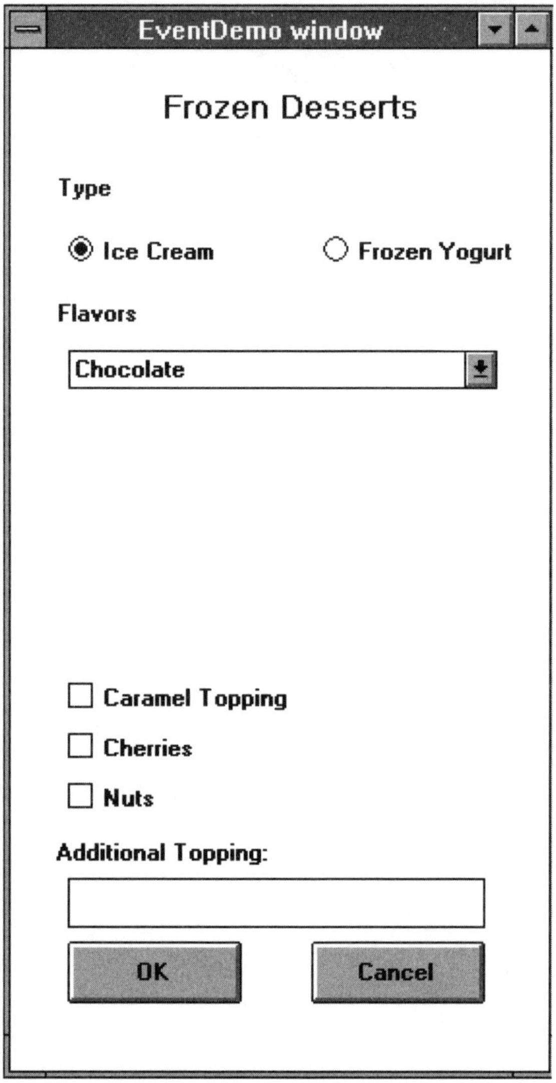

Figure 9-1

```
java.awt.Event[id=1001,x=34,y=114,target=java.awt.Checkbox[34,114
   ,120x26,label=Ice Cream,state=true],arg=true]
java.awt.Event[id=403,x=34,y=179,key=1005,target=java.awt.Choice
   [34,179,150x30,current=Chocolate]]
java.awt.Event[id=1001,x=34,y=179,target=java.awt.Choice[34,179,1
   50x30,current=Dutch Apple],arg=Dutch Apple]
```

```
java.awt.Event[id=404,x=34,y=179,key=1005,target=java.awt.Choice
 [34,179,150x30,current=Dutch Apple]]
java.awt.Event[id=403,x=34,y=179,key=1005,target=java.awt.Choice
 [34,179,150x30,current=Dutch Apple]]
java.awt.Event[id=404,x=34,y=179,key=1005,target=java.awt.Choice
 [34,179,150x30,current=Dutch Apple]]
java.awt.Event[id=1001,x=34,y=179,target=java.awt.Choice[34,179,1
 50x30,current=Mocha],arg=Mocha]
java.awt.Event[id=1001,x=34,y=179,target=java.awt.Choice[34,179,1
 50x30,current=Mandarin Orange],arg=Mandarin Orange]
java.awt.Event[id=1001,x=34,y=348,target=java.awt.Checkbox[34,348
 ,126x20,label=Caramel Topping,state=true],arg=true]
java.awt.Event[id=1001,x=34,y=374,target=java.awt.Checkbox[34,374
 ,120x20,label=Cherries,state=true],arg=true]
java.awt.Event[id=1001,x=34,y=400,target=java.awt.Checkbox[34,400
 ,120x20,label=Nuts,state=true],arg=true]
java.awt.Event[id=401,x=34,y=452,key=66,shift,target=java.awt.
 TextField[34,452,216x26,text=,editable,selection=0-0]]
java.awt.Event[id=402,x=34,y=452,key=66,shift,target=java.awt.
 TextField[34,452,216x26,text=B,editable,selection=1-1]]
java.awt.Event[id=402,x=34,y=452,target=java.awt.TextField[34,
 452,216x26,text=B,editable,selection=1-1]]
java.awt.Event[id=401,x=34,y=452,key=97,target=java.awt.Text
 Field[34,452,216x26,text=B,editable,selection=1-1]]
java.awt.Event[id=402,x=34,y=452,key=97,target=java.awt.Text
 Field[34,452,216x26,text=Ba,editable,selection=2-2]]
java.awt.Event[id=401,x=34,y=452,key=110,target=java.awt.Text
 Field[34,452,216x26,text=Ba,editable,selection=2-2]]
java.awt.Event[id=402,x=34,y=452,key=110,target=java.awt.Text
 Field[34,452,216x26,text=Ban,editable,selection=3-3]]
java.awt.Event[id=401,x=34,y=452,key=110,target=java.awt.Text
 Field[34,452,216x26,text=Ban,editable,selection=3-3]]
java.awt.Event[id=402,x=34,y=452,key=110,target=java.awt.Text
 Field[34,452,216x26,text=Bann,editable,selection=4-4]]
java.awt.Event[id=401,x=34,y=452,key=97,target=java.awt.Text
 Field[34,452,216x26,text=Bann,editable,selection=4-4]]
java.awt.Event[id=402,x=34,y=452,key=97,target=java.awt.Text
 Field[34,452,216x26,text=Banna,editable,selection=5-5]]
java.awt.Event[id=401,x=34,y=452,key=110,target=java.awt.Text
 Field[34,452,216x26,text=Banna,editable,selection=5-5]]
java.awt.Event[id=402,x=34,y=452,key=110,target=java.awt.Text
 Field[34,452,216x26,text=Bannan,editable,selection=6-6]]
java.awt.Event[id=401,x=34,y=452,key=97,target=java.awt.Text
 Field[34,452,216x26,text=Bannan,editable,selection=6-6]]
java.awt.Event[id=402,x=34,y=452,key=97,target=java.awt.Text
 Field[34,452,216x26,text=Bannana,editable,selection=7-7]]
java.awt.Event[id=1001,x=34,y=485,target=java.awt.Button[34,485,
 90x32,label=OK],arg=OK]
java.awt.Event[id=201,x=0,y=0,target=EventDemo[50,50,287x557,
 resizable,title=EventDemo window]]
```

Below is a discussion of the key points of the example:

- Since `EventDemo` is a stand-alone Java application (not applet), class `EventDemo` (comment `/* (1) */`) is subclassed from AWT class `Frame`. The `Frame` class represents a top-level window that can accept a menu and other window components. It is not an applet because it is a free-floating window that cannot be embedded into the window of a browser.

- The no-argument default constructor `EventDemo()` (comment `/* (2) */`) instantiates, initializes and locates the window components displayed on the frame. To simplify the discussion, I will not dwell on the details of each type of Java component. For now, the important activity of the constructor is to create a `PrintStream` object to collect the diagnostic output and the `show();` statement at the end of the body. The call to `show()` means to make the frame and all of its child components visible. It is a required statement for all stand-alone AWT applications.

- The `action()` method (comment `/* (3) */`) is where window control selection messages are trapped for any special processing. In this example, no real work is being done, so the incoming messages are rerouted to the default `action()` method of the base class `Component` (which is an ancestor of class `Frame`):

```
return super.action(event, arg);
```

- The `handleEvent(Event)` method (comment `/* (4) */`) is where <u>all</u> messages come through. The default method is in class `Component`, an ancestor class to `Frame`. In a real application, this method would be overwritten to deal with Scrollbar-related events.

  The `handleEvent` method receives an object of type `Event`. The `Event` object would have information like the type of the object that initiated the event, the x and y coordinates of the event and the time stamp of the event. The actual combination of properties would vary depending on the event type (for example, if it involves the mouse, the x and y coordinates are recorded at the time of the event). All of the state information about the `Event` object can be outputted and viewed by calling the `toString()` method.

  To keep things simple, the `handleEvent()` method of `EventDemo` avoids recording the MOUSE_MOVE events, since such events are extremely numerous (and not terribly exciting). The `event id` is an integral value and represents the actual event type. These event types are represented as `final` variables and they can be found in the source file `Event.java` (this is provided with the Java Developer's Kit). For instance, values 403 and 404 are the KEY_ACTION and KEY_ACTION_RELEASE messages, respectively. These messages are generated as the result of the user typing within the text field under the label "`Additional Flavors.`" Value 1001 is the `ACTION_EVENT` message, which is the result of the user clicking on the radio buttons, check boxes, push buttons and choice control. Finally, there is the `WINDOW_DESTROY` message (value 201) which is the result of the user closing the main application window.

It should be noted that the default `handleEvent()` method of class `Component` routes all non-Scrollbar-related events to another default method called `action()`. Method `action()` would have been implemented in `EventDemo` if we had serious work to perform in response to button and choice selections.

Events in a Microsoft Foundation Class Environment

In this section, we will look at an equivalent example written with C++ and the Microsoft Foundation Classes™ (from Visual C++ 4.0 Professional Edition). It is not my intention to dwell on the minute details of the MFC architecture since this is really a subject deserving its own book. Rather, the purpose of the example is to show the similarities between the Java messaging system and that of Microsoft Windows 95™ or NT.

The following MFC code was built with the help of the Class Wizard™ tool of the Microsoft Developer Studio™ (the name of the development environment). Whenever a new project is created in Studio, a number of source files are generated. Only those relevant to this topic are listed. All of the sources and their make file can be found on the included media.

To keep the example relatively simple, the window of figure 9-1 is implemented as a dialog-based application. The relevant listings follow (the highlighted code represent the main points of the example):

Listing 9-2: EventDemo.h

```
// EventDemo.h : main header file for the EVENTDEMO application
//

#ifndef __AFXWIN_H__
        #error include 'stdafx.h' before including this file for
        PCH
#endif

#include "resource.h"// main symbols


/////////////////////////////////////////////////////////////////
 //////////////
// CEventDemoApp:
// See EventDemo.cpp for the implementation of this class
//
```

```
class CEventDemoApp : public CWinApp                    /* (1) */
{
public:
    CEventDemoApp();

// Overrides
// ClassWizard generated virtual function overrides
//{{AFX_VIRTUAL(CEventDemoApp)
public:
    virtual BOOL InitInstance();
//}}AFX_VIRTUAL

// Implementation

//{{AFX_MSG(CEventDemoApp)
// NOTE - the ClassWizard will add and remove member functions
 here.
//   DO NOT EDIT what you see in these blocks of generated code !
//}}AFX_MSG
DECLARE_MESSAGE_MAP()
};
```

Listing 9-3: EventDemo.cpp

```
// EventDemo.cpp : Defines the class behaviors for the
 application.
//

#include "stdafx.h"
#include "EventDemo.h"
#include "EventDemoDlg.h"

#ifdef _DEBUG
#define new DEBUG_NEW
#undef THIS_FILE
static char THIS_FILE[] = __FILE__;
#endif

/////////////////////////////////////////////////////////////////
 ///////////
// CEventDemoApp

BEGIN_MESSAGE_MAP(CEventDemoApp, CWinApp)
//{{AFX_MSG_MAP(CEventDemoApp)
// NOTE - the ClassWizard will add and remove mapping macros
 here.
//   DO NOT EDIT what you see in these blocks of generated code!
//}}AFX_MSG
```

```
ON_COMMAND(ID_HELP, CWinApp::OnHelp)
END_MESSAGE_MAP()

/////////////////////////////////////////////////////////////////
//////////
// CEventDemoApp construction

CEventDemoApp::CEventDemoApp()
{
    // TODO: add construction code here,
    // Place all significant initialization in InitInstance
}

/////////////////////////////////////////////////////////////////
//////////
// The one and only CEventDemoApp object

CEventDemoApp theApp;

/////////////////////////////////////////////////////////////////
//////////
// CEventDemoApp initialization

BOOL CEventDemoApp::InitInstance()
{
    // Standard initialization
    // If you are not using these features and wish to reduce the
 size
    //  of your final executable, you should remove from the
 following
    //  the specific initialization routines you do not need.

#ifdef _AFXDLL
    Enable3dControls();     // Call this when using MFC in a shared
 DLL
#else
    Enable3dControlsStatic();     // Call this when linking to MFC
 statically
#endif

    CEventDemoDlg dlg;
    m_pMainWnd = &dlg;
    int nResponse = dlg.DoModal();                    /* (2) */
    if (nResponse == IDOK)
    {
        // TODO: Place code here to handle when the dialog is
        //  dismissed with OK
    }
    else if (nResponse == IDCANCEL)
    {
```

```
    // TODO: Place code here to handle when the dialog is
    //  dismissed with Cancel
    }

    // Since the dialog has been closed, return FALSE so that we
exit the
    //  application, rather than start the application's message
pump.
    return FALSE;
}
```

Listing 9-4: EventDemoDlg.h

```
// EventDemoDlg.h : header file
//

/////////////////////////////////////////////////////////////////////
///////////
// CEventDemoDlg dialog

class CEventDemoDlg : public Cdialog                    /* (3) */
{
// Construction
public:
    CEventDemoDlg(CWnd* pParent = NULL);    // standard constructor
    ~CEventDemoDlg();                                  /* (6) */
    virtual BOOL OnWndMsg( UINT message, WPARAM wParam, /* (7) */
  LPARAM lParam, LRESULT* pResult );

// Dialog Data
//{{AFX_DATA(CEventDemoDlg)
    enum { IDD = IDD_EVENTDEMO_DIALOG };
// NOTE: the ClassWizard will add data members here
//}}AFX_DATA

// ClassWizard generated virtual function overrides
//{{AFX_VIRTUAL(CEventDemoDlg)
protected:
    virtual void DoDataExchange(CDataExchange* pDX);    // DDX/DDV
 support
//}}AFX_VIRTUAL

// Implementation
protected:
    HICON m_hIcon;

// Generated message map functions
//{{AFX_MSG(CEventDemoDlg)
    virtual BOOL OnInitDialog();
    afx_msg void OnPaint();
```

```
    afx_msg HCURSOR OnQueryDragIcon();
//}}AFX_MSG
    DECLARE_MESSAGE_MAP()

private:

    CStdioFile  rfile;                                      /* (3) */
};
```

Listing 9-5: EventDemoDlg.cpp

```cpp
// EventDemoDlg.cpp : implementation file
//

#include "stdafx.h"
#include "EventDemo.h"
#include "EventDemoDlg.h"

#ifdef _DEBUG
#define new DEBUG_NEW
#undef THIS_FILE
static char THIS_FILE[] = __FILE__;
#endif

/////////////////////////////////////////////////////////////////
///////////
// CEventDemoDlg dialog

CEventDemoDlg::CEventDemoDlg(CWnd* pParent /*=NULL*/)
    : CDialog(CEventDemoDlg::IDD, pParent)
{
    //{{AFX_DATA_INIT(CEventDemoDlg)
// NOTE: the ClassWizard will add member initialization here
    //}}AFX_DATA_INIT
    // Note that LoadIcon does not require a subsequent
DestroyIcon in Win32
    m_hIcon = AfxGetApp()->LoadIcon(IDR_MAINFRAME);        /* (4) */
    if (!rfile.Open("RESULTS.TXT", CFile::modeCreate |
CFile::modeWrite)) {
        MessageBox("Cannot open file RESULTS.TXT", NULL, MB_OK);
        rfile.Abort();
      }
}

CEventDemoDlg::~CEventDemoDlg()                            /* (6) */
{
    rfile.Close();
}
```

```cpp
BOOL CEventDemoDlg::OnWndMsg( UINT message, WPARAM wParam,
                                                              /* (7) */
        LPARAM lParam, LRESULT* pResult )
{

    char buffer[256];
    switch (message) { // (A)

    case WM_COMMAND:
strcpy(buffer, "Message = WM_COMMAND, Window Control = ");
switch (wParam) { // (B)
case IDC_ICE_CREAM:
    strcat(buffer, "Ice Cream");
    break;
case IDC_FROZEN_YOGURT:
    strcat(buffer, "Frozen Yogurt");
            break;
case IDC_FLAVOR_SELECTION:
    strcat(buffer, "Flavors");
            break;
        case IDC_CARAMEL_TOPPING:
    strcat(buffer, "Caramel Topping");
        break;
        case IDC_CHERRIES:
    strcat(buffer, "Cherries");
            break;
        case IDC_NUTS:
    strcat(buffer, "Nuts");
            break;
        case IDC_OK:
    strcat(buffer, "Ok");
            break;
        case IDC_CANCEL:
    strcat(buffer, "Cancel");
            break;
default:
if (LOWORD(wParam) == IDC_ADD_TOPPING) {
    strcat(buffer, "Add Topping, Code = ");
   if (HIWORD(wParam) == EN_CHANGE)
    strcat(buffer, "EN_CHANGE");
   else
   if (HIWORD(wParam) == EN_UPDATE)
  strcat(buffer, "EN_UPDATE");
   else
   if (HIWORD(wParam) == EN_SETFOCUS)
  strcat(buffer, "EN_SETFOCUS");
   else
 return CWnd::OnWndMsg(message,
   wParam, lParam, pResult);
   }
```

```
else
if (LOWORD(wParam) == IDC_FLAVOR_SELECTION) {
    strcat(buffer, "Flavors, Code = ");
  if (HIWORD(wParam) == CBN_SELCHANGE)
    strcat(buffer, "CBN_SELCHANGE");
   else
  if (HIWORD(wParam) == CBN_DROPDOWN)
    strcat(buffer, "CBN_DROPDOWN");
   else
  if (HIWORD(wParam) == CBN_SETFOCUS)
    strcat(buffer, "CBN_SETFOCUS");
   else
  if (HIWORD(wParam) == CBN_CLOSEUP)
    strcat(buffer, "CBN_CLOSEUP");
   else
 return CWnd::OnWndMsg(message,
    wParam, lParam, pResult);
    break;
          }
else
    return CWnd::OnWndMsg(message, wParam, lParam, pResult);
    }  // (B)
    strcat(buffer, "\n");
    rfile.Write(buffer, strlen(buffer));
    break;
case WM_CREATE:
    strcpy(buffer, "Message = WM_CREATE");
    strcat(buffer, "\n");
    rfile.Write(buffer, strlen(buffer));
    break;
case WM_INITDIALOG:
    strcpy(buffer, "Message = WM_INITDIALOG");
    strcat(buffer, "\n");
    rfile.Write(buffer, strlen(buffer));
    break;
case WM_CLOSE:
    strcpy(buffer, "Message = WM_CLOSE");
    strcat(buffer, "\n");
    rfile.Write(buffer, strlen(buffer));
    break;
case WM_DESTROY:
    strcpy(buffer, "Message = WM_DESTROY");
    strcat(buffer, "\n");
    rfile.Write(buffer, strlen(buffer));
    break;
    }  // (A)

    return CWnd::OnWndMsg(message, wParam, lParam, pResult);
}
```

```
void CEventDemoDlg::DoDataExchange(CDataExchange* pDX)
{
    CDialog::DoDataExchange(pDX);
    //{{AFX_DATA_MAP(CEventDemoDlg)
    // NOTE: the ClassWizard will add DDX and DDV calls here
    //}}AFX_DATA_MAP
}

BEGIN_MESSAGE_MAP(CEventDemoDlg, CDialog)
    //{{AFX_MSG_MAP(CEventDemoDlg)
    ON_WM_PAINT()
    ON_WM_QUERYDRAGICON()
    //}}AFX_MSG_MAP
END_MESSAGE_MAP()

//////////////////////////////////////////////////////////////////
///////////
// CEventDemoDlg message handlers

BOOL CEventDemoDlg::OnInitDialog()
{
    CDialog::OnInitDialog();

    // Set the icon for this dialog. The framework does this
     automatically
    //  when the application's main window is not a dialog
    SetIcon(m_hIcon, TRUE);                     // Set big icon
    SetIcon(m_hIcon, FALSE);                    // Set small icon
                                                /* (5) */
    CButton * pIceCreamButton = (CButton *)
     GetDlgItem(IDC_ICE_CREAM);
    pIceCreamButton->SetCheck(1);

    CComboBox * pFlavorsComboBox =
        (CComboBox *) GetDlgItem(IDC_FLAVOR_SELECTION);
    pFlavorsComboBox->SelectString(-1, "Dutch Apple");

    // TODO: Add extra initialization here

    return TRUE;    // return TRUE  unless you set the focus to a
    control
}

// If you add a minimize button to your dialog, you will need the
 code below
//  to draw the icon. For MFC applications using the
document/view model,
//  this is automatically done for you by the framework.
```

```
void CEventDemoDlg::OnPaint()
{
    if (IsIconic())
    {
            CPaintDC dc(this); // device context for painting

            SendMessage(WM_ICONERASEBKGND,
                    (WPARAM) dc.GetSafeHdc(), 0);

            // Center icon in client rectangle
            int cxIcon = GetSystemMetrics(SM_CXICON);
            int cyIcon = GetSystemMetrics(SM_CYICON);
            CRect rect;
            GetClientRect(&rect);
            int x = (rect.Width() - cxIcon + 1) / 2;
            int y = (rect.Height() - cyIcon + 1) / 2;

            // Draw the icon
            dc.DrawIcon(x, y, m_hIcon);
    }
    else
    {
            CDialog::OnPaint();
    }
}


// The system calls this to obtain the cursor to display while
 the user drags
//  the minimized window.
HCURSOR CEventDemoDlg::OnQueryDragIcon()
{
    return (HCURSOR) m_hIcon;
}
```

In form, the window produced is visually identical to the one for the Java example. As the user tracks the mouse and works with the controls, the various messages are collected into file "RESULTS.TXT." Below is an example of what the contents might look like:

```
Message = WM_CREATE
Message = WM_INITDIALOG
Message = WM_COMMAND, Window Control = Frozen Yogurt
Message = WM_COMMAND, Window Control = Ice Cream
Message = WM_COMMAND, Window Control = Flavors, Code =
 CBN_SETFOCUS
Message = WM_COMMAND, Window Control = Flavors, Code =
CBN_DROPDOWN
Message = WM_COMMAND, Window Control = Flavors, Code =
 CBN_CLOSEUP
```

```
Message = WM_COMMAND, Window Control = Flavors, Code =
  CBN_SELCHANGE
Message = WM_COMMAND, Window Control = Caramel Topping
Message = WM_COMMAND, Window Control = Cherries
Message = WM_COMMAND, Window Control = Nuts
Message = WM_COMMAND, Window Control = Add Topping, Code =
  EN_SETFOCUS
Message = WM_COMMAND, Window Control = Add Topping, Code =
  EN_UPDATE
Message = WM_COMMAND, Window Control = Add Topping, Code =
  EN_CHANGE
Message = WM_COMMAND, Window Control = Add Topping, Code =
  EN_UPDATE
Message = WM_COMMAND, Window Control = Add Topping, Code =
  EN_CHANGE
Message = WM_COMMAND, Window Control = Add Topping, Code =
  EN_UPDATE
Message = WM_COMMAND, Window Control = Add Topping, Code =
  EN_CHANGE
Message = WM_COMMAND, Window Control = Add Topping, Code =
  EN_UPDATE
Message = WM_COMMAND, Window Control = Add Topping, Code =
  EN_CHANGE
Message = WM_COMMAND, Window Control = Add Topping, Code =
  EN_UPDATE
Message = WM_COMMAND, Window Control = Add Topping, Code =
  EN_CHANGE
Message = WM_COMMAND, Window Control = Ok
Message = WM_CLOSE
Message = WM_DESTROY
```

Below are the essential points of the Windows MFC example:

- In the Microsoft Windows 95™ or NT environment, there is a window procedure that controls the behavior of each window (roughly equivalent to the Java `Frame`). The MFC classes hide these window procedures with a series of wrapper classes, beginning with one called `CWnd`. In conventional C programming for Windows applications, there is an overall window procedure called `WinMain()` that controls processing for the "main" window. `WinMain()` also has responsibility for instantiating other windows-like dialog boxes and also routing messages to such windows. In MFC, `WinMain()` is concealed by a derived class of `CWinApp`, which for our example is class `CEventDemoApp` (comment `/* (1) */`).

  For our example, class `CEventDemoApp` is "windowless" (i.e., it has no visible components). The main purpose of this class is to instantiate a `CEventDemoDlg` object, which represents the dialog box of Figure 9-1.

This activity is done in `CEventDemoApp::InitInstance()`. The Class Wizard™ actually adds the highlighted code at the time the project is created. The key statement is:

```
int nResponse = dlg.DoModal();
```

which is a call to transfer control to our dialog box object `dlg` until the user closes the dialog box (comment `/* (2) */`).

- Our main class of interest is `CEventDemoDlg`, which is derived from `CDialog` (comment `/* (3) */`). `CDialog` is the predefined base class for displaying dialog boxes on the screen. Such boxes may be *modal* or *modeless*. *Modal* dialog boxes must be closed by the user before other application windows may be used. A *modeless* dialog box on the other hand will allow a user to work with functions of other windows without closing the box.

  For the header file of `CEventDemoDlg`, we add function prototypes for the destructor `~CEventDemoDlg()` and for another member function called `OnWndMsg()`. The latter is where all window messages pass through and by overriding this function, we can selectively examine certain ones. These two function prototypes are entered manually.

  A private data member `rfile` of type `CStdioFile` is added for class `CEventDemoDlg`. Class `CStdioFile` is the MFC interface for writing ASCII text to external disk files.

- The member function implementations reside in source file `CEventDemoDlg.cpp`. Within constructor `CEventDemoDlg::CEventDemoDlg(CWnd *)`, an output file called `"RESULTS.TXT"` (comment `/* (4) */`) is created to receive output with `CFile::Open()` (which is inherited by `CStdioFile`).

- When the program ends and the `CEventDemoDlg` object goes out of scope, it would be necessary to close the file handle in our `CStdioFile` object `rfile`. This is done by calling `Close()` in destructor `~CEventDemoDlg()` (comment `/* (6) */`).

- When a `CEventDemoDlg` object is instantiated, a `WM_INITDIALOG` message is sent to the object. The underlining message mapping mechanism of MFC routes the message in such a way that the `CDialog::OnInitDialog()` will get called. Since `CEventDemoDlg` is a subclass of `CDialog`, we can override this member function and provide custom initializations of our own. In this case, we use some of the MFC functions to enable the `IDC_ICE_CREAM` radio button and select "Dutch Apple" for the edit field of the combo box (comment `/* (5) */`).

- The member function `CEventDemoDlg::OnWndMsg()` (comment
  `/* (7) */`) is where all window messages are passed to the
  `CEventDemoDlg` object. The windows message dispatch mechanism will
  route all window messages to `CWnd::OnWndMsg()`. Class `CWnd` is the
  ancestor class to `CEventDemoDlg`. By overriding this member function,
  we can get an idea of the types of messages that come in.

  On a Win32 environment the message argument is a 32-bit unsigned integer. The `wParam` and `lParam` arguments are 32-bit integers. The `pResult`
  argument is a pointer to a 32-bit value which is returned by a window procedure.

  For this example, we check only the `message` and the `wParam` arguments
  to find what type of event and from whom. As the reader can see, breaking
  down the incoming information with `switch` statements can get rather
  tedious. Fortunately, the MFC environment does disperse these messages
  further and they can be dealt with on a function-by-function basis. The
  purpose of this example is to just show what sort of messages a window
  can receive and the main pipeline for this information.

  Messages from the child controls come in as `WM_COMMAND` messages and
  we would need to inspect `wParam` to see from which control the message
  had originated. All of the controls were drawn with the help of the Class
  Wizard (figure 9-2). As each control is created, the user assigns a unique
  integral identifier (such as `IDC_ICE_CREAM`, `IDC_FLAVOR_SELECTION`,
  etc.). These identifiers are used by the underlining MFC message map.
  For `WM_COMMAND` messages, the `wParam` argument contains this integral
  identifier.

  For the various types of buttons, the entire 32 bits of `wParam` represents
  the id. For combo boxes and text fields, we would need to inspect the
  low word (`LOWORD`) of `wParam` to find the id of the control and the high
  word of `wParam` to determine the exact message (text field change notification, the receiving of the focus, the dropping down of the combo box,
  etc.).

  There are a number of standard messages, such as `WM_CREATE`,
  `WM_INITDIALOG`, `WM_CLOSE` and `WM_DESTROY`. `WM_CREATE` is sent
  when the window has been created but is yet to be visible. For dialog
  boxes, there is an additional `WM_INITDIALOG` message that is sent before
  the box becomes visible (for dialog boxes, initialization of controls is done
  in response to `WM_INITDIALOG`). `WM_CLOSE` is sent when the user closes
  the dialog box from the system menu. Finally, `WM_DESTROY` is sent after a
  window or dialog box has been removed from the screen.

Figure 9-2

Converting a Stand-Alone Java Application to an Applet

The process of taking a Java application and converting it into an applet is pretty straightforward. The bulk of the application's code remains intact, but there are a few things of which the developer should be aware. In this section, we will take a simple AWT-based application and convert it to an applet.

The stand-alone Java program is called `LogonAppDemo`, which is a dialog box for the user to enter his personal identifier and a password. As he types the password, the keystrokes are masked by asterisks. Below is what the box looks like (figure 9-3):

The following is the listing for this stand-alone program:

Listing 9-6: LogonAppDemo.java

```java
import java.awt.*;

public class LogonAppDemo extends Frame {        /* (1) */

    public LogonAppDemo() {                       /* (2) */
```

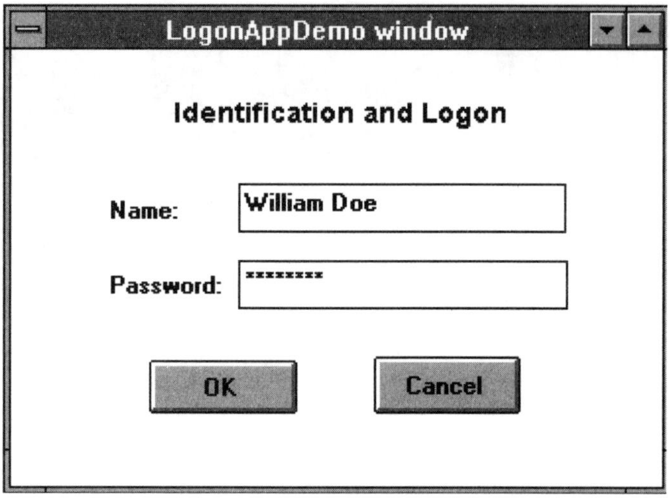

Figure 9-3

```
super("LogonAppDemo window");
name = "";
password = "";

addNotify();
resize(insets().left + insets().right + 333,
 insets().top + insets().bottom + 222);
nameField=new TextField(20);
add(nameField);
nameField.reshape(insets().left + 117,insets().top +
 68,167,25);
logonLabel=new Label("Identification and Logon");
logonLabel.setFont(new Font("Helvetica",Font.BOLD,14));
add(logonLabel);
logonLabel.reshape(insets().left + 72,insets().top +
 23,186,18);
nameLabel=new Label("Name:");
nameLabel.setFont(new Font("Dialog",Font.BOLD,12));
add(nameLabel);
nameLabel.reshape(insets().left + 39,insets().top +
 73,47,18);
passwordField=new TextField(20);
add(passwordField);
passwordField.reshape(insets().left + 117,insets().top +
 107,168,25);
OKButton=new Button("OK");
OKButton.setFont(new Font("Dialog",Font.BOLD,12));
add(OKButton);
OKButton.reshape(insets().left + 72,insets().top +
 158,75,27);
```

```
        passwordLabel=new Label("Password:");
        passwordLabel.setFont(new Font("Dialog",Font.BOLD,12));
        add(passwordLabel);
        passwordLabel.reshape(insets().left + 39,insets().top +
         112,69,16);
        cancelButton=new Button("Cancel");
        cancelButton.setFont(new Font("Dialog",Font.BOLD,12));
        add(cancelButton);
        cancelButton.reshape(insets().left + 186,insets().top +
         156,75,29);

        show();

}    // LogonAppDemo

public synchronized void show() {
        move(50, 50);
        nameField.requestFocus();
        super.show();
}    // show

public boolean handleEvent(Event event) { /* (3) */
        if (event.id == Event.KEY_PRESS && event.target ==
         OKButton) {
         enterOKButton(event);
         return true;
         }
        else
        if (event.id == Event.KEY_PRESS && event.target ==
         cancelButton) {
         enterCancelButton(event);
         return true;
         }
        else
        if (event.id == Event.KEY_PRESS && event.target ==
         nameField) {
        keyPressNameField(event);
        return true;
        }
        else
        if (event.id == Event.KEY_PRESS && event.target ==
         passwordField) {
         keyPressPasswordField(event);
         return true;
            }
        else
        if (event.id == Event.WINDOW_DESTROY) {
            hide();
            dispose();
            System.exit(0);
            return true;
```

```java
            }
            return super.handleEvent(event);

    }   // handleEvent

    public boolean action(Event event, Object arg) {
        if (event.target instanceof Button) {
            String caption = (String)arg;
            if (caption.equals("OK")) {
                handleEvent(new Event(this, Event.WINDOW_DESTROY,
                null));
                }
            if (caption.equals("Cancel"))
                handleEvent(new Event(this, Event.WINDOW_DESTROY,
                null));
            }

        return super.action(event, arg);

    }   // action


    public void keyPressNameField(Event ev) { /* (4) */

    String tmp = "";
    char ch = (char)ev.key;
    if ((SPACE <= ev.key) && (ev.key <= TILDE)) {
        name += ch;
        nameField.setText(name);
        }
    if (ev.key == BACKSPACE) {
        if (name.length() > 0)  {
            tmp += name.substring(0, name.length()-1);
            name = tmp;
            nameField.setText(name);
            tmp = "";
            }
        }
    if ((ev.key == TAB) || (ev.key == NEWLINE)) {
        if (ev.shiftDown())
            cancelButton.requestFocus();
        else
            passwordField.requestFocus();
        }

    }   // keyPressNameField

    public void keyPressPasswordField(Event ev) {    /* (4) */
    String tmp = "";
    char ch = (char)ev.key;
```

```
    if ((EXCLAMATION <= ev.key) && (ev.key <= TILDE)) {
        password += ch;
        passwordField.setText(passwordField.getText()+"*");
        }
    if (ev.key == BACKSPACE) {
        if (password.length() > 0)  {
            tmp += password.substring(0, password.length()-1);
            password = tmp;
            tmp = "";
            for (int index = 0; index < password.length();
             index++)
                tmp += "*";
            passwordField.setText(tmp);
            tmp = "";
            }
        }
    if ((ev.key == TAB) || (ev.key == NEWLINE)) {
        if (ev.shiftDown())
            nameField.requestFocus();
        else
            OKButton.requestFocus();
        }

    }   // keyPressPasswordField

public void enterOKButton(Event ev) {/* (4) */
    if (ev.key == TAB) {
        if (ev.shiftDown())
            passwordField.requestFocus();
        else
            cancelButton.requestFocus();
        }
    if (ev.key == NEWLINE) {
        handleEvent(new Event(this, Event.WINDOW_DESTROY, null));
        }
    }   // enterOKButton

public void enterCancelButton(Event ev) { /* (4) */
    if (ev.key == TAB) {
        if (ev.shiftDown())
            OKButton.requestFocus();
        else
            nameField.requestFocus();
        }
    if (ev.key == NEWLINE) {
        handleEvent(new Event(this, Event.WINDOW_DESTROY, null));
        }
    }   // enterCancelButton
```

```
public static void main(String args[]) {
    new LogonAppDemo();
}

private int BACKSPACE     =     8;
private int TAB           =     9;
private int NEWLINE       =    10;
private int SPACE         =    32;
private int EXCLAMATION   =    33;
private int TILDE         =   126;

private Label logonLabel;
private Label nameLabel;
private Label passwordLabel;
private TextField nameField;
private TextField passwordField;
private Button OKButton;
private Button cancelButton;

private String name;
private String password;

}
```

First, a few points about the stand-alone program.

- The main class of every stand-alone Java AWT program is subclassed from class `Frame` (comment /* (1) */). The `Frame` is a top-level window that has a title and can support a menu bar. The `Frame` class uses `BorderLayout` as the default layout manager. The `BorderLayout` scheme uses a North-East-South-West-Center approach to aligning controls, where the last control is placed in a vacant spot within the middle of the frame.

- The constructor `LogonAppDemo()` (comment /* (2) */) handles the creation, sizing, font selection and placement of all of the Java window controls. Each type of control has its own peculiar set of attributes, but the one activity that is common to every control after it is created is that it must be added to the frame object. For instance:

```
nameField = new TextField(20);
add(nameField);                        // Attach control to the frame
```

- As we have seen before, the `handleEvent()` method must be overridden to trap the events of interest (comment /* (3) */). If the message is `KEY_PRESS` (which means the user had pressed a key), we want to find which control (`OKButton`, `cancelButton`, `nameField` or `passwordField`) had sent the message and then process the message accordingly.

- From `handleEvent()`, the flow of control goes to any of the helper methods: `keyPressNameField()`, `keyPressPassword()`, `enterOKButton()` or `enterCancelButton()` (comment /* (4) */). If the event originated from a `TextField` object, then we are interested in getting the keystroke value if it is a displayable character and then display the character from the `TextField` object. In the process, we would update the complete string that the user has input up to this point. If the user presses the backspace key, then the last character is removed from the internal string and the contents of the `TextField` object are displayed accordingly.

  If the user is typing within the password field, we would record the characters he has typed, but the output of each character would be masked by an asterisk.

  One aspect of the helper methods is that the developer has to do a bit of work to manage the focus of the controls. The `tab` and `enter` keys are given special significance to shift the focus from one control to another (`nameField` to `passwordField` to `OKButton` to `cancelButton` to `nameField`). The simultaneous pressing of the `tab` or `enter` keys with the `shift` key will reverse the focus traversal. The key method for transferring the focus to a control is `requestFocus()` from class `Component`, which is a superclass to class `Frame`. The following code fragment is from method `keyPressPasswordField()`:

  ```
  if ((ev.key == TAB) || (ev.key == NEWLINE)) {
     if (ev.shiftDown())
       nameField.requestFocus();      // return focus to name
                                       // field
     else
       OKButton.requestFocus();       // forward focus to the
                                       // OK button
  }
  ```

- In the case of the buttons, the `enter` key is given the special meaning to accept (`"Ok"`) or reject (`"Cancel"`) the text field data (in both cases, nothing special is done, the dialog box simply closes). The `action()` method is overridden for this purpose. The body of the method determines which button had sent the message and passes a new `Event` object with the `WINDOW_DESTROY` message to `handleEvent()`.

Now that we have an understanding of the features of this sample application, we will convert it to an applet called `LogonAppletDemo`.

One thing to keep in mind about applets is that they are part of the makeup of Hypertext Markup Language (HTML) files, which are retrieved from server machines by Java-aware browsers like Netscape Navigator 2.0™ or higher. The following simple HTML source will load the bytecode file LogonAppletDemo.class:

```
<HTML>
<HEAD>
<TITLE> Logon Demonstration </TITLE>
</HEAD>
<BODY>

<APPLET CODE="LogonAppletDemo.class"  WIDTH=370  HEIGHT=210>
</APPLET>

</BODY>
</HTML>
```

The bytecode file is loaded with the <APPLET CODE = ...> tag and must be terminated with the </APPLET> tag. The name of the bytecode file must be bounded by double quotes. There are two required tags to support the first one, namely WIDTH and HEIGHT, which establish the dimensions of the rectangle to contain the applet. These magnitudes are measured in pixels. The loading of the HTML file into Netscape Navigator™ would appear something like figure 9-4.

Now, it is time to examine the code that produces the applet. The highlighted portions indicate a change or addition from the LogonAppDemo version. The code that is unchanged from the original is not listed:

Listing 9-7: LogonAppletDemo.java

```java
import java.awt.*;
import java.applet.Applet;

public class LogonAppletDemo extends Applet {

    public void init() {

        super.init();
        name = "";
        password = "";

        setLayout(new BorderLayout());

        // Other statements unchanged

        // show();

    }   // LogonAppDemo

    public synchronized void show() {          // Unchanged
```

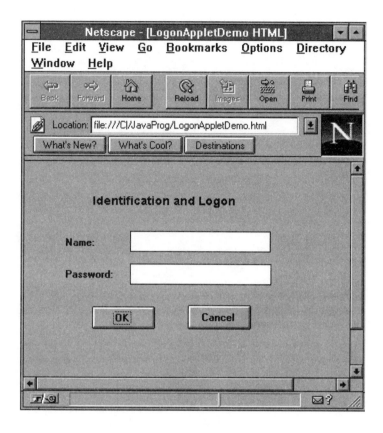

Figure 9-4

```
    move(50, 50);
    nameField.requestFocus();
    super.show();
}  // show

public boolean handleEvent(Event event) {
    if (event.id == Event.KEY_PRESS && event.target ==
    OKButton) {
        enterOKButton(event);
        return true;
        }
    else
    if (event.id == Event.KEY_PRESS && event.target ==
    cancelButton) {
        enterCancelButton(event);
        return true;
        }
    else
    if (event.id == Event.KEY_PRESS && event.target ==
```

```
    nameField) {
        keyPressNameField(event);
        return true;
        }
    else
    if (event.id == Event.KEY_PRESS && event.target ==
     passwordField) {
        keyPressPasswordField(event);
        return true;
        }
    else
    if (event.id == Event.WINDOW_DESTROY) {
        hide();
        return true;
        }

    return super.handleEvent(event);

}   // handleEvent

public boolean action(Event event, Object arg) {

// Statements unchanged

}   // action

public void keyPressNameField(Event ev) {

// Statements unchanged

}   // keyPressNameField

public void keyPressPasswordField(Event ev) {

// Statements unchanged

}   // keyPressPasswordField

public void enterOKButton(Event ev) {

// Statements unchanged

}   // enterOKButton

public void enterCancelButton(Event ev) {

// Statements unchanged

}   // enterCancelButton
```

```
    // Private fields unchanged
}   // End of LogonAppletDemo
```

Comparing `LogonAppletDemo` against `LogonAppDemo`, we note the following differences:

- Instead of subclassing from class `Frame`, `LogonAppletDemo` is subclassed from class `Applet`. `Applet` is actually a subclass of `Panel`, which is a subclass of `Container`.

  To use class `Applet`, remember to `import` the class with:

  ```
  import java.applet.Applet;
  ```

- For applets, one does not use a constructor. The `init()` method is automatically called and all initializations, such as the creation of window controls, their placements and sizings, are done within `init()`.

  Within the body of our `init()` method, we should call the base class `init()` with:

  ```
  super.init();
  ```

  to make sure the `Applet` subobject is properly initialized.

  Since applets are embedded within an existing window (the browser's), it has no window title (in `LogonAppDemo`, this was done with statement `super("LogonAppDemo window");`). Setting a title in the browser window would be done with something like:

  ```
  <TITLE> Logon Demonstration </TITLE>
  ```

  in the HTML file.

  Another important aspect to account for in the initialization is the choosing of the layout manager. A layout manager governs how the window controls would be placed in the `Container` object (both `Frame` and `Applet` are ultimately subclassed from `Container`). The default layout manager for `Frame` is `BorderLayout`, while the default for `Applet` is `FlowLayout`. The `BorderLayout` scheme allows for controls to be aligned with the edges or center ("North," "East," "South," "West" and "Center"). On the other hand, the `FlowLayout` scheme is one where all the controls are placed on a row and wrap around to the next row depending on the size of the total window. If the window is sizable, then the controls would be realigned as the window is sized. However, applets are embedded within a window and, by themselves, they cannot be resized. Hence, an application based on the `BorderLayout` manager would probably not look very pleasing in the `FlowLayout` mode. To correct this, we must have the following statement in the body of `init()`:

```
setLayout(new BorderLayout());
```

One final point about `init()` is that there is no need to call:

```
show();
```

since the browser window is already visible. For a stand-alone application, `show()` must be called, otherwise nothing appears.

- Unlike stand-alone applications, there is no `public static main()` method. The browser will automatically instantiate the applet object because of the `APPLET` tag mentioned earlier.

Simple Layout Managers

Whenever developers create interactive applications with graphical user interface components, one of the issues that inevitably surfaces is how the components should be adjusted to account for different display resolutions, different fonts and user activities like window resizing. In Java, there are five types of layout managers to assist the developer in the placement or sizing of components. In a native windowing environment like OSF Motif™, this is called "widget management." Up to now, most of the sample Java applications and applets have not used a layout manager. This is the case where a statement such as:

```
setLayout(null);
```

appears in the constructor of an application or in the `init()` method of an applet. This is fine for demonstrating the main topic of the moment and fine for situations of rapid prototyping. However, if the application is intended for production, serious thought should be given to accommodating different display devices and how the window might look when its attributes and resources change.

It is seldom that one layout manager would suffice for an entire window or dialog box. Rather, the desired result is usually a combination of layout managers, where each layout manager governs a particular region of a window. Each region is usually a `Panel` object (represented as a borderless rectangle) that contains other components like text fields, buttons or images.

In this section, we will examine some of the simple layout managers of Java. Occasionally, we will do a rough comparison with a Motif equivalent. I have chosen Motif instead of MS Windows because Motif has some very sophisticated schemes for widget layout. One fundamental difference in approach between Java and Motif is that layout managers are special objects in Java, created solely for the purpose of managing widget layout. In Motif, certain types of container widgets, such as `form` and `row-column` widgets, have layout managers built into them. Another important difference is that Java is based on the object-oriented paradigm, whereas Motif is an event-driven but procedural C language API.

The first simple layout manager is called the `FlowLayout`, which is the default layout manager for `Panel` objects (and for applets, since applets are `Panel` objects). With `FlowLayout`, the approach is to place as many controls as possible on a row for a window of a given width. If there are more controls than can be placed on one row, then the remainder will be placed on a subsequent row and so on. Figure 9-5 below illustrates a window containing twelve buttons with `FlowLayout` management.

If the window above is resized by stretching or shrinking, then the number of buttons per row will change according to the scheme mentioned. The code for `FlowLayoutDemo` appears as follows:

Listing 9-8: FlowLayoutDemo.java

```
import java.awt.*;

public class FlowLayoutDemo extends Frame {
```

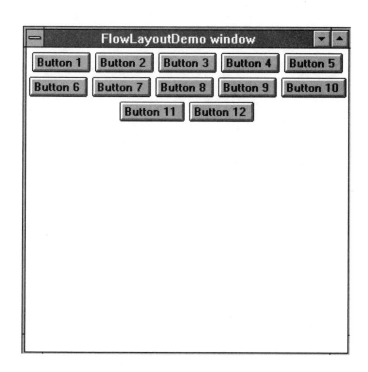

Figure 9-5

```
public FlowLayoutDemo() {

    super("FlowLayoutDemo window");
    setLayout(new FlowLayout());

    button1  = new Button("Button 1");
    button2  = new Button("Button 2");
    button3  = new Button("Button 3");
    button4  = new Button("Button 4");
    button5  = new Button("Button 5");
    button6  = new Button("Button 6");
    button7  = new Button("Button 7");
    button8  = new Button("Button 8");
    button9  = new Button("Button 9");
    button10 = new Button("Button 10");
    button11 = new Button("Button 11");
    button12 = new Button("Button 12");
    add(button1);
    add(button2);
    add(button3);
    add(button4);
    add(button5);
    add(button6);
    add(button7);
    add(button8);
    add(button9);
    add(button10);
    add(button11);
    add(button12);
    resize(350, 350);
    show();
}

public synchronized void show() {
    move(75, 75);
    super.show();
}

public boolean handleEvent(Event event) {
    if (event.id == Event.WINDOW_DESTROY) {
        hide();
        dispose();
        System.exit(0);
        return true;
    }
    return super.handleEvent(event);
}

public boolean action(Event event, Object arg) {
```

```
        if (event.target instanceof MenuItem) {
            String label = (String) arg;
        }
        return super.action(event, arg);
    }

    public static void main(String args[]) {
        new FlowLayoutDemo();
    }

    private Button button1;
    private Button button2;
    private Button button3;
    private Button button4;
    private Button button5;
    private Button button6;
    private Button button7;
    private Button button8;
    private Button button9;
    private Button button10;
    private Button button11;
    private Button button12;
}
```

The statement:

```
setLayout(new FlowLayout());
```

establishes `FlowLayout` as the management scheme for the controls contained within the `Frame` object.

The approximate equivalent in a windowing environment like Motif would be the use of something called a `XmRowColumn` widget. The following C program and Motif resource files are rough equivalents to the Java sample:

Listing 9-9: FlowLayoutDemo.c

```
/* Source File: FlowLayoutDemo.c */

#include <X11/StringDefs.h>
#include <X11/Intrinsic.h>
#include <Xm/Xm.h>
#include <Xm/RowColumn.h>
#include <Xm/PushB.h>

static char * btns[] = {
                        "btn1", "btn2", "btn3",
                        "btn4", "btn5", "btn6",
                        "btn7", "btn8", "btn9",
                        "btn10", "btn11", "btn12"
                        };
```

```
void main(argc,   argv)
int argc;
char * argv[];
}
Widget mainLevel, rowcolWidget, buttonWidget[XtNumber(btns)]
int index;

mainLevel = XtInitialize(argv[0], "Flow", NULL, 0, &argc, argv);

rowcolWidget =
   XtCreateManagedWidget("rowcol", xmRowColumnWidgetClass,
    mainLevel, NULL, 0);

for (index=0; index<XtNumber(btns); index++)
   buttonWidget[index] =
       XtCreateWidget(btns[index], xmPushButtonWidgetClass,
        rowcolWidget, NULL, 0);

XtManageChildren(buttonWidget, XtNumber(btns));

XtRealizeWidget(mainLevel);
XtMainLoop();
}
```

Listing 9-10: Flow

```
/* Resource File: Flow */

Flow*resizable:              TRUE

Flow*btn1.labelString:       Button 1
Flow*btn2.labelString:       Button 2
Flow*btn3.labelString:       Button 3
Flow*btn4.labelString:       Button 4
Flow*btn5.labelString:       Button 5
Flow*btn6.labelString:       Button 6
Flow*btn7.labelString:       Button 7
Flow*btn8.labelString:       Button 8
Flow*btn9.labelString:       Button 9
Flow*btn10.labelString:      Button 10
Flow*btn11.labelString:      Button 11
Flow*btn12.labelString:      Button 12


Flow*orientation:            horizontal
Flow*rowcol*packing:         pack_tight
```

The execution of the C-based Motif program could produce a window like figure 9-5 after some manual resizing. There is a slight difference in behavior in that Button 11 and Button 12 each would be stretched vertically to fill the remaining height of the window and both would be justified from the left side (see figure 9-6).

One unique aspect of the Motif windowing system is that widget attributes can be separated into an ASCII-based resource file. The resource file is read by the Motif window manager and the manager applies the attributes to the widgets created within the C source file. By putting widget attributes into a resource file, one can change the values (like label strings) without the need to recompile the source code. The following statement initializes the underlining X toolkit (of which Motif is based):

```
mainLevel = XtInitialize(argv[0], "Flow", NULL, 0, &argc, argv);
```

The second argument to XtInitialize() refers to the name of the resource file.

The next statement:

```
rowcolWidget = XtCreateManagedWidget("rowcol",
                  xmRowColumnWidgetClass, mainLevel, NULL, 0);
```

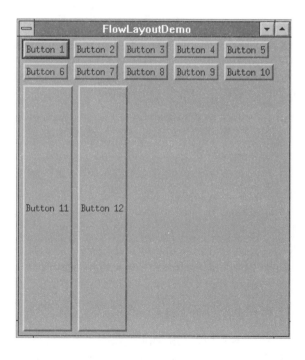

Figure 9–6

creates a `XmRowColumn` widget with variable `rowcolWidget` as the reference to the widget. The name `rowcol` is the resource name given to the widget.

In turn, a `for` loop creates a number of buttons to be contained within `rowcolWidget`:

```
for (index=0; index<XtNumber(buttons); index++)
  buttonWidget[index] =
       XtCreateWidget(btns[index],xmPushButtonWidgetClass,
                       rowcolWidget, NULL, 0);
```

The next statement:

```
XtManageChildren(buttonWidget, XtNumber(btns));
```

instructs the window manager that the `rowcolWidget` will manage its child components. By management, we mean that the parent widget would be responsible for regulating the child control's input focus, size, location and visibility.

The creation of the widgets creates the data structures. In addition, these widgets must be realized with:

```
XtRealizeWidget(mainLevel);
```

The statement would create a window for the main widget represented by `mainLevel` (including windows for each of its child components).

Finally, the statement:

```
XtMainLoop();
```

represents the event loop, where the application picks up an event from the event queue and dispatches it to the proper event handler.

The widget attribute settings in resource file `Flow` play a major role in the behavior of the resulting window. Besides giving each button a label, the following two lines are very significant:

```
Flow*orientation:              horizontal
Flow*rowcol*packing:           pack_tight
```

The `orientation` is set to `horizontal`, which means that the `XmRowColumn` widget would fill by row (starting from the upper left-hand corner of the window and going to the right). This is in contrast to `vertical`, which would mean to fill by column (beginning from the same location but going down). The `packing` attribute is set to `pack_tight`, which means to fill as many child controls as possible per row (or column) before proceeding to the next row (or column).

The interesting aspect about this Java-Motif comparison is that both can produce similar results with a particular layout scheme, but each has its own approach to implementing the scheme.

Now, let us look at another Java layout called `BorderLayout`. We have seen earlier that `BorderLayout` is the default for `Frame` objects (from which stand-alone Java applications originate). Figure 9–7 shows a Java window of five buttons managed by the `BorderLayout` scheme.

The Java code for `BorderLayoutDemo` would look like:

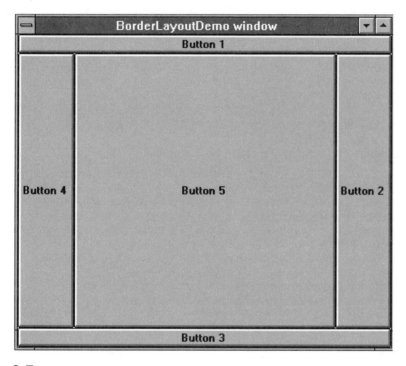

Figure 9-7

Listing 9-11: BorderLayoutDemo.java

```java
import java.awt.*;

public class BorderLayoutDemo extends Frame {

    public BorderLayoutDemo() {

        super("BorderLayoutDemo window");
        setLayout(new BorderLayout());

        resize(450, 350);
        button1=new Button("Button 1");
        add("North", button1);
        button2=new Button("Button 2");
        add("East", button2);
```

```
        button3=new Button("Button 3");
        add("South", button3);
        button4=new Button("Button 4");
        add("West", button4);
        button5=new Button("Button 5");
        add("Center", button5);

        show();
    }

  public synchronized void show() {
    move(75, 75);
    super.show();
  }

  public boolean handleEvent(Event event) {

  if (event.id == Event.WINDOW_DESTROY) {
            hide();
            dispose();
            System.exit(0);
            return true;
          }
  return super.handleEvent(event);
  }

  public boolean action(Event event, Object arg) {
  if (event.target instanceof MenuItem) {
      String label = (String) arg;
      }
  return super.action(event, arg);
  }

      public static void main(String args[]) {
      new BorderLayoutDemo();
    }

  private Button button1;
  private Button button2;
  private Button button3;
  private Button button4;
  private Button button5;

}
```

The first place where `BorderLayoutDemo` differs from `FlowLayoutDemo` is how the layout manager is chosen from the constructor:

```
setLayout(new BorderLayout());
```

Furthermore, as each `Button` object is created, a special implementation of the `add()` method is called to determine how it would be positioned against the main window:

```
add("North", button1);
...
add("East ", button2);
...
add("South ", button3);
...
add("West ", button4);
...
add("Center ", button5);
```

The first argument should be a legal string such as `"North,"` `"East,"` `"South,"` `"West"` and `"Center."` The strings are <u>case-sensitive</u>. Respectively, the first four strings mean to flush the control to the top, right, bottom or left of the main window. String `"Center"` means to put the control in whatever space that remains.

Warning: In order to use the `BorderLayout` manager properly, only one control should use any one of these positional parameters. If two controls are designated as `"North,"` then the last one will dominate the position (the first will not appear). If two buttons are to share the same border, then the approach would be to put the buttons on a `Panel` object and then align the `Panel` object to the border.

The equivalent to the Java `BorderLayoutDemo` for Motif might be something like the following:

Listing 9-12: BorderLayoutDemo.c

```c
/* Source File: BorderLayoutDemo.c */

#include <X11/StringDefs.h>
#include <X11/Intrinsic.h>
#include <Xm/Xm.h>
#include <Xm/Form.h>
#include <Xm/PushB.h>

static char * btns[] = {
                        "btn1", "btn2", "btn3", "btn4", "btn5"
                        };
```

```
void main(argc,  argv)
int argc;
char * argv[];
{
Widget mainLevel, formWidget, buttonWidget[XtNumber(btns)];
int index, n;
Arg wargs[10];

mainLevel = XtInitialize(argv[0], "Border", NULL, 0, &argc,
 argv);

formWidget =
    XtCreateManagedWidget("form", xmFormWidgetClass, mainLevel,
     NULL, 0);

for (index=0; index<XtNumber(btns); index++)
   buttonWidget[index] =
     XtCreateWidget(btns[index], xmPushButtonWidgetClass,
      formWidget, NULL, 0);

n = 0;
XtSetArg(wargs[n], XmNtopAttachment, XmATTACH_FORM); n++;
XtSetArg(wargs[n], XmNleftAttachment, XmATTACH_FORM); n++;
XtSetArg(wargs[n], XmNrightAttachment, XmATTACH_FORM); n++;
XtSetValues(buttonWidget[0], wargs, n);

n = 0;
XtSetArg(wargs[n], XmNrightAttachment, XmATTACH_FORM); n++;
XtSetArg(wargs[n], XmNtopAttachment, XmATTACH_WIDGET); n++;
XtSetArg(wargs[n], XmNtopWidget, buttonWidget[0]); n++;
XtSetArg(wargs[n], XmNbottomAttachment, XmATTACH_WIDGET); n++;
XtSetArg(wargs[n], XmNbottomWidget, buttonWidget[2]); n++;
XtSetValues(buttonWidget[1], wargs, n);

n = 0;
XtSetArg(wargs[n], XmNbottomAttachment, XmATTACH_FORM); n++;
XtSetArg(wargs[n], XmNleftAttachment, XmATTACH_FORM); n++;
XtSetArg(wargs[n], XmNrightAttachment, XmATTACH_FORM); n++;
XtSetValues(buttonWidget[2], wargs, n);

n = 0;
XtSetArg(wargs[n], XmNleftAttachment, XmATTACH_FORM); n++;
XtSetArg(wargs[n], XmNtopAttachment, XmATTACH_WIDGET); n++;
XtSetArg(wargs[n], XmNtopWidget, buttonWidget[0]); n++;
XtSetArg(wargs[n], XmNbottomAttachment, XmATTACH_WIDGET); n++;
XtSetArg(wargs[n], XmNbottomWidget, buttonWidget[2]); n++;
XtSetValues(buttonWidget[3], wargs, n);

n = 0;
XtSetArg(wargs[n], XmNtopAttachment, XmATTACH_WIDGET); n++;
```

```
XtSetArg(wargs[n], XmNtopWidget, buttonWidget[0]); n++;
XtSetArg(wargs[n], XmNrightAttachment, XmATTACH_WIDGET); n++;
XtSetArg(wargs[n], XmNrightWidget, buttonWidget[1]); n++;
XtSetArg(wargs[n], XmNbottomAttachment, XmATTACH_WIDGET); n++;
XtSetArg(wargs[n], XmNbottomWidget, buttonWidget[2]); n++;
XtSetArg(wargs[n], XmNleftAttachment, XmATTACH_WIDGET); n++;
XtSetArg(wargs[n], XmNleftWidget, buttonWidget[3]); n++;
XtSetValues(buttonWidget[4], wargs, n);

XtManageChildren(buttonWidget, XtNumber(btns));

XtRealizeWidget(mainLevel);
XtMainLoop();
}
```

Listing 9-13: Border

```
/* Resource File: Border */

Border*resizable:          TRUE

Border*btn1.labelString:   Button 1
Border*btn2.labelString:   Button 2
Border*btn3.labelString:   Button 3
Border*btn4.labelString:   Button 4
Border*btn5.labelString:   Button 5
```

The execution of the Motif version of BorderLayoutDemo would produce a window like figure 9-7. All of the five buttons would assume the same relative positions.

This Motif version of BorderLayoutDemo differs from the Motif version of FlowLayoutDemo in a number ways:

The main widget at the highest level is a XmForm widget, not a XmRowColumn widget:

```
formWidget =
     XtCreateManagedWidget("form", xmFormWidgetClass,
     mainLevel, NULL, 0);
```

After five button widgets have been created, the relative position of each is established with the XtSetArg() macro and XtSetValues() function. For instance, the following code establishes the location for Button 2:

```
n = 0;
XtSetArg(wargs[n], XmNrightAttachment, XmATTACH_FORM); n++;
XtSetArg(wargs[n], XmNtopAttachment, XmATTACH_WIDGET); n++;
XtSetArg(wargs[n], XmNtopWidget, buttonWidget[0]); n++;
XtSetArg(wargs[n], XmNbottomAttachment, XmATTACH_WIDGET); n++;
```

```
XtSetArg(wargs[n], XmNbottomWidget, buttonWidget[2]); n++;
XtSetValues(buttonWidget[1], wargs, n);
```

Without dwelling on the details, the code means to flush the right side of
`Button 2` against the main window, its top against the bottom of `Button 1`
and its bottom against the top of `Button 3`. Setting these positional attributes
can also be done in the resource file.

Child controls can also be arranged on a grid within a parent widget. The next
Java example, `GridLayoutDemo`, organizes twelve buttons into a 4-by-3 matrix
(four rows and three columns) as shown in Figure 9-8:

If the user sizes the window, each button would stay in its relative position and
all of them would remain tiled against each other. The code appears as:

Listing 9-14: GridLayoutDemo.java

```
import java.awt.*;

public class GridLayoutDemo extends Frame {
```

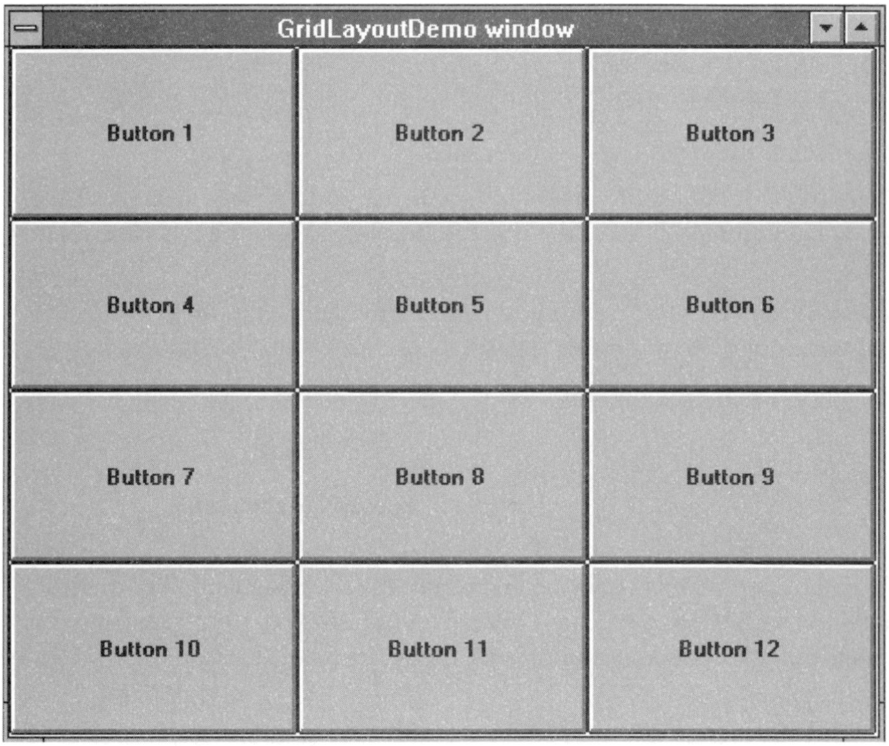

Figure 9-8

```
public GridLayoutDemo() {

    super("GridLayoutDemo window");
    setLayout(new GridLayout(4,3));

    resize(480,400);

    for (int index = 0; index < 12; index++) {
        button[index] = new Button("Button "+(index+1));
        add(button[index]);
        }

    show();
}

public synchronized void show() {
    move(75, 75);
    super.show();
}

public boolean handleEvent(Event event) {
  if (event.id == Event.WINDOW_DESTROY) {
        hide();
        dispose();
        System.exit(0);
        return true;
        }
return super.handleEvent(event);
}

public static void main(String args[]) {
    new GridLayoutDemo();
}

private Button [] button = new Button[12];

}
```

The `GridLayoutDemo` program is similar to `FlowLayoutDemo` except for the choice of the layout manager in the constructor:

```
setLayout(new GridLayout(4,3));
```

The constructor for the `GridLayout` class takes two `int` arguments: the number of rows and the number of columns.

An equivalent to the Java version of `GridLayoutDemo` for Motif might look like:

Listing 9-15: GridLayoutDemo.c

```c
/* Source File: GridLayoutDemo.c */

#include <X11/StringDefs.h>
#include <X11/Intrinsic.h>
#include <Xm/Xm.h>
#include <Xm/Form.h>
#include <Xm/PushB.h>

static char * btns[] =  {
        "btn1", "btn2", "btn3",
        "btn4", "btn5", "btn6",
        "btn7", "btn8", "btn9",
        "btn10", "btn11", "btn12"
        };
void main(argc,  argv)
int argc;
char * argv[];
{
Widget mainLevel, formWidget, buttonWidget[XtNumber(btns)];
int index;

mainLevel = XtInitialize(argv[0], "Grid", NULL, 0, &argc, argv);

formWidget =
     XtCreateManagedWidget("form", xmFormWidgetClass, mainLevel,
      NULL, 0);

for (index=0; index<XtNumber(btns); index++)
   buttonWidget[index] =
      XtCreateWidget(btns[index], xmPushButtonWidgetClass,
       formWidget, NULL, 0);

XtManageChildren(buttonWidget, XtNumber(btns));

XtRealizeWidget(mainLevel);
XtMainLoop();
}
```

Listing 9-16: Grid

```
/* Resource File: Grid */

Grid*resizable:         TRUE
Grid.form*width:        400
Grid.form*height:       400
Grid*topAttachment:     attach_position
Grid*bottomAttachment:  attach_position
```

```
Grid*leftAttachment:            attach_position
Grid*rightAttachment:           attach_position

Grid*btn1.labelString:          Button 1
Grid*btn1.leftPosition:              1
Grid*btn1.rightPosition:            33
Grid*btn1.topPosition:               1
Grid*btn1.bottomPosition:           25

Grid*btn2.labelString:          Button 2
Grid*btn2.leftPosition:              1
Grid*btn2.rightPosition:            33
Grid*btn2.topPosition:              26
Grid*btn2.bottomPosition:           50

Grid*btn3.labelString:          Button 3
Grid*btn3.leftPosition:              1
Grid*btn3.rightPosition:            33
Grid*btn3.topPosition:              51
Grid*btn3.bottomPosition:           75

Grid*btn4.labelString:          Button 4
Grid*btn4.leftPosition:              1
Grid*btn4.rightPosition:            33
Grid*btn4.topPosition:              76
Grid*btn4.bottomPosition:          100

Grid*btn5.labelString:          Button 5
Grid*btn5.leftPosition:             34
Grid*btn5.rightPosition:            66
Grid*btn5.topPosition:               1
Grid*btn5.bottomPosition:           25

Grid*btn6.labelString:          Button 6
Grid*btn6.leftPosition:             34
Grid*btn6.rightPosition:            66
Grid*btn6.topPosition:              26
Grid*btn6.bottomPosition:           50

Grid*btn7.labelString:          Button 7
Grid*btn7.leftPosition:             34
Grid*btn7.rightPosition:            66
Grid*btn7.topPosition:              51
Grid*btn7.bottomPosition:           75

Grid*btn8.labelString:          Button 8
Grid*btn8.leftPosition:             34
Grid*btn8.rightPosition:            66
Grid*btn8.topPosition:              76
Grid*btn8.bottomPosition:          100
```

```
Grid*btn9.labelString:       Button   9
Grid*btn9.leftPosition:               67
Grid*btn9.rightPosition:             100
Grid*btn9.topPosition:                 1
Grid*btn9.bottomPosition:             25

Grid*btn10.labelString:      Button  10
Grid*btn10.leftPosition:              67
Grid*btn10.rightPosition:            100
Grid*btn10.topPosition:               26
Grid*btn10.bottomPosition:            50

Grid*btn11.labelString:      Button  11
Grid*btn11.leftPosition:              67
Grid*btn11.rightPosition:            100
Grid*btn11.topPosition:               51
Grid*btn11.bottomPosition:            75

Grid*btn12.labelString:      Button  12
Grid*btn12.leftPosition:              67
Grid*btn12.rightPosition:            100
Grid*btn12.topPosition:               76
Grid*btn12.bottomPosition:           100
```

The execution of the Motif-based `GridLayoutDemo` program gives a window like figure 9–8 with the same behaviors as the Java version.

The `GridLayoutDemo` program is like the Motif-based `BorderLayoutDemo` in that the main window uses a `XmForm` widget:

```
formWidget =
    XtCreateManagedWidget("form", xmFormWidgetClass, mainLevel,
    NULL, 0);
```

Where `GridLayoutDemo` differs from `BorderLayoutDemo` is in the settings of certain widget attributes. To force all of the buttons to assume the same relative dimensions, we would need to specify `attach_position` for all widgets of the form:

```
Grid*topAttachment:     attach_position
Grid*bottomAttachment:  attach_position
Grid*leftAttachment:    attach_position
Grid*rightAttachment:   attach_position
```

The window is then mapped to a conceptual coordinate system where the height is divided into quarters (four rows) and the width is divided into thirds (three columns). The upper left-hand corner of the window would be (0,0) and the lower right-hand corner would be (100,100). If we examine the settings for Button 12:

```
Grid*btn12.leftPosition:     67
Grid*btn12.rightPosition:   100
Grid*btn12.topPosition:      76
Grid*btn12.bottomPosition:  100
```

The settings would show that Button 12 would be contained within the rectangular region bounded by points (67,76) to (100,100).

Summary: One observation about Java is that it is fairly simple to choose and use layout managers because they are distinct objects. In Motif, the choice of a layout scheme requires one to know the type of widgets to use and how to set the attributes. The Motif approach offers flexibility in allowing the developer to build his own layout scheme, but this work requires much more thought and detailed coding than the Java layout managers we have seen thus far. One definite advantage about Motif is that the setting of widget attributes can be isolated into resource files so that any special customizations (like names of labels) can be made without forcing changes to source code.

Stacking the Deck: The CardLayout Manager of Java

Java offers some more sophisticated layout schemes for finer grain control of the interface components. In this section, we are going to examine how the Java `CardLayout` manager works.

With `CardLayout`, a number of window controls are basically stacked together like a deck of cards. All of the controls would be fully instantiated, but only the top control would be visible. With a little work, any of the other hidden controls could be made to surface to the top.

The Java-based `CardLayoutDemo` example I am about to present features three panels superimposed on each other. Each of the panels contains four buttons. All of the buttons are flushed to the left, top and right edges of the main window. Only one panel with its four buttons is visible at any given time. Another button labeled "Forward" is located at the bottom of the main window. It is used to toggle forward to the next panel. Figure 9-9 below shows the main window at start up.

The following is the code for `CardLayoutDemo`:

Listing 9-17: CardLayoutDemo.java

```java
import java.awt.*;

public class CardLayoutDemo extends Frame {

    public CardLayoutDemo() {

        super("CardLayoutDemo window");
```

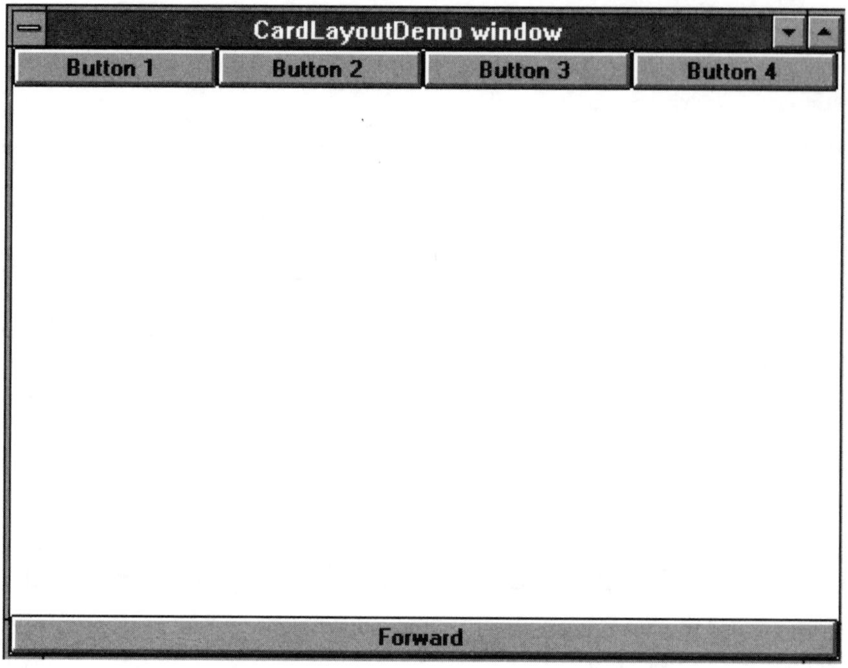

CardLayoutDemo window

| Button 1 | Button 2 | Button 3 | Button 4 |

Forward

Figure 9-9

```
setLayout(new BorderLayout());                    /* (3) */

cardPanel = new Panel();                           /* (2) */
cardPanel.setLayout(layout = new CardLayout());

Panel p1 = new Panel();                            /* (1) */
p1.setLayout(new GridLayout(1,4));
button1=new Button("Button 1");
p1.add(button1);
button2=new Button("Button 2");
p1.add(button2);
button3=new Button("Button 3");
p1.add(button3);
button4=new Button("Button 4");
p1.add(button4);
cardPanel.add(p1);

Panel p2 = new Panel();                            /* (1) */
p2.setLayout(new GridLayout(1,4));
button5=new Button("Button 5");
p2.add(button5);
```

```
        button6=new Button("Button 6");
        p2.add(button6);
        button7=new Button("Button 7");
        p2.add(button7);
        button8=new Button("Button 8");
        p2.add(button8);
        cardPanel.add(p2);

        Panel p3 = new Panel();                          /* (1) */
        p3.setLayout(new GridLayout(1,4));
        button9=new Button("Button 9");
        p3.add(button9);
        button10=new Button("Button 10");
        p3.add(button10);
        button11=new Button("Button 11");
        p3.add(button11);
        button12=new Button("Button 12");
        p3.add(button12);
        cardPanel.add(p3);

        add("North",cardPanel);

        forwardButton=new Button("Forward");
        forwardButton.setFont(new Font("Dialog",Font.BOLD,12));
        add("South", forwardButton);

        resize(400, 350);
        show();
    }

public synchronized void show() {
    move(75, 75);
    super.show();
}

public boolean handleEvent(Event event) {

  if (event.id == Event.WINDOW_DESTROY) {
    hide();
    dispose();
    System.exit(0);
    return true;
    }
return super.handleEvent(event);
}

public boolean action(Event event, Object arg) {
    if (event.target instanceof Button) {
        String label = (String) arg;
```

```
            if (label.equals("Forward")) {
                layout.next(cardPanel);
            }
        }
        return super.action(event, arg);
    }

    public static void main(String args[]) {
        new CardLayoutDemo();
    }

    private CardLayout layout;
    private Panel       cardPanel;
    private Button      forwardButton;
    private Button      button1;
    private Button      button2;
    private Button      button3;
    private Button      button4;
    private Button      button5;
    private Button      button6;
    private Button      button7;
    private Button      button8;
    private Button      button9;
    private Button      button10;
    private Button      button11;
    private Button      button12;


}
```

Demonstrating the behavior of the CardLayout manager is not quite as simple as the examples for BorderLayout, FlowLayout or GridLayout. This example also incorporates some of the layouts already discussed (see the previous topic, *Simple Layout Managers*). The highlighted code represent the main points of the example.

- Each of the Panel objects (reference variables p1, p2 and p3 - see comment /* (1) */) with its four buttons is managed by a GridLayout manager of one row and four columns. This is done to give all the buttons common dimensions and to fill the entire width of the Panel object from left to right.

- Each of the Panel objects represented by p1, p2 and p3 is added to another Panel object referenced by private variable cardPanel (comment /* (2) */). The object referenced by cardPanel is one of the key components of the example since cardPanel is managed by a CardLayout manager:

```
cardPanel = new Panel();
```

```
cardPanel.setLayout(layout = new CardLayout());
```

The `CardLayout` manager object is retained in the private variable `layout`.

- At the very top level, the main window is managed by a `BorderLayout` manager (comment `/* (3) */`) and its child components are the `Panel` object referenced by `cardPanel` and the `Button` object referenced by private variable `forwardButton`. The `Panel` object is aligned to the top of the main window while the `Button` object with label "Forward" is aligned to the bottom.

- An `action()` method is provided to trap mouse clicks on the "Forward" button. The main code appears as:

```
if (label.equals("Forward")) {
    layout.next(cardPanel);
    }
```

To bring the next button panel to the surface, the layout manager would use the `next()` method and pass it a single `Container` argument representing the parent `Container` object. When the user reaches the last `Panel` object, the `next()` method would cycle back to the beginning.

A native windowing system such as Motif does not use layout manager objects. Rather, the layout schemes are built into certain predefined widgets such as `XmForm` or `XmRowColumn` containers. An approximate Motif equivalent to the Java `CardLayoutDemo` example might look like the following:

Listing 9-18: CardLayoutDemo.c

```
/* Source File: CardLayoutDemo.c */

#include <X11/StringDefs.h>
#include <X11/Intrinsic.h>
#include <Xm/Xm.h>
#include <Xm/Form.h>
#include <Xm/RowColumn.h>
#include <Xm/PushB.h>

static char * btns[] = {
        "btn1", "btn2", "btn3",
        "btn4", "btn5", "btn6",
        "btn7", "btn8", "btn9",
        "btn10", "btn11", "btn12"
        };

void nextPanel(widget, rowcolWidget, callback)
Widget widget;
```

```
WidgetList rowcolWidget;
XmAnyCallbackStruct * callback;
{
int n;
Arg wargs[10];
static int curr_widget = 0;
XtUnmanageChild(rowcolWidget[curr_widget]);
curr_widget++;
curr_widget %= 3;

n = 0;
XtSetArg(wargs[n], XmNtopAttachment, XmATTACH_FORM); n++;
XtSetArg(wargs[n], XmNtopWidget, rowcolWidget[curr_widget]); n++;
XtSetArg(wargs[n], XmNleftAttachment, XmATTACH_FORM); n++;
XtSetArg(wargs[n], XmNrightAttachment, XmATTACH_FORM); n++;
XtSetValues(rowcolWidget[curr_widget], wargs, n);
XtManageChild(rowcolWidget[curr_widget]);

n = 0;
XtSetArg(wargs[n], XmNtopAttachment, XmATTACH_WIDGET); n++;
XtSetArg(wargs[n], XmNtopWidget, rowcolWidget[curr_widget]); n++;
XtSetValues(rowcolWidget[3], wargs, n);
}

void main(argc, argv)
int     argc;
char * argv;
{
Widget      mainLevel, mainFormWidget;
Widget      forwardButtonWidget, buttonWidget[XtNumber(btns)];
WidgetList rowcolWidget[4];
int index, n;
Arg wargs[10];

mainLevel = XtInitialize(argv[0], "Card", NULL, 0, &argc, argv);

mainFormWidget =
    XtCreateManagedWidget("mainform", xmFormWidgetClass, mainLevel,
    NULL, 0);

rowcolWidget[0]   =
    XtCreateWidget("rowcol1", xmRowColumnWidgetClass,
    mainFormWidget, NULL, 0);
rowcolWidget[1]   =
    XtCreateWidget("rowcol2", xmRowColumnWidgetClass,
    mainFormWidget, NULL, 0);
rowcolWidget[2]   =
    XtCreateWidget("rowcol3", xmRowColumnWidgetClass,
    mainFormWidget, NULL, 0);
rowcolWidget[3]   =
```

```
        XtCreateWidget("rowcol4", xmRowColumnWidgetClass,
         mainFormWidget, NULL, 0);

for (index=0; index<=3; index++) {
    buttonWidget[index] =
    XtCreateWidget(btns[index], xmPushButtonWidgetClass,
     rowcolWidget[0], NULL, 0);
    XtManageChild(buttonWidget[index]);
    }

for (index=4; index<=7; index++) {
    buttonWidget[index] =
    XtCreateWidget(btns[index], xmPushButtonWidgetClass,
     rowcolWidget[1], NULL, 0);
    XtManageChild(buttonWidget[index]);
    }

for (index=8; index<=11; index++) {
    buttonWidget[index] =
    XtCreateWidget(btns[index], xmPushButtonWidgetClass,
     rowcolWidget[2], NULL, 0);
    XtManageChild(buttonWidget[index]);
    }

forwardButtonWidget =
    XtCreateWidget("forward", xmPushButtonWidgetClass,
     mainFormWidget, NULL, 0);

for (index=0; index<3; index++) {
    n = 0;
    XtSetArg(wargs[n], XmNtopAttachment, XmATTACH_FORM); n++;
    XtSetArg(wargs[n], XmNtopWidget, rowcolWidget[index]); n++;
    XtSetArg(wargs[n], XmNleftAttachment, XmATTACH_FORM); n++;
    XtSetArg(wargs[n], XmNrightAttachment, XmATTACH_FORM); n++;
    XtSetValues(rowcolWidget[index], wargs, n);
    }

XtManageChild(rowcolWidget[0]);    /* Make visible the parent of */
                                   /* buttons 1, 2, 3, & 4 */

n = 0;
XtSetArg(wargs[n], XmNtopAttachment, XmATTACH_WIDGET); n++;
XtSetArg(wargs[n], XmNtopWidget, rowcolWidget[0]); n++;
XtSetArg(wargs[n], XmNleftAttachment, XmATTACH_FORM); n++;
XtSetArg(wargs[n], XmNrightAttachment, XmATTACH_FORM); n++;
XtSetValues(rowcolWidget[3], wargs, n);

XtManageChild(rowcolWidget[3]);    /* Make visible the separator */
                                   /* widget */
```

```
n = 0;
XtSetArg(wargs[n], XmNtopAttachment, XmATTACH_WIDGET); n++;
XtSetArg(wargs[n], XmNtopWidget, rowcolWidget[3]); n++;
XtSetArg(wargs[n], XmNbottomAttachment, XmATTACH_FORM); n++;
XtSetArg(wargs[n], XmNleftAttachment, XmATTACH_FORM); n++;
XtSetArg(wargs[n], XmNrightAttachment, XmATTACH_FORM); n++;
XtSetValues(forwardButtonWidget, wargs, n);

XtManageChild(forwardButtonWidget);        /* Make visible the */
                                           /* "Forward" button */

XtAddCallback(forwardButtonWidget, XmNactivateCallback, nextPanel,
 rowcolWidget);

XtRealizeWidget(mainLevel);
XtMainLoop();
}
```

Listing 9-19: Card

```
/* Resource File: Card */

Card*resizable:                     TRUE
Card.width:                         360
Card.mainform.topAttachment:        attach_position
Card.mainform.bottomAttachment:     attach_position
Card.mainform.leftAttachment:       attach_position
Card.mainform.rightAttachment:      attach_position

Card.mainform.rowcol1.orientation:  horizontal
Card.mainform.rowcol1.packing:      pack_ tight
Card.mainform.rowcol2.orientation:  horizontal
Card.mainform.rowcol2.packing:      pack_ tight
Card.mainform.rowcol3.orientation:  horizontal
Card.mainform.rowcol3.packing:      pack_ tight
Card.mainform.forward.orientation:  horizontal
Card.mainform.forward.packing:      pack_ tight

Card*btn1.labelString:              Button  1
Card*btn2.labelString:              Button  2
Card*btn3.labelString:              Button  3
Card*btn4.labelString:              Button  4
Card*btn5.labelString:              Button  5
Card*btn6.labelString:              Button  6
Card*btn7.labelString:              Button  7
Card*btn8.labelString:              Button  8
Card*btn9.labelString:              Button  9
Card*btn10.labelString:             Button 10
Card*btn11.labelString:             Button 11
Card*btn12.labelString:             Button 12
Card*forward.labelString:           Forward
```

The execution of the Motif version of `CardLayoutDemo` yields a window that appears very similar to the Java version of figure 9-9. The approach taken to construct the window is also similar to the Java example, except we are using C functions that are part of the Motif toolkit. The following is a summary of the Motif-based example:

- An array of four `XmRowColumn` widgets is created. The first three would each contain four buttons and would be stacked together. Each of these three widgets would be flushed to the left, top and right of the main window, thereby forcing each to be superimposed on the other. The fourth `XmRowColumn` widget would serve as a separator between the visible top panel and the "Forward" button, which is flushed to the left, bottom and right of the main window.

- After all of the `XmRowColumn` widgets have been created with the `mainFormWidget` as the parent, each `XmRowColumn` widget has its border attributes adjusted with the `XtSetArg()` macro and the `XtSetValues()` function.

- All of the `XmRowColumn` widgets and the `XmPushButton` widget labeled "Forward" are placed against a `XmForm` widget (represented by variable `mainFormWidget`). By doing this, we can specify the following in the resource file so that the top, middle and bottom rows of the window would assume relatively even spacing on the initial start-up:

```
Card.mainform.topAttachment:      attach_position
Card.mainform.bottomAttachment:   attach_position
Card.mainform.leftAttachment:     attach_position
Card.mainform.rightAttachment:    attach_position
```

- To give the "Forward" button functionality, a callback function is associated with the button:

```
XtAddCallback(forwardButtonWidget, XmNactivateCallback,
              nextPanel, rowcolWidget);
```

The `XmNactivateCallback` argument means to invoke the callback function `nextPanel()` if the "Forward" button is clicked. The `WidgetList` represented by variable `rowcolWidget` would be passed to the callback function.

The callback function `nextPanel()` would look like the following:

```
void nextPanel(widget, rowcolWidget, callback)
Widget widget;
WidgetList rowcolWidget;
XmAnyCallbackStruct * callback;
{
int n;
Arg wargs[10];
static int curr_widget = 0;
XtUnmanageChild(rowcolWidget[curr_widget]);
```

```
curr_widget++;
curr_widget %= 3;
n = 0;
XtSetArg(wargs[n], XmNtopAttachment, XmATTACH_FORM); n++;
XtSetArg(wargs[n], XmNtopWidget, rowcolWidget[curr_widget]);
 n++;
XtSetArg(wargs[n], XmNleftAttachment, XmATTACH_FORM); n++;
XtSetArg(wargs[n], XmNrightAttachment, XmATTACH_FORM); n++;
XtSetValues(rowcolWidget[curr_widget], wargs, n);
XtManageChild(rowcolWidget[curr_widget]);
n = 0;
XtSetArg(wargs[n], XmNtopAttachment, XmATTACH_WIDGET); n++;
XtSetArg(wargs[n], XmNtopWidget, rowcolWidget[curr_widget]);
 n++;
XtSetValues(rowcolWidget[3], wargs, n);
}
```

Like all callback functions, there is no return value (void). Of the three arguments, the second one, the WidgetList rowcolWidget is used within the body of the function. A static int is used to track the last visible widget, so the first task is to hide the current widget with XtUnmanageChild(). Next, the index value, curr_widget is cycled forward by one (modulo 3). The border attributes of the successor XmRowColumn widget is attached to the left, top and right of the main window. This widget is then made visible with a call to XtManageChild(). Finally, the top of the middle widget is set to the bottom of the newly visible XmRowColumn widget.

Optimizing Flexibility with the Java GridBagLayout Manager

The most flexible and the most complicated of the Java layout managers is the GridBagLayout manager. Using this manager requires some planning and experimentation since there are a number of interdependent, visual parameters to take into account. The GridBagLayout manager is quite unique to Java and is difficult to mimic in other native windowing systems.

Before presenting the sample program using the GridBagLayout manager, it would be helpful to look at a conceptual sketch of the user interface (figure 9-10). During the planning stage, the developer must envision a logical Cartesian coordinate system where the x values (horizontal) increase by moving right and the y values (vertical) increase by moving down. Each window control would be placed within a rectangular block of cells. In figure 9–10, each of these controls is represented by the name of the reference variable (which we will see in the code later). Each control will occupy a certain amount of area in the rectangular block of cells, but it will always be contained within that block. The block to which the control is attached is determined by the coordinate in the upper left hand corner. For instance, the `Label` object represented by `dressingLabel` is attached to coordinate (1,0).

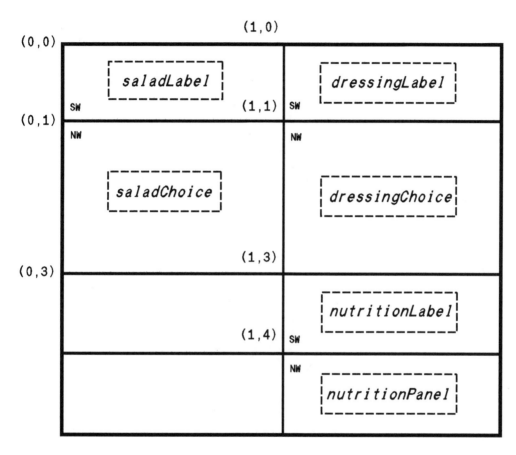

NW - Nouthwest   SW - Southwest

Figure 9-10

After a control is attached to a block, its area can be centered (the default, as illustrated by the dashed rectangles) or anchored to one of the corners. In the example, all of the controls are anchored to the lower left hand corner (southwest) or to the upper left hand corner (northwest). There are also parameters to control the amount of block area a control should occupy (the stretching of the control) and the amount of relative white space between any two adjacent controls.

Once all of the desired parameters have been set and passed to the `GridBagLayout` manager, the manager would handle the calculations and the placement of the controls.

With this preliminary understanding of the user interface, I will now present the Java example, `GridBagLayoutDemo`. When the program begins execution, the main window would look something like figure 9-11.

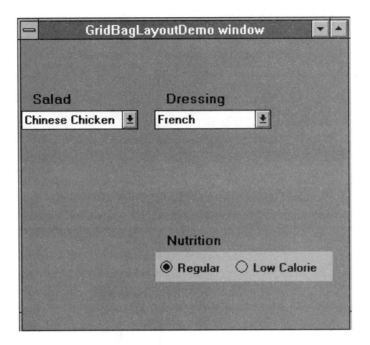

Figure 9-11

If the reader were to mentally superimpose the grid of figure 9-10 onto the figure 9-11, he would envision the relative locations of the controls. In figure 9-11, each control is anchored to a corner of its cell (southwest or northwest).

Below is the listing of `GridBagLayoutDemo`:

Listing 9-20: GridBagLayoutDemo.java

```java
import java.awt.*;

public class GridBagLayoutDemo extends Frame {

    public GridBagLayoutDemo() {

        super("GridBagLayoutDemo window");
```

```
GridBagLayout gbl = new GridBagLayout();/* (1) */
setLayout(gbl);

GridBagConstraints gbc = new GridBagConstraints();

int weightX = 10;
int weightY = 10;

resize(350,330);
nutritionGroup = new CheckboxGroup();
Panel nutritionPanel = new Panel();

// Row 0    (gridy == 0)

saladLabel=new Label("Salad");
saladLabel.setFont(new Font("Dialog",Font.BOLD,14));
saladLabel.setBackground(Color.lightGray);
add(saladLabel, gbl, gbc,                       /* (2) */
   GridBagConstraints.NONE, GridBagConstraints.
    SOUTHWEST,
   weightX, weightY, 0, 0, 1, 1);

dressingLabel=new Label("Dressing");
dressingLabel.setFont(new Font("Dialog",Font.BOLD,14));
dressingLabel.setBackground(Color.lightGray);
add(dressingLabel, gbl, gbc,                     /* (2) */
   GridBagConstraints.NONE, GridBagConstraints.
    SOUTHWEST,
   weightX, weightY, 1, 0, 1, 1);

// Row 1    (gridy == 1)

saladChoice= new Choice();
saladChoice.setFont(new Font("Dialog",Font.BOLD,12));
add(saladChoice,gbl, gbc,                        /* (2) */
    GridBagConstraints.NONE, GridBagConstraints.NORTHWEST,
        weightX, weightY, 0, 1, 1, 2);
saladChoice.addItem("Chinese Chicken");
saladChoice.addItem("Little Caesar");
saladChoice.addItem("Smoked Turkey");
saladChoice.addItem("Tossed Green");
saladChoice.addItem("Tuna 'N Shrimp");

dressingChoice= new Choice();
dressingChoice.setFont(new Font("Dialog",Font.BOLD,12));
add(dressingChoice, gbl, gbc,                    /* (2) */
   GridBagConstraints.NONE, GridBagConstraints.NORTHWEST,
   weightX, weightY, 1, 1, 1, 2);
```

```
        dressingChoice.addItem("French");
        dressingChoice.addItem("Italian");
        dressingChoice.addItem("Oil 'N Vinegar");
        dressingChoice.addItem("Ranch");
        dressingChoice.addItem("Russian");
        dressingChoice.addItem("Thousand Island");

        // Row 2   (gridy == 2)   is empty

       // Row 3    (gridy == 3)

        nutritionLabel=new Label("Nutrition");
        nutritionLabel.setFont(new Font("Dialog",Font.BOLD,14));
        nutritionLabel.setBackground(Color.lightGray);
        add(nutritionLabel, gbl, gbc, /* (2) */
            GridBagConstraints.NONE, GridBagConstraints.SOUTHWEST,
            weightX, weightY, 1, 3, 1, 1);

        // Row 4    (gridy == 4)

        regularButton=new Checkbox("Regular",nutritionGroup,
         true);
        regularButton.setFont(new Font("Dialog",Font.BOLD,12));

        lowcalButton=new Checkbox("Low Calorie",nutritionGroup,
         false);
        lowcalButton.setFont(new Font("Dialog",Font.BOLD,12));

        nutritionPanel.add(regularButton);
        nutritionPanel.add(lowcalButton);
        nutritionPanel.setBackground(Color.lightGray);

        add(nutritionPanel, gbl, gbc, /* (2) */
            GridBagConstraints.NONE, GridBagConstraints.NORTHWEST,
            weightX, weightY, 1, 4, 1, 1);
        setBackground(new Color(150, 150, 150));

        show();

    }

public synchronized void show() {
    move(75, 75);
    super.show();
}

public boolean handleEvent(Event event) {
if (event.id == Event.WINDOW_DESTROY) {
    hide();
```

```
        dispose();
        System.exit(0);
        return true;
        }
    return super.handleEvent(event);
    }

    public boolean action(Event event, Object arg) {
    if (event.target instanceof MenuItem) {
      String label = (String) arg;
      }
    return super.action(event, arg);
    }


    private void add(Component comp, GridBagLayout gridBagLayout,
                                                /* (3) */
                    GridBagConstraints gridBagParms,
                    int fl, int an,
                    int wx, int wy,
                    int gx, int gy,
                    int gw, int gh)  {
    gridBagParms.fill        = fl;
    gridBagParms.anchor      = an;
    gridBagParms.weightx     = wx;
    gridBagParms.weighty     = wy;
    gridBagParms.gridx       = gx;
    gridBagParms.gridy       = gy;
    gridBagParms.gridwidth   = gw;
    gridBagParms.gridheight  = gh;
    gridBagLayout.setConstraints(comp, gridBagParms);
    add(comp);
    }


    public static void main(String args[]) {
        new GridBagLayoutDemo();
    }


    private CheckboxGroup  nutritionGroup;
    private Choice         saladChoice;
    private Label          saladLabel;
    private Label          dressingLabel;
    private Choice         dressingChoice;
    private Checkbox       regularButton;
    private Checkbox       lowcalButton;
    private Label          nutritionLabel;
}
```

The highlighted code illustrates the main points of the example. The following is
a discussion of the main points:

- The `GridBagLayoutDemo` program is a stand-alone application (since class `GridBagLayoutDemo` is subclassed from class `Frame`). The constructor for `GridBagLayoutDemo` creates a `GridBagLayout` manager object (comment `/* (1) */`) to manage its controls with statements:

```
GridBagLayout gbl = new GridBagLayout();
setLayout(gbl);
```

  The constructor also creates a `GridBagConstraints` object, which actually holds all of the layout properties mentioned earlier. This is done with the statement:

```
GridBagConstraints gbc = new GridBagConstraints();
```

  The remaining code of the `GridBagLayoutDemo` constructor instantiates the `Label`, `Choice` and `Button` objects and adds them to the `GridBagLayoutDemo` frame. To help with organization, the `Button` objects are grouped into a `Panel` object (reference variable `nutritionPanel`) and the `Panel` object is added to the main frame.

- After each child control of `GridBagLayoutDemo` has been instantiated, a call is made to a custom-written `add()` method (comment `/* (2) */`) to set the layout properties. For instance, the setting of the properties for the list box `saladChoice` is done with the statement:

```
add(saladChoice, gbl,  gbc,
    GridBagConstraints.NONE,  GridBagConstraints.NORTHWEST,
    weightX,  weightY,
    0,  1,
    1,  2);
```

- To make the setting of these properties a little easier, the custom-written `add()` method was created (comment `/* (3) */`):

```
private void add(Component comp, GridBagLayout gridBagLayout,
                 GridBagConstraints gridBagParms,
                 int fl, int an
                 int wx, int wy,
                 int gx, int gy
                 int gw, int gh)     {
gridBagParms.fill        = fl;
gridBagParms.anchor      = an;
gridBagParms.weightx     = wx;
gridBagParms.weighty     = wy;
gridBagParms.gridx       = gx;
gridBagParms.gridy       = gy;
gridBagParms.gridwidth   = gw;
gridBagParms.gridheight  = gh;
gridBagLayout.setConstraints(comp, gridBagParms);
```

```
add(comp);
}
```

The following is a summary of the various parameters of the
`GridBagConstraints` object:

- `fill`: this variable determines whether the area of the control would
  stretch to fill the cell and how the stretching would be done. Possible
  values for this variable would be `GridBagConstraints.NONE`,
  `GridBagConstraints.HORIZONTAL`, `GridBagConstraints.`
  `VERTICAL` and `GridBagConstraints.BOTH`.

- `anchor`: this variable determines whether the area of the control
  would be flushed against an edge or corner of its cell. Possible values
  for variable `anchor` would be `GridBagConstraints.CENTER`,
  `GridBagConstraints.EAST`, `GridBagConstraints.SOUTH-`
  `EAST`, `GridBagConstraints.SOUTH`,
  `GridBagConstraints.SOUTHWEST`, etc.

- `weightx, weighty`: these variables determine the relative amount of
  white space between the various components. The setting of these
  variables is rather tricky since the anticipated behaviors from these
  settings is not obvious. The recommendation is to give all controls the
  same non-zero `weightx` and non-zero `weighty`, say a value of 10
  each, just to get the other properties established first. After that, the
  developer can choose to assign different weight values to individual
  controls and experiment with the overall results. A general rule to
  keep in mind is that if control A has greater `weightx` and `weighty`
  values than the corresponding `weightx` and `weighty` values of control B, then control A will "possess" more horizontal and vertical
  white space than control B.

- `gridx, gridy`: these variables represent the upper left hand corner of
  the logical cell in which the control is to be placed.

- `gridwidth, gridheight`: these variables determine how many logical cells the control should occupy. When there are "large" controls,
  such as list boxes and text fields, such controls should be mapped to a
  number of logical cells. In these cases, the other properties, such as
  `fill`, `anchor`, `weightx` and `weighy`, apply to the entire control's
  domain or block of cells.

  Once the desired parameters have been given appropriate values, the
  values are applied to the control in question with the
  `setConstraints()` method of the `GridBagLayout` manager:

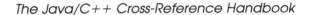

```
gridBagLayout.setConstraints(comp, gridBagParms);
```

Summary: The `GridBagLayout` manager offers the greatest degree of control of the user interface components, but it requires planning and experimentation to achieve a relatively platform-independent result. The parameters of the `GridBagConstraints` object determine the sizing and positioning of the components. Many of these parameters are interrelated. In the effort to find a combination of values that will give the most optimal results, default values for most of the properties should be chosen initially. The process is very much like focusing the lens of a camera on an image. Once the contours of the basic image have come into view, the developer can work on the details to sharpen the image.

CHAPTER
10

- The World of Client-Server Computing

- A File Retrieval Service in C

- The File Retrieval Service in Java

- Accessing Uniform Resource Locators

Networking the Java Environment

The World of Client-Server Computing

Over the years there has been a major push by many businesses to go to a client-server computing environment. The phrase "client-server" basically means a networked environment where potentially heterogeneous computing equipment can communicate with each other. Each piece of equipment would be given a role that it could do well. For instance, traditional mainframe computers are generally good at managing large databases and such machines would be used to house and manage data. On the other hand, personal computers are very capable in their ability to display data, especially with multicolor, high-resolution graphics. The idea is to optimize all of the computing resources so that a business can reap the greatest benefits from its investments.

The terms "client" and "server" have often been confused with particular types or brands of computing hardware. Rather, the terms really refer to the software behind the equipment. A server is a *provider* of a service, while a client is a *requester* of a service. Either type of software can run on a mainframe, workstation or personal computer. Generally speaking, servers run on expensive, multi-processor, multiuser systems, while clients run on single-processor, single-user systems. New, faster and more powerful hardware appear all of the time, so the placement of a client or server would change all of the time.

For years, UNIX has provided a means for different platforms to communicate with each other through a common interface called sockets. Microsoft Windows 95™ and NT also support sockets through the WINSOCK interface. In line with these traditions, Java supports sockets programming through the various classes of its standard `java.net` package.

The Java classes support the OSI network specification for the Internet Protocol (IP) and that includes the User Datagram Protocol (UDP) and the Transmission Control Protocol (TCP). For all practical purposes, most developers will program with TCP/IP, since it offers the greatest reliability for the delivery of information over a network. TCP/IP has more overhead than UDP, but its protocol will insure that data packets will not be dropped, duplicated or delivered out-of-order. TCP/IP can also be used over a wide area network. In this chapter, we will focus on TCP/IP-based examples.

For developers who have written client-server programs in C using sockets, the use of Java will be a very refreshing change. Many of the tedious details of managing a socket connection are handled by the Java classes. In this chapter, we will look at a sample client-server application written in C with Berkeley (BSD) sockets and compare it to an equivalent Java example.

A File Retrieval Service in C

Providing the user with the ability to retrieve remote files from a client application is a very common type of service. In this section, we will look at a complete client-server example using C and BSD sockets under the UNIX operating system. There are two complete C programs for the overall system and each is intended to run on separate machines. The server program is called `ClipArtServer` and the client program is called `ClipArtSelector`.

As the program names suggest, this is a system for the retrieval of clip art images, something that might be very useful within a corporate environment. Today, any user of a graphical word processor is likely to import images into a document. Instead of distributing every clip art conceivable to every user, the image files would be stored on a central repository and the user would retrieve whatever he needs and whenever he needs it. A server program would perform the retrieval per request and the end-user would make his request via a client program.

The reader will find that there are a lot of details to setting up a TCP/IP connection. Some of these details pertain to the server while others pertain to the client. To simplify the whole effort for writing either clients or servers, a function common to both was written to handle all of the typical and mundane details of socket connections. Let us first examine the common code:

Listing 10-1: common.h

```
/* File: common.h */

#define NOSOCK                      -1
#define UDP_SERV                     0
```

```
#define TCP_SERV                    1
#define QLEN                        5
#define LINELGTH                  128
#define BUFFSIZE                  256
#define PORT                    27000
#define FALSE                       0
#define TRUE                        1


#ifndef  MAX
#define  MAX(x,y)  ((x)>(y)?(x):(y))
#endif


#ifndef    INADDR_NONE
#define    INADDR_NONE     0xFFFFFFFF
#endif
```

Listing 10-2: common.c

```
/* File: common.c */

#include <stdio.h>
#include <varargs.h>
#include <sys/types.h>
#include <sys/socket.h>
#include <netinet/in.h>
#include <netdb.h>
#include <fcntl.h>
#include "common.h"

extern int errno;
extern char * sys_errlist[];

u_long inet_addr();

int notify_exit(msg, va_alist)                      /* (1) */
char * msg;
va_dcl
{
va_list parms;
va_start(parms);
_doprnt(msg, parms, stderr);
va_end(parms);
exit(1);
}

int createTCPSocket(host, port, backlog)            /* (2) */
char * host;
int    port;
int    backlog;
{
```

```
struct hostent    *   pHostEnt;
struct protoent *   pProtoEnt;
struct sockaddr_in sin;
int     sock;

bzero((char*)&sin, sizeof(sin));
sin.sin_family = AF_INET;
sin.sin_port = htons((u_short)port);

if (host == NULL)                          /* server portion */
   sin.sin_addr.s_addr = INADDR_ANY;
else {                                     /* client portion */
   if (pHostEnt = gethostbyname(host))
      bcopy(pHostEnt->h_addr, (char*)&sin.sin_addr,
       pHostEnt->h_length);
   else
   if ((sin.sin_addr.s_addr = inet_addr(host)) == INADDR_NONE)
      notify_exit("Cannot get \"%s\" protocol entry\n", host);
   }

if ((pProtoEnt = getprotobyname("tcp")) == 0)
   notify_exit("Cannot get \"tcp\" protocol entry\n");

sock = socket(PF_INET, SOCK_STREAM, pProtoEnt->p_proto);
if (sock < 0)
   notify_exit("Cannot create socket: %s\n", sys_errlist[errno]);

if (host == NULL) {                        /* server portion */
   if (bind(sock, (struct sockaddr *)&sin, sizeof(sin)) < 0)
      notify_exit("Cannot bind to port %d: %s\n", port,
       sys_errlist[errno]);

   printf("Successful bind to port %d\n", port);

   if (listen(sock, backlog) < 0)
      notify_exit("Cannot listen on port %d: %s\n", port,
       sys_errlist[errno]);
   }
else {                                     /* client portion */
   if (connect(sock, (struct sockaddr *)&sin, sizeof(sin)) < 0)
      notify_exit("Cannot connect to host %s on port %d: %s\n",
       host, port, sys_errlist[errno]);
   }

return sock;
}
```

Here are the main points of what the code has in common:

- Macros that are application-specific are placed within their own header files (.h files). For this example, the header file common.h is associated with common.c, which is the source file for the functions common to the client and server programs.

- The notify_exit() function (comment /* (1) */) is used to handle fatal situations such as not being able to translate a host name to the Internet (IP) address or not being able to connect to a socket. The function is very similar to the standard printf() function. The first argument, msg, is a string (char *) with the standard format descriptions. The second argument, va_alist (of type va_list) represents an indefinite number of parameters, each mapped to a format descriptor of msg (the mapping goes from left to right). The identifiers with the prefix va_ represent predefined macros from the header file varargs.h.

- The createTCPSocket() function (comment /* (2) */) is the key function of common.c. It takes three arguments: host, port and backlog. The host variable represents the domain name or dotted decimal name for the physical computer and it is used by the client program to identify the machine to which it wants to talk. The port variable represents the protocol port number that the server program is monitoring for client connections. Finally, the backlog variable is the length of the queue for deferred client requests while the server is busy filling a request. Variable host is only meaningful to the client while variable backlog is only meaningful to the server. Both client and server use variable port.

- Within the body of function createTCPSocket(), a number of predefined struct variables or pointer to struct variables (pHostEnt, pProtoEnt and sin) are declared. These data structures are predefined types in netinet/in.h and netdb.h and are used to receive or pass parameters for various socket functions.

- Variable sin is of type struct sockaddr_in. The members of this struct must be given a set of values so that sin can be passed as a parameter to the bind() function after the socket has been created. The following statement:

```
sin.sin_family = AF_INET;
```

establishes the protocol family, which is always AF_INET for TCP/IP. The next statement:

```
sin.sin_port = htons((u_short)port);
```

uses the htons() function to make sure the protocol port field takes a short value converted from native host byte order to standard network byte order (most significant byte first). Using `htons()` and sipling functions like `ntohs()`, `htonl()` and `ntohl()` will insure that the source is portable to any machine.

- The next set of statements has to do with obtaining the binary address of the host:

```
if (host == NULL)                /* server portion */
    sin.sin_addr.s_addr = INADDR_ANY;
else {                           /* client portion */
    if (pHostEnt = gethostbyname(host))
        bcopy(pHostEnt->h_addr, (char*)&sin.sin_addr,
        pHostEnt->h_length);
    else
    if ((sin.sin_addr.s_addr = inet_addr(host)) ==
    INADDR_NONE)
        notify_exit("Cannot get \"%s\" protocol entry\n",
        host);
}
```

If the program is the server, the `host` variable would contain a `NULL`. In this case, the address field of `sin`, `sin.sin_addr.s_addr`, would be given value `INADDR_ANY`, which is a wild card address of `0.0.0.0`. This address means the server can receive messages from any system attached to it via the network (including itself).

If the program is the client, then the `host` variable would be given a host name or an IP address in textual dotted decimal form. If the address is a host name (such as `snoopy.pets.com`), then the `gethostbyname()` function would be used to obtain the IP address. The return value is a pointer to `struct hostent`, where a member of the `struct`, `h_addr`, holds the IP address. If `gethostbyname()` is successful (not zero), then the `bcopy()` function is used to copy `pHostEnt->h_addr` to (`&sin.sin_addr`). The `bcopy()` function is the proper way to copy binary values.

The `gethostbyname()` function gets its address from the `/etc/hosts` file of the local system, a Yellow Pages (yp) map or from a domain name server.

If the `gethostbyname()` function is unsuccessful, the `host` variable could have the IP address in textual, dotted decimal notation already. If so, the `inet_addr()` function is used to convert that string format to binary. If the `inet_addr()` function fails, a value of `INADDR_NONE` is returned.

- The following set of statements leads to the construction of a socket:

```
if ((pProtoEnt = getprotobyname("tcp")) == 0)
    notify_exit("Cannot get \"tcp\" protocol entry\n");
```

```
sock = socket(PF_INET, SOCK_STREAM, pProtoEnt->p_proto);
if (sock < 0)
    notify_exit("Cannot create socket: %s\n",
      sys_errlist[errno]);
```

The getprotobyname() function must be used to obtain the official protocol number given the string name of the protocol (such as "tcp" or "udp"). The function returns a pointer to struct protoent where the member p_proto contains the protocol number.

The pProtoEnt->p_proto member is then passed as one of the parameters to the socket() function, which, if successful, returns a socket. The predefined value, PF_INET, must be passed for TCP/IP. In addition, the predefined value, SOCK_STREAM, must be passed for TCP.

- After a socket has been successfully created, the next portion of code would associate the parameters of variable sin to the socket through the bind() function (for the server) or the connect() function (for the client):

```
if (host == NULL) {                          /* server portion */
    if (bind(sock, (struct sockaddr *)&sin, sizeof(sin)) < 0)
        notify_exit("Cannot bind to port %d: %s\n", port,
          sys_errlist[errno]);

    printf("Successful bind to port %d\n", port);

    if (listen(sock, backlog) < 0)
        notify_exit("Cannot listen on port %d: %s\n", port,
          sys_errlist[errno]);

}
else {                                       /* client portion */
    if (connect(sock, (struct sockaddr *)&sin, sizeof(sin))
      < 0)
        notify_exit("Cannot connect to host %s on port %d:
          %s\n", host, port, sys_errlist[errno]);
}


return   sock;
```

After the server has successfully called function bind(), it would call listen() on the socket to wait for incoming client requests. The second parameter, backlog, represents the length of the queue for the retention of client requests while the server is busy processing a request.

The connect() function is used by the client program to make a request to the server.

When the end of the `createTCPSocket()` function has been reached, the newly created socket, `sock`, is returned.

Now, it is time to examine the main source files for both the server and client programs. The following is the main source for the server:

Listing 10-3: ClipArtServer.c

```c
/* File: ClipArtServer.c */

#include <sys/types.h>
#include <sys/param.h>
#include <sys/socket.h>
#include <sys/time.h>
#include <sys/resource.h>
#include <sys/errno.h>
#include <sys/signal.h>
#include <sys/wait.h>
#include <netinet/in.h>
#include <netdb.h>
#include <varargs.h>
#include <string.h>
#include <stdio.h>
#include <fcntl.h>
#include "common.h"

int errno;
char * sys_errlist[];

void reaper(int status)                    /* (2) */
{
while (wait3(&status, WNOHANG, 0) >= 0);
}

int transfer(fd)                           /* (4) */
int fd;
{
char filename[BUFFSIZE];
char buffer[BUFFSIZE];
int  lgth;
int  filedes;
int  count;

bzero(filename, sizeof(filename));
bzero(buffer, sizeof(buffer));

while (lgth = read(fd, buffer, sizeof(buffer))) {
   if (lgth < 0)
      notify_exit("Transfer read: %s\n", sys_errlist[errno]);
```

```c
        if (buffer[lgth-1]=='\n') {
            buffer[lgth-1]='\0';
            strcat(filename, buffer);
            break;
            }
        else
            strcat(filename, buffer);
        }

if (strlen(buffer)==0)
    return(0);

filedes = open(filename, O_RDONLY);

if (filedes < 0)
    notify_exit("Unable to get file descriptor for file %s\n",
     filename);

bzero(buffer, sizeof(buffer));

while (count = read(filedes, buffer, sizeof(buffer))) {
    if (count == -1)
        notify_exit("Read failed on file %s", filename);
    if (write(fd, buffer, count)<0)
        notify_exit("Write failed on file %s", filename);
    }

close(filedes);

printf("Done transferring file %s\n", filename);

return(0);
}

int main(argc, argv)
int argc;
char *argv[];
{
struct sockaddr_in  fsin;
int                 alen;
int                 msock;
int                 ssock;
int                 port_no = PORT;

switch(argc) {
    case 1:
        break;
    case 2:
        port_no = (u_short) atoi(argv[1]);          /* (1) */
        break;
```

```
        default:
            notify_exit("Usage: FileServer [portbase]\n");
        }

msock = createTCPSocket(NULL, port_no, QLEN);

(void) signal(SIGCHLD, reaper);                        /* (2) */

while(1) {                                             /* (3) */
    alen = sizeof(fsin);
    ssock = accept(msock, (struct sockaddr *)&fsin, &alen);
    if (ssock < 0) {
        if (errno == EINTR) continue;
        notify_exit("accept: %s\n", sys_errlist[errno]);
        }
    switch (fork()) {
        case 0:     /* child */
            (void) close(msock);
            exit(transfer(ssock));
        default:  /* parent */
            (void) close(ssock);
            break;
        case -1:
            notify_exit("fork: %s\n", sys_errlist[errno]);
        } /* switch */
    }
}
```

Below are the main points of the server program:

- The server program is started from the command line by typing:

  `ClipArtServer`

  or by typing:

  `ClipArtServer   port_number`

  where `port_number` is a valid and available integral port number above 1024. If an explicit port number is given, the string for this value would be contained in `argv[1]` (comment `/* (1) */`). Without an explicit port number, the server will use the predefined value for PORT in file `common.h`.

- The next statement:

  `msock = createTCPSocket(NULL, port_no, QLEN);`

  creates and returns a socket to variable `msock` with the TCP protocol.

- As the main program continues, the parent process will create a child process to handle each request. After a child process has completed its assignment and exits, its entry in the process table remains until its parent process waits on it. If the parent process fails to wait on a child, then the child process will never exit gracefully. When that happens, the child enters a zombie state.

As the child exits, the operating system will send a SIGCHLD signal to the parent process. That being the case, the parent process needs to trap the SIGCHLD signal (comment /* (2) */):

```
(void) signal(SIGCHLD, reaper);
```

The above statement says that when a SIGCHLD signal is sent to the parent, the reaper() function should be executed. The reaper() function simply calls library function wait3(), which will complete the termination of an exiting child. To avoid deadlocks, the WNOHANG parameter is used so that the parent process will not be suspended into a sleep state while waiting for some child process to exit.

Function wait3() will return zero to indicate there are no children in the zombie state. A return value of -1 means there are no children at all.

• The flow of control of the server then enters an endless while loop (comment /* (3) */) where the first statement is the accept() function:

```
ssock = accept(msock, (struct sockaddr *)&fsin, &alen);
```

The parent process of the server blocks on this function until a client request has been received. The underlying TCP protocol software then creates a socket for the new connection and returns it to variable ssock.

The parent server process then calls fork() to divide itself into two processes:

```
switch (fork()) {
   case 0:    /* child */
         (void) close(msock);
         exit(transfer(ssock));
   default: /* parent */
         (void) close(ssock);
         break;
   case -1:
         notify_exit("fork: %s\n", sys_errlist[errno]);
   }    /* switch */
```

The parent process and the child process both share the same code. The return value of fork() determines which is the parent and which is the child. The fork() routine creates a new process table for the child where resources like socket descriptors are duplicated. That being the case, the child process should close the master socket descriptor (msock) and the parent process should close the slave socket descriptor (ssock). The parent process would then go back to the accept() routine to wait for another incoming connection. The child process would call the function, trans-fer(), to perform service for the client. The newly created socket, ssock, is passed as a parameter to function transfer().

- The transfer() function (comment /* (4) */) is where the child process does its work to find and deliver the desired file to the client. The first order of business is to construct the file name that was sent by the client:

```
while (lgth = read(fd, buffer, sizeof(buffer))) {
    if (lgth < 0)
        notify_exit("Transfer read: %s\n", sys_errlist[errno]);
    if (buffer[lgth-1]=='\n') {
        buffer[lgth-1]='\0';
        strcat(filename, buffer);
        break;
        }
    else
        strcat(filename, buffer);
    }

if (strlen(buffer)==0)
    return(0);
```

The read() routine is applied to the socket descriptor that was passed from main(). The read() function continues until there are zero characters in the internal buffer or until there is a terminating newline character in the incoming buffer. All of the meaningful buffer contents are concatenated into variable filename.

- Once the file name has been constructed, the file is opened in read-only mode. The contents of the file are then iteratively read and written to the socket:

```
filedes = open(filename, O_RDONLY);

if (filedes < 0)
    notify_exit("Unable to get file descriptor for file %s\n",
        filename);

bzero(buffer, sizeof(buffer));

while (count = read(filedes, buffer, sizeof(buffer))) {
    if (count == -1)
        notify_exit("Read failed on file %s", filename);
    if (write(fd, buffer, count)<0)
        notify_exit("Write failed on file %s", filename);
    }
```

```
    close(filedes);

    printf("Done transferring file %s\n", filename);
```

When the reading and writing has completed, the file descriptor for the file is closed. When the child process exits, the system will automatically close the descriptor for the TCP connection.

To complete the entire system, the client program is now introduced. The following is the source for the client, ClipArtSelector:

Listing 10-4: ClipArtSelector.c

```c
/* File: ClipArtSelector.c */

#include <stdio.h>
#include <varargs.h>
#include <sys/types.h>
#include <sys/socket.h>
#include <netinet/in.h>
#include <netdb.h>
#include <fcntl.h>
#include "common.h"

extern int errno;
extern char * sys_errlist[];

void get_file(host, port)                          /* (1) */
char * host;
int    port;
{
char buff[LINELGTH+1];
char filename[LINELGTH+1];
int  sock, count, fdes;

do {
    bzero(filename, sizeof(filename));
    sock = createTCPSocket(host, port, 0);
    printf("Enter the name of a file and press <return> (Type a
     single <return> to exit): ");

    fgets(buff, sizeof(buff), stdin);
    buff[LINELGTH] = '\0';
    if (buff[0]=='\n')
        return;
    write(sock, buff, strlen(buff));
    if (buff[strlen(buff)-1] == '\n')
        buff[strlen(buff)-1] = '\0';
```

```
            strcat(filename, buff);

            fdes = open(filename, O_WRONLY | O_CREAT, S_IRUSR | S_IWUSR);

        if (fdes < 0)
            notify_exit("Unable to get file descriptor for file %s\n",
              filename);

        while  (count = read(sock, buff, sizeof(buff))) {
            if (count < 0)
                notify_exit("Socket read failed: %s\n",
                sys_errrlist[errno]);
            if (write(fdes, buff, count)<0)
                notify_exit("Write failed on file %s", filename);
            }
        close(fdes);
        } while (TRUE);
}

int main(argc, argv)
int   argc;
char *argv[];
{
char * host = "localhost";
int     port_no = PORT;

switch (argc) {
    case 1: host = "localhost";
                  break;
    case 3: port_no = atoi(argv[2]);
    case 2: host = argv[1];
                  break;
    default: fprintf(stderr, "Usage: FileGet [host [port]]\n");
                  exit(1);
    }

get_file(host, port_no);
exit(0);
}
```

Below are the main points of the client program:

- The client program is started from the command line by typing:

  ```
  ClipArtSelector
  ```

  or:

  ```
  ClipArtSelector   host   port_no
  ```

  The first option without parameters will select the local system as the default host and a default port number (macro PORT). The second option allows for the choice of a host and a well-known port number that the server program is listening. The host could be a domain name or an IP address in dotted decimal format.

- The main function for file retrieval is `get_file()` (comment `/* (1) */`). This routine is given the host and port number. The body of the function is a `do` loop of repetitive activities. The loop first makes a connection to the server program:

```
sock = createTCPSocket(host, port, 0);
```

On the server side, the server program will return a new socket connection from its `accept()` call. A child server process then waits for the incoming file name from the client.

- The client program will then prompt the user to enter a file name and to terminate his input with an `<enter>` from the command line. The file name is written to the socket descriptor and the name is retained in variable `filename` so that when the server returns the contents the file can be properly saved:

```
bzero(filename, sizeof(filename));
...
printf("Enter the name of a file and press <return>
          (Type a single <return> to exit): ");

fgets(buff, sizeof(buff), stdin);
buff[LINELGTH] = '\0';
if (buff[0]=='\n')
    return;

write(sock, buff, strlen(buff));
if (buff[strlen(buff)-1] == '\n')
    buff[strlen(buff)-1] = '\0';

strcat(filename, buff);
```

- Next, a new file with `filename` is prepared for the arrival of the file contents:

```
fdes = open(filename, O_WRONLY | O_CREAT, S_IRUSR | S_IWUSR);
```

The file is opened in write-only mode (`O_WRONLY`) with a request to create the file if it does not already exist (`O_CREAT`). The user who creates the file is given read and write permissions (`S_IRUSR | S_IWUSR`).

- The client program then reads the socket for incoming data from the server and writes the contents to the file:

```
while (count = read(sock, buff, sizeof(buff))) {
        if (count < 0)
```

```
        notify_exit("Socket read failed: %s\n",
         sys_errlist[errno]);
      if (write(fdes, buff, count)<0)
         notify_exit("Write failed on file %s", filename);
      }

  close(fdes);
```

The loop finishes when the number of bytes returned is zero. The file descriptor is then properly closed.

When the user has finished with the retrieval of the desired files, he simply presses <enter> at the prompt to exit the client program. When that happens, the system will close the socket descriptor.

Summary: As the reader may sense, writing even a simple client-server application in C for file retrieval is not exactly a trivial task. There are an immense number of details to consider if the work is to be done properly. The next section will show a Java equivalent to this system and will offer the reader a sign of relief.

The File Retrieval Service in Java

As I had mentioned in the previous section (*A File Retrieval Service in C*), giving end-users the ability to retrieve files remotely is a common type of service. In this section, I will present a Java equivalent to the clip art file retrieval system.

I will first start with the server program, `ClipArtServer`. This program has no graphical user interface. It is started on the command line and runs forever until it is interrupted with a CTRL-C:

```
java ClipArtServer 5000
```

The only argument to `ClipArtServer`, 5000, is a port number. The port is the entry point that the server program monitors for client requests. The number 5000 is chosen since all integers 1024 and lower are reserved for special system services (such as `echo` and `datetime`).

Below is the listing for `ClipArtServer`:

Listing 10-5: ClipArtServer.java

```java
import java.io.*;
import java.net.*;

class ClipArtAssistant extends Thread {

    ClipArtAssistant(Socket s) {
        sock = s;
    }
```

```
    public void run() {                                       /* (3) */
        try {
            DataOutputStream out = new
             DataOutputStream(sock.getOutputStream());
            DataInputStream  in  = new
             DataInputStream(sock.getInputStream());

            filename = in.readLine();
            File fobj = new File(filename);
            FileInputStream fis = null;

            int count;
            byte [] barray = new byte[8192];

            if (fobj.exists() && fobj.isFile()) {
                fis = new FileInputStream(fobj);
                while ((count = fis.read(barray)) != -1) {
                    out.write(barray, 0, count);
                    out.flush();
                    sleep(5);
                    }
                }
            in.close();
            out.close();
            sock.close();
            }
        catch(Exception err) {
            System.err.println(err.toString());
            System.exit(-1);
            }
    }

    private Socket sock;
    private String filename;

}   // ClipArtAssistant

public class ClipArtServer {

    public static void main(String args[]) {
        Socket sock = null;
        FileInputStream fis = null;
        ClipArtAssistant ca = null;
        try {
            ServerSocket servsock =                            /* (1) */
                new ServerSocket(new
                  Integer(args[0]).intValue());
            while (true) {
                sock = servsock.accept();
```

```
            ca = new ClipArtAssistant(sock);       /* (2) */
            ca.start();
            }
        }
      catch (Exception err) {
            System.out.println(err.toString());
            System.exit(-1);
            }


    }
}   // ClipArtServer
```

The following is a discussion of the main points of the server program:

- The purpose of class ClipArtServer is to listen for client requests on the port. ClipArtServer itself never fills any request. Rather, it takes each request and hands it off to a ClipArtAssistant object that fills the request. The ClipArtAssistant class is actually subclassed from class Thread. By taking this approach, it is possible to provide service to many clients. No client is blocked waiting for another client's request to be filled.

- The bulk of activity for class ClipArtServer is its main() method. The first thing this method does is to create a socket object called servsock using class ServerSocket (comment /* (1) */). Next, the socket object servsock calls method accept(), which means the object will block until there is a client connection. When a connection does come in, accept() will return a Socket object and this would be assigned to variable sock.

- A ClipArtAssistant object is instantiated and given the socket connection represented by variable sock (comment /* (2) */). The ClipArtAssistant object is actually subclassed from class Thread, so it would be activated by sending it the start() message.

- The threads mechanism of Java is such that the call to the start() method will eventually call the object's run() method. So we must implement a run() method for class ClipArtAssistant (comment /* (3) */). Every Socket object is bidirectional, i.e., it has an input stream as well as an output stream. To get references to both, we execute the following statements:

```
DataOutputStream out = new
 DataOutputStream(sock.getOutputStream());
DataInputStream  in  = new
 DataInputStream(sock.getInputStream());
```

We first read the input stream to obtain the name of the file the client application had sent:

```
filename = in.readLine();
```

and then make a `File` object from the name:

```
File fobj = new File(filename);
```

The application will block on the `readLine()` method until there is a stream of characters within the input stream buffer. The method returns when a '\r,' '\n,' '\r\n ' or end-of-file is detected.

* Next, a few checks are performed to insure that the `File` object representing the file name exists and whether it is a real file (and not a directory):

```
if (fobj.exists() && fobj.isFile()) {
    fis = new FileInputStream(fobj);
  while ((count = fis.read(barray)) != -1) {
        out.write(barray, 0, count);
      out.flush();
      sleep(5);
    }
  }
```

Assuming the `File` object is valid, a `FileInputStream` object, `fis`, is created from it. Using the `read()` method, an array of bytes is read and then written to the socket via the `DataOutputStream` object, `out`. To insure that all of the bytes are transmitted, the `flush()` method is used after every `write()`. Finally, since `ClipArtAssistant` is a thread object, we must call `sleep()` to give other threads a chance to run.

* Finally, after the contents of the file have been written to the socket, the `ClipArtAssistant` thread closes its resources with:

```
in.close();
out.close();
sock.close();
```

That is what goes on the server side. Now, we will look at the client program, `ClipArtSelector`. The Java version of the client utilizes the AWT controls. When `ClipArtSelector` is run, the window shown in figure 10-1 appears.

The mouse or up-down arrow keys would be used to select the desired image and the Ok button would start the file transfer process. Once the process has completed, a message such as:

```
File transfer for FISHERMEN.TIF done
```

will appear within the status text field located at the bottom of the window.

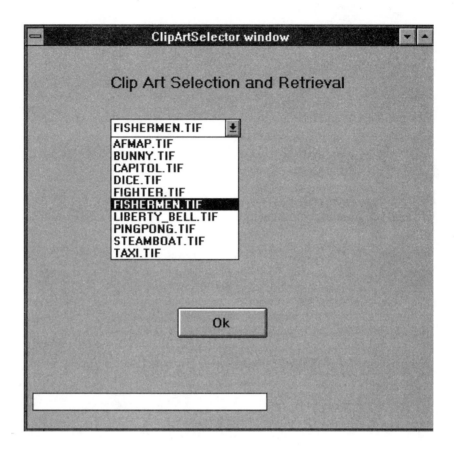

Figure 10-1

The following is the code for the client application:

Listing 10-6: ClipArtSelector.java

```
import java.awt.*;
import java.net.*;
import java.io.*;

class FileRequest {

    FileRequest(String hostname, int port, String fn) {/* (5) */
        try {
            sock = new Socket(hostname, port);
            filename = fn;
            }
        catch(Exception err) {
```

```java
                System.err.println(err.toString());
                System.exit(-1);
                }
        }

    void retrieve() {                                       /* (6) */

        DataInputStream dis = null;
        PrintStream out = null;
        File fobj = null;
        FileOutputStream fos = null;
        byte bdata;

        try {
                dis = new DataInputStream(sock.getInputStream());
                out = new PrintStream(sock.getOutputStream());

                fobj = new File(filename);
                fos = new FileOutputStream(fobj);

                out.println(filename);
                out.flush();

                int count;
                byte [] barray = new byte[8192];

                while ((count = dis.read(barray)) != -1) {
                    fos.write(barray, 0, count);
                    fos.flush();
                    }

                fos.close();
                dis.close();
                out.close();
                sock.close();
                }
        catch (Exception err) {
                System.out.println(err.toString());
                System.exit(-1);
                }

        }

    private Socket sock;
    private String filename;
}

public class ClipArtSelector extends Frame {         /* (1) */
```

```
public ClipArtSelector() {

    super("ClipArtSelector window");
    setBackground(Color.lightGray);

    setLayout(null);
    addNotify();
    resize(insets().left + insets().right + 435,
      insets().top + insets().bottom + 410);
    mainLabel=new Label("Clip Art Selection and Retrieval");
    mainLabel.setFont(new Font("Dialog",Font.BOLD,16));
    add(mainLabel);
    mainLabel.reshape(insets().left + 78,insets().top +
      26,270,26);
    clipartChoice= new Choice();
    clipartChoice.setFont(new Font("Dialog",Font.BOLD,12));
    add(clipartChoice);
    clipartChoice.reshape(insets().left + 90,insets().top +
      78,240,176);
    okButton=new Button("Ok");
    okButton.setFont(new Font("Dialog",Font.BOLD,14));
    add(okButton);
    okButton.reshape(insets().left + 162,insets().top +
      280,96,32);
    statusField=new TextField(30);
    statusField.setFont(new Font("Dialog",Font.PLAIN,10));
    statusField.disable();
    add(statusField);
    statusField.reshape(insets().left + 6,insets().top +
      371,252,19);

    FileInputStream fis = null;                          /* (2) */
    DataInputStream dis = null;
    String filename = null;

    try {
        fis = new FileInputStream("images.txt");
        dis = new DataInputStream(fis);

        while ((filename = dis.readLine()) != null)
            clipartChoice.addItem(filename);
        }

    catch(Exception err) {
        System.err.println(err.toString());
        System.exit(-1);
        }

    show();
}
```

```
public synchronized void show() {
    move(50, 50);
    super.show();
}

public boolean handleEvent(Event event) {            /* (3) */
    if (event.id == Event.ACTION_EVENT && event.target ==
    okButton) {
        clickedOkButton();
        return true;
        }
    else
    if (event.id == Event.WINDOW_DESTROY) {
        hide();
        dispose();
        System.exit(0);
        return true;
        }
return super.handleEvent(event);
}

public void clickedOkButton()                    {/* (4) */
    String selectedFile = clipartChoice.getSelectedItem();
    fileRequest = new FileRequest("micron1", 5000,
     selectedFile);
    statusField.setText("");
    fileRequest.retrieve();
    statusField.setText("File transfer for "+selectedFile+"
     done");
}

public static void main(String args[]) {
    new ClipArtSelector();
}

private Label    mainLabel;
private Choice   clipartChoice;
private Button   okButton;
private TextField   statusField;
private FileRequest   fileRequest;
}
```

This sample for the client is fairly long, so we will focus our discussion on the essentials (highlighted code), especially the communication between the client and the server.

- The first observation is that class `ClipArtSelector` is subclassed from class `Frame` (comment `/* (1) */`) and not from class `Applet`. Hence, `ClipArtSelector` represents an application and not an applet. Since applets will not allow the creation of files on the user's system (because of security), the example must be made an application.

- The constructor `ClipArtSelector()` performs the usual creation and initialization of the controls contained within the frame. One of the controls is represented by reference variable `clipartChoice`, which is the list box of graphics file names. Instead of hardcoding the file names into the program, the names are placed into an ASCII file, `images.txt`, and read into the `Choice` object (comment `/* (2) */`):

```
fis = new FileInputStream("images.txt");
dis = new DataInputStream(fis);

while ((filename = dis.readLine()) != null)
    clipartChoice.addItem(filename);
```

This is done by first creating a `FileInputStream` object from the file name and then a `DataInputStream` object from the `FileInputStream` object. The `readLine()` method is then applied to the `DataInputStream` object to obtain each file name (each name is on its own line).

- The clicking or pressing of the Ok button would start the process of initiating the request and the file transfer from the server. This would cause an `Event.ACTION_EVENT` to be passed to method `handleEvent()` (comment `/* (3) */`):

```
if (event.id == Event.ACTION_EVENT && event.target ==
 okButton) {
    clickedOkButton();
    return true;
    }
```

If the event originated from `okButton`, then `clickedOkButton()` would be called.

- The `clickedOkButton()` method (comment `/* (4) */`) basically instantiates a `FileRequest` object to open a connection to the server and initiate the file retrieval. The constructor of `FileRequest` is passed the name of the host, the port number and the file name to be retrieved. As we will see shortly, the `FileRequest` object handles all of the details of the client request:

```
public void clickedOkButton() {
    String selectedFile = clipartChoice.getSelectedItem();
    fileRequest = new FileRequest("micron1", 5000,
     selectedFile);
    statusField.setText("");
```

```
    fileRequest.retrieve();
    statusField.setText("File transfer for "+selectedFile+"
    done");
  }
```

The `clickedOkButton()` will also clear the `statusField` (a `TextField` object) before the transfer and write the notification message into `statusField` when the transfer is complete.

- The constructor of class `FileRequest` (comment /* (5) */) takes the host name and port number to create a `Socket` object that is referenced by private variable, `sock`. The file name is also retained in private variable, `filename`.

The creation of the `Socket` object with the given parameters will trigger the server program to return the `Socket` object from the statement:

```
sock = servsock.accept();
```

within its `main()` method.

The server program will then block on the statement:

```
filename = in.readLine();
```

of its `run()` method until the file name is sent by the client.

- The bulk of the client's work is within the body of its `retrieve()` method (comment /* (6) */). From the `Socket` object, `sock`, the input stream and the output stream are retrieved to create a `DataInputStream` object and a `PrintStream` object:

```
dis = new DataInputStream(sock.getInputStream());
out = new PrintStream(sock.getOutputStream());
```

With the `PrintStream` object, `out`, the client would send the name of the desired file to the server:

```
out.println(filename);
out.flush();
```

Warning: It is important to use the `println()` method instead of `print()` since the server is blocking on `readLine()`, which expects a newline character to indicate the end-of-stream. The use of `print()` will cause the server to block on `readLine()` forever. In addition, every write to the socket should be followed by a `flush()` just to insure that the contents of the internal buffers are passed into the socket.

The `retrieve()` method will also create a `FileOutputStream` object that will collect the contents of the file that the server sends back:

```
fobj = new File(filename);
fos = new FileOutputStream(fobj);
```

The method then blocks on the `read()` method until all of the contents of the file sent by the server have arrived:

```
int count;
byte [] barray = new byte[8192];

while ((count = dis.read(barray)) != -1) {
    fos.write(barray, 0, count);
    fos.flush();
    }
```

The `DataInputStream` object, `dis`, reads the data into an array of bytes and the array is written to the file with the `FileOutputStream` object, `fos`.

- Finally, when all of the contents have been read and written to the file, the socket and the various streams are closed:

```
fos.close();
dis.close();
out.close();
sock.close();
```

Summary: Compared to the C language version of the file retrieval system, the Java version is remarkably easy! In Java, the developer does not need to worry about essentials like network byte order (the read and write methods of `DataInputStream` and `DataOutputStream` handle these details by making sure everything will be in network byte order). There are none of the complicated C-style `struct`s used to pass or receive the numerous socket parameters (such as the protocol family value). Furthermore, Java does not require any special `bind()` method for servers or special `connect()` method for clients. The creation of a `ServerSocket` object or a `Socket` object, respectively, automatically handles these tasks.

Note: There is a Java class called InetAddress in package java.net. This class represents IP addresses and has a variety of methods to get host names and internet addresses of local and remote machines. In addition, each of the ServerSocket and Socket classes supports a getInetAddress() method to obtain an InetAddress object of the system from which the ServerSocket object or the Socket object is running.

Accessing Uniform Resource Locators

One of the most useful aspects of the `java.net` package is the support for accessing a `Uniform Resource Locator` (URL) on the Internet. Usually, URLs are names that refer to HTML pages (which are retrieved by your browser from a HTTP server), but URLs would also include files local to your machine and files intended for downloading from a FTP server.

In this section, we will look at a Java example called `URLDemo`. The example shows how to use the URL class to traverse to different points of interest on the Internet. The example also carries a few other Java programming tidbits.

One should note that the URL is very specific to programming for the Internet and is not part of any standard ANSI C function library or standard ANSI C++ class library. The reason is mostly historical: interest in the Internet came well after these languages were established in the industry. Java, on the other hand, is part of the Internet revolution.

`URLDemo` is written as an applet. When it is accessed via its own HTML page, it would look something like figure 10-2.

When a selection is made from the list box, the browser will retrieve the desired URL (see figure 10-3).

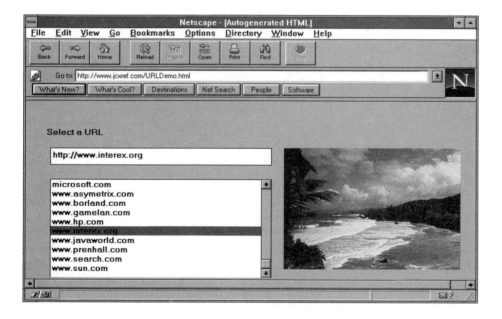

Figure 10-2

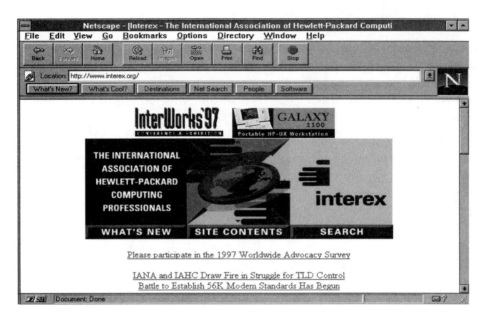

Figure 10-3

Below is the listing of the URLDemo applet. The highlighted code represent the main points of the example:

Listing 10-7: URLDemo.java

```java
import java.awt.*;
import java.applet.*;
import java.io.*;
import java.net.*;
import java.util.*;

public class URLDemo extends Applet {

        void URLListSelected(Event event) {                  /* (3) */

            AppletContext context = getAppletContext();
            String URLName = null;
            URL selectedURL = null;
            try {
                URLName = "http://"+URLList.getSelectedItem().
                 trim();
                selectedURLField.setText(URLName);
                selectedURL = new URL(URLName);
                context.showDocument(selectedURL);
                }
```

```
        catch(MalformedURLException err) {
            showStatus("Error: "+err);
            }
    }

public void init() {

        super.init();
        setLayout(null);
        addNotify();
        resize(738,309);
        setBackground(new Color(12632256));
        URLList = new java.awt.List(0,false);
        add(URLList);
        URLList.reshape(30,120,360,170);
        URLList.setFont(new Font("Dialog", Font.BOLD,
         14));
        URLList.setBackground(new Color(16777215));
        selectedURLField = new java.awt.TextField();
        selectedURLField.reshape(30,66,360,30);
        selectedURLField.setFont(new Font("Dialog",
         Font.BOLD, 14));
        selectedURLField.setBackground(new
         Color(16777215));
        selectedURLField.setEditable(false);
        add(selectedURLField);
        selectedURLLabel = new java.awt.Label("Select a
         URL");
        selectedURLLabel.reshape(24,24,120,31);
        selectedURLLabel.setFont(new Font("Dialog",
         Font.BOLD, 14));
        add(selectedURLLabel);

        nativeURL = getDocumentBase();            /* (1) */

        DataInputStream dis = null;
        String item = null;
        URL url = null;
        try {
            url = new URL(nativeURL, "URLData.txt");
            dis = new DataInputStream
             (url.openStream());
            while ((item = dis.readLine()) != null)
                URLList.addItem(item);
            picture = getImage(nativeURL,
             "tropical.gif");
            }
        catch(IOException err) {
            showStatus("Error: "+err);
            }
    }
```

```
public boolean handleEvent(Event event) {
        if (event.target == URLList && event.id ==
        Event.LIST_SELECT) {
            URLListSelected(event);                    /* (3) */
            return true;
        }
        return super.handleEvent(event);
}
public void paint(Graphics graph){                     /* (2) */
    Rectangle rect = selectedURLField.bounds();
    graph.drawImage(picture, rect.x+rect.width+20,
    rect.y , this);
}

private    Image         picture;
private    URL           nativeURL;
private    List          URLList;
private    TextField     selectedURLField;
private    Label         selectedURLLabel;

}
```

The following are the main points of the URLDemo applet:

- The init() method is the main entry point for the applet. Here is where the Label, List and TextField objects are instantiated and placed on the applet (which is a subclass of class Panel). The Applet method, getDocumentBase() (comment /* (1) */), is used to retrieve the URL of the HTML document where the applet is embedded. The retrieved URL object is then assigned to reference variable nativeURL.

- Another URL object, url, is created based on the URL object referenced by nativeURL:

  ```
  url = new URL(nativeURL, "URLData.txt");
  ```

  The second argument to the URL constructor is the file containing URL string names, such as www.hp.com. The creation of the URL object referenced by variable url is the first step to obtaining the contents of file URLData.txt.

- In order to read the contents of file "URLData.txt," which is in the URL object, url, an input stream must be obtained with url.openStream(). The next step would be to create a DataInputStream object, read each line item and then add each item into the List object URLList:

  ```
  dis = new DataInputStream(url.openStream());
  while ((item = dis.readLine()) != null)
     URLList.addItem(item);
  ```

- The next statement would be to use the URL object, nativeURL, to obtain an image called "tropical.gif." This image basically is a decoration and will be rendered on the applet:

```
picture = getImage(nativeURL, "tropical.gif");
```

Private variable `picture` is a reference to an `Image` object.

- Both constructors for `URL` and `DataInputStream` must be bounded within a `try` block. Both can throw an exception of type `IOException`. Specifically, the constructor for `URL` can throw a `MalformedURLException`, which is a subclass of `IOException`.

- After method `init()` completes, the Java environment will send a paint message to the applet, in which case the statements in method `paint()` will be executed (comment `/* (2) */`). The only incoming parameter is a `Graphics` object, `graph`, which is similar to a device context from the Microsoft Windows™ system. The area chosen for drawing is offset by 20 pixels from the right edge of `selectedURLField` and offset from the top edge of the applet by the same amount as the upper edge of `selectedURLField`:

```
// Get attributes of bounding rectangle
Rectangle rect = selectedURLField.bounds();

// Render the image
graph.drawImage(picture, rect.x+rect.width+20, rect.y ,
  this);
```

- When the user clicks on `List` object `URLList`, a message is sent to the `handleEvent()` method. From there, the method `URLListSelected()` is called to handle the processing (comment `/* (3) */`). Within the body of `URLListSelected()`, the item name is selected and a URL object is instantiated from the name:

```
URLName = "http://"+URLList.getSelectedItem().trim();
selectedURLField.setText(URLName);
selectedURL = new URL(URLName);
```

The `trim()` method is from class `String`. The method will rid any spaces preceding the actual string and any spaces following the string.

Note: The use of the `trim()` method is a smart way to get rid of extra spaces and invisible characters from your text input. It is a way to prevent `MalformedURLException` objects from being thrown as the result of using the URL constructor.

For this example, all of the URLs are of the HTTP type.

- After the URL object, `selectedURL`, has been created, it is used by an `AppletContext` object to retrieve the desired resource:

```
AppletContext context = getAppletContext();
...
try {
    ...
    context.showDocument(selectedURL);
}
```

The showDocument() method will cause the browser containing the applet to retrieve the resource named by the URL object. If the URL represented by the URL object is not valid, then a browser such as Netscape Navigator will display a message such as the following:

```
The requested item could not be loaded by the proxy.
```

Summary: The Java URL class is the vehicle for tapping into any known resource on the Internet. One interesting aspect about the URL class is that it has methods like getDocumentBase() to support relative URLs, which means the absolute locations of the resources do not have to be hardcoded into the applet (or application). We have also seen an example where a file of parameter data for a List object can be stored on the server and retrieved on demand. This is a great feature where changes can be made to one file without the need to recompile the applet.

References

Advanced C++ Programming Styles and Idioms
by James O. Coplien
Addison-Wesley Publishing Company
ISBN 0–201–54855–0

The Annotated C++ Reference Manual
by Margaret A. Ellis and Bjarne Stroustrup
Addison-Wesley Publishing Company
ISBN 0–201–51459–1

Core Java (Second Edition)
by Gary Cornell and Cay S. Horstmann
Prentice-Hall SunSoft Press Series
ISBN 0–13–596891–7

C++ and C Debugging, Testing and Reliability
by David A. Spuler
Prentice-Hall, Inc.
ISBN 0–13–308172–9

C++ IOStreams Handbook
by Steve Teale
Addison-Wesley Publishing Company
ISBN 0–201–59641–5

C++ Programming Guidelines
by Thomas Plum and Dan Saks
Plum Hall, Inc.
ISBN 0–911537–10–4

The Design and Evolution of C++
by Bjarne Stroustrup
Addison-Wesley Publishing Company
ISBN 0–201–54330–3

Effective C++
by Scott Meyers
Addison-Wesley Publishing Company
ISBN 0–201–56364–9

The Evolution of C++
edited by Jim Waldo
MIT Press
ISBN 0–262–73107-X

Internetworking with TCP/IP, Volume 3
by Douglas E. Comer and David L. Stevens
Prentice-Hall, Inc.
ISBN 0–13–474222–2

Java by Example (Second Edition)
by Jerry R. Jackson and Alan L. McClellan
Prentice-Hall SunSoft Press Series
ISBN 0–13–272295-X

Java in a Nutshell: A Desktop Quick Reference for Java Programmers
by David Flanagan
O'Reilly & Associates, Inc.
ISBN 1–56592–183–6

Java Networking and AWT API
by Nataraj Nagaratnam, Brian Maso and Arvind Srinivasan
Waite Group Press
ISBN 1–57169–031-X

Java Unleashed
by Michael Morrison and sixteen other authors
Sams Net
ISBN 1–57521–049–5

Just Java (Second Edition)
by Peter van der Linden
Prentice-Hall SunSoft Press Series
ISBN 0–13–272303–4

MFC Internals
by George Shepherd and Scot Wingo
Addison-Wesley Publishing Company
ISBN 0–201–40721–3

The X Window System: Programming and Applications with Xt
    (OSF/MOTIF Edition)
by Douglas A. Young
Prentice-Hall, Inc.
ISBN 0–13–497074–8

Index

About the Software

An installation program on the CD-ROM media has been provided to create the directory structure of sample programs on your Microsoft Windows 95™ or Windows NT™ environment. When the installation has completed, you should see the following directory tree from where you have chosen your point of installation:

```
..\JCppXref\JAVA
..\JCppXref\JAVA\JAVA1_1
..\JCppXref\JAVAPAKS
..\JCppXref\Unix_C
..\JCppXref\WinNTCpp\Borland
..\JCppXref\WinNTCpp\Microsoft
```

Below is a summary of what each of the relative paths contains:

- Directory JCppXref\JAVA contains all of the Java examples. Each example includes the sources, bytecode files and project file.

- Directory JCppXref\JAVA\JAVA1_1 contains all of the Java examples for version 1.1.1 of the JDK.

- Directory JCppXref\JAVAPAKS contains all of the custom Java packages that are necessary to support some of the sample Java programs. Please refer to the topic, "Organizing Java Classes into a Package" in Chapter 4 or the README.TXT file on the CD-ROM media about how to properly configure the CLASSPATH environment variable to recognize the packages.

- Directory JCppXref\Unix_C contains a small collection of UNIX-based C samples. Each example includes the sources and shell scripts to create the executable. Some of these examples also have Motif-based resource files. These examples require an ANSI-compliant C compiler.

- Directory JCppXref\WinNTCpp\Borland contains a small collection of C++ programs intended for Borland C++™ version 5.0 or higher. These programs should also work in a UNIX environment with a current ISO/ANSI-compliant C++ compiler.

- Directory JCppXref\WinNTCpp\Microsoft contains the major collection of C++ programs intended for Microsoft Visual C++ 4.0™ or higher. These programs should also work in a UNIX environment with a current ISO/ANSI-compliant C++ compiler.

The README.TXT file from the CD-ROM media will contain any last-minute instructions the reader may need to know.

Please refer to the Preface for additional information about the CD-Rom contents.

Additional Software on the Distribution Media

Along with the sample programs mentioned in the previous section, the CD-ROM media also contains the Java Development Kit (JDK) version 1.1.4 for Windows™ 95 and NT and for Macintosh from Sun Microsystems, Inc.

The JDK comes with its own unarchiving and installation programs.

Note: After the installation of a Java development environment, the PATH and JAVA_HOME environment variables must be properly set up. Setting up these variables is very similar to setting up the CLASSPATH variable for Java packages. Refer to the README.TXT file for further information.

Exhibit A
Java™ Development Kit
Version 1.1.x
Binary Code License

This binary code license ("License") contains rights and restrictions associated with use of the accompanying software and documentation ("Software"). Read the License carefully before installing the Software. By installing the Software you agree to the terms and conditions of this License.

1. **Limited License Grant.** Sun grants to you ("Licensee") a non-exclusive, non-transferable limited license to use the Software without fee for evaluation of the Software and for development of Java™ compatible applets and applications. Licensee may make one archival copy of the Software. Licensee may not re-distribute the Software in whole or in part, either separately or included with a product. Refer to the Java Runtime Environment Version 1.1 binary code license (http://www.javasoft.com/products/JDK/1.1/index.html) for the availability of runtime code which may be distributed with Java compatible applets and applications.

2. **Java Platform Interface.** Licensee may not modify the Java Platform Interface ("JPI", identified as classes contained within the "java" package or any subpackages of the "java" package), by creating additional classes within the JPI or otherwise causing the addition to or modification of the classes in the JPI. In the event that Licensee creates any Java-related API and distributes such API to others for applet or application development, Licensee must promptly publish an accurate specification for such API for free use by all developers of Java-Based software.

3. **Restrictions.** Software is confidential copyrighted information of Sun and title to all copies is retained by Sun and/or its licensors. Licensee shall not modify, decompile, disassemble, decrypt, extract, or otherwise reverse engineer Software. Software may not be leased, assigned, or sublicensed, in whole or in part. **Software is not designed or intended for use in on-line control of aircraft, air traffic, aircraft navigation or aircraft communications; or in the design, construction, operation or maintenance of any nuclear facility. Licensee warrants that it will not use or redistribute the Software for such purposes.**

4. **Trademarks and Logos.** This License does not authorize Licensee to use any Sun name, trademark or logo. Licensee acknowledges that Sun owns the Java trademark and all Java-related trademarks, logos and icons including the Coffee Cup and Duke ("Java Marks") and agrees to: (i) comply with the Java Trademark Guidelines at http://java.com/trademarks.html; (ii) not do anything harmful to or inconsistent with Sun's rights in the Java Marks; and (iii) assist Sun in protecting those rights, including assigning to Sun any rights acquired by Licensee in any Java Mark.

459

5. Disclaimer of Warranty. Software is provided "AS IS," without a warranty of any kind. ALL EXPRESS OR IMPLIED REPRESENTATIONS AND WARRANTIES, INCLUDING ANY IMPLIED WARRANTY OF MERCHANTABILITY, FITNESS FOR A PARTICULAR PURPOSE OR NON-INFRINGEMENT, ARE HEREBY EXCLUDED.

6. Limitation of Liability. SUN AND ITS LICENSORS SHALL NOT BE LIABLE FOR ANY DAMAGES SUFFERED BY LICENSEE OR ANY THIRD PARTY AS A RESULT OF USING OR DISTRIBUTING SOFTWARE. IN NO EVENT WILL SUN OR ITS LICENSORS BE LIABLE FOR ANY LOST REVENUE, PROFIT OR DATA, OR FOR DIRECT, INDIRECT, SPECIAL, CONSEQUENTIAL, INCIDENTAL OR PUNITIVE DAMAGES, HOWEVER CAUSED AND REGARDLESS OF THE THEORY OF LIABILITY, ARISING OUT OF THE USE OF OR INABILITY TO USE SOFTWARE, EVEN IF SUN HAS BEEN ADVISED OF THE POSSIBILITY OF SUCH DAMAGES.

7. Termination. Licensee may terminate this License at any time by destroying all copies of Software. This License will terminate immediately without notice from Sun if Licensee fails to comply with any provision of this License. Upon such termination, Licensee must destroy all copies of Software.

8. Export Regulations. Software, including technical data, is subject to U.S. export control laws, including the U.S. Export Administration Act and its associated regulations, and may be subject to export or import regulations in other countries. Licensee agrees to comply strictly with all such regulations and acknowledges that it has the responsibility to obtain licenses to export, re-export, or import Software. Software may not be downloaded, or otherwise exported or re-exported (i) into, or to a national or resident of, Cuba, Iraq, Iran, North Korea, Libya, Sudan, Syria or any country to which the U.S. has embargoed goods; or (ii) to anyone on the U.S. Treasury Department's list of Specially Designated Nations or the U.S. Commerce Department's Table of Denial Orders.

9. Restricted Rights. Use, duplication or disclosure by the United States government is subject to the restrictions as set forth in the Rights in Technical Data and Computer Software Clauses in DFARS 252.227-7013(c) (1) (ii) and FAR 52.227-19(c) (2) as applicable.

10. Governing Law. Any action related to this License will be governed by California law and controlling U.S. federal law. No choice of law rules of any jurisdiction will apply.

11. Severability. If any of the above provisions are held to be in violation of applicable law, void, or unenforceable in any jurisdiction, then such provisions are herewith waived to the extent necessary for the License to be otherwise enforceable in such jurisdiction. However, if in Sun's opinion deletion of any provisions of the License by operation of this paragraph unreasonably compromises the rights or increases the liabilities of Sun or its licensors, Sun reserves the right to terminate the License and refund the fee paid by Licensee, if any, as Licensee's sole and exclusive remedy.

LICENSE AGREEMENT AND LIMITED WARRANTY

READ THE FOLLOWING TERMS AND CONDITIONS CAREFULLY BEFORE OPENING THIS CD PACKAGE. THIS LEGAL DOCUMENT IS AN AGREE-MENT BETWEEN YOU AND PRENTICE-HALL INC. (THE "COMPANY"). BY OPEN-ING THIS SEALED CD PACKAGE, YOU ARE AGREEING TO BE BOUND BY THESE TERMS AND CONDITIONS. IF YOU DO NOT AGREE WITH THESE TERMS AND CON-DITIONS, DO NOT OPEN THE CD PACKAGE. PROMPTLY RETURN THE UNOPENED CD PACKAGE AND ALL ACCOMPANYING ITEMS TO THE PLACE YOU OBTAINED THEM FOR A FULL REFUND OF ANY SUMS YOU HAVE PAID.

1.   **GRANT OF LICENSE:** In consideration of your purchase of this book, and your agreement to abide by the terms and conditions of this Agreement, the Company grants to you a nonexclusive right to use and display the copy of the enclosed software program (hereinafter the "SOFTWARE") on a single computer (i.e., with a single CPU) at a single location so long as you comply with the terms of this Agreement. The Company reserves all rights not expressly granted to you under this Agreement:

2.   **OWNERSHIP OF SOFTWARE:** You own only the magnetic or physical media (the enclosed CD) on which the SOFTWARE is recorded or fixed, but the Company and the software developers retain all the rights, title, and ownership to the SOFTWARE recorded on the original CD copy(ies) and all subsequent copies of the SOFTWARE, regardless of the form or media on which the original or other copies may exist. This license is not a sale of the original SOFTWARE or any copy to you.

3.   **COPY RESTRICTIONS:** This SOFTWARE and the accompanying printed materials and user manual (the "Documentation") are the subject of copyright. The indi-vidual programs on the CD are copyrighted by the authors of each program. You may not copy the Documentation or the SOFTWARE, except that you may make a single copy of the SOFTWARE for backup or archival purposes only. You may be held legally responsible for any copying or copyright infringement which is caused or encouraged by your failure to abide by the terms of this restriction.

4.   **USE RESTRICTIONS:** You may not network the SOFTWARE or otherwise use it on more than one computer or computer terminal at the same time. You may phys-ically transfer the SOFTWARE from one computer to another provided that the SOFT-WARE is used on only one computer at a time. You may not distribute copies of the SOFTWARE or Documentation to others. You may not reverse engineer, dissassemble, decompile, modify, adapt, translate, or create derivative works based on the SOFTWARE or the Documentation without the prior written consent of the Company.

5.   **TRANSFER RESTRICTIONS:** The enclosed SOFTWARE is licensed only to you and may not be transferred to any one else without the prior written consent of the Company. Any unauthorized transfer of the SOFTWARE shall result in the immediate ter-mination of this Agreement.

6.   **TERMINATION:** This license is effective until terminated. This license will terminate automatically without notice from the Company and become null and void if you fail to comply with any provisions or limitations of this license. Upon termination, you shall destroy the Documentation and all copies of the SOFTWARE. All provisions of this Agreement as to warranties, limitation of liability, remedies or damages, and our owner-ship rights shall survive termination.

7.   **MISCELLANEOUS:** This Agreement shall be construed in accordance with the laws of the United States of America and the State of New York and shall benefit the Company, its affiliates, and assignees.

8.   **LIMITED WARRANTY AND DISCLAIMER OF WARRANTY:** The Company warrants that the SOFTWARE, when properly used in accordance with the Documentation, will operate in substantial conformity with the description of the SOFTWARE set forth in the Documentation. The Company does not warrant that the

SOFTWARE will meet your requirements or that the operation of the SOFTWARE will be uninterrupted or error-free. The Company warrants that the media on which the SOFT-WARE is delivered shall be free from defects in materials and workmanship under normal use for a period of thirty (30) days from the date of your purchase. Your only remedy and the Company's only obligation under these limited warranties is, at the Company's option, return of the warranted item for a refund of any amounts paid by you or replacement of the item. Any replacement of SOFTWARE or media under the warranties shall not extend the original warranty period. The limited warranty set forth above shall not apply to any SOFTWARE which the Company determines in good faith has been subject to misuse, neglect, improper installation, repair, alteration, or damage by you. EXCEPT FOR THE EXPRESSED WARRANTIES SET FORTH ABOVE, THE COMPANY DISCLAIMS ALL WARRANTIES, EXPRESS OR IMPLIED, INCLUDING WITHOUT LIMITATION, THE IMPLIED WARRANTIES OF MERCHANTABILITY AND FITNESS FOR A PARTICULAR PURPOSE. EXCEPT FOR THE EXPRESS WARRANTY SET FORTH ABOVE, THE COM-PANY DOES NOT WARRANT, GUARANTEE, OR MAKE ANY REPRESENTATION REGARDING THE USE OR THE RESULTS OF THE USE OF THE SOFTWARE IN TERMS OF ITS CORRECTNESS, ACCURACY, RELIABILITY, CURRENTNESS, OR OTHERWISE.

IN NO EVENT, SHALL THE COMPANY OR ITS EMPLOYEES, AGENTS, SUPPLIERS, OR CONTRACTORS BE LIABLE FOR ANY INCIDENTAL, INDIRECT, SPE-CIAL, OR CONSEQUENTIAL DAMAGES ARISING OUT OF OR IN CONNECTION WITH THE LICENSE GRANTED UNDER THIS AGREEMENT, OR FOR LOSS OF USE, LOSS OF DATA, LOSS OF INCOME OR PROFIT, OR OTHER LOSSES, SUSTAINED AS A RESULT OF INJURY TO ANY PERSON, OR LOSS OF OR DAMAGE TO PROPERTY, OR CLAIMS OF THIRD PARTIES, EVEN IF THE COMPANY OR AN AUTHORIZED REPRE-SENTATIVE OF THE COMPANY HAS BEEN ADVISED OF THE POSSIBILITY OF SUCH DAMAGES. IN NO EVENT SHALL LIABILITY OF THE COMPANY FOR DAMAGES WITH RESPECT TO THE SOFTWARE EXCEED THE AMOUNTS ACTUALLY PAID BY YOU. IF ANY, FOR THE SOFTWARE.

SOME JURISDICTIONS DO NOT ALLOW THE LIMITATION OF IMPLIED WARRANTIES OR LIABILITY FOR INCIDENTAL, INDIRECT, SPECIAL, OR CONSE-QUENTIAL DAMAGES, SO THE ABOVE LIMITATIONS MAY NOT ALWAYS APPLY THE WARRANTIES IN THIS AGREEMENT GIVE YOU SPECIFIC LEGAL RIGHTS AND YOU MAY ALSO HAVE OTHER RIGHTS WHICH VARY IN ACCORDANCE WITH LOCAL LAW.

ACKNOWLEDGMENT

YOU ACKNOWLEDGE THAT YOU HAVE READ THIS AGREEMENT, UNDERSTAND IT, AND AGREE TO BE BOUND BY ITS TERMS AND CONDITIONS. YOU ALSO AGREE THAT THIS AGREEMENT IS THE COMPLETE AND EXCLUSIVE STATEMENT OF THE AGREEMENT BETWEEN YOU AND THE COMPANY AND SUPERSEDES ALL PROPOSALS OR PRIOR AGREEMENTS, ORAL, OR WRITTEN, AND ANY OTHER COMMUNICATIONS BETWEEN YOU AND THE COMPANY OR ANY REPRESENTATIVE OF THE COMPANY RELATING TO THE SUBJECT MATTER OF THIS AGREEMENT.

Should you have any questions concerning this Agreement or if you wish to contact the Company for any reason, please contact the Company in writing at the address below.

Robin Short
Prentice Hall PTR
One Lake Street
Upper Saddle River, New Jersey 07458